Emotions

An Essay in Aid of Moral Psychology

Day-to-day life is a sequence of emotional states: hope, disappointment, irritation, anger, affection, envy, pride, embarrassment, joy, sadness, and many more. We know intuitively that these states express deep things about our character and our view of the world. But what are emotions, and why are they so important to us?

In one of the most extensive investigations of the emotions ever published, Robert C. Roberts develops a novel conception of what emotions are and then applies it to a large range of types of emotion and related phenomena. In so doing, he lays the foundations for a deeper understanding of our evaluative judgments, our actions, our personal relationships, and our fundamental well-being.

Aimed principally at philosophers and psychologists, this book will certainly be accessible to readers in other disciplines such as religion and anthropology.

Robert C. Roberts is Distinguished Professor of Ethics at Baylor University, Texas.

D1600213

Emotions

An Essay in Aid of Moral Psychology

ROBERT C. ROBERTS

Baylor University

CAMBRIDGE
UNIVERSITY PRESS

PUBLISHED BY THE PRESS SYNDICATE OF THE UNIVERSITY OF CAMBRIDGE
The Pitt Building, Trumpington Street, Cambridge, United Kingdom

CAMBRIDGE UNIVERSITY PRESS
The Edinburgh Building, Cambridge CB2 2RU, UK
40 West 20th Street, New York, NY 10011-4211, USA
477 Williamstown Road, Port Melbourne, VIC 3207, Australia
Ruiz de Alarcón 13, 28014 Madrid, Spain
Dock House, The Waterfront, Cape Town 8001, South Africa

http://www.cambridge.org

First published 2003

Printed in the United Kingdom at the University Press, Cambridge

Typeface ITC New Baskerville 10/12 pt.   *System* LaTeX 2$_\varepsilon$ [TB]

A catalog record for this book is available from the British Library.

Library of Congress Cataloging in Publication data
Roberts, Robert C., 1942–
Emotions : an essay in aid of moral psychology / Robert C. Roberts.
p.   cm.
Includes bibliographical references and index.
ISBN 0-521-81978-4 – ISBN 0-521-52584-5 (pbk.)
1. Emotions (Philosophy)   I. Title.
B105.E46 B76   2002
128′.37–dc21   2002025620

ISBN 0 521 81978 4 hardback
ISBN 0 521 52584 5 paperback

This book is dedicated to my daughter Beffie

Contents

Acknowledgments

This book has been an embarrassingly long time in the making, and along the winding way I have collected more debts than I can hope to remember. But it's a pleasure to remember the ones I can. At one or more points in the book's redaction history, each of the following persons made some contribution: Bill Alston, Steve Bilynskyj, Harold Brown, Tony Celano, Justin D'Arms, John Deigh, Alan Donagan, Mark Drost, Mylan Engel, Steve Evans, Dan Farrell, Patricia Greenspan, John Hare, Bennett Helm, Paul Holmer, Arthur Holmes, Daniel Jacobson, Tom Kennedy, Jim King, Richard Kyte, Burt Louden, Rick McCarty, Paul Moser, Martha Nussbaum, Bernard Reginster, Nate Roberts, Amélie Rorty, William Schroder, Richard Shweder, David Solomon, Michael Stocker, Mark Talbot, Bill Tolhurst, Cliff Williams, Nicholas Wolterstorff, Jay Wood, and Linda Zagzebski.

I am also indebted to academic and funding institutions for abundant support. Early stages of the work were supported by a sabbatical leave from Wheaton College, a grant from the Institute for Advanced Christian Studies, and the hospitality of the Catholic University of Leuven (1987–1988) and Juniata College, where I was J. Omar Good Visiting Professor (1989–1990). In 1992–1995 I was supported in this and other work by a generous grant from the Pew Charitable Trusts. In 1998–1999 I enjoyed a Fellowship for College Teachers from the National Endowment for the Humanities, another sabbatical from Wheaton College, and the hospitality of Alvin Plantinga's Center for Philosophy of Religion at the University of Notre Dame. In the summer of 2000, Calvin College's Center for Christian Scholarship enabled John Hare, Linda Zagzebski, and me to spend a week discussing one another's books-in-progress. Finally, I am grateful to Baylor University for a sabbatical leave during my first year of employment that enabled me to finish the volume.

I have incorporated bits and pieces, in sometimes deeply revised form, from the following earlier work: "Solomon on the Control of Emotions" *Philosophy and Phenomenological Research* **44** (1984): 395–403; "What An

Emotion Is: A Sketch" *The Philosophical Review* **97** (1988): 183–209; "Is Amusement an Emotion?" *American Philosophical Quarterly* **25** (1988): 269–274; review of Robert M. Gordon's *The Structure of Emotions: Investigations in Cognitive Philosophy* in *The Philosophical Review* **99** (1990): 266–268; review of Patricia S. Greenspan's *Emotions and Reasons* in *Philosophical Books* **31** (1990): 233–235; "Feeling One's Emotions and Knowing Oneself" *Philosophical Studies* **77** (1995): 319–338; "Propositions and Animal Emotion" *Philosophy* **71** (1996): 147–156; "Emotions as Judgments," contribution to a book symposium on Martha Nussbaum's *The Therapy of Desire*, in *Philosophy and Phenomenological Research* **59** (1999): 793–798; and review of David Pugmire, *Rediscovering Emotions*, in *The Philosophical Quarterly* **51** (2001): 116–119.

1

Studying Emotions

1.1. WHAT THIS BOOK IS ABOUT

Anthony Trollope comments about an unsavory character who looms large in his novel *The Prime Minister* (Chapter 58):

The abuse which was now publicly heaped on the name of Ferdinand Lopez hit the man very hard; but not so hard perhaps as his rejection by Lady Eustace. That was an episode in his life of which even he felt ashamed, and of which he was unable to shake the disgrace from his memory. He had no inner appreciation whatsoever of what was really good or what was really bad in a man's conduct.... In a sense he was what is called a gentleman. He knew how to speak, and how to look, how to use a knife and fork, how to dress himself, and how to walk. But he had not the faintest notion of the feelings of a gentleman. He had, however, a very keen conception of the evil of being generally ill spoken of.

Without directly mentioning any of Lopez's actions, Trollope here unmistakably sketches a man of momentous moral defects, just by indicating his patterns of emotional responsiveness – that he is more ashamed of being rejected by a classy female adventurer than of being the object of public moral opprobrium, but not at all ashamed of his shameful deeds. His lack of appreciation for good and bad action, suggests Trollope, is due to his emotional unresponsiveness to actions in moral terms (notice how Trollope mixes descriptions of Lopez's emotional dispositions with cognitive ascriptions like "no inner appreciation," "not the faintest notion," "a very keen conception"). The structure of his emotions explains why he does so much evil, why he has so little moral understanding, and why his life and the lives of those he touches closely are so miserable.

The involvement of emotions in what may be broadly termed the "moral" character of our lives is pervasive and deep. Because emotions are often impulses to act, their quality strongly affects the quality of what we do. Those who are prone to strong and inappropriate fear and anger tend to act and behave in a certain set of familiar ways, while compassion and the emotions of friendship incline people to actions of another kind. These two sorts of emotional tendencies, and many others, may coexist in a single person, thus making people complex and morally puzzling. But emotions are not *just* "causes" of actions; they may also determine the identity of our actions. The very "same" action of shoving a person into a ditch may be done from anger at the shoved person or fear for her life; in the first case the agent is *getting revenge* (let us say), and in the second he is *protecting against danger*. What I have said has already suggested that our character or personality is in large part a disposition to be affected in one set of ways or another: One who is regularly angered by trivial offenses to his private person but seldom or never by significant offenses against others or against the public good is a mean-spirited person. Someone who rejoices in the flourishing of family and friends, for their sake, has a nobler character than one who is unaffected by their weal, or who is affected by it, not for their sake but, say, for the sake of his own convenience. To be emotionally unsusceptible to an-other's well- or ill-being for the other's sake is to be incapable of friendship with that other, on at least one conception of friendship; the most important relationships of our lives are constituted, in large part, by our dispositions to react with specific emotions to the other and his vicissitudes. Besides these connections to action, character, and relationships, emotions are a kind of eye for value and the import of situations, a mode of spiritual per-ception that may be deep and wise, or shallow and foolish. Because of these and other types of importance, certain regular patterns of emotional re-sponse are characteristic of the flourishing, mature, and "happy" human life, while alternative patterns constitute ill-function and immaturity and tend to misery.

This volume and its projected companion aim to contribute to our under-standing of moral personality conceived in a broad sense of "moral," with a particular focus on the place of emotions and emotional formation in that personality. The conception of *moral* to which I refer includes not only our responses to duties and permissions, but also our happiness (which certainly does not imply always feeling good) – what kind of life, and in particular what formation of personality, and thus of relationships with others, consti-tutes human well-being all around. The work is divided into two parts. The present volume is on the nature of emotions and feelings and, in Chapter 4, begins to treat their connections to the moral life. The projected second volume begins with a general account of the relation of emotions to moral-ity in my broad sense of the word, and then it offers accounts of a number of particular traits of the flourishing personality with special reference to the emotions and emotionlike states that exemplify or interact with them.

The project of understanding the good life in terms of the virtues, and the virtues in terms of their relationships to the emotions, is nothing new. Aristotle says that moral virtue is concerned with passions and actions, and in his accounts of particular virtues the passions often figure even more prominently than the actions. The association of the virtues with the passions (many of which we would call emotions in modern English) recurs almost wherever the virtues are carefully reflected on in the history of philosophy. Thus Thomas Aquinas devotes Questions 22–48 of the first part of the second part of his *Summa Theologiæ* to a study of the passions, preparatory to his general discussion of virtue in Questions 55–67 and his detailed discussions of the virtues and vices in the second part of the second part, Questions 1–170, many of which themselves involve discussions of passions such as hope, fear, despair, joy, love, hatred, and envy. Book II of David Hume's *A Treatise of Human Nature* – "Of the Passions" – prepares the reader for Book III, in which he presents his ethics of virtue. Adam Smith's ethics, as presented in *The Theory of Moral Sentiments*, is likewise an ethics of virtue that focuses strongly on the passions. In our own period, when John Rawls turns to address justice as a trait of persons (rather than a structural feature of institutions), he finds it necessary to speak not just of dispositions to act, but of moral sentiments such as anger and guilt.[1]

This book is not a historical work, but I intend it as a contribution to this long discussion. I hope that it is in some ways a refinement of its predecessors. At any rate, it is dependent on them for direction and inspiration, as well as for the proposals that have fueled my thought, even when I disagree with them. As befits its historical location at the beginning of the 21st century, this book is more sensitive than its forebears to the possibility that neither emotions nor virtues are the same in every cultural setting, but instead vary to some extent with systems of custom, interest, and belief. While attempting to credit the diversity or potential diversity of human emotions and virtues, my discussions are also more resolutely particularistic. It seems to me that the way to study virtue is to study the virtues, and to do so rather in depth. "Virtue theory," especially in our time but also earlier, has often been long on generalizing accounts and short on careful exploration of particular virtues. Particular virtues are treated as illustrations of general theory, rather than as a fund of insight out of which any generalizations that are possible may emerge.

Accordingly, much of the second volume will study particular virtues, with special emphasis on their dynamic and internal connections with emotions and emotion dispositions. I comment on more general theoretical questions because they seem naturally to arise out of the particular discussions of virtues. Thus the method is "empirical" in the broad sense that it follows Wittgenstein's dictum, "Don't think. Look!", though lots of the looking in this sort of case is a kind of thinking – thinking about examples, as Wittgenstein's also is. Similarly, in the present volume, Chapter 3 is devoted to an extensive detailing of particular emotion types as well as of

---

[1] *A Theory of Justice* (Oxford: Oxford University Press, 1972), Sections 66–67 and 73–74.

emotionlike phenomena that are sometimes treated as emotions, such as
surprise, amusement (at what is comical), and vanity.

1.2. THE SUPPOSED POVERTY OF CONCEPTUAL ANALYSIS

How shall we conduct an inquiry into the emotions that will serve well the
study of the virtues? The methods of many disciplines have been used to
study the emotions. Philosophers, from Aristotle[2] to the present, have used
an approach that today would be called conceptual or philosophical analysis, one that I want to examine closely in this opening chapter because
recently it has been under attack and I will argue that it is still the central
approach for our purposes. But in the 19th and 20th centuries a number
of other approaches have been developed. Emotions have been examined
by the methods of evolutionary biology, experimental psychology, brain science, psychoanalysis and other clinical approaches, cultural anthropology,
and cultural history and the history of ideas. In each case, one or another of
a variety of theories forms a more or less definite background of the examination and shapes its results. For example, evolutionary biologists tend to
think of emotions as behavioral response mechanisms that (at least in our
evolutionary past, and in some cases also now) promote physical survival,
while many anthropologists think of emotions as culturally determined patterns of experience and behavior that serve various social functions (though
some anthropologists are psychoanalytic, and so stress less the determina-
tions of culture). Brain scientists tell a rather different story about emotions, one in terms of brain circuitry and neurotransmitters, but typically
lean on the evolutionary conception of emotion, while historians of the
emotions may exploit psychoanalytic theory or perhaps a more cognitive-
behavioral framework. In addition to these disciplines, fiction writing should
be mentioned, though it is not theoretical or academic in the way the other
disciplines are. Nevertheless, writers such as Jane Austen, Fyodor Dostoevsky,
Leo Tolstoy, Charles Dickens, and George Eliot are very astute observers of
emotions in the context of the narrative flow of human life, and are especially important for our purposes since they so often depict the emotions as
expressing traits of persons' character. Most of the other disciplines focus
much less on emotions that differentiate persons of one moral formation
from persons of another, and seldom are emotions set in as rich a narrative
context as they are in literature. A possible exception is psychoanalysis.

Conceptual analysis is an approach to the investigation of emotions that
takes major clues about them from the ways people talk about the emotions
in the contexts of their life. As I understand the practice and as the word
"clue" suggests, it is not a purely lexicographical or syntactical/semantic

[2] See Aristotle's *Rhetoric*, especially Book II, Chapters 1–11 (1377b15–1388b30).

approach. It is not as though we could expect to find out what emotions are by looking up "emotion" and/or words like "anger" and "nostalgia" in the dictionary, nor could we expect to "analyze" such concepts merely by summarizing the various conditions under which the most proficient speakers of English ascribe emotion or anger to themselves and others. Such information about how the best speakers of English use the emotion words is an important part of conceptual analysis, but the analyst is very much in the business of *interpreting* these facts of usage. For one thing, even the best English speakers use vocabulary loosely and shiftingly, so conceptual analysis will involve normative decisions about what is the right and central usage. But beyond this, the conceptual analyst typically offers some general schema by which he or she proposes to make sense of the "data" of linguistic usage. (Consider the various schemata that have been offered by such philosophers as Robert Solomon,[3] Patricia Greenspan,[4] and Robert Gordon.[5]) Furthermore, as a person who not only speaks about emotions, but also experiences them and experiences their connections with actions, perceptions, desires, sensations, and the like, the analyst is also very concerned to make sense of his or her experience and the experiences of other human beings. Thus as I conceive conceptual analysis, it is particularly based on collection of and reflection about examples from everyday human life, many of which can be understood only in the light of a fairly rich narrative background. This preoccupation represents an overlap with literary and psychoanalytic examinations of emotion and a rather strong contrast with biological and neuroscientific examinations. The conceptual analyst, as I understand his *métier*, will look for formulations regarding emotion and particular emotion types, and will be particularly interested in potential counterexamples, also from everyday life, to his formulations.

Conceptual analysis has been criticized as an inadequate approach to the emotions along two different lines by Amélie O. Rorty and Paul E. Griffiths. The two lines of criticism have in common the suggestion that the conceptual scheme provided by our ordinary language about the emotions is a deeply misleading, and perhaps even internally incoherent, indicator of the nature of emotions. Thus any analysis that takes that scheme at face value and as a point of departure is doomed to deep error. Each of these authors promotes an alternative approach. Rorty proposes that we study the history of the philosophies of the emotions because in her view those variegated philosophies have *constituted* the incoherent or apparently incoherent concept of emotion that analysts try vainly to make sense of. Griffiths thinks that the best scientific accounts of the phenomena that we call "emotions" – essentially, accounts from evolutionary biology and its

---

3 *The Passions* (Garden City, New York: Doubleday, 1976).
4 *Emotions and Reasons* (New York: Routledge, 1988).
5 *The Structure of Emotions* (Cambridge, England: Cambridge University Press, 1987).

auxiliary experimental psychology – show that "emotions" form such a qualitatively diverse set of phenomena that the concept *emotion* and the concepts
of particular types of emotion are useless for the purpose of genuine knowledge. I shall examine the arguments and proposals of Rorty and Griffiths,
bringing into my critique of Griffiths some observations about the best recent work on the neuroscience of emotions. I shall then end this Introduction with a sketch of a kind of conceptual analysis that avoids the legitimate
criticisms that have been leveled against conceptual analysis of the emotions
as it was practiced in the 20th century.

1.3. DECONSTRUCTING *EMOTION* VIA THE HISTORY OF PHILOSOPHY

Amélie Rorty begins her paper, "Aristotle on the Metaphysical Status
of *Pathe*,"[6] by commenting on the deplorable state of present-day
philosophical theorizing about the passions and emotions. The discussions
are "arbitrary and factitious" and "puzzlingly pulled in what appear to be
opposing directions" (p. 521); these "persistent and unresolvable contemporary polemical debates carry an air of a chimaeral construction" (p. 545).
The reason for this apparent impasse is that the concept under discussion itself contains these "opposing directions"; the discussions only reflect
tensions internal to the concept:

We sometimes hold people responsible for their emotions and the actions they
perform from them. Yet normal behavior is often explained and excused by the
person 'suffering' an emotional condition. We treat emotions as interruptions or
deflections of normal behavior, and yet also consider a person pathological if he
fails to act or react from a standard range of emotions. Sometimes emotions are
classified as a species of evaluative judgments whose analysis will be given in an
adequate theory of cognition. But sometimes the cognitive or intentional character
of an emotion is treated as dependent on, and ultimately explained by, a physical
condition (p. 521).

We can easily think of a few more "opposing directions" that the concept
of emotion can pull us in: Some emotions bond people together, others
sunder them; some emotions are recognizable via facial expressions, others are not; some emotions disappear as soon as contrary information is
heard and believed, others persist in the face of such information; some
emotions have an identifiable propositional content, others have none;
some emotions (like shame) are intrisically reflexive or self-referring, others (like joy) are not; some emotions are based in the most excellent, others
in the most cock-eyed reasoning, while still others are based in no reasoning at all; some emotions are disruptive episodes, relatively unintegrated

[6] *Review of Metaphysics* **38** (1984): 521–546.

into the characteristic concerns and purposes and intentional actions of a person's life, while others are continuous with those leading concerns and express them; some emotions involve discernible bodily arousal, others do not; some emotions are conscious states, others are not; some emotions are pleasurable, others are painful, and perhaps still others are neither the one nor the other; some emotion types are pancultural, others are culture-specific or culture-determined; some emotions are intentional, brought on by the subject for some purpose of her own, while others are not intentional; some emotions are motivations, while others are not. Rorty points out that these "opposing" divisions within the concept of emotion do not tend to be marked by our lexicalized emotion categories ("anger," "nostalgia," "solicitude," "joy"). For example, there might be instances of anger that fall on each of the sides of most of these divisions. Perhaps this fact helps to hide from us the rampant disorder internal to the concept of emotion.

Rorty's thesis that the seeming unresolvability of the debates about the nature of emotions somehow stems from the extraordinary variety and oppositions among the phenomena that we call emotions seems plausible to me, if we add the further premise that the debating theorists base their positions on hasty generalizations from their favored ranges of cases. For example, one kind of theorist fixes on cases of emotion that have highly definite conceptual content, that respond flexibly to changes of information and reasoning, and that are highly integrated into the individual's conscious purposes and explicit worldview. Another kind of theorist fixes on cases of emotion that respond poorly or not at all to information and reasoning, have a strong component of bodily arousal, and have close analogues in beasts and babies. Both theorists then ignore the "opposite" kinds of cases as long as they can, or they authorize their theories by finding clever ways to explain away the counterexamples or assimilate them to their own paradigm, or they just deny that those are "really" emotions. Without the hasty generalizations, followed by digging in of theoretical heels, we would presumably get descriptively richer, less theoretical, monolithic or reductive accounts, ones that would be less controversial because the generalizations would be spare and cautious, always keeping a welcoming lookout for the instructive counterexample. Among people who practiced this more descriptive philosophy of emotion, there would presumably be far less of the unyielding disagreement that Rorty deplores. In making this proposal I am supposing that the concept of emotion is not internally incoherent, and that its apparent incoherence comes from the hasty generalizations of theorists.

But this is not Rorty's proposed resolution of the difficulty. Although she does not go quite so far as to say that the concept itself is incoherent, she does blame the concept at least as much as its analysts. She thinks that our current concept of an emotion is a contraption whose ill-assorted parts are accretions traceable to diverse periods of the history of philosophy in which very divergent agendas shaped the claims that were made about the emotions. If we lack a clear view of that history, we are doomed to a conceptual muddle, because we take the concept of emotion at "face value"; that is, we treat it as though it is a single, coherent concept.

> The history of discussions of the passions does not form a smooth continuous history, which expands or narrows the class of *pathe* by following a single line of thought. Sometimes the transformations (say from Aristotelian *pathe* to Stoic *passiones*) arise from moral preoccupations concerning voluntary control; sometimes the transformations (say from Renaissance *amor* to Hobbesian passions and desires) are impelled by metaphysical and scientific preoccupations; sometimes the transformations (say from Hobbesian passions and desires to Humean and Rousseauean sentiments) have a political direction. If nothing else, this should show that *pathe*, *passiones*, affects, emotions, and sentiments do not form a natural class. Additions to that class were made on quite distinctive grounds. Before we can evaluate the competing claims of current polemical debates, before we can understand the force of their various claims, we must first trace the philosophic preoccupations in which they originated (p. 545).

Again, it is not entirely clear whether Rorty is claiming that, for example, the Stoics merely noticed and emphasized that some emotions are subject to voluntary control and had a theory about it and built further theory on it, perhaps overgeneralizing from it, or whether the Stoics *invented* voluntary control of emotions and then passed that trait of emotions (or at least of the concept of emotion) on to us. If the former is so, then it might be *interesting* to know what the Stoics said about voluntary control, but it would not be *necessary* for a contemporary conceptual analyst, as Rorty seems to suggest it is. The analyst would be looking at an emotion like anger and noticing the same feature that the Stoics exploited, namely that people can often control their anger if they have a modicum of understanding of their emotion and make some effort. Since the conceptual analyst would be doing essentially the same kind of thing the Stoic was doing, the analyst would be under no necessity to advert to what the earlier theorist had said.

   If the present-day theorist really needs to know the Stoic discussion, the latter must be somehow constitutive of the very subject matter of the present discussion. In that case when Rorty says, "Before we can evaluate the competing claims of current polemical debates, . . . we must first trace the philosophic preoccupations in which they originated," she must be saying that the "opposing" features that set the parameters of our debate actually *originated* in the earlier philosophical discussions. For example, if we can't appreciate the notion that emotions are subject to voluntary control without knowing the Stoic contribution to the subject, then the fact that emotions are subject to voluntary control is not just *noticed* by the Stoics but *created* by them. Even this would not be enough, strictly speaking, to make acquaintance with historical Stoicism a necessary condition for understanding current debates because the voluntariness of emotions might take on a life of its own after having been socially constructed in terms of Stoic theory. On this interpretation, Rorty's claim that we cannot understand emotions without history of philosophy implies that this history not only created such features of emotions as their voluntariness, reliance on judgments, power to deflect normal behavior, grounding in physiological conditions, and so on, but created these features in such a way that they are *internally tied to the originating theories.*

What kind of understanding of the concept of emotion would emerge from a study of the history of the philosophy of emotion, on the second interpretation of Rorty's thesis? Since by hypothesis our concept of emotion is socially constructed in such a way as to make conceptual–analytical accounts of it chimaeral, the result of the historical studies that Rorty envisages would be our understanding of an incoherent "concept" *as incoherent.* If we wrote the history of the concept of emotion, we would understand *emotion* to be a philosophically constructed chimaera (my dictionary says a chimera is "an imaginary monster compounded of incongruous parts"). We would see that the concept of emotion has no real referent, but only this constructed, chimaeral one. This history would explode a myth, exposing a *purported* concept for the monstrous contraption that it is.

We might wonder why, on this interpretation, the unmasking of the "concept" of emotion could not proceed ahistorically, just by showing the internal contradictions in the concept. Perhaps the idea is that this procedure would never decisively show the concept to be incoherent since a conservative could always fall back on the hope of a future account that will show the concept's coherence. The genealogy of *emotion* might be thought capable of laying this hope finally to rest, by showing once and for all where the contradictory strands in the "concept" came from.

It is not clear to me that Rorty endorses the rather implausible view that I have just sketched. Perhaps she thinks that the influence of philosophical theories on our concept of emotion is of some looser variety, and that phrases like "must first trace the philosophical preoccupations" and "necessary to trace the history" should be taken more weakly than I have done. She does make one remark that seems to make the history of philosophy less crucial:

Officially we are preoccupied with determining whether emotions can be evaluated for their rationality; or whether they are voluntary; or whether they can be "reduced" to cognitions; or whether they are interruptions of behavior that is normally purposeful. But in fact we know better: when we are really thinking, rather than making pronouncements, we know that we evaluate the appropriateness of emotions by criteria that are much richer than those of logical consistency: we are interested in determining whether they are inadequate or excessive, crude or subtle; whether they are harmoniously balanced with one another; whether we admire the character traits they reveal and the motives that usually accompany them. And when we are careful, we usually also distinguish passions, emotions, affects, sentiments (pp. 521–522).

While I would not describe in just Rorty's terms the kind of conceptual analysis I commend, I agree with the direction of her thought in this quotation. She is saying, in effect, that if we stop crudely theorizing and look carefully at the human emotions and our modes of describing and evaluating them, if we stop thinking in terms of simplistic questions about emotions and *look* to see how they actually and richly function in the course of our lives, then the seeming incoherence in the concept of emotion begins to disappear and we see not incoherence and in principle irresolvable debates, but subtle and rich variety linked by family resemblances. So perhaps Rorty is admitting that we may not strictly *need* the history of philosophy after all, but just a more astute and careful and "empirical" and less theoretically hidebound application of philosophical analysis. But because philosophers have historically picked up on some features of emotions to the exclusion of others, the history of philosophy might help in our analysis by alerting us to features that need accommodating and abstractions we need to avoid. On this interpretation, which we might call the "history of philosophy as aid to conceptual analysis" view, Rorty would not be saying that the concept of emotion is an imaginary monster, nor that the history of philosophy is strictly necessary to its analysis. The history of the philosophy of emotions is *a useful but non-necessary adjunct* to philosophical analysis (along with several other adjunct disciplines), in heading off theoretical dead-ends, raising interesting questions, and making interesting proposals.

My purpose is not to adjudicate the interpretation of Rorty's provocative paper, but to defend a kind of conceptual analysis of the emotions. Since the second interpretation allows for conceptual analysis with a recommendation of aid from the history of philosophy, I have no quarrel with it. And I am interested in the first interpretation, not because I ascribe it with confidence to Rorty, but because it is a challenge to my project.

Let us try out an argument, which we might call the realist common sense objection, against the historically constructed chimaera theory (HCCT). As a proposal for examination why not say the following:

Proposal:
We can explain the "opposing" features of emotions much more straightforwardly. We needn't posit that the history of philosophy has created these features, because we can observe them in our everyday experience. For example, we can explain why people have thought that emotions are strongly connected with judgments by noting that people, in any historical period, including our own, can be roused to anger or fear or nostalgia by narratives, and that their anger or fear can often be dispelled instantaneously by telling them something. We needn't resort to the history of philosophy to explain why people think emotions are grounded in physical conditions such as fatigue or the influence of drugs; appeal to their experience is enough. We do not need the history of philosophy to explain why people are sometimes held responsible for their emotions and sometimes exonerated because of them. Nor do we need it to show us why people think that both normal

and abnormal human functioning depend on emotional states and dispositions. These judgments about emotion can be nicely attributed to the human experience of living. And clearly, the philosophers who built their theories on one or another of these features did so by observing them, just as we do. HCCT reverses the order of priority: the philosophers' theories came from the features, not the features from the theories. And if our attributions of these seemingly opposed features to emotions are results of observation rather than of theory construction, then we may have some confidence that they only seem opposed – that the concept of emotion is not a chimaera but a consistent body of attributions. After all, reality, even psychological reality, is not likely to be incoherent.

The weakness of this response is that on HCCT, the fact that we can observe the opposing features is not evidence that they were not created (in the strong sense required by HCCT) by the history of philosophy. As Rorty says, "All these views are embedded in our common speech and common sense, as well as in the literary works that form our understanding of ourselves" (p. 545). So the position is insulated against the common-sense realist objection. But HCCT needs to have more going for it, if we are to abandon common-sense realism for it, than that it is insulated against objections from common-sense realism. We need some positive reason to accept it, since common-sense realism is common sense. If philosophical reference to each of the features of passions that Rorty finds identified and exploited in the history of philosophy can be as well accounted for on the hypothesis that the philosopher in question identifies a previously existent feature as on the hypothesis that the philosopher invents the feature and then passes it down to us in the form of common sense, then the history of philosophy gives us no reason to accept HCCT rather than common-sense realism about emotion features. In that case we just have an evidential stand-off; and since common sense takes natural precedence, we have no reason to abandon it.

But other considerations seem to weaken further the appeal of HCCT. We might wonder where philosophers got the idea of the feature – say, that emotions are dependent on judgments or that emotions disrupt normal behavior or that emotions are necessary to fully normal behavior – if they did not get it from observation. Philosophers are typically pretty creative people, and so we might think there's no mystery here, but my guess is that if we looked at the contexts in their writings in which philosophers identify the features that have come to play roles in modern discussions of the emotions, we would see that they often appeal to examples and observations. This is certainly true of Aristotle and Hume, and I would guess that it is true of most of the main players in Rorty's history of the emotions.

Also, we might wonder why these features have had such sticking power in human life and why they are sustainable at pretty much all educational levels and with so little direct influence from the history of philosophy. We might think that where concepts are invented more or less out of whole cloth and without much of an observational basis, they require more direct and continuous intervention from theorists than the concept of emotion seems to enjoy. Another possible argument might be launched by examining anthropologists' studies of emotions among peoples who cannot have been influenced by the history of philosophy. If such studies show the natives identifying features of emotions like the ones that generate the controversies in recent Western intellectual discussions, that would be evidence that these are observable features antedating philosophical theories that exploit them (see Sections 3.2b, 3.3b, and 3.3c).

Yet another potential argument is that if we expand the list of "opposing" features, as I did at the beginning of this section, we may begin to have a hard time finding plausible originating points for them in the history of philosophy. We may wonder why Rorty selects just four oppositions, and whether all four even of these are plausibly explained in terms of the history of philosophy. In any case, the project of showing that the "opposing" features of emotions were born in the history of philosophical discussions of the emotions has yet to be done. The hypothesis cannot be fully evaluated in the absence of a more or less full, book-length demonstration.

Let us consider the history of philosophy as an aid to conceptual analysis. Rather than think of the history of the philosophy of emotions as *constituting* or creating our concepts and experiences of emotions, we might think of this history as *influencing* them, in the course of responding to the phenomena. Different players in that history respond according to their own particular agendas and theoretical frameworks, so that they highlight different features of the emotions, which, as we have seen, do have many diverse features. The anthropologist Robert Levy has proposed that societies may "hypercognize" or "hypocognize" emotion types. For example, the Tahitians, among whom Levy did field work, hypercognize anger but hypocognize sadness. They have a subtle vocabulary for describing, explaining, evaluating, and prescribing for anger but not even a word that denotes sadness. The Tahitians do become sad, but they are less likely to notice it and do not identify it with the same precision as societies in which it is more "cognized."[7] Something similar might be true of the generic features of emotions: For theorists with differing interests, different features will be salient, and the saliencies will both influence and result from their theories; but this is not to say the features are created by the theories. Perhaps Aristotle, the Stoics, Augustine, and others did not create the features that our concept of an emotion attribute to emotions; instead, they all more or less successfully describe phenomena that have been relatively stable through human history, the same kind of thing that contemporary analytical philosophers, anthropologists, psychologists, neuroscientists, and evolutionary biologists are giving

---

[7] See "Emotion, Knowing, and Culture," in Richard A. Shweder and Robert A. LeVine (eds.), *Culture Theory: Essays on Mind, Self, and Emotion* (Cambridge, England: Cambridge University Press, 1984), pp. 214–237.

their accounts of. Emotions invite highly perspectival accounts because they are many-sided phenomena. On this picture we may admit possible influences from Aristotle, the Stoics, and so on, on our way of thinking about the emotions, but it would be an exaggeration to talk about the transformation of Aristotelian *pathe* into Stoic *passiones,* as though the subject matter of their discussions is not the rather old familiar facts of anger, fear, joy, and hope. Instead, we could talk about Aristotelian *ideas* about emotions and Stoic *ideas.* In that case the puzzles we experience when we study the emotions as philosophers would be not just products of this history but, more importantly, products of the phenomena – the emotions that we observe in human beings. And the supposed conflicts that we find within the Aristotelian account, or the conflicts between that account and, say, the Stoic account, would be due as much to the actual features of emotions and passions as to theorists' accounts of them. An imperialistically social constructivist account of emotions is as far from the truth about them as a purely neurological account. Each, according to its special interests, "hypercognizes" certain features.

Let us distinguish emotion category concepts from emotion type concepts. Examples of category concepts are ones that have roughly the same degree of generality as *emotion: sentiment,* πάθος, *passio, affect, affectus, passion,* and so on. Type concepts are concepts of subclasses within the categories of emotion, passion, affect, and so on. Examples are *anger, dismay, sorrow, shame,* τὸ νεμεσᾶν,[8] *liget,*[9] and so on. Emotion category concepts encompass a range of type concepts. Thus *emotion* is the class that includes anger, nostalgia, shame, joy, and perhaps (on the periphery) puzzlement, amusement (at humor), surprise, and the startle response. Because *emotion* and *passio* and πάθος encompass partially different ranges of types, they will be different, though largely overlapping, concepts. For example, Thomas Aquinas lists desire (*concupiscentia*) as a type of *passio,* whereas we would probably not regard it as a kind of emotion (though we might include it among the passions); and as Rorty makes abundantly clear in the main body of her paper, the concept of a πάθος in Aristotle's society was much broader than our concept of emotion, encompassing such things as bodily wounds and states of sense perception. I think that the studies in the history of philosophy that Rorty commends can sensitize us to the variability of the category concepts related to that of emotions (passions, sentiments, etc.) and to the relativity of such variation to human interests; they can mitigate a certain platonizing tendency in the study of emotions, a tendency that natural languages

---

[8] An emotion type discussed by Aristotle, different from envy (φθόνος), characterized by discomfort about someone else's undeserved good fortune. See *Rhetoric,* Book II, Chapter 9 (pp. 1386b10–1387b20).

[9] A dominant emotion in the moral psychology of the Ilongots, a head-hunting group in the Philippines (see Section 3.3b).

seem to engender. The history of philosophy and psychology is full of lists of "basic" emotions, and these lists differ remarkably from one another; the best explanation of this diversity seems to be that the lists reflect different sets of theoretical interests (see Section 3.1c). Also, the history of philosophy, like cultural anthropology, can moderate our naive tendency to think that our emotion type vocabulary divides the world of the emotions in the natural and only possible way (see Section 1.5e).

So the concept of emotion can be thought of as determined by the range of type concepts that it encompasses, but it must be admitted to be somewhat indeterminate because of questionable types on the outer fringes, such as surprise, startle, amusement (e.g., at jokes), interest (e.g., in philosophical ideas), and others. The intuitions of good speakers of English vary as to whether these states are emotions. But the bare question of English usage is not in itself a very interesting one; we want to know *why* type concepts like *anger, fear,* and *envy* are solidly in everybody's paradigm of emotion while *surprise* and *startle* are only in some people's. One way to get at an answer to this question will be to take seriously the various "opposing" features of the paradigm cases that Rorty's essay invites us to highlight, as well as others that I have indicated. If we can come up with a broad unifying conception of emotion that accommodates all these opposing features, then we will have a conception that unifies at least the paradigm cases and gives us a plausible account of why English speakers group this range of mental states together under a single class name. That is the main task of Chapter 2.

In Chapter 3 I will then test the conception by analyzing a wide range of type concepts, including not only the paradigm types but pretty much anything that anybody is inclined to call an emotion, including the contested types. My strategy will be not so much to try to decide whether each type belongs to the category of emotion as to try to see in what ways each type is similar, and in what ways dissimilar, to the undisputed paradigm cases. Thus I do not offer my account as a "theory," as implying that all and only what we would properly call an emotion fits the proffered conception. Instead I shall argue that the conception is superior to its competitors in making sense of all the "opposing" features in the paradigm cases. I shall try to show fairly precisely the various ways in which the other cases deviate from the paradigm. But despite the fuzziness on the edges, I think I will have shown that the concept of emotion is not a monster.

1.4. DECONSTRUCTING *EMOTION* VIA THE LIFE SCIENCES

There is a strong movement these days to subsume psychology under biology and related disciplines such as physiology and especially neurophysiology. Paul Griffiths's *What Emotions Really Are: The Problem of Psychological*

Categories,[10] is an especially explicit, philosophically sophisticated, and uncompromising example of this trend. Besides this, the book is focused on emotions and directly attacks conceptual analysis as an approach to understanding emotions. For all these reasons, it is interesting for our purposes, and I hope I will be forgiven for paying so much attention to it.

a. Science Fractures a Concept?

Griffiths's thesis is reminiscent of Rorty's proposal that we deconstruct the concept of emotion using the history of philosophy because, trading on some of the "oppositions" that are present in the ordinary concept of emotion, he proposes that under scientific study the concept of emotion will "fracture" into three radically distinct concepts. Recent science shows that the vernacular concept of emotion covers a range of things that have as little to recommend their assimilation under a single concept as the hodgepodge in Aristotle's class of superlunary objects.

Emotion is like the category of "superlunary" objects in ancient astronomy. There is a well-defined category of "everything outside the orbit of the moon" but it turns out that superlunary objects do not have something specially in common that distinguishes them from other arbitrary collections of objects. . . . what we know about ["emotions"] suggests that there is no rich collection of generalizations about this range of phenomena that distinguishes them from other psychological phenomena. They do not constitute a single object of knowledge (p. 14).

In particular, he is impressed by the "opposition" between (a) emotions that show a clear physiological syndrome, are reflexlike, pancultural, and phylogenetically ancient, and do not require higher cognitive processing and (b) emotions that do require such processing and may be quite culturally specific and do not show any clear physiology.

The first group he calls (following Paul Ekman) "affect program responses." . . . the affect program theory deals with a range of emotions corresponding very roughly to the occurrent instances of the English terms "surprise," "fear," "anger," "disgust," "contempt," "sadness," and "joy." The affect programs are short-term, stereotypical responses involving facial expression, autonomic nervous system arousal, and other elements. The same patterns of response occur in all cultures and homologues are found in related species. These patterns are triggered by a cognitive system which is "modular" in the sense that it does not freely exchange information with other cognitive processes (p. 8).

"Higher cognitive emotions" are divided into two discrete categories. Griffiths calls the first category "irruptive motivations," following Robert Frank.[11] These are like the affect program responses in that both kinds of

---

[10] Chicago: University of Chicago Press, 1997.
[11] *Passions Within Reason: The Strategic Role of the Emotions* (New York: Norton, 1988).

emotion "produce a form of passivity" (p. 245); that is, they are not intentionally produced but *come over* the subject in response to something.
These states, which include instances of loyalty, jealousy, and guilt, as well as
episodes that vernacular speech would identify with the same names as are
used for the affect programs, are "states which interfere with the smooth
unfolding of plans designed to secure our long-term goals" (p. 246). Thus
they are not only *irruptive* (i.e., passive states) but also *disruptive* of long-term
goal-seeking. An example of irruptive motivational anger would be the emotion of a man that drives him to take revenge on people for trespassing his
rights even when taking revenge undermines his considered long-term goals
(e.g., making money, keeping his friends). Frank argues that such an emotion is evolutionarily adaptive, despite first appearances, because people will
be disinclined to trespass the rights of a person who is likely to go ballistic
in this way. The irruptive motivations have surface irrationality that hides
a deeper function. These "emotions" may occur in the absence of facial
expression and autonomic arousal and do involve higher cognitive processing. In our example, the concept of a violated right, which the angry subject
deploys in his response to the situation, clearly requires the functioning of
"higher" parts of the brain, not just the "informationally encapsulated" ones
that operate in the affect programs.

The second kind of higher cognitive "emotions" are "socially constructed." Griffiths distinguishes two kinds of social construction, the "social
concept model" and the "social role model," and dismisses the former as
trivial. He points out that many social constructionists in emotion theory
think that a society constructs emotions by providing categories in terms
of which its people respond emotionally to objects and situations. But this
"is a model of the emotions themselves only because an emotion is identified with the thought that the eliciting situation is present" (p. 139; here
Griffiths refers to a version of the propositional attitude theory that we will
discuss in the next subsection). The kind of socially constructed emotions
that fill a significant category are the ones he calls *disclaimed actions*. These
are essentially fake emotions – behavioral patterns that one produces, under
the guidance of cultural rules, for the sake of achieving some goal. Thus,
according to Griffiths, they lack the "passivity" that he finds common to
the affect programs and the irruptive motivations. Far from disrupting goal-
directed behavior, these are stratagems to purpose. Griffiths hastens to point
out that the subject of such an "emotion" is not merely pretending: "The
subject does not have conscious access to the causes of their [*sic*] behavior
and provides an erroneous explanation of their behavior that masquerades
as an introspective report" (p. 158). Borrowing from Robert Solomon, he
says,

A good example is the display of anger as an unconsciously implemented "strategic
behavior" in a marital quarrel. The agent has reasoned that they can improve their

position by adopting the role of someone who believes themselves wronged. The agent is not simply acting, because although they are motivated by these considerations they are not aware of this motivation. In such a case the agent will behave as if they had judged themselves to be wronged. There is all the difference in the world between this and actually believing oneself to have been wronged (p. 233).

These "emotions" are so different from the items that belong in his other two categories that Griffiths has some doubts about whether to include this class as one of the kinds of things into which the vernacular concept of emotion fractures:

> The disclaimed action emotions cannot be placed in a single category with the other emotions because they are essentially pretenses. It would be like putting ghost possession in the category of parasitic diseases. Averill and Boothroyd (1977) suggest that "falling in love" is the adoption of a social role which licenses the performance of certain behaviors. If so, then just as there are no ghosts to explain ghost possession, there is no state of love to explain love behavior (p. 246).

But since Griffiths is sometimes willing to countenance their inclusion, let us say that, according to him, what folks call emotion, when subjected to scientific pressure, fractures into three concepts: affect program responses, irruptive motivations, and disclaimed actions.

We will want to ask two questions about this schema. First, what is the scientific rationale for it, and how does that rationale impinge on the project of giving an account of the emotions for purposes of a psychology of the virtues? And second, are the proposed categories really discrete? Do they "carve nature at its joints"? Are they natural kinds? Do they neatly divide the area that folks call "emotions" and provide a replacement schema that makes more sense of the phenomena? But before we turn to these questions, we must look at Griffiths's direct critique of conceptual analysis as an approach to understanding the emotions.

b. Conceptual Analysis as Propositional Attitude Analysis

Griffiths thinks that conceptual analysis is strongly, if not essentially, tied to what he calls the "propositional attitude" theory of emotions. According to the variants of this theory, emotions are either simply evaluative beliefs, or evaluative beliefs plus some added feature such as physiological perturbation, desire, or "affect." Thus a person's being in the state of fear is equivalent to her believing she is in danger, or to this belief plus an appropriate kind of physiological arousal, or the desire not to be in danger, or a certain phenomenological tone called "affect." Griffiths raises a number of objections to the propositional attitude theories, such as that a subject's beliefs often conflict with his emotions (he believes earthworms to be harmless but still fears them), that people can have the relevant evaluative beliefs yet feel no emotion (I believe I have sinned, but I don't feel guilty), that people respond with emotion to presentations of what they know to be fiction (e.g., in novels and movies), and so on. It is true that conceptual analysis of emotions has been dominated, since the 1960s, by propositional attitude theories, and these objections and others devastate the propositional attitude theories. But the objections require nothing beyond the resources of conceptual analysis: a rich enough fund of examples from ordinary experience and some careful reflection. I have previously raised these objections and others[12] and will discuss them in Section 2.4.

A somewhat more significant objection to conceptual analysis is that it "can tell us only what people currently believe about emotion" (p. 39), not about what emotions really are, in a sense that is determined by their underlying causal mechanisms. This strong association of what emotions really are with a certain kind of underlying causal mechanism is the crux of Griffiths's argument against conceptual analysis. The kind of causal mechanism he has in mind is the kind that evolutionary biology and neuroscience, as branches of physical science, try to establish. Let us say that some state or syndrome of states that we could call "fear" in human beings can be shown to be present (with variations) in all animal species that bear a certain evolutionary proximity to us (say, the primates, or, less proximately, the mammals). This would yield a causal explanation of human fear in terms of the mechanism of *descent*: Humans have this syndrome because their ancestors had something like it. That humans' ancestors had something like it and that we have retained the trait can perhaps be explained by a second explanatory strategy, *adaptation*: Because fear involves avoidance of and escape from dangers, fear seems to promote survival. Associated with these kinds of explanation would be the expectation of cross-species neurological similarities in the fear response. For example, we would expect to find significant parallels in the neurological circuitry and chemistry of fear in rhesus monkeys and human beings and somewhat weaker but still significant parallels in rats. Explanations of fear in terms of the causal mechanisms of *neural circuitry and chemistry* would thus be another kind of explanation that, in Griffiths's view, would count as contributing to our knowledge of what an emotion "really is." Since these patterns of explanation require stable and determinately structured causal mechanisms ("causal homeostatic mechanisms") and since such mechanisms determine natural kinds, Griffiths is preoccupied with establishing natural kinds as a basis for explanation in psychology. The fear affect program is such a natural kind, as is, presumably, irruptive motivational fear (though Griffiths admits that we have little solid information about what the homeostatic causal mechanism is in this case). Clearly, if what we mean by "what an emotion really is" is the homeostatic physical

---

[12] "Solomon on the Control of Emotions." *Philosophy and Phenomenological Research* **44** (1984): 395–403; "What an Emotion Is: A Sketch." *The Philosophical Review* **97** (1988): 183–209; "Propositions and Animal Emotion." *Philosophy* **71** (1996): 147–156.

mechanism that underlies the emotion, then we will not get very close to an answer by asking what ordinary people, in the ordinary course of their ordinary experience, have come to believe about emotions.

On the other hand, if What is an emotion? is not a question about underlying physical mechanism (whether thought of in terms of distant history or present operation), but about emotions as experienced by human subjects, as structures of meaning and explanation in the course of social life, as entering into our actions and reasoning, as evaluated to be proper or improper, praiseworthy, blameworthy, or morally indifferent, and as bearing on our happiness and maturity and relationships with one other and with God (see the passage from Trollope with which this chapter begins), then conceptual analysis may be the central approach to determining "what an emotion really is."

According to Griffiths, conceptual analysis of fear is just a description of how people in the analyst's society use the word or what they believe about the word's supposed referent. Something analogous but presumably more general would be true of conceptual analysis of "emotion." Analysts of this ilk dismiss empirical findings about fear, such as Paul Ekman's evidence that facial expressions of fear are pancultural and interculturally recognizable and Joseph LeDoux's discoveries about the neural circuitry involved in the production of fear. They regard this information as irrelevant because it is not known to most users of the word "fear" and therefore cannot be part of the meaning of "fear." They are, according to Griffiths, not *au courant* of the philosophy of language which, since the work of Saul Kripke and Hilary Putnam, sees that linguistic usage can change in response to scientific discoveries. For example, "fish" once included whales, but the discovery that whales are mammals has changed that, at least for sophisticated speakers.

If fear is a putative natural kind like water or crustacean then a causal theory [of meaning] would say that "fear" has as part of its meaning a schema awaiting the results of future research. Fear is "whatever is happening to people in these paradigm cases" (pp. 4–5).

If it turns out that "fear" is ambiguous as between more than one naturally distinct category of states as defined by their homeostatic causal mechanisms, then science might lead to a revision of the extension of "fear," in much the way that it has led us to exclude whales from the extension of "fish." For example, if affect program fear is as different from disclaimed action fear as Griffiths thinks it is, biology and neuroscience might lead us to stop thinking of disclaimed action fear as a sort of fear. We might instead adopt the policy of calling it "fake danger response."

In the following sections I shall argue that it is implausible to suppose that the field of things that folks call emotions can be divided, for scientific purposes, into the three categories that Griffiths has proposed. The phenomena interlock in ways that make these categories very awkward and artificial. To put the matter in Griffiths's terms, affect programs, irruptive motivations, and disclaimed actions are not natural kinds. Or, to put the matter in Rorty's terms, the "oppositions" of attribute among the things that we call human emotions do not divide them into the kind of neatly discrete categories that Griffiths's theory needs them to divide into. His categories might be useful for certain restricted purposes; for example, one might undertake a study of just those things that fit the category of irruptive motivations, simply because they fit the pattern of explanation that Robert Frank proposes for them. But to do so would be to leave out a number of other kinds of "higher cognitive" emotions that do not fit the category, including some that we might call "higher cognitive affect programs."

I shall argue that, given the ways that the various "opposite" attributes of emotions criss-cross the whole field, defeating any neat categorial scheme, it is better to think of what folks call emotions as not fracturing into several natural kinds, but as belonging to one category, albeit one that is fuzzy on the edges and held together in part by family resemblances and in part by a "homeostatic causal mechanism" of a kind rather different from what Griffiths has in mind. I shall argue that while studies of emotion by physical science, along the lines commended by Griffiths and LeDoux, are possible for certain ranges of emotions (especially the affect programs) and will no doubt yield interesting results, they are not likely to account for the whole range of emotions as well as the best conceptual analysis, supplemented with scientific knowledge, can do. And especially for purposes of moral psychology of the virtues and vices, where the higher cognitive shaping of the emotions (including the affect programs) is so important, conceptual analysis is the indispensable central method.

c. Affect Programs

The affect program responses are clearly the most encouraging kind of emo-tion for the biologically oriented psychologist because they yield more read-ily to biological explanatory strategies than do the items that fit in Griffiths's other two categories or other emotions that fit in none of these categories. Paul Ekman has spent more than thirty years studying responses that he calls "anger," "fear," "sadness," "enjoyment," "disgust," and "surprise," and he has gathered empirical evidence that the "emotions" he studies are sim-ilar to one another but distinct from other kinds of psychological states (e.g., beliefs) in having characteristic facial expressions that can be cross-culturally recognized with fairly high reliability and distinctive autonomic arousal, among other marks; he has also gathered empirical evidence that these states differ from one another by the *particular* facial expressions and *particular* patterns of autonomic arousal that are characteristic of them. Griffiths adds that these emotions are "informationally encapsulated" – that is, controlled by a kind of information processing that is very rapid and largely unconscious and not susceptible to direct modification by higher cognitive processes. This is one of the chief ways in which Griffiths keeps the affect program responses distinct in kind from the "higher cognitive" emotions. Griffiths and Ekman both stress that states strongly homologous to these six emotions can be found in species evolutionarily close to *homo sapiens.*

Joseph LeDoux's neuroscientific work on fear[13] is a good example of the kind of emotion research that Griffiths commends. A chief research strategy used to locate brain functions is to destroy, by highly selective surgery, some part of the brain and then to observe which functions have been lost. Another technique is to inject a kind of stain into one part of the brain and scare the subject, then to kill the subject and look at other parts of the brain under a microscope to see where the stain got projected through the neural network. Because humans have been slow to volunteer as subjects in this kind of research, much of it is done on animals such as monkeys, rabbits, rats, and pigeons, who are not consulted. We have seen that Griffiths stresses the importance of homologies, and not just of adaptive strategies, in explanations of emotion, and he ties homologies to homeostatic causal mechanisms. Species evolutionarily distant from human beings, such as wasps and clams, have response patterns that are analogous to fear inasmuch as they are responses to potential harm and involve avoidance of the harm. It even turns out that a surprisingly wide range of animals (including the fruit fly and marine snails) can be conditioned to respond with fear to new stimuli (p. 147). Presumably these responses, like human affect program fear, are an adaptation to dangerous environments, and there is some kind of causal mechanism by which the response operates. But wasps are so unlike human beings that it would not be a very promising research strategy to correlate surgical ablations of wasp counterparts of brains with the resulting functional deficits, if the purpose was to discover the causal mechanism underlying *human* fear. Wasp fear and human fear are only analogous, while monkey fear and human fear are homologous: because monkeys and people are evolutionarily closely related, their fears (at least a certain range of what we call fears) have very similar underlying causal mechanisms. Where we are not sure of the extent of similarity between the two mechanisms, the best bet, Griffiths is saying, will be with organisms that are known to be closer in descent.

Let me give you an example of the kind of explanation LeDoux's work yields. Wanting to discover the brain mechanisms underlying fear responses to a conditioned auditory stimulus, he applied the surgical and staining techniques I mentioned above to rats that he conditioned (or tried to condition, after surgery that sometimes prevented conditioning) to a sound by pairing it with an electrical shock. A normal rat, so conditioned, would respond to

---

[13] *The Emotional Brain: The Mysterious Underpinnings of Emotional Life* (New York: Simon and Schuster, 1998).

the sound, in the absence of the electrical shock, with the marks of affect
program fear: muscular "freezing," increased blood pressure and heart rate,
reduced pain responsivity, and elevated stress hormones from the pituitary
gland (p. 144). To find out how the normal rat's brain works, LeDoux systematically damaged various brain parts, starting with the "highest" part of
the auditory pathway. At each stage he would attempt to condition the damaged rat to see whether it could still be conditioned and, if so, whether any
parts of the fear response were missing. He started by damaging the auditory
cortex, and he found that this damage had no effect on the rat's condition-
ability. So he then damaged "the next lower station, the auditory thalamus,
and these lesions completely prevented fear conditioning" (p. 152). From
this combination of effects he inferred that the auditory stimulus had to pass
through the thalamus but could bypass the "higher," more discriminating,
auditory cortex. Where did it go from the auditory thalamus? To find out,
he injected stain into the rat's auditory thalamus, scared the rat by using the
conditioned stimulus, and put slices of the rat's brain under the microscope.
The stain he had injected into the thalamus could be seen in four different
subcortical regions, so one of these areas was probably where the responses
characteristic of fear are generated. A process of further elimination was
needed to determine which one, so LeDoux damaged each of these parts in
some more rats' brains, to see which kind of damage prevented fear conditioning. He found that damage to the amygdala was the kind that prevented
such conditioning. More particularly, damage to the central nucleus of the
amygdala interfered with all the different measures of conditioned fear, but
he also discovered that each of these responses is brought about by different
outputs of the central nucleus.

For example, I demonstrated that lesions of different projections of the central nucleus separately interfered with freezing and blood pressure conditioned responses –
lesions of one of the projections (the periaqueductal gray) interfered with freezing
but not blood pressure response, whereas lesions of another (the lateral hypothalamus) interfered with the blood pressure but not the freezing response (pp. 158–159).

The circuitry identified for conditioned fear by the investigations I have
summarized is thus something like the following: (1) A conditioned stimulus activates neurons in the ear, which project to (2) the auditory cortex
and (3) the auditory thalamus. The auditory thalamus sends signals to (4)
the central nucleus of the amygdala, which then projects to (5, etc.) several
other parts of the brain which, no doubt by yet other mediations, bring about
the bodily and behavioral marks of fear. This is of course only a crude and
partial account of the causal mechanism underlying fear. Neuroscientists
have much to say about the mechanics of the transmission of signals along
the neural pathways, and we have said nothing about the feeling of fear (if
rats do feel fear), which involves the complicated and controversial neuroscience of consciousness. But I think I have reported enough to indicate

the *kind* of explanation of emotions that biologically oriented psychologists look for. They are explanations in terms of physical underlying causal mechanisms.

Clearly, LeDoux's scientific work is limited to the emotions that Ekman calls affect program responses. The importance of the sensory thalamus and relatively less importance of the sensory cortex and complete absence of essential involvement of language centers in LeDoux's fear reflects what Griffiths calls its "informationally encapsulated" nature. The fact that conditioning is the only strategy for emotional learning that is in view for LeDoux's research is another indicator that he is dealing exclusively with "lower" cognitive processes. The fact that LeDoux can conduct his research almost entirely by manipulating and observing rats reflects the evolutionary homology that Griffiths attributes to the affect programs. And it is equally clear that any emotion that lacked clear and distinctive physiological markers would be quite foreign to LeDoux's research program.

But we can here raise a question that Griffiths's metaphysics discourages us from asking: Are the boundaries of the category of affect programs set by the nature of the phenomena under investigation, or by the limitations of scientific technique and interests? It is one of Griffiths's main theses that natural kinds are the posits of our best scientific theories. But this will not be so if science ignores certain cases simply because they do not fit the theory or are not susceptible to currently available research techniques. In that case it may be better to admit that current science cannot explain all the cases that seem to belong together.

LeDoux does not deny the possibility that some instances of adult human fear may depend on some of the highest cognitive functions. In other words, he does not hold that the fear that he researches is "informationally encapsulated," though he does show that fear *can* occur without the involvement of the "higher" brain centers. But his research does not purport to give a full neural explanation for instances of fear that do involve "higher" brain centers. Although he does not speak of natural kinds, it is as though he allows that there may be instances of the natural kind fear that his neurological theory of fear does not explain. Antonio Damasio[14] is even more explicit in denying that what Griffiths calls affect program fear is necessarily informationally encapsulated.

We have seen that one of the defining characteristics of affect program states as a supposed "natural kind" is that they are "informationally encapsulated" and that they thus belong in an entirely separate category from the "higher cognitive emotions." Othello's sexual jealousy cannot be an affect program, because it is mediated by Othello's understanding a narrative or implied narrative. For his jealousy to be an affect program, "he would

---

[14] *Descartes' Error: Emotion, Reason, and the Human Brain* (New York: Avon Books, 1994).

have had to catch Desdemona in bed with Cassio, or at least have seen the handkerchief, before his jealousy was initiated" (Griffiths, p. 117). As Griffiths says at the end of the book, "no one expects discoveries about the fear affect program to apply to responses to danger mediated by higher cognition" (p. 242), speaking presumably of someone who has been convinced by the argument of his book. (Calling both these kinds of things "emotions" is on a par with calling the sun and some Martian fossilized bacteria "superlunary objects.")

But if natural kind concepts are supposed to carve nature at its joints, these do not seem to be natural kinds because many cases of emotions span the categories. Consider the following case. Just prior to lunch time, a hungry philosopher, browsing in the library, comes on a review of his recent book in a prominent journal and, as he reads, he realizes that the reviewer has found a fatal objection to his central argument, an argument on which he has built his career, his reputation, and his sense of his own professional worth. He breaks out in a cold sweat, his heart starts pounding and his blood pressure goes up, the muscles in his back and neck tense up, his mouth goes dry, and his appetite disappears. His involuntary facial expression is one of extreme distress. This appears to be an affect program emotion mediated by higher cognitive processes. It looks for all the world as though the information from his cerebral cortex (the philosopher is reading sophisticated theoretical material and understanding both its theoretical significance and the significance it has for his career, his reputation, and his sense of importance) is getting through very nicely to his amygdala and having quite an impact on it. Furthermore, the philosopher is sophisticated enough to realize that he is in a state of panic, and exactly why. Here, then, is an affect program state that appears not to be "informationally encapsulated." Furthermore, the affect program is not "triggered" in a reflexlike way as Griffiths's affect programs are supposed to be triggered but comes on gradually as the realization dawns on our philosopher that the jig is up for his theory. It is an affect program state that is also a higher cognitive emotion.

It is just this kind of case that Antonio Damasio is trying to explain when he claims that the "limbic system" (the more "primitive" and evolutionarily older part of the brain in which much of emotional processing is supposed to go on, and includes the amygdala) is accessible to the cerebral cortex (see Damasio, pp. 131–139):

In many circumstances of our life as social beings...we know that our emotions are triggered only after an evaluative, voluntary, nonautomatic mental process. Because of the nature of our experience, a broad range of stimuli and situations has become associated with those stimuli which are innately set to cause emotions. The reaction to that broad range of stimuli and situations can be filtered by an interposed mindful evaluation. And because of the thoughtful, evaluative filtering process, there is room for variation in the extent and intensity of preset emotional patterns...(Damasio, p. 130).

Griffiths is aware that his "natural kinds" threaten to blend together under influence from the phenomena, and he defends the border by two strategies. First, he admits and then minimizes the point I have made. He says,

It seems clear that emotions [read: affect programs] are sometimes triggered as a result of higher cognitive processes. A complex chain of reasoning may reveal that an entirely novel stimulus is dangerous, and fear ensues (p. 92).

After the brief admission in these two sentences, Griffiths turns away from the point and for several pages discusses affect programs that are "triggered despite, or in opposition to, higher cognitive processes" (p. 92). And note the rather evasive and reducing locution he uses in his admission: "triggered as a result of." The expression is designed to dissociate the higher cognition from the emotion, to suggest that it is somewhat incidental to it – certainly not defined by it – but not even really triggered by it but only triggered as a result of it. Five pages later he comes back to the admission and expands it in such a way as to confirm the distance between the higher cognition and the emotion. Here he rather confusingly says that "In some cases higher cognitive processes may be able to trigger emotional responses directly" (p. 97) and then in a footnote takes this back a bit:

Creating emotion by imagining emotionally significant stimuli may be an example of the direct effect of central cognitive processes. On the other hand, this may work via the generation of visual and other sensory imagery. It would then be an internal analogue of the triggering of emotion by the visual arts (p. 97, note).

Surely there are cases of autonomically vigorous emotions about objects accessed via higher cognition that are not cases of "imagining emotionally significant stimuli." And what if emotions *are* occasioned by visual and other sensory imagery? Would this suggest, as Griffiths's "on the other hand" seems to imply, that higher cognitive processing is not involved? Many paintings have a narrative background the understanding of which contributes significantly to their emotional impact. Might Griffiths say that such a narrative background, as contrasted with the supposedly lower cognitive mere sensory impression, cannot contribute to the autonomic arousal characteristic of the affect programs? In any case, he goes on:

The modular system which triggers emotion has an interestingly biased mechanism for learning. The biased nature of the learning mechanism provides a further reason for thinking of *the emotion-triggering system as independent of higher cognitive processes*, since the biases seem to be specific to the learning of emotional responses. The isolation of the triggering system from cognition need not be complete. It may be that rational evaluations of stimuli as emotionally significant can cause the triggering system to be sensitive to those stimuli in future instances. I know of no experimental literature that would allow this to be determined at present. There are also results which seem to show that higher cognitive processes can affect the initiation of emotions in much the same way that they affect the perception of pain (Melzack 1973). . . . Finally,

Ekman's work on cultural display rules suggests that other cognitive processes can block the display of automatic emotional responses by recruiting the bodily systems involved for other purposes (p. 97f, italics added).

So we seem to have four ways that Griffiths admits higher cognition to be possibly involved in the "triggering" of the affect program responses. The first is that affect programs might be triggered via imagination, though it is possible that this is not really higher cognition because such imagining may just produce sensory imagery. Let us clarify his second, third, and fourth possibilities with examples. A man might have an ordinary untutored fear of snakes. Let us say this is unreflective and automatic, thus conforming to the basic paradigm of the affect programs. But then he reads about the poisonous properties of copperheads in his district, thus possibly overlaying his lower cognitive responsiveness with higher cognitive information. Griffiths is admitting that such higher processing of the "stimulus" might enhance the basic responsiveness. The third kind of case would be a higher cognitive assessment, not of the "stimulus" but of the emotion itself. For example, a therapist might tell a client who has a mild phobia of snakes that, because of the therapy he has received, he will respond less violently to a snake the next time he encounters one. Griffiths is admitting that such higher cognitive "input" might actually affect the emotional response. An example of the fourth kind would be a traditional Japanese person whose culture has taught him that it is impolite to look sad. Consequently, when he is impinged upon by a sadness-evoking stimulus, he automatically checks himself after an instantaneous facial expression of sadness and puts on a happy face. Griffiths seems to admit that the effect of the cultural teaching, which is presumably higher cognitive, on the duration of his sad facial expression might thereby reduce other marks (say, blood pressure) of the syndrome.

I submit that the involvement of higher cognitive processes in the panic of our hypothetical professor does not fit any of the four models of involvement that Griffiths admits. He is shy to acknowledge cases in which the very object of an affect program response is wholly and fundamentally presented via higher cognition and could be presented in no other way.[15] To admit this

---

[15] Besides this kind of case, there seem to be "lower" cognitive emotions that also fail to fit the paradigm. LeDoux says, in a comment that is reminiscent of the affect program thesis, that there is probably no such thing as the neurophysiology of *emotion*, but instead each of the basic emotion types has its own neurochemistry and circuitry. Thus separate investigations must be undertaken for fear, sadness, anger, disgust, and so on. But interestingly, LeDoux mentions a basic emotion that is not included in Ekman's list or in Griffiths's, namely, lust or sexual arousal. An essential mark of the affect programs, as Griffiths defines them following Ekman's work, is that they have a distinctive facial expression that is panculturally recognizable. It seems likely that lust, despite its obvious attractiveness from an evolutionary point of view and the plausibility of supposing it to have a distinctive physiology, gets left off the list of affect programs because it lacks such a facial expression.

kind of case would be to give up the most significant part of the "fracturing" of the concept of emotion that is the fundamental thesis of Griffiths's book.

Perhaps Griffiths will respond that such imagined cases and anecdotal evidence as my panic stricken professor are insufficient to establish the claim that his supposed "natural kind" emotion categories overlap. Damasio, too, offers only an imagined case:

> If you hear of an acquaintance's death, your heart may pound, your mouth dry up, your skin blanch, a section of your gut contract, the muscles in your neck and back tense up while those in your face design a mask of sadness. In either case, there are changes in a number of parameters in the function of viscera (heart, lungs, gut, skin), skeletal muscles (those that are attached to your bones), and endocrine glands (such as the pituitary and adrenals). A number of peptide modulators are released from the brain into the bloodstream. The immune system also is modified rapidly. The baseline activity of smooth muscles in artery walls may increase, and produce contraction and thinning of blood vessels (the result is pallor); or decrease, in which case the smooth muscle would relax and blood vessels dilate (the result is flushing) (Damasio, p. 135).

But the supposition that such cases occur, and occur in abundance in human life, is so much a part of common sense and is so well supported by everyday experience that I should think it is Griffiths who needs to supply empirical evidence that people do *not* experience autonomic arousal in response to objects accessed essentially through higher cognitive processing. He supplies no such empirical backing and indeed seems to try to prevent the reader from looking at the obvious evidence.

Another example of this evasiveness is his discussion of Damasio (Griffiths, pp. 102–106), who, as we have seen, believes that the "lower" parts of the brain, like the amygdala, are susceptible to inputs from the parts of the brain that mediate language and reasoning. Damasio does, admittedly, make a couple of mistakes in his account of the relation between the higher and the lower processes. The first is not quite the mistake of which Griffiths accuses him – that of supposing that all emotions involve visceral activation. Instead, Damasio posits an "as if" circuit that enables the brain to read visceral activation even when there is none, analogous to the pains that amputees sometimes experience in their missing limbs. This allows him to posit that even emotions involving no visceral activation are experienced as "somatic markers" – pleasant or unpleasant somatic sensations. Griffiths's objection that some episodes that fall under the ordinary concept of emotion do not involve any measurable visceral change can be translated into a correct objection, namely that some emotions do not even involve any experience "as if" of visceral change. Another mistake is that Damasio has a somewhat confused concept of *innate* (see Griffiths, pp. 55–64, 104–106). But Damasio's basic thesis that organs like the amygdala can be activated by higher cognitive processes is almost certainly correct and devastating for the basic thesis of Griffiths's book. One would expect Griffiths to aim all his fire power at *that* thesis, but instead he presents arguments against the weaker spots in Damasio's picture, arguments that create a bit of smoke to keep the reader from seeing clearly that Griffiths did not answer the crucial argument against his view that the affect programs and the higher cognitive emotions are two completely discrete classes of things.

The fact seems to be that some emotions exhibiting the physiological syndromes that Griffiths ascribes to the affect programs are informationally encapsulated, and others are not. Instances of phobic fear are good examples of the former group; our panic-stricken professor is an example of the latter. And there are many intermediate and mixed cases, in which higher and lower cognition work in tandem or the emotion is partially but not wholly susceptible to rational modification. Brain scientists such as Damasio and LeDoux have partial explanations of these phenomena in terms of the modularity of the brain. The phenomena do not lend themselves to Griffiths's neat two-part fracturing of the concept of emotion into discrete natural kinds. For all that we have seen so far, the concept of emotion is more like a mosaic with a variety of "opposites" such as Rorty identified, opposites that do not divide the whole mosaic into two or three separate and complete pictures, but opposites that occur more or less throughout the mosaic. The question remains whether the mosaic has any overall order in it or whether it is just a great, nondescript agglomeration of oppositions of light and dark, of color, and of shape, as Rorty's thesis, on one interpretation, proposes.

I would like to comment on Griffiths's vocabulary before going on to the category of irruptive motivations. Like many biologically oriented psychologists, he is fond of speaking of the objects of emotions as "stimuli" or "triggers." In Griffiths's case, this is perhaps in part a reaction against the propositional attitude theorists, for whom the subject's situation, as it is believed by the subject to be, determines the identity of the emotion (its type-identity, but also its particular identity – see Section 2.5c) and perhaps is constitutive of it. But biologically oriented psychologists who are unconcerned about the menace of conceptual analysis also speak in Griffiths's way because they think of the emotion essentially as behavior rather than as a mental state. Only behavior, after all, will affect the environment, and effects on some piece of the environment (making it ignore you, scaring it off, running from it, planting some of your seed it, etc.) are what is significant for survival and reproduction and thus evolution. But such behavior has to be correlated with environmental variables or occasions – that is to say, stimuli or triggers of the behavior in question. So the biological psychologist is really interested in two things: behavior and behavioral triggers. Now among nonhumans, certain stereotypical situations will pretty reliably trigger the fear response. For example, rats can be reliably predicted to exhibit fear upon perceiving the approach of a cat. But for humans, the situation is different, as Griffiths notes:

Emotions in humans . . . are elicited by an enormously wide range of stimuli. A mere light on a control panel may precipitate fear or joy. The only thing which all eliciting situations for fear have in common is the extremely abstract property that, in the light of the organism's past learning history, they can be evaluated as dangerous. This makes it unlikely that each of these situations possesses a range of common features of a fairly immediate perceptual kind (p. 86).

So it is not quite right to call the situation that a human being fears the "trigger." The "trigger," instead, is the situation *as perceived as dangerous*. But the situation as perceived is not the trigger *of the emotion*; it is a subjective state of the subject that "triggers" at best *part* of the emotion – for example, the visceral markers and the behavior. Thus it is really better to think of the perception of the situation in the terms distinctive of the emotion (e.g., dangerous for fear, offensive for anger, disgusting for disgust, etc.) as part of the emotion. It seems to me that this would be a natural way for a brain scientist to think of the matter, if she were thinking just in terms of the brain processes and not in terms of their evolutionary significance: The perception that mediates the onset of the various neural events is itself a neural event and one that may, as we have seen, involve input from very sophisticated, indeed distinctively human, parts of the brain. But as soon as we start thinking of human emotions in such a way that neither the situation that elicits the emotion nor the perception of the situation is the trigger of the emotion, then we see that the same thing is true of the other animals. For them, too, the emotion is not triggered by the situation simply but by the situation as perceived by the animal in a certain way; but the animal's perception of the situation in the distinctively emotional way is not the trigger *of the emotion* but part of it.

d. Higher Cognitive Emotions

According to Griffiths, under the influence of science the vernacular concept of emotion fractures into two parts, the affect programs and the higher cognitive emotions, and this latter category again fractures into two, irruptive motivations and disclaimed actions. In this subsection, first I look at the category of irruptive motivations, and then I look more broadly at higher cognitive emotions. In the next subsection I will address disclaimed actions.

The idea of irruptive motivations comes from Robert Frank's *Passions Within Reason*, which is a development of sociobiology theory. According to Frank, emotions are episodic adaptive departures from means-end reasoning. They are adaptive, despite the fact that they disrupt the ordinary rational pursuit of the subject's goals, because they secure the longer-term success of those goals by their effect on one's conspecifics (namely, other people). The sense of fairness is one of Frank's examples. He has shown experimentally that people will often refuse to accept an unfair distribution of goods to themselves even when they know the alternative is to receive nothing at all. Out of commitment to being treated fairly, they eschew the (short-term) rational strategy of maximizing their benefits. Similarly, loyalty to a friend who has been fired may lead a person to turn down the job when it is offered to himself. If we look only at the short term, these actions seem irrational. But if a person is known by his fellows to be willing to sacrifice significantly to be treated fairly, he puts his conspecifics on notice that they had better treat him fairly, and this is a long-term gain. Similarly, a person reaps many social advantages by becoming known as a loyal friend. Griffiths points out that such "emotions" as loyalty and a sense of fairness are quite different from the affect programs, in that they are mediated by higher cognition and do not have the same physiological marks. He is attracted to this theory because of its evolutionary bent, though he criticizes it, with other forms of evolutionary psychology, for being insufficiently disciplined in the use of adaptationist explanations. These psychologists speculatively spin "just so" stories that are unrestrained by knowledge of the ecological context in which the trait developed or by interspecies homologies. For example, the sense of justice is explained, as a trait of the species, by the adaptiveness of being fearsome to one's conspecifics when not treated fairly – the conspecifics are deterred from unfairness by anticipatory fear. But if people had the trait of becoming friendly and affectionate when treated unfairly, then the evolutionary psychologist would explain this trait as adaptive, say, by one's conspecifics being wheedled into treating one more fairly by friendliness and affection. Thus it seems that with sufficient imagination, any trait that a species actually *has* can be explained by *some* kind of adaptivity (and there may be competing adaptive "just so" stories that can be told, especially when the ecological context of adaptation is not known). This method of explanation is thus too "easy," not sufficiently controlled by the data. By contrast, the affect programs can be explained evolutionarily, not just as adaptive but as having homologues in related species whose ecological contexts can be known. Thus, by contrast with the scientific work that has been done on the affect programs, Griffiths goes so far as to say that we do not know what the higher cognitive emotions are (see pp.229, 241) because we do not know what their underlying homeostatic causal mechanism is.

We may wonder whether loyalty and a sense of fairness even belong in the vernacular concept of an emotion. But some of the things that Frank attempts to explain using the strategy I have just described do seem to belong in the category: Jealousy, guilt, shame, and vengefulness are examples. Griffiths, however, is offering the category of irruptive motivations as one of three that exhaust the field covered by the ordinary concept of emotion (the third being disclaimed actions). So we must ask whether all higher cognitive emotions that are not ways of faking emotion so as to justify some otherwise unjustifiable action are irruptive motivations.

Griffiths glosses "irruptive motivational states" as "states that interfere with the smooth unfolding of plans designed to secure our long-term goals" (p. 246). But there seem to be plenty of higher cognitive emotions that do not interfere with the unfolding of our plans but are a direct consequence of our plans and fit smoothly into them. Consider the gratitude a person feels when, endeavoring to accomplish some task, a friend comes along and offers welcome help. This is certainly a higher cognitive emotion, may have very little of the physiological markers characteristic of the affect programs, and is not a fake (let us say). The accomplishing of the task is enhanced, rather than impeded, by the feelings and expression of gratitude. Or consider hope. Someone in the family has been injured, and several phone calls have been made without securing medical help. Then finally, one call gets through to the doctor, and a feeling of hope comes over the family. This emotion depends on a sophisticated conceptual understanding of the situation; it is not fake; but neither is it disruptive of anybody's long-term goals. I submit that countless instances of higher cognitive emotions are neither irruptive motivations nor social pretenses.

We might also wonder whether nonfake higher cognitive emotions are all motivational. Take the quiet satisfaction a person feels in having solved a difficult and important engineering problem. It is clearly an emotion, yet it does not seem to lead to any action (other than further contemplation of the accomplishment). Furthermore, the kind of examples in which Frank specializes seem tendentious. Goal disruption is relative to some particular goal. But we typically have many goals, of different kinds, between which we may be torn by the situations of life. Loyalty to one's sacked friend may "disrupt" one's goal of getting the best job one can, but it may *express* the goal of friendship. Why suppose that friendship is not a perfectly real goal of people who are loyal to their friends? And to suppose that such loyalty is irrational is to accept a very narrow conception of rationality as narrow self-interest. Guilt may "disrupt" the "goal" of feeling good about oneself, but it may express the perfectly rational "goal" of being a morally upright person.

Some higher cognitive emotions that are not fake are disruptive and motivational, but not all are, by a long shot. I submit that the concept of an irruptive motivation is far too narrow to do the categorial work that Griffiths assigns it. Besides this, there is the conceptual difficulty that the category seems to reflect a very particular ideology of rationality: It is only by this contestable standard that these emotions can be construed as short-term irrational or disruptive.

e. Disclaimed Actions

The third category into which Griffiths thinks the vernacular concept of emotion fractures under scientific pressure consists of "emotions" that are unconscious strategic pretenses imitative of emotions belonging in the other two categories but lacking the "passivity" characteristic of the affect programs and the irruptive motivations, pretenses that are reinforced by local culture and serve the purpose of licensing behaviors that would not be socially acceptable if performed without the excuse provided by the fake "passivity" of the fake emotion. Griffiths is not fully confident that this third category should be allowed, and nowhere does he claim that disclaimed actions are a natural kind. But in claiming that this category is discrete in that its states are strategic and therefore not passive, Griffiths does invite us to propose counterexamples and critical questions about the discreteness. I shall argue that the inference "strategic therefore not passive" is fallacious, that countless human emotions that seem to fall in the categories of affect programs and higher cognitive emotions have an intentional element, and that being intentional does not mark a neat division among kinds of emotions, but on the contrary many human emotions fall on a *continuum* of intentionalness. We can also question whether intentional emotions are all strategic, whether the subject is always unconscious of his own role in getting them up, and whether they are always "reinforced by local culture."

The passiveness that Griffiths thinks is characteristic of the affect programs and the irruptive motivations must not be merely that they are not intentionally brought on by their subject. If only that were meant, then got-up emotions would be uninterestingly unpassive by definition. If passivity is not to be thus trivialized, it must be an attribute of the subject under the influence of the emotion, and it must consist in something like inertia, in the emotion's not being purely under the volition of the subject and instead having a "life of its own," causing the subject to feel and behave in certain ways. In other words, for a subject to be passive to an emotion is for the subject to be *in its grip.* Part of this may be affect program type grip – heart beating faster, and so on; part of it may be motivational – you feel like hitting somebody, and so on; part of it may be what Stocker calls affectivity[16] – feeling a certain way characteristic of the emotion, where this feeling is not to be identified with bodily sensation. Passivity means that the subject has a sense of *being* compelled in such ways *by* the emotion. Thus the question whether everything that is done intentionally lacks the passivity characteristic of emotions is an empirical question.

Non-emotional analogues of this are not contrary to deliberation and strategic intention. For example, when you sled down a hill, you may carefully choose a position from which to start the descent, strategizing how to get the effect you want (a slow smooth safe ride, a fast exciting bumpy one, etc.) and pushing off hard or gently. But once on your way you may be carried along, without volitional control, by the sled. Or you may be partially in control (say, you can steer it a bit) and partially not in control (you can't

[16] See Michael Stocker and Elizabeth Hegeman, *Valuing Emotions* (Cambridge, England: Cambridge University Press, 1996), pp. 17–55 and *passim.*

stop it). Human experience suggests that many got-up emotions (perhaps all of them, to some degree) are like this: They take hold of you, some very gently and some violently.

Dostoevsky's underground man is especially prone to getting up emotions and is unusually astute about his own states and the relationship between his deliberate production of the emotion and its "passivity." His remarks suggest that his got-up emotions are quite capable of taking him over in the way characteristic of real emotions.

> I used to invent my own adventures, I used to devise my own life for myself, so as to be able to carry on somehow. How many times, for instance, used I to take offence without rhyme or reason, deliberately; and of course I realised very well that I had taken offence at nothing, that the whole thing was just a piece of play-acting, but in the end I would work myself up into such a state that I would be offended in good earnest. All my life I felt drawn to play such tricks, so that in the end I simply lost control of myself. Another time I tried hard to fall in love. This happened to me twice, as a matter of fact. And I can assure you, gentlemen, I suffered terribly. In my heart of hearts, of course, I did not believe that I was suffering, I'd even sneer at myself in a vague sort of way, but I suffered agonies none the less, suffered in the most genuine manner imaginable, as though I were really in love. I was jealous. I made scenes. And all because I was so confoundedly bored, gentlemen, all because I was so horribly bored.[17]

The underground man's got-up emotions are strategic, with at least two aims: making life miserable for others and dispelling his own boredom. But the strategy works best when the emotion is not *mere* play-acting, but the passivity of the emotion supervenes, as it often does in his case. His emotions are a clear counterexample to Griffiths's "strategic, therefore no passivity" inference. He is also a counterexample to the principle that disclaimed action emotions require that the subject be unconscious of the strategizing. The underground man is often transparent in the getting-up of his emotions up and in why he is doing it. We might also wonder to what extent the underground man's strategies are sanctioned or reinforced by local culture. Dostoevsky himself thinks that the underground man is a cultural product,[18] but it is not clear that the culture functions as a sanctioner or reinforcer of the sort that Griffiths envisions.

The method of acting developed by Constantin Stanislavski[19] presupposes that people can be trained to bring themselves into the states of emotion of the characters they are playing on stage. For Stanislavski this means that they do not merely reproduce the facial and bodily movements and

---

[17] *Notes from the Underground*, in *The Best Short Stories of Dostoevsky*, translated with an Introduction by David Magarshack (New York: Modern Library, no date), p. 122.

[18] See the author's note at the beginning of the story.

[19] *An Actor Prepares*, translated E. R. Hapgood (New York: Routledge, 1948). I thank Sarah Borden and Lance Wilcox for alerting me to Stanislavski's writings.

vocal inflections that a character in a given emotional state would produce, but the actors themselves *feel* the emotions. Stanislavski believes that without this "inner experience" (p. 164) the acted behavioral expression will always be somewhat wooden and artificial: "All external production is formal, cold, and pointless if it is not motivated from within" (*ibid.*). If we apply this insight about acting to the kind of cases of disclaimed action that Griffiths cites, then, far from "strategic" implying "not passive," "not passive" (that is, not genuinely felt as an inner motivation, a lived experience of emotion) implies "not strategic" (that is, not very likely to be a successful strategy). If romantic love is a social role that licenses certain behaviors, then, on Stanislavski's principle, the license will not be very effective if "there is no state of love to explain love behavior" (Griffiths, p. 246). Stanislavski thinks that human beings have memories of a variety of emotional experiences that they can learn to trigger and apply to new situations. The memories are somewhat schematic, so that in triggering them one is not just reliving the original experience, but is having a new experience that fits the schema. As an actor practices a part, he may deliberately recall emotional situations of his own past that are formally similar to the situations of his character in the play. The physical movements of the actor on stage, if they are well-executed and attended by receptivity to memory, can trigger the appropriate emotional memories and thus reproduce the experience of the character. Another stimulus is "the text of the play, the implications of thought and feeling that underlie it and affect the inter-relationship of the actors...," and another is "all the external stimuli that surround us on the stage, in the form of settings, arrangement of furniture, lighting, sound and other effects, which are calculated to create an illusion of real life and its living *moods*" (p. 191, Stanislavski's italics).

Paul Ekman, Robert Levenson, and Wallace Friesen have supplied some empirical evidence that supports Stanislavski's theory. They instructed actors to contract their facial muscles in ways that (unknown to the actors) are characteristic of expression of various emotions, and they monitored their heart rate and finger temperatures. They found that autonomic responses characteristic of the expressed emotions occurred with no other provocation than such "acting."[20] But regardless of the accuracy of Stanislavski's theory about *how* professionally enacted emotions are produced, he is clearly right that actors do sometimes experience their characters' emotions, thus reproducing the "passivity" involved in them, and that they do this deliberately.

A case in which an emotion comes on partly spontaneously and partly intentionally is found in Jane Austen's *Sense and Sensibility*. The subject is Marianne Dashwood ("sensibility"), a partisan of the romantic ideology of strong feelings. Willoughby, with whom Marianne has recently fallen madly

---

[20] "Autonomic Nervous System Activity Distinguishes Among Emotions." *Science* **221** (1983): 1208–1210.

in love, has suddenly and inexplicably departed from the county for an indefinite period. She is wrenched with grief. Her sister Elinor ("sense") tries in vain to understand the departure and the relationship:

But whatever might be the particulars of their separation, her sister's affliction was indubitable; and she thought with the tenderest compassion of that violent sorrow which Marianne was in all probability *not merely giving way to as a relief, but feeding and encouraging as a duty* (Chapter 15, italics added).

It is implausible to suggest that Marianne's affliction is nothing but a pretense, even if it is supposed to be an unconscious and therefore sincere one. Her violent sorrow shows the passivity characteristic of genuine emotion; and we may suppose that her facial expression is panculturally recognizable, and physiological measurements would suggest that she is in the affect program state that Ekman calls "sadness" – this despite the fact that romantic love does not seem to be pancultural. Furthermore, her emotion is clearly a higher cognitive one because her ability to conceptualize *an indefinitely long period of time* is essential to its situational object. If we accept Elinor's description of Marianne as intensifying her romantic sadness out of a sense of duty, then we can see that the intention with which a subject brings on his emotion is not always strategic (unless we think of people's dutiful actions as strategies for getting their duty done).

In mixing spontaneity and intention, Marianne's emotion seems to be typical of an enormous number of the emotions of sophisticated human beings. In subtle ways we engineer our emotions (or deengineer them), sometimes strategically and sometimes under ideological (religious, antireligious, political, ethical, aesthetic) inspiration (or pressure). All such emotions seem to violate the supposedly neat fracture lines that Griffiths thinks science produces in the concept of emotion. Griffiths will no doubt respond that my data are all anecdotal or, worse, literary. But the examples are true to our experience. If someone proposes that experience is fundamentally inaccurate, then we need strong empirical justification for the claim. To justify the particular fracture lines that Griffiths posits, we need empirical studies showing that no emotion that requires higher cognition for its onset has the physiological characteristics of the so-called affect programs. We need studies showing that all emotions that are neither fake nor informationally encapsulated are both disruptive of the subject's long-range goals and motivational. We need studies showing that no emotions that the subject intentionally brings on himself have the character of "passivity." Griffiths cites no study of any of these kinds.

The impression I have tried to convey in this and the preceding two subsections is the complexity of the phenomena that we call emotions, a criss-crossing of properties in the field that foils any effort to divide the emotions into neat, mutually exclusive nonoverlapping categories. It is a complexity to which Amélie Rorty drew attention and which she tried to

reduce in a very different way. If present-day biology seems to demand such
a division (because of its relative success in dealing with certain instances of
the affect programs and its awkwardness in dealing with much of anything
else), it seems to me that this may indicate that biology has its explanatory
limits. It is good at some kinds of things and not so good at others, and it is
not very good at explaining a great deal that belongs to the field of emotion.

1.5. CONCEPTUAL ANALYSIS OF EMOTIONS

In the present section I describe and defend the kind of conceptual analysis I will employ in this book. I argue that the study of emotions can be
legitimately undertaken from a variety of disciplinary angles and with a
variety of methods. These disciplines include anthropology, experimental
psychology, neuroscience, evolutionary biology, and conceptual analysis, to
mention just some of the main ones. No one of these disciplines is omni-
competent to gather knowledge about emotions, but each is especially fitted
to answer its own kind of questions. For example, neuroscience is uniquely
well-fitted to answer questions about the neural circuits and the neurochemistry involved in the production of emotions, anthropology is able to answer
questions about how emotions vary or do not vary with culture, and evolutionary biology may be able to provide very long-term historical explanations of the presence of certain human emotion dispositions. Furthermore,
some disciplines may be especially competent with some kinds of emotions,
while being relatively incompetent to deal with others. For example, neuroscience seems well-equipped to deal with the kinds of emotions that Ekman
calls the affect programs, and (so far, at least) it has less power to explain
emotions that depend on the understanding of narratives.

Griffiths laments the complacency of philosophers of emotion, who stay
in the rut of conceptual analysis when other parts of the philosophy of mind
have ventured to connect with more scientific inquiries. Why might philosophers of emotion have been prone to such complacency? One plausible
answer is that philosophers of emotion tend to have a somewhat different
set of interests backing up their interest in emotions than do other philosophers of mind, who are perhaps most typically interested in epistemology
and metaphysics. As I survey the crop of philosophers who have been occupied with the emotions in the last twenty-five years, it strikes me that
almost all of them (I think of Michael Stocker, Patricia Greenspan, Robert
Solomon, Martha Nussbaum, Aaron Ben-Ze'ev, John Deigh, Amélie Rorty,
Charles Taylor, Gabriele Taylor, Richard Wollheim, and Ronald de Sousa)
are interested in emotions for their applications to ethics, taking ethics in
a broad sense. Perhaps the kinds of questions that life scientists have been
most proficient at answering are ones that ethicists are less interested in
asking: For example, are surprise, anger, fear, and other emotions systematically and cross-culturally differentiated by the sets of facial muscles that are

contracted in their expression? What evolutionary advantages were provided to our distant human and prehuman ancestors by the counterparts of shame, anger, jealousy, and so on? How do fear and anger (for example) differ with regard to typical blood pressure, skin conductance, dilation of irises, muscle contraction, heart rate, and so on? What brain circuitry is involved in fear (anger, surprise, lust, etc.), and how exactly does it work? For one thing, scientific investigation of a biological and physiological kind has had its chief successes with the human emotions that have strong homologues in monkeys, cats, and rats – namely, emotions that do not require much sense of self or much in the way of higher cognitive processing, emotions that have clear and strong physiological concomitants and are responses to present, sense perceptible objects. These are some of the emotions that are least explicable in terms of conceptual analysis[21] and most susceptible to Darwinian and neurological science, but they are also the emotions that are least interesting to ethicists. Ethicists tend to be more interested in emotions that are physiologically more subtle or unpredictable and whose objects can only be identified in fairly complex conceptual and narrative terms – emotions that depend heavily on language and are thus prime candidates for conceptual analysis (or psychoanalysis[22]).

Conceptual analysis has its own special virtues, in particular a greater sensitivity and skill for conceptual refinement than is found in related disciplines, such as anthropology and literary history. I think of conceptual analysis of emotions as the investigation of them from the point of view of human participants. Conceptual analysis has sometimes been construed as a purely linguistic exercise that asks how words (like "emotion" and "regret") are used. Some conceptual analysts even eschew any pretension to investigate to what the words in question refer. But I take investigation of linguistic usage to be just one among several strategies of conceptual analysis. Other strategies are 2) paying careful imaginative attention to the narrative contexts in which emotions or the emotion in question occur; 3) consulting the analyst's own experience (introspection, if you will); 4) careful comparison with neighboring phenomena (e.g., an analysis of jealousy would likely be conducted in conjunction with an analysis of envy; and somewhat differently, an analysis of an emotion in our cultural context might be carried on in comparison with a somewhat similar emotion in an exotic culture); 5) investigating connections to related phenomena such as actions, judgments, moods, desires, and other kinds of concerns; 6) concerted use of examples,

---

[21] As I will explore in Sections 2.5g–2.5j, emotions in response to music, though they are often "high" in some sense, share this attribute.

[22] Psychoanalysis deals in emotions about which the analysand may initially be quite inarticulate, but its assumption is that articulation is in principle possible and that such articulation can express the actual structure of the emotions. Furthermore, the sentences in which the emotions are articulated in psychoanalysis strongly tend to constitute narratives.

especially narrative examples, and counterexamples. A conceptual analysis making expert use of these and other analytic strategies is no substitute for evolutionary biology or neurophysiology, but it is a discipline capable of supplying a set of insights and information about emotions that no other discipline can supply, or supply so well.

a. A Mentalist Proposal

The concept of emotion can be divided in an indefinitely large number of ways, along the lines of hedonic tone, sophistication of cognition, motivationality, rationality, informational encapsulation, intentionalness, pancultural recognizability, reflexivity, disruptiveness, involvement of autonomic changes, homology in related species, and perhaps others, as well as indefinitely various combinations of the above. But none of these divisions threatens the integrity and singleness of the concept of emotion because all such divisions cross-cut one another in various ways and thus do not produce clean, mutually exclusive categories such as are needed for a genuine fracture. The concept of emotion may hold together by virtue of the complex partial attribute overlaps of the various items that fall under it.

But so far I have proposed no way to introduce any simplifying order into this apparent chaos. The fact that the vernacular concept of emotion does not fracture neatly does not keep it from being quite a mess. I want now to suggest a way to introduce some larger order into it – an order beyond the mini-orders that are created by the attribute overlaps. My suggestion will be reminiscent of the earlier conceptual analysts without being a version of the propositional attitude theory. It will differ from that theory, first, in not making either beliefs or propositions fundamental to emotions, while nevertheless making a place for propositions; and second, in not pretending to the reductivity of a "theory." It will be interesting to reflect why conceptual analysis is able to find something like a "theoretical structure that accounts for the projectability" of the category (Griffiths, p. 188), while biology and neuroscience cannot do so. I shall suggest that the key is that conceptual analysis, and not biology or neuroscience, conceives emotions essentially as mental states. This, in turn, will be because ordinary human beings conceive them as mental states that play varied and complex roles in ordinary human experience, action, and explanation.

Griffiths comments that "the three-way fracturing of the emotion category into socially sustained pretenses, affect program responses and higher cognitive states extends to many specific emotion categories, such as anger. Some instances of anger fall into each of these three categories" (p. 17). Let us look at an instance of each of these categories of anger to see whether we can discern any commonality among them despite the categorial differences. Our affect program example is this: Little Fred trips little Sam, who falls down and hurts his knee; Sam gets an angry expression on his face and kicks Fred in the shin. In this case the object of anger is perceptually present to the subject and the offense against him is simple, not requiring sophisticated conceptualization. The response is similarly simple and physical. A higher cognitive version of anger will involve conceptualizing the offender in culturally determined ways, will not require the perceptual presence of the offender, and may involve sophisticated, culturally determined methods of revenge. For example, an abbot is offended by one of his monks' repeatedly addressing him as "Francis" rather than as "Father" and later withholds from him a promotion in the order. The commonality between the affect program response and the higher cognitive emotion, in virtue of which they are both thought to be cases of anger and thus of emotion, is patent to anyone who grasps the roles of *offender* and *revenge* in the logic of the emotion. It is clear that the abbot's state of mind has the same "logic" as that of the child who was tripped. A case of "pretense" anger is similar: The intentionally angry person ascribes some offense to the object of his anger, and to get revenge is disposed to harm, hurt, or deprive her in some way. To revert to the example from Solomon, a husband wants to avoid going out in the evening and thus intentionally gets angry with his wife for not picking up his shirts at the laundry (presumably his refusal to go out with her is his revenge on her for not picking up the shirts).[23] The husband may very well not "judge" (really believe) his wife to have offended against him in not picking up the shirts; nevertheless, if he has succeeded in making himself angry about this trumped-up offense, she will *appear* to him to have offended him. If she does not even appear to him in this light, then he is *only* play-acting an emotion, and is not really in an emotional state, not even a got up one.[24] (This distinction between *S believes of R that p* and *R appears to S in terms of p* is developed in Sections 2.3 to 2.4.) And so what is common to the child, the abbot, and the husband, insofar as they are all angry, is that some person appears to them as having offended them in some way, and that they therefore want to do harm or cause pain or inconvenience to the offender.[25]

Here again we have attributes that overlap the supposedly discrete categories of affect program, higher cognitive emotions, and disclaimed actions, except that now the attributes seem, when taken together as a package, to be ordinary people's reason for calling all three kinds of case anger. Now that we know that whales give live birth to their young and suckle them, we are not inclined to think of them as fish. The mere fact that they look somewhat like fish is not enough to sustain their inclusion in the category, in many ordinary people's minds. Let us suppose that LeDoux turns his

---

[23] "Emotions and Choice," in A. Rorty (ed.), *Explaining Emotions* (Berkeley: University of California Press, 1980), p. 263.

[24] In Chapter 4 I will call such got-up emotions "false feelings." For further discussion of this example from Solomon, in pursuit of a different issue, see Section 4.5.

[25] This is a simplified account. See Section 3.3 for a fuller one.

attention next to anger and maps its neurology, in the affect program form, as neatly as he has done for affect program fear. Then he investigates higher cognitive and disclaimed action anger and finds that their neurological mappings are quite different – in fact, as different as whales are from fish. How likely is it that when ordinary people assimilate this information, they will be inclined to quit calling all three things by the single term "anger"? In view of the subjective logical structure that holds the three cases together, it seems to me highly unlikely that ordinary people will ever come to think of these kinds of anger as not even all instances of anger. Anger has deep and ramified significance in ordinary human life, but it is not as a neurological phenomenon that it has this significance, but as a mental structure of meaning and personal interaction. As long as that structure is common to the three kinds of case, it seems likely that ordinary people will group them together because that is what interests them. (What interests us as people may be quite different from what interests us in our special role as scientists.) In a way, the foregoing speculation is academic because, as we have seen, it is highly unlikely that affect programs are neatly discrete from higher cognitive and disclaimed action emotions in anything like the way that whales are neatly discrete from fish. So conceptual analysis, of the kind that I have been doing in this chapter and will pursue throughout the book, both (a) undermines the reasons for thinking that ordinary people may someday abandon the category of *emotion* and categories like *anger* and (b) reveals something like ordinary people's positive reason for thinking the physiologically, evolutionarily, and motivationally diverse items all to be solidly cases of anger. In Chapter 2 I shall develop a general account of emotions as mental structures of meaning, and in Chapter 3 I shall apply it to, and test it by, a wide range of emotion types. We might say that Chapter 2 proposes a conceptual analysis of *emotion*, whereas Chapter 3 proposes conceptual analyses of *regret, envy, contempt, admiration*, and the like.

Sometimes scientific researchers into emotion suggest that scientific research of their favored kinds is the only access to real knowledge about emotions. My remarks in the preceding paragraph appeal to the concept of *the interest relativity of categories and explanations*. Griffiths and Rorty have pointed out some kinds of diversity among emotions, and I have pointed out others. Rorty points out that the diverse aspects of emotions become especially salient to people who have particular theoretical interests to which those aspects are relevant (see Section 1.3). Some of the kinds of diversity that Griffiths points out are more salient to someone concerned with scientific studies of emotions (e.g., the characteristic facial expressions of the so-called affect programs), and others are available only to scientific study (e.g., the neurological differences between fear and other emotion types that LeDoux posits). It would be quite understandable if a scientist like LeDoux were attracted by the thesis that higher cognitive fear that lacks a salient autonomic component is a completely different phenomenon from the fear that he studies in rats and of which he finds a homologue in humans. This will be (as Rorty might point out) because LeDoux is interested in the neurological dimension of emotions. But emotions may differ from and resemble one another in many ways, and we may be interested in emotions from many angles, angles from which one or another similarity or difference will be crucial.

As an example of interest relativity, consider the following comment from LeDoux:

Many but not all people who encounter a snake [on a woodland path] will have a full-blown emotional reaction that includes bodily responses and emotional feelings. This will only occur if the visual representation of the snake triggers the amygdala. A whole host of output pathways will then be activated. Activation of these outputs is what makes the encounter with the snake an emotional experience, and the absence of activation is what prevents the encounter with the rabbit from being one (LeDoux, P. 284).

But a person might be afraid of the snake without having what LeDoux calls "a full-blown emotional reaction." A person might feel some fear without having much, if any (at least not any sensible), autonomic arousal and might keep his eye on the snake, making sure he stays out of its way. If asked why he behaved as he did, he will say he was afraid of the snake, and if asked whether he felt afraid of the snake, or just cold-bloodedly circumvented it, he will say that he felt afraid of it. Perhaps the amygdala is involved in such fear; maybe not. But in both the kinds of case that involve amygdala reactions and ones that do not, the ordinary person will explain the emotion and the behavior by speaking about the subject's perceiving *danger* in the snake, and if that concept is subjected to clarification, it will be in terms of his not wanting to get bitten, or his wanting to get away from the snake, or his concern not to be harmed. In other words, we can subsume the "full-blown emotional reaction" case with the other kind of case by speaking of the subject's concern (instinctive or learned, conscious or unconscious) not to be harmed. But LeDoux seems to suggest that people who do not have the full complement of physiological reactions are not having "an emotional experience."

Why would a thinker about the emotions[26] feed on so narrow a diet of examples? The answer is pretty obvious in LeDoux's case, and it has to do with his professional competency: He is a physiologist and will naturally be chiefly focused on cases where the physiological aspect is salient and where physiological explanations can be pursued. This is also why he focuses on fear rather than on such emotions as regret or awe or respect. It fits better with his physiological program, and it is more susceptible to Darwinian

---

[26] The title, *The Emotional Brain*, gives the impression that the book is about emotions in general; but in view of the fact that the book is almost entirely about fear, and indeed almost entirely about one *kind* of fear, it might better have been titled *The Frightened Brain*.

explanation in terms of survival than many other emotions. But a diet of
emotions that have a strong physiological component and are capable of
being investigated with rats as subjects will hardly be adequate for someone
interested in moral psychology, or indeed for anyone broadly interested in
the nature and place of emotions in human life.

Different angles of interest are evident in a bone that Carl Ratner picks
with Carroll Izard. Citing a facial expression experiment like the ones Paul
Ekman performs, Ratner comments:

One photo was variously described as amusement, gratitude, optimism, serenity,
and satisfaction (Izard, p. 204). Yet the authors inexplicably state that the subjects
expressed a common judgment that the photograph manifested joy![27]

Here it is pretty clear that Izard is just not interested in what he would
regard as the fine shades of joy. Instead, he is interested in the fact that
people are able to recognize, pretty reliably, a certain facial behavior as
expressing some kind of positive emotion that he is happy, not putting too
fine a point upon it, to call joy. Izard's lack of interest in the finer shades is
a function of the question he is asking in his research. Ratner, by contrast,
as a social constructionist, is interested in the variety of emotions, and so
he is shocked by Izard's conceptual roughness. What about ordinary folks?
Sometimes they are a bit like Izard. A mother casts a glance out the window
and sees the smiles on her children's faces; she is not concerned at the
moment whether they are amused, excited, gratified, or grateful (she might
turn to her husband and comment that the kids are "happy"). But very
often, an ordinary man is more like Ratner. He is intensely interested in
knowing whether the lady with him is smiling at some incongruity (say, the
spinach lodged ridiculously between his teeth) or smiling a benevolent and
admiring approval of his recent clever remark. Her smile may be beautiful,
but her mental state is what concerns him. The distinctions among the many
emotions that can be expressed by smiling are often crucial in everyday life,
even if they are not for Izard's science. Because the fine points are crucial in
everyday life, they are also crucial in this book; and because the most direct
and precise avenue to the fine points is conceptual analysis, that is the chief
method of this book.

LeDoux seems to classify hunger and lust with emotions like fear. Many
people, both ordinary and scientific, will hesitate to class hunger with emotions (they may call it an "appetite" instead). I think that one reason for this
hesitation is that emotions like fear can be morally qualified, but hunger
does not seem to have this property. For example, we might admire and
praise a North American, personally unconnected with the Sudan, who
feared a famine in the Sudan. But I don't suppose that anyone was ever

---

[27] "A Social Constructionist Critique of the Naturalistic Theory of Emotion." *The Journal of
Mind and Behavior* **10** (1989): 211–230, 222f.

morally praised for being hungry. On the other hand, because LeDoux sees a strong analogy between the neurological and other physiological syndromes characteristic of hunger and the kind of fear that he investigates, he is inclined to class them together as emotions. I can see no objection to his doing so, as long as we keep in mind that the classification is relative to his interests.

LeDoux makes one remark that seems to be not only motivated by his special interests but straightforwardly erroneous: "Emotional feelings result when we become consciously aware that an emotion system of the brain is active" (p. 302). This formula cannot be right, inasmuch as people felt emotions before they ever became "consciously aware than an emotion system of the brain [was] active"; indeed, many people who have been feeling emotions for years will have become consciously aware of the existence of emotion systems in the brain only upon reading LeDoux's fascinating book. Emotion systems in the brain are posits of theories, and no such theory is necessary for feeling emotions. What people are aware of in feeling an emotion is not the activity of a brain system, but the *emotion*, for which the activity of the brain system may plausibly be thought to be a necessary condition. Once we have read LeDoux's book, we may *infer* that our amygdala is active when we feel strong anxiety or fear. But nobody feels his amygdala being active. Instead, he feels afraid.

But now Griffiths will point out that if science can show us that when we think we're drinking water we're really drinking H_2O, then scientists like LeDoux can show us that what we're really feeling when we feel fear is the activity of the amygdala. I think we can concede the point, if we resist the suggestion of the word "really" in the previous sentence. The "really" is attempted imperialism. This imperialism is unrealistically heavy-handed, ontologically. When we feel fear we are aware of some situation of our world as having a special kind of significance for us (in this case, the negative significance of being a threat to something important in our life), a significance that does not seem even remotely to be captured by a story about electrical impulses coursing along strings of neurons between various parts of the brain. So not only are we not aware of what is going on in our brain except by inference in virtue of a theory, the place that the feeling of fear has in our lives is lost if we think of fear as (nothing but) the activation of the amygdala, and so on. But even when we know that the chemical analysis of water is H_2O, much of the significance of water in our lives remains the same: When we are thirsty, water is tremendously welcome; when we look at an ocean scene, we still see its awesomeness and beauty; we want to get in out of the rain but are glad for its influence on the crops; a swim on a hot summer day is a delight; and so forth; and all this has precious little to do with the chemical analysis of the stuff. We have learned that water is H_2O, but we are very far from having learned that it is not water. From a human point of view, it would therefore be better not to say that water is nothing but H_2O, or that water is "*really* [just] H_2O," but rather that the chemical analysis of water is H_2O. This preserves the everyday human ontology of water, which is surely as important to us as any scientific analysis, and implies the interest relativity of the claim that water is H_2O. Similarly, even if we learned that fear is a consequence of a certain activation of the amygdala, we would not have shown that fear is therefore not a perception of threat. And, outside certain rather narrow contexts of brain science and psychotherapy, the characterization of fear as a perception of threat will be far more to the point than the characterization of it as amygdala activation.

Consider one last example from LeDoux. "The brain states and bodily responses are the fundamental facts of an emotion, and the conscious feelings are the frills that have added icing to the emotional cake" (LeDoux, p. 302). This statement is correct only if indexed to a scientific context: It should be formulated as "*Given the interests of brain science with Darwinian presuppositions,* then the brain states and bodily responses are the fundamental facts, and so on." The brain states and bodily responses are certainly not, in the ordinary contexts of life, including the moral contexts, the fundamental facts of an emotion; the conscious feelings (and their unconscious counterparts) are not merely frills, but are the very substance of the emotion. This is not to reject science but to place it with respect to a certain set of interests.

The angle of interest I take in the present project is moral or ethical. It asks questions like, by what standards do we judge emotions to be proper or improper, and what is it about them that makes them subject to moral evaluation? What role have emotions in the formation of moral judgments? What set of emotion dispositions is characteristic of the honest person (the generous, the humble, the truthful, the just, etc.)? When, if ever, is it virtuous to act out of fear? anger? shame? What do emotional feelings have to do with moral self-knowledge? Do people have responsibility for their emotions, and, if so, how does one go about controlling and shaping one's emotions, as happens in such moral virtues as self-control, temperance, courage, perseverance, and patience? These are very different questions from those of LeDoux and the evolutionary psychologists. It is appropriate for these thinkers to focus their interest on the physiological aspects of emotions or their adaptiveness and biological history and to make distinctions and offer explanations that fit these interests. It may even be appropriate for them to ignore those subjective commonalities among physiologically and evolutionarily diverse emotions that I pointed out at the beginning of this section because the observation of those commonalities may not help them to focus their research. But it would not be appropriate for *me* to ignore them, or for *them* to legislate that *I* ought to ignore them, or to suggest that an investigation driven by my kind of interests is less likely to yield objective knowledge than an investigation driven by theirs.

The three instances of anger with which I began this subsection have in common not a single physiology, a single biological history, or a single biological function but *the form of a mental state.* The fact that this common-ality is revealed by conceptual analysis and is not revealed by the methods of biological psychology is significant. Conceptual analysis is a kind of in-quiry that is eminently suited to reveal the structures of lived experience – what we might call "primary psychology." We might also call it subjectivity or internal or real psychology, or the psychology of meanings. By contrast, biological psychology focuses on behavior and physiological mechanisms and the history of these.

b. Emotions and Explanations

I now apply the themes of the previous subsection – the notions of inter-est relativity and of a mentalist account and their relation to conceptual analysis – to an important aspect of inquiry into emotions, that of emo-tions as explanations of behavior and action and emotions as things to be explained. Let us begin with emotions as explanations.

We can distinguish broadly two ways that emotions cause behavior. I illustrate with a comment by LeDoux:

The conscious fear that can come with fear conditioning in a human is not a cause of the fear responses; it is one consequence (and not an obligatory one) of activating the defense system in a brain that also has consciousness (p. 147).

Due to his interest, LeDoux has in mind a certain *kind* of "fear responses": increased heart rate and blood pressure, muscular "freezing," and the like, and not, for example, the rational precautions a person might take after becoming afraid that an intruder is in the dark house to which he has just returned. Suppose that the homeowner has both kinds of responses. His body tenses, his heart is pounding, and his brow is wet. Some of these events can occur before he feels afraid. But in addition, he retreats quietly from the house and calls the police. He knows his chances are slim of overcom-ing, unarmed, an intruder who has the prior advantage of concealment. So he decides to go for help and to do so, if possible, without arousing the intruder's attention. These actions are also "fear responses," but it seems plausible to suppose that they *are* caused (i.e., motivated) by the conscious[28]

---

[28] Strictly speaking, the fear, even when it gives rise to sophisticated rational action, need not be conscious. Freudian unconscious motivation by emotion is commonplace. But the causation of the behavior in this kind of case is still radically different from the kind that LeDoux has in view. Here we are speaking of true *motivation*, the explanation of whose nonstereotypical behavioral consequences requires reference to a mental state with a broadly rational structure; the LeDoux kind of causation, by contrast, has the character of *reflex*. Our knowledge of the rational structure of unconscious fear – that the subject seeks by some effective means to avoid or eliminate or reduce some perceived threat – is drawn by analogy from conscious experience of fear and confirmed by the character of the behavior in relation to a plausible reconstruction of the subject's "take" on his situation.

fear – the awareness that the situation poses a threat. Here, the person feels fear and is led by this experience to search for a good way to avoid the danger.

Neuroscientific explanations are of unparalleled power if the "behavior" to be explained is reflexlike (heart rate, etc.), but much of human behavior that is to be explained by emotions seems to result from properly mental activity. In such cases, explanations that appeal (at least implicitly) to the "logic" of the emotion are much more powerful than ones that appeal to its neurocircuitry; though the logical and the reflexlike are often intricately intertwined, as in the case of our fearful homeowner. Consider a causal attribution of complex and puzzling behavior to jealousy, in Jane Austen's *Persuasion.*

Frederick Wentworth, whom Anne Elliot has not ceased to love in the several years since she was persuaded to reject him because of discrepancy in rank, has returned to the region with improved rank. But he treats her coldly and seems to be forming an attachment with a younger woman, Louisa Musgrove. Then at a concert he makes a point of telling Anne that he has no interest in Louisa, who is about to be married to someone else. Anne reflects about the encounter:

His choice of subjects, his expressions, and still more his manner and look, had been such as she could see in only one light. His opinion of Louisa Musgrove's inferiority, an opinion which he seemed solicitous to give, his wonder at Captain Benwick [Louisa's fiancé], his feelings as to a first, strong attachment – sentences begun which he could not finish – his half-averted eyes, and more than half-expressive glance – all, all declared that he had a heart returning to her at last . . . (Chapter 8).

But before she and Wentworth can come to a full understanding of one another, Anne is thrown together, in public view, with an eligible cousin, William Elliot, whom Wentworth has earlier heard speculatively matched with Anne. Wentworth avoids her:

She saw him not far off. He saw her too; yet he looked grave, and seemed irresolute, and only by very slow degrees came at last near enough to speak to her. . . . The difference between his present air and what it had been in the octagon room was strikingly great. – Why was it? . . . He began by speaking of the concert, gravely; more like the Captain Wentworth of Uppercross; owned himself disappointed, had expected better singing; and in short, must confess that he should not be sorry when it was over. Anne replied, and spoke in defence of the performance so well, and yet in allowance for his feelings, so pleasantly, that his countenance improved, and he replied again with almost a smile. They talked for a few minutes more; the improvement held; he even looked down towards the bench, as if he saw a place on it well worth occupying; when, at that moment, a touch on her shoulder obliged Anne to turn round (Chapter 8).

The touch is from Mr. Elliot, who enlists her to translate Italian for a singer. When she returns from this task, Wentworth coldly and formally takes his leave:

"Is not this song worth staying for?" said Anne, suddenly struck by an idea which made her yet more anxious to be encouraging.

"No!" he replied impressively, "there is nothing worth my staying for"; and he was gone directly.

Jealousy of Mr. Elliot! It was the only intelligible motive (Chapter 8).

Anne explains this sequence of starkly contrasting behaviors, some more reflexlike and some highly intentional, displayed within a very short period of time, by reference to the emotion of jealousy. It is "the only intelligible motive." What is the reasoning here? How does one explain behavior by reference to jealousy?

Anyone who knows, from a participant's point of view, what jealousy is, knows that it is based on an attachment that demands something like exclusivity, and that when a person is jealous, he sees a third party as a rival for that exclusive attention or favor (see Section 3.9 for more precision). Signs of attachment, like those that Wentworth gives in the earlier encounter, and the presence of a plausible candidate rival, like Mr. Elliot, will therefore encourage a jealousy hypothesis. Furthermore, someone who understands the logic of jealousy knows that the jealous perception of the rival's success or potential success in securing the affection of the beloved is painful to the subject, and by experience he knows which reflexlike expressions are typical of this pain; he will also know that the pain can be partially masked by bravado, formality, and so on. The otherwise puzzling combinations of Wentworth's behavior make sense when construed as symptoms of jealousy because they, plus circumstantial facts, fit the logic of this emotion. But the logic of jealousy is not a logic of the objective situation but of the subject's *construal* of the situation, a *subjective* logic. We might wonder whether, given the rational (nonstereotypical, socially complex, non-reflexlike) character of much of Wentworth's behavior, any purely neurological explanation of it – analogous to the kind that LeDoux can give of a rat's "freezing" in response to a conditioned fright stimulus – will ever be producible. But whether or not such explanations are possible, the difference between them and explanations in terms of emotions' subjective logic is patent. The latter kind is commonplace and highly successful; the former currently a dream of science fiction. So the emotion, in its subjective logic, is used to explain the behavior. Here the question to be answered is "Why is Wentworth behaving in these ways?" and the answer is "He is feeling jealous...."

But the emotion itself may be an object of explanation, and its internal logic or conceptual structure may be crucial in this kind of explanation as well. Here the question would be "Why is Wentworth jealous?" and the immediate answers will follow the form "He is in love with Anne" and "He sees William Elliot as a rival." These are perfectly good and precise explanations, for ordinary human purposes. For more specialized purposes, further explanatory probes of different kinds can be made. Some are biographical. We might wonder what, in Wentworth's upbringing, makes him susceptible to Anne's charms, rather than Louisa's; or what makes him especially quick to construe himself as abandoned. Here we might explain by reference to his character, his intellect, and his past history with Anne (these explanations are suggested by the novel). There are also questions about the origins of human nature. What evolutionary adaptiveness and line of biological descent account for the general human disposition to jealousy (and thus for Wentworth's in particular)? And there are neuroscientific questions: What kind of anatomy does an organism have to have to be susceptible to jealousy like Wentworth's? and What patterns of neurological activity underlie this emotion? I will comment now on the nature and relations of these various ways of explaining emotions.

I point out first that perfectly satisfactory explanations of behavior in terms of the subjective logic (SL) of the emotion can be produced in complete ignorance of whatever neurophysiological underpinnings and evolutionary history the emotion may possess. Nor does it appear that, given the interests and purposes served in everyday life by SL explanations, they would be significantly improved by adjoining such scientific explanations to them (though perhaps we should reserve judgment on this point until the scientific explanations are produced). On the other hand, it is hard to see how the scientific explanations are going to be implemented apart from the resources out of which the SL explanations are constructed. Both Griffiths and LeDoux speak of fear as a response to danger, and this is a primitive sort of conceptual analysis. An evolutionary or neuroscientific explanation of fear cannot get started apart from some such identification of the emotion under investigation. LeDoux's explanations are of only one or two kinds of fear, namely conditioned and unconditioned fright and a related version of anxiety; it is misleading to say that he has given a neurological explanation of fear, and only a sophisticated conceptual analysis of fear would show the precise limitations of his explanations. Such an analysis would also show, with some precision, the kinds of things that remain to be scientifically explained in the future. Similarly, if jealousy like that displayed by Wentworth is to be explained biologically or neuroscientifically, it will be important to know what is under investigation; consequently, something like the conceptual analysis of jealousy offered in Section 3.9 will be a prerequisite to such an explanation.

Second, evolutionary and neuroscientific explanations of jealousy are no substitute for SL explanations; if Anne Elliot wants to explain Captain Wentworth's behavior, and jealousy is the best explanation, it will get her nowhere to know the adaptive-historical or descent-historical truth about the phenomenon of jealousy or its neurocircuitry and neurochemistry; she needs to know about his state of mind: what he cares about and other features of his construal of his situation. Third, SL explanations are neither more nor less capable of being true than the scientific explanations; they serve *different* interests and answer different kinds of questions. I hope that this point will be made forceful by an analogy that I develop in Section 1.5d. Fourth, conceptual analysis is uniquely qualified to display the structure of SL explanations. It would be quite backward to suppose that one could learn the subjective logic of an emotion type by investigating its neural underpinnings or its evolutionary history. Fifth, SL explanations are especially relevant to discussions of ethics and the virtues, appealing as they do to what subjects care about and how they construe the situations of their lives. The standards of ethics are, in part, standards for what one cares about and how one construes potential offenses (e.g., it is often thought that a person's anger has low ethical value if it is based on trivial concerns and thus lacks a proper sense of what is really an offense, but has higher ethical value if it is based on important concerns).

Finally, the subjective logic of an emotion is a species of what Griffiths calls a "causal homeostatic mechanism." He points out that causal homeostasis is not all of one kind. "The concept of causal homeostasis entails a very broad conception of the essence of a category. An essence can be *any theoretical structure that accounts for the projectability of a category*" (p. 188, italics added). The causal homeostasis of chemical elements is their internal microstructure, while that of biological taxa is external and historical (biological descent). If the concept is this flexible, we can extend it to mental events. An emotion type like jealousy brings together a set of objects with correlated properties that have an underlying explanation that makes them projectable. Patterns of behavior like Wentworth's, with their many variations, will have a unified explanation in terms of a mental state with a certain structure that is appealed to in SL explanations of jealous behavior. If so, perhaps the causal homeostasis of emotions in general is the logical subjectivity of concern-based construal, and the causal homeostasis of particular emotion types is their particular structures of concern-based construal. If this is indeed the causal homeostasis of emotions, then it is one that is most appropriately investigated, not through the methods of the life sciences, but through conceptual analysis.

c. Stimulus and Narrative

A "stimulus," as the word is used in scientific contexts, is a simple, usually external (i.e., environmental) trigger of change in organisms. Thus a loud noise with sudden onset is a stimulus to the startle response, and an electrical shock is used as an unconditioned fear stimulus in many of LeDoux's experiments; the sound of a buzzer can be the stimulus conditioned in rats by pairing it with the electric shock. Furthermore, the learning that goes with responses to stimuli is paradigmatically *conditioning*. Fright lends itself well to discussion in terms of stimulus and response and conditioning; other emotions, like higher cognitive fear, or remorse and envy and hope, lend themselves less naturally to discussion in terms of stimulus, both because they are not "triggered" by a simple physical occurrence or perceptual experience and because the preparation for them (the learning) is not principally conditioning. We speak more naturally of the *occasions* of such emotions or the situations they are *about*. And we are less inclined to think of these occasions as stimuli because they are narratively complex. It is only when the situation is "taken in" (understood) by the subject that the emotion takes full shape, and the situation may be such that only by piecing together diverse narrative strands can the subject "assemble" an object that will evoke *this* emotion.

Consider a case of anger. George Knightley stops by to tell Emma of her protégée Harriet's good fortune in being courted by his friend Robert Martin, a "respectable, intelligent gentleman-farmer" (Jane Austen, *Emma*, Chapter 8). He has advised Robert to propose to the good-looking girl. He doesn't think her quite worthy of his friend, she being an illegitimate child without fortune or much in the way of intellect or education. But Robert, encouraged by Harriet, is deeply in love, and Knightley is pretty convinced that in time his good sense can make a decent wife of her. So Knightley becomes indignant when Emma tells him that Harriet has already refused Robert's offer. He becomes angry with Emma when it emerges that the refusal is a result of Emma's having put it into Harriet's head that she is too good for Robert. Knightley's anger (and the reader's) grows as the folly and injustice of Emma's meddlesome, snobbish, impertinent, and self-satisfied manipulations of Harriet's love life come to light in the conversation.

Where is the "stimulus" of this emotion? There is nothing closely analogous to the electric shock or the sound of the buzzer that "trigger" the rat's fear in LeDoux's experiments. We can certainly speak of what *elicits* Knightley's anger (and the reader's). It is the known and understood *situation* composed of Robert's and Harriet's relative merits, Robert's proposal, Harriet's refusal, the reasonableness of Robert's hopes, the causes of Harriet's refusal in Emma's manipulations, and so forth. In other words, what elicits the anger is a situation that cannot be depicted otherwise than by a narrative, and which must be understood in moral terms ("folly," "injustice," "meddlesome," etc.). To be presented with this "object" requires a language-mediated cognitive sophistication that seems qualitatively different from the mental equipment needed to respond to a "stimulus." Or, if we are comfortable extending the word "stimulus" to cover the text as visually read or the conversation between Emma and Knightley as it impinges on their auditory receptors, then we must sever the usual scientific connection between the concepts of *stimulus* and *conditioning*. For we must resist the suggestion that conditioning is the kind of learning by which we come to be able to understand narratives of this sort. No amount of the process of associating stimuli can account for human beings' syntactical ability to understand language[29] and thus to have the kind of emotions that depend on the ability to understand narratives. Human emotions typically involve putting together narrative elements in the way that Knightley's anger does. Only seldom is human fear purely the kind of conditioned or unconditioned response to a stimulus that LeDoux so ably studies in rats.

Another respect in which emotions are "logical" creates a third complication for explaining emotions in terms of conditioning. Take a typical case of fear – say, a basketball fan's fear that his team's most important player will foul out before he is able to make the needed points; a patriot's fear that a certain candidate will win the election; a doctor's fear that his patient will take a turn for the worse during the night. Each of these fears is logically coordinate with a variety of other possible emotions, in the following way. A doctor who fears that his patient will take a turn for the worse in the night can be expected to be glad if he finds out the next morning that the patient is significantly better. He can also be expected to feel hopeful if he is given reason to think it probable that the patient will be better in the morning. With a few other assumptions, we can be expect him to feel grateful to another doctor who gives him advice that enables him to help the patient make it through the night, or angry at a nurse who by culpable negligence lets the patient take a turn for the worse. In everyday emotion explanations, this coordination is explained by saying that the doctor *cares* about his patient or *desires* the patient to make it through the night (further counterfactual specification of his emotion disposition would be required to decide which of these two attributions is preferable). Emotions of different types are yielded as different "readings" of the patient's situation impinge on this single concern of the doctor. Given this logical coordination characteristic of so many human emotions, the explanation of individual differences of emotion response in terms of a history of associations of stimuli seems woefully unpromising.[30]

I do not deny that narratively structured, concern-based emotions will ever be understood in detail in neuroscientific terms. But the terms in which they will be understood (if they ever are) will be, in part, of a very different kind than the fear whose circuitry LeDoux has mapped. The circuitry involved will include, in significant part, the language centers in the cerebral

---

[29] See Noam Chomsky, "A Review of B.F. Skinner's *Verbal Behavior*," in J. A. Fodor and J. J. Katz (eds.), *The Structure of Language* (Englewood Cliffs, New Jersey: Prentice-Hall, 1964), pp. 547–578.

[30] It is not surprising that conditioning theories of fear – which admittedly are powerful explanations of certain kinds of fear – are most successful as explanations of *irrational* fear (classical conditioning) and irrational behavior associated with fear (operant conditioning). See LeDoux, *The Emotional Brain*, Chapter 8. Conditioning as such seems to be rationality-blind. Because many emotions, like those of a good doctor in relation to his patient or like George Knightley's moral anger, are in the very weave of a rational life, it is hardly to be expected that conditioning theories will take us very far in explaining them.

cortex, and the mapping will have to show how narrative elements such as those constituting the object of George Knightley's anger are assembled into a single situational object. They will also need to identify the neurological structures underlying the concerns that coordinate emotions and the connection of these concerns to higher cognitive states (the doctor's concern *that the patient make it through the night,* or Knightley's concern *that justice be done to Robert Martin,* obviously exploits sophisticated brain centers). Because the forms of narrative of the higher cognitive emotions differ from one type of emotion to another, the structural difference will presumably have to be reflected in the neurological mappings. The differences of concerns from one another would also need to be reflected in any fine-grained mapping. Currently, neuroscience is nowhere near any such account. On the other hand, we already have a discipline that subtlely investigates and differentiates mental states with a narrative structure – conceptual analysis.

d. Physical Basis and Emotions Themselves[31]

Let us suppose that the fondest dreams of neuroscience have come true. By the year 2050, scientists have mapped fifty different emotion types in as much detail as LeDoux has done for conditioned fright, managing to distinguish each emotion type from all others by purely neurological markers (along with the other bodily changes they effect and record). In addition to envy, jealousy, nostalgia, indignation, resentment, umbrage, exasperation, awe, gladness, reverence, admiration, shame, embarrassment, guilt, schadenfreude, puzzlement, bewilderment, astonishment, and many others, they can give precisely differentiating neurological maps of such exotic and culture-bound states as Ilongot *liget* and Japanese *amae.* I don't know whether such a feat is even in principle possible, but let us imagine it's been done.

What is the status of this achievement? What kind of advance in our understanding has occurred? Does it make sense to say that we have now discovered the precise nature of the emotions *themselves,* whereas before we were only acquainted with their conscious epiphenomena (their "phenomenology," as some philosophers like to say)? Will such knowledge function as a substitute for the "knowledge" of these emotions (or as we might think, largely erroneous guesswork) that Jane Austen displays in her novels? Or does Austen's knowledge stand, pretty much unrevised but supplemented? Or is some other description of the new state of our knowledge more accurate? I propose an analogy.

Physically speaking, music is nothing but temporally extended and divided sequenced mixtures of air vibrations of various frequencies and

---

[31] I am indebted to Jay Wood for suggesting the analogy that I exploit in this subsection.

amplitudes or, alternatively, mixtures of atmospheric compression wave trains of varying wavelengths and amplitudes. An exact physical account of any performance can in principle be given in these and related terms, and an approximate such account can be given of any musical work [it would be approximate because different performers, different individual instruments (e.g., different violins), and different performance rooms, among other variables, yield physical variations]. However, musicians do not construe works and performances of them in the terms of physics, but in musical terms. They hear and speak of melodies, harmonies and counterpoint, rhythms, themes and their development, musical structure, dynamics, evocation and musical meanings, phrases, cadences, dissonances and resolutions of dissonances, and much more. It is only incidentally and occasionally that they hear and speak of frequencies, amplitudes, and wavelengths.

Similarly, ordinary people, as well as less ordinary ones like Jane Austen and conceptual analysts of emotion, attribute states like jealousy and nostalgia to people under particular circumstances of behavior, bodily change, and social situation, and they explain the behavior or bodily changes in terms of the emotion and explain the emotion in terms of the person's concerns, beliefs, thoughts, perceptions, personal history, present situation, and other factors. Even when they know something about the neuroscience of emotion, they discuss and experience emotions – their own and other people's – primarily in these traditional terms.

Notice that the acoustical account of music, while a sophisticated scientific achievement, is not a more sophisticated *substitute* for the terms of musical analysis. A fairly detailed physics of music has been around for a couple of hundred years, and for certain purposes it is far more precise and objective than the language of musical analysis, yet musicians show little inclination to abandon the traditional terms of musical analysis in favor of a physical one. Musical analysis of a work of music is analogous to conceptual analysis of emotions, while physical analysis of music is analogous to neurological analysis of emotions. Musical analysis is an account of music, in terms that are fairly close to the viewpoint of what we may call the "musical subject" (including in this term educated listeners as well as composers and performers), in much the way that conceptual analysis of emotions is an account of them in terms fairly close to the viewpoint of the "emotional subject," the person who experiences his own and other people's emotions in the contexts in which they are appropriate or inappropriate, in which they express other things about the person, in which they create expectations regarding behavior and have consequences for social relations, and so on. Just as musical analysis borders regularly on evaluation of the music under analysis *as music*, so conceptual analysis borders regularly on evaluation of the emotions under analysis *as emotions*. The language and concepts of musical analysis are a way of regimenting what people hear when they listen to music, what composers do when they compose it, what performers attend to as they perform it, and what teachers point out as they try to convey an understanding of it. The terms of analysis that are taught in conservatories of music are more precise than those in which ordinary musically aware listeners and performers hear music, but there is much continuity here. When a neophyte is taught the notion of a cadence, she is given a term for a category of musical occurrence with which she has been long familiar. It is part of musical culture. Few ordinary listeners are able to distinguish a French sixth from a German sixth, but this ability is a sophistication of the ordinary framework of musical appreciation; the physics of sound waves, by contrast, is not, regardless of how important it may be in the building of organs and acoustically optimal performance rooms.

Notice, too, that the physical account, insofar as it is an account of music, is parasitic on the musical account, but not vice versa. Imagine a physical account of a performance of Stravinsky's *Rite of Spring* – say, as rendered on a graph produced by an oscilloscope. It will show patterns of repetition and variation that "match" an account that a musician might give in terms of themes and development, phrases, cadences, and climaxes – at least it will show this to someone who knows how to read the graph and also has some musical understanding of the piece. But the musical meaning of those patterns would be utterly inaccessible to someone who lacked the kind of understanding that comes with the human subjectivity of a *musically* intelligent listener. In other words, an expert acoustician, giving a physical account of the *Rite of Spring*, will be able to make musical sense of it only if she has, in addition to her physical conceptual framework, some musical appreciation of the piece. On the other hand, an intelligent listener can fully appreciate a performance, in musical terms, without having the foggiest notion of what is happening at the level of physics.

If the analogy holds, a neurological account of the emotions will help us to understand *emotions*, rather than just their physical substructure, only if it can be subordinated to (i.e., interpreted in terms of) the ordinary terms in which we experience and discuss our emotions, the terms of which conceptual analysis of emotions is a technical upgrade. That the analogy does hold seems to be borne out by the fact that neuroscientists like LeDoux and Damasio refer regularly to the emotions they are dealing with in the terms of ordinary emotional life (fear is a response to danger and motivates behavior designed to protect from danger or escape from it). Indeed, it is hard to see how they would otherwise locate the objects of their research.

In one sense the physical account tells us what is really happening, what the performance of the *Rite of Spring* really amounts to, in a way that pointing to the themes and their developments, the thematic structure of the piece, the use of harmony, dissonance, counterpoint, and rhythm will not do. Such an account is the only kind that tells us what the performance "really is," *in case our question is about the physics* of the piece and the performance. But in case our question about the piece and the performance is musical, the physical account by itself does not tell us what we want to know. It is not more "objective"; it is simply not to the point. To suppose that atmospheric compression waves are "real" while pieces of music are only epiphenomenal is itself a judgment that is relative to a certain world view. It is true that without the compression waves there would be no music. But from there one can go on to say *either* that the compression wave trains are real and the music is not, *or* that the music is real and so are the compression wave trains that constitute its physical substratum. The latter attitude leaves it open that the interesting thing might be (for some people, at any rate) the music rather than its physical substratum. About the emotion analog, LeDoux seems to be of two minds. On the one side he says, "The brain states and bodily responses are the fundamental facts of an emotion, and the conscious feelings are the frills that have added icing to the emotional cake" (p. 300). On the other side, the subtitle of his book is *The Mysterious Underpinnings of Emotional Life.*

Paul Churchland, trading on the fact that scientific advances, when assimilated, can change our perception of things, has suggested that it might be possible to eliminate "folk ontology" altogether and to experience our world in terms of the latest scientific theories.[32] One aspect of such an education would presumably eliminate the musical conceptual framework in favor of that of acousticians. Thus when listening to what we currently call music, such aficionados would hear mixtures of atmospheric wave trains of given lengths (frequencies) and amplitudes and would *no longer* hear melodies, harmonies, dissonances, thematic developments, and the like. I doubt that this is possible: There are natural limits to our "plasticity of mind"; and musical understandings, even when they are culturally mediated (as they always are), are vastly more natural to us than acoustical ones. But even if we could eliminate music as music, why would we want to do so? Are we really committed enough to the imperialism of science to desire this elimination? That, I suppose, is a matter of taste. To me, it is obvious that to educate ourselves to "appreciate" music only as physics would be self-impoverishment. Presumably, the supposed advance would be in objectivity and truth: Music *really is* air vibrations, so the perception of it in musical terms is in some sense a misperception, like the perception of the evening sun as sinking below the horizon. But to insist that objectivity favors the air vibration construal seems to be physicalist prejudice. Perhaps there is no physical theory according to which a certain sequence of air vibrations is a beautiful melody tastefully harmonized; but why think *that* consideration would prevent its being such? Why not conclude instead that excellence of physical theory is not always the measure of objectivity? Why should we not suppose that music is as real as air vibrations and that if the best language in which to understand it is not

---

[32] See his *Scientific Realism and the Plasticity of Mind* (Cambridge, England: Cambridge University Press, 1979).

a physical theory, then a framework other than physical theory is sometimes needed for objectivity?

And the same may be said of the emotions. We have a rich vocabulary and explanatory framework referring to emotional phenomena, which is not scientific any more than our framework for understanding music is. Jane Austen and Charles Dickens are masters of this framework in much the way that Johannes Bach and Johannes Brahms are masters of the musical. It is very unlikely that any advances in neuroscience will cause us to stop explaining Frederick Wentworth's jealousy by pointing out that he is in love with Anne and that she seems to him to be attracted to William Elliot, and to start explaining it by referring to electrochemical changes transmitted from one part of Wentworth's brain to another and down into his trunk and back again. But if it were possible to make this transition, by some heroic effort of social training and popularization of science, should we desire it? Should we trade in our Austens and Trollopes for LeDouxes and Damasios? Would eliminating our conceptual framework of the emotions promote our understanding of them, making it more objective? In Austen and Dickens, the mastery of the conceptual framework of the emotions is a crucial element in their understanding of moral character. If we wish to retain their moral insights, we will hamper our understanding, rather than enhance it, by eliminating the language that supports and expresses that understanding.

e. Conceptual Analysis in This Book

I have argued that for people with certain human interests, there is no substitute for the kind of conceptual framework of the emotions that ordinary people make daily use of. As a consequence of this, conceptual analysis of the sort that philosophers have more or less always practiced is an irreplaceable central discipline in the study of the emotions. Let me comment, by way of conclusion, about analysis as I practice it in this book.

Early in this chapter I noted the many "opposite" attributes that items falling under the concept *emotion* can have. Some theorists have taken this fact to signal an internal incoherency that precludes straightforward conceptual analysis. I have argued that two strong versions of this hypothesis are not compelling, and I have suggested that if we think of emotions as mental events, we may find a central core to the concept that will hold all the diversity and "opposition" more or less together. I say "more or less" because my proposed central core analysis works best for the paradigm cases of human emotions, while leaving some items of human emotion (e.g., some instances of love – see Section 3.15) a little bit off the core analysis, some kinds of human emotion (like responses to nonverbal music – see Section 2.5j) pretty far off the core analysis, and the emotions of animals and preverbal human infants somewhat off the core analysis but assimilable to it by analogy (see Sections 2.5e and 2.5f). I want to discuss all these kinds of emotion, as well as others that do not quite fit the paradigm, so as to meet head-on and assess the counterexamples to my analysis and to display both its power and its limits. I have also argued that some emotions are better adapted to conceptual analysis than others – in particular, ones that have a strongly narrative structure and depend on narrative understanding. My analysis, like any conception or explanation of emotions, will be interest-relative and not absolute. I am especially interested in the narrative emotions and treat them as paradigmatic because of their dominance in adult human life and their consequent special relevance to the moral life and the moral and intellectual virtues.

Clearly, I am supposing that a concept can have the kind of coherency that is needed for it to be *a* concept without being susceptible to analysis in terms of strictly necessary and sufficient conditions. Still, I will work for all reasonable strictness and precision. I will be keenly interested in counterexamples, both as applied to the proposed core analysis of *emotion* and as applied to the defining propositions for emotion types. These propositions are intended as somewhat rough approximations, not because there is a shining diamond-hard and spanking clean Platonic essence to which they do not quite attain, but because there are borderline cases and the concepts have somewhat rough edges.

Sometimes conceptual analysis is conceived as merely the process of noting and arranging in order the kind of things that ordinary English speakers say about the matter under analysis or the ways we use the word in question ("emotion," "regret," "resentment"). Such a method, while a useful beginning, has three notable limitations. It is culturally myopic, is limited by the limitations of insight of the persons whose speech is taken as the starting point, and appears to remain removed from the thing under analysis (examining not emotions but what is said about them).

Cultural myopia can be mitigated by looking at analogous concepts from other cultures and other times. While I am interested chiefly in emotion concepts as they are found in modern Western societies, I will also consider concepts from other cultures, such as the Ilongot *liget* and the Ifaluk *metagu*, as well as the ancient and medieval Christian concept of *acedia*, and I will comment from time to time on historical changes in emotion concepts.

The second limitation of mere linguistic analysis is that it may not discriminate sufficiently between ordinary speakers of the language and really insightful people. People vary in the powers of observation that inform their speech, and the conceptual analyst of emotion will want to be an unusually sensitive user of language himself and to enlist the help of others who are even more sensitive. The ideal helper will be someone who is especially observant and sensitive, without being in thrall to a technical theory. While novelists are not necessarily without theoretical prejudices, their business – the observation of human beings in settings of action and

interaction – predisposes them to be careful and sensitive observers. Some of
the best are stunning in their insights. I must also commend something that
might go by the opprobrious name of "introspection." Conceptual analysis
of emotions, like musical analysis, is analysis from a participant's point of
view. Thus, much of the "observing" that the analyst does will be an observing
of what it is like to be the subject of emotions.

The third limitation of conceptual analysis is that it is about our *concept*
of the thing in question, whereas we may be interested in the thing *itself*. As
is evident from the history and anthropology of astronomical concepts, it is
possible for a given society's concept of *x* to be wildly at variance with the
real nature of *x*. But as I argued in Section 1.5c, some objects of investigation
are not as independent of the human experience of them as astronomical
objects are. If we do nonscientific analysis of emotions – say, the kind that
is implicit in Austen – we risk our concept of emotion being parochial and
idiosyncratic in a way *distantly* analogous to the wild miss characteristic of
primitive astronomical concepts. But the likelihood of such distortion is
initially far less than in the astronomy case,[33] and it is further reduced if we
are careful analysts, if we do our analysis in conversation with historical and
cross-cultural sources and with persons of first-rate emotional sensitivities
like the great novelists, and if we ourselves are sensitive "introspectors."

But if conceptual analysis is the most fundamental of the "theoretical"
disciplines for acquiring an understanding of emotions as they play out in
current human life, it is possible and salutary for it to be supplemented by
the kind of scientific information that we have discussed in this chapter.
While it is not crucial to our understanding of joy to know that the facial
expression characteristic of it (or, more precisely, characteristic of a range of
emotions related to joy) has the kind of rough cultural universality that Paul
Ekman has demonstrated, it is no doubt interesting to know this; it adds a
bit of genuine information to the richer and more internal knowledge of joy
and the other "joyful" emotions that can be achieved through conceptual
analysis. Dostoevsky and Austen knew that emotions with "passivity" could be
got up by play-acting, but still it is nice to have the experimental confirmation
that Ekman and his colleagues achieved in the study that I discussed in
Section 1.4e. If Robert Frank's claims about the social adaptiveness of moral
anger could be made less speculative (perhaps through the establishment of
historical homologies, as Griffiths urges), and detached from his ideological
concept of rationality, this too would be a bit of interesting information
collateral to the richer and more internal understanding of anger that can

---

[33] Just as a nonprobative aside, I would note that both Michelle Rosaldo and Catherine Lutz,
in their anthropological studies of emotion, think that sophisticated Westerners can learn
something *about emotions* from these rather primitive peoples. But no one in his right mind
would think we have anything to learn about the nature of planets and stars from the Ilongots
or the Ifaluk.

be achieved through conceptual analysis. It is always interesting to know the historical backgrounds, including evolutionary, of the things we study. Most interesting of all, it seems to me, is the supplementation of knowledge of emotions that comes (or may come) from neuroscience. It is part of the ordinary observation of our emotions, and thus a part of conceptual analysis as I understand it, that we often react behaviorally to a frightful object before we feel afraid, that we feel anxious in certain situations without our being consciously aware of any real danger, and that we can continue to react with fear to an object that we positively and firmly believe to pose no threat. These aspects of the concept of fright and anxiety can be explained with a fairly high degree of scientific confidence and in some detail by reference to the neural pathways involved in the generation of these emotions. To revert to the analogy of the previous subsection, this explanation is parallel to a physicist's explanation of why the interval of a diminished fifth sounds the way it does, by reference to the interaction of the frequencies of the two compression wave trains. In other words, the mechanics underlying the experience has been given in each case. This kind of knowledge strikes me as being closer to the knowledge of the emotion itself than that yielded by the other two kinds of scientific inquiry. Obviously, however, this knowledge gains much of its interest from its power to explain things that are already known about fright and anxiety (or diminished fifths) by careful observers – the kind of things in which conceptual analysis of fear and anxiety trades.

The next chapter provides an account of the nature of emotions that exemplifies what I have been calling conceptual analysis. It begins with a dozen or so general observations about emotions, observations that ordinary emotional subjects can make simply by being intelligent and observant human beings. In the rest of the chapter I develop the mentalist account of emotions that was foreshadowed in Sections 1.5a and 1.5c as a way of making unified sense of these and related features. I do not take the account presented there to be a mere "phenomenology" of emotion, by comparison with which the neuroscientist or the evolutionary psychologist offers an account of "what emotions really are."[34] Instead, I take this to be an account of what emotions really are, from a particular point of view – namely, human life as it is actually lived and viewed from the angle of broadly moral concerns.

---

[34] Damasio gets it right when he says of consciousness, "The appearance *is* the reality – the human mind as we directly sense it." *The Feeling of What Happens: Body and Emotion in the Making of Consciousness* (New York: Harcout Brace and Company, 1999), p. 27, Damasio's italics.

2

The Nature of Emotions

At a department meeting, my colleague George suggests that I should have last choice of upper-division course assignment, because I'm nothing but a middle-aged white protestant male, and besides that, ethics is a soft discipline and not serious philosophy. I get mad. I shall treat this as a paradigm case of emotion, making twelve remarks about it and cases of emotion that are unlike it in various ways. In doing so, I want to mark features of emotions that will need to be accommodated in any account of the nature of emotion. Some of these claims are controversial. Arguments for the more controversial ones will be found throughout this book. Remarks E1–E12 are not in any special order, particularly not in order of importance.

E1. I begin by noting that not only *am* I mad, I also *feel* mad. In feeling angry, I am aware of being angry. In English "feeling" functions, in some contexts, as a synonym for "emotion." Yet "feel an emotion" is not redundant in the way that "feel a pain" is. A "pain" that is not felt is not a pain, but unfelt emotions are common. Novelists describe, and psychotherapists regularly confront, people who are angry, resentful, envious, and anxious, yet do not feel these emotions. Not only can a person have an emotion he does not feel, he can feel an emotion he does not have. For example, a person might feel pity for a sufferer when he does not in fact pity the sufferer, or feel anxious when in fact he is not anxious but is in the early stages of flu (see Section 4.7). *Summary*: Emotions are paradigmatically felt, but emotions may occur independently of the corresponding feeling, and the feeling of an emotion can be nonveridical, illusory.

E2. When George offers his reasons for my being given last choice of upper-division course assignment, a number of things happen in my body: My blood pressure goes up, the muscles of my forehead and around my eyes contract in a characteristic formation, my heart rate increases, my neck and hand muscles tighten up, and so on. I feel some, but not all, of these bodily occurrences. Of the ones I do feel, none is necessarily felt: For example, after a couple of minutes of not being aware that my hand muscles are tight, I might come to feel their tightness. People sometimes identify the feeling of an emotion with the feeling of these bodily states. But this seems to be wrong, because one can feel this configuration, or a subjectively indistinguishable configuration, of bodily states without feeling the emotion (perhaps the states are induced by a dose of caffeine or epinephrine); and one can feel an emotion while unaware of some, and perhaps all, of the members of the configuration. On the other hand, the feeling (i.e., the sensation) of these physiological states, when it exists, forms *part* or an *aspect* of the feeling of the emotion. *Summary:* Physiological changes often accompany emotions; sometimes they are felt; the feeling of them is not the feeling of the emotion, though it is characteristically an aspect of that feeling.

E3. My anger is *directed at* George, *on account of* his remark. Emotions are like a number of other kinds of mental states in being "intentional" – that is, taking some "object" beyond themselves. Just as every belief is *that* such-and-such is the case, or *in* such-and-such, and every desire is *for* something or other, and every wondering is *about* something or *whether* such-and-such is the case, to be angry is to be angry at someone, about something; to hope is to hope for something, usually on some basis; to envy is to envy someone something; and so forth. In this respect, too, emotions differ from sheer sensations: The throbbing in my left foot is not *that, about,* or *whether* something beyond itself (though when sensations function as perceptions, they are intentional: feeling the light switch in the dark, smelling the coffee, hearing the howl of the wolf). *Summary:* Paradigm cases of adult human emotions take "objects."

E4. George, as the object of my anger, is not merely singular, but part of a situation. I am angry at *him,* for an *offense,* performed in a certain kind of *way* (in this case intentionally), in a certain *setting* (right there in front of my other colleagues), and so on. If someone unacquainted with the situation (or better, my mental construction of the situation) asks, What are you angry about? I shall answer with a story – a set of propositions – in which these various features are drawn together and interconnected in such a way as to draw a "picture" of the situation as I see it in my anger. Furthermore, different parts of the picture can be focal or salient to the view that I take of the situation. The offender may be primarily in mind, with what he has done in the background, or the offense may be salient for me with the offender in the background, or the way the offense was committed (right there in front of everybody) or his mental state (he had been planning that for days and did it out of spite) may be the focus of my anger. Each picture has the same elements, but it is a shifting one, less like a painting or photograph and more like a stage presentation in which various players may come forward and others recede to the background, possibly in rapid succession. Not all emotions take situational objects (some forms of love do not), but the vast majority do. *Summary:* Emotional objects are typically situational or composite, with unequal and shifting focus on the various elements of the situational object.

E5. The type of emotional state that a person is in is determined by the *kind* of story one tells in explaining it (the kind of elements that the picture has). For example, in explanations of anger we expect to hear about *culpable offenses*; in explanations of fear we expect to hear about *threats* to the subject's well-being or the well-being of things that matter to him or her; in explanations of grief we expect to hear about *loss* of something important to the subject, and so on. *Summary:* We could say that emotion type is determined by certain leading concepts that define it.

E6. If asked whether, in addition to my anger's being shaped by the story in terms of which I picture the situation that angers me, I also believe or judge that story to be true, I will probably say "yes." I may go through the various propositions composing the story and ask about each: Do I believe that George said that I should be given last choice of upper-division course assignment? Do I believe that in saying this he insulted me, demeaning my work and my field? Do I believe he was intentionally malicious or otherwise culpable in doing so? After such a critical examination of my mind, I may conclude that I believe all the propositional content of my emotion: I believe the situation to be as my emotion pictures it. Perhaps this is the typical case. It is not the only kind of case. I may have some reason to doubt that the colleague was being malicious: In fact, I think in my heart of hearts that the colleague was just joking, and my reason for thinking so is that some of my other colleagues took the remark that way. But this colleague has been rubbing me the wrong way and I prefer the more anger-engendering construction of his remark, and hang onto it, yet without believing it. If somebody confronts me, saying "Roberts, you don't really think George was being malicious, do you?" I may be reluctant to admit it but I may know that I really don't think that. I admit to myself that my anger is "irrational," but I still hang onto it. *Summary:* In the paradigm cases, the subject of an emotion believes the propositional content of his emotion, but in some cases of genuine emotion the subject does not believe all of that content.

E7. As I have told the story about my anger, I have pictured myself as perfectly articulate about my emotion: I can produce the "story" that gives my reasons. But people are often inarticulate about their emotions, for various kinds of reasons. Some of the propositional content of the emotion may be unconscious (it may be not just in the background but completely off stage), and some of the content may not be propositional at all. For example, the kind of ecstatic joy or awe that one may experience while sitting on the shore of a deserted mountain lake at sunset or listening to one of the Brandenburg Concerti seems not even to *have* a "story." Perhaps even the most articulate and articulable emotions typically have some nonpropositional content.

Summary: It is possible to have emotions without being able to articulate (all of) their content; some of the content may be nonpropositional.

E8. I have not yet said what I want to *do* when George suggests that I be given last choice of upper-division course assignment because of my low social status and the softness of my discipline. I will tell you now: It is a toss-up between punching him out, insulting him back, and getting him fired. There is a pattern here: Every action that comes to mind is punitive. Other emotions motivate other kinds of action: Fear to protect something, envy to put the rival down, embarrassment to hide from view, and so on. Thus references to such emotions are often a powerful way to explain actions. But not all emotions are motivational: Joy and grief, for example, do not seem to generate (or contain) desires for particular kinds of action (though they do have characteristic facial, vocal, and gestural expressions). *Summary:* Many types of emotion are motivational in the sense that they involve a desire to perform characteristic types of action, but not all emotions are motivational in this sense.

E9. We sometimes speak of "hanging on" to our anger, or giving in to anger that we feel coming on, or letting ourselves be carried away. We also speak of giving up our anger (say, in an act of forgiveness) or not allowing ourselves to get angry. We often speak as though we have some control over our emotions, at least part of the time – that we can sometimes choose whether to go into an emotional state, or whether to remain there. But we also sometimes speak as though the emotion has control of us, partial or even complete. We are sometimes paralyzed by fear, possessed by anger. *Summary:* The subject of an emotion is sometimes able to exercise voluntary control over it, and sometimes unable to do so.

E10. I have pictured my anger at George as quite intense. A measure of its intensity is how I would like to punish him; we can imagine that instead of wanting to punch him or get him fired, I only have an urge to annoy him with a little snide remark or a dirty look. Other indicators of intensity are degree of autonomic arousal, duration, intensity of feeling, and dominance over other mental contents. *Summary:* Emotions come in degrees of intensity.

E11. Let us say that my anger at George is not very intense, and I respond to his proposal with a mildly cutting remark of my own about *his* discipline. And I find that my anger has disappeared. This is one kind of case. In another kind of case, the more I act punitively, the angrier I get. *Summary:* Expression of an emotion in behavior and action sometimes causes an emotion to subside, but sometimes expression intensifies and/or prolongs the emotion.

E12. After the meeting at which I show visible anger at George, one of my other colleagues commends me for it, saying, "I was glad to see that you got so angry about what George said; he deserved it. I can remember a time when you would have taken that remark in stride." We can also imagine cases of anger that would be properly censured as morally unfitting. Almost all of the emotion types (hope, joy, fear, contempt, etc.) exhibit some instances that are morally praiseworthy, and others that are morally reprehensible. *Summary*: Emotions, like actions, are subject to moral praise and blame.

The foregoing is just a sampling of facts about emotions. Others will be uncovered as we proceed, but these twelve should be enough to get us started. Any adequate account of the nature of emotion must accommodate these facts. No theory of emotion that I know of accommodates them gracefully. By "theory" I mean an account that purports to specify the necessary and sufficient conditions for anything's membership in the class *emotion*. Accordingly, I shall not offer a theory of emotion. I shall offer, instead, what I call an "account," that is, a series of discussions that test a certain paradigm for emotions – that emotions are concern-based construals – that I think does accommodate fairly well the vast majority of cases of mental states that would be agreed by most English speakers to count as emotions. The cases that deviate from the paradigm will be discussed in terms of the paradigm: that is, the ways they fit and fail to fit it will be noted. The result, I hope, will be to shed considerable light on the nature or natures of emotions, but without in the strictest sense offering a theory.

Amélie Rorty has asserted that "emotions do not form a natural class." In stressing their resistance to classification, she gives this list: fear, religious awe, exuberant delight, pity, loving devotion, panic, pride, remorse, indignation, contempt, disgust, resignation, compassion.[1] If no true theory of emotion is possible, then Rorty is right about classification. But I think that much in the field can be conceptually regimented, and that we forestall understanding by giving up too early on the effort to find a fundamental conception or paradigm. So the present chapter, in which I conceptualize emotions as concern-based construals, can be read as a qualified challenge to Rorty's thesis. Loving devotion, if thought of as a disposition, will escape my account, but the phrase may also (somewhat awkwardly) refer to an episode of consciousness, as when I contemplate my daughter's school band performance with loving devotion. Since it is plausible to limit emotions to mental episodes, it seems reasonable to designate the latter loving devotion, and not the former, as an emotion. In this case the emotion seems to be a version of joy or pride, and I think my proposal handles it well. Exuberant delight, if it is so generalized as not to be "about" anything (perhaps it is due to artificial – or natural but abnormal – chemical alteration of the central nervous system), will not fit the account, but it seems to me useful to distinguish this kind of state of mind from emotions proper and call it "mood." "Resignation" may be a character trait term or the name of a mental act, in which case it will not fit my account of emotions, but one can also feel resigned, and I think my account will handle that kind of case.

---

[1] Amélie O. Rorty (ed.), *Explaining Emotions* (Berkeley: University of California Press), p. 1.

Emotion words are often used in contexts where no emotion is referred to, or seriously referred to: "Adelaide is a jealous person" makes no claim that she is currently experiencing any emotion; "I envy you your red socks," "I'm sorry you had to wait," "I pity the woman who marries him," and "I am grateful to my critics for their penetrating comments" are often not serious references to emotions of envy, regret, pity, or gratitude.

A number of items that do not appear in Rorty's list, but would appear in lists of some theorists, may also not be captured by my proposal. Theorists occasionally include such reflexes as the startle response (see Section 3.16c) and the orienting reflex as emotions, as well as amusement at jokes (see Section 3.16b). Others would consider clinical depression and clinical euphoria to be emotions. Robert Solomon, in his "emotional register,"[2] includes a number of items that don't seem to me to be emotions, though I acknowledge that they are all closely related to, or involve, emotions, being dispositions to emotions or dispositions not to experience certain emotions: indifference, duty, faith, friendship, innocence, and vanity. Gilbert Ryle lets in avarice, considerateness, patriotism, kindliness, and laziness,[3] and Steven Ross includes generosity, obsequiousness, and loyalty.[4] All these words seem to me more naturally construed as trait terms than as emotion terms.

I do not claim that just anything any philosopher or psychologist calls an emotion is a concern-based construal. But I think my account encompasses occurrences of what paradigmatically counts as episodes of embarrassment, anger, shame, envy, gratitude, hope, anxiety, jealousy, grief, despair, remorse, joy, and resentment, as well as the items from Rorty's list about which I expressed no doubt – that is, a great deal of what is indisputably and paradigmatically emotion. In Chapter 3 I test the model I am proposing in an analysis of a fairly wide range of the paradigmatic emotions and also some of the items more on the periphery of the class. The chapter will bear out Rorty's thesis in showing that some of what some people are inclined to call emotions lack some of the central features of my paradigm, as do some of what anybody not driven by a reductive theory would call emotion.

2.2. FEELINGS

It is almost a truism among certain philosophers that "emotions aren't feelings."[5] Seldom is much trouble taken to say what *kind* of feelings emotions aren't, but items that come to mind are tightness in the chest, a

---

[2] *The Passions* (Garden City, New York: Doubleday, 1977), pp. 280–371.
[3] *The Concept of Mind* (New York: Harper and Row, 1949), p. 85.
[4] "Evaluating the Emotions" *The Journal of Philosophy* **81** (1984): 309–326.
[5] For efforts to resist this trend, see David Pugmire's *Rediscovering Emotion* (Edinburgh: Edinburgh University Press, 1998) and Peter Goldie's *The Emotions* (Oxford: Clarendon Press, 2000). I have reviewed these books in, respectively, *The Philosophical Quarterly* **51** (2001): 116–119 and *Philosophia Christi* **3** (2001): 543–552.

prickly or flushing sensation on the neck or face, awareness of perspiring or clamminess, an uncomfortable glowing sensation midbody, and generally the sensations of what psychologists call "arousal."[6] That *such* feelings are not emotions follows from E3: Anger, hope, fear, and gratitude, like beliefs and desires, are necessarily about, of, or for something, while feelings of flushes, prickles, gnawings, and constrictions make no such reference beyond themselves.

If E1 is true and not all emotions are felt, then the generalization *emotions are feelings* has to be false, no matter what kind of feelings are in question. But the fact remains that ordinary people are strongly inclined unreflectively to identify emotions and feelings. Let us speculate a moment why this is so. Perhaps we can find a sense of "feeling" that will put us on a track of what emotions are. Gilbert Ryle displays part of the variety of feelings in an essay[7] in which he distinguishes seven different senses of "feeling": (1) *Perceptual.* Someone feels the temperature of the bathwater. (2) *Exploratory.* I feel in my pocket for my keys. (3) *Mock perceptual.* The condemned man "feels" the noose around his neck, though he is eating breakfast in his cell. (4) *Sensory.* We feel aches and tickles. (5) *Of general condition.* We have a nonlocalized feeling of being depressed, lazy, or sleepy. (6) *Of tentative judgment.* Ryle feels there's a flaw in some argument. (7) *Of inclination.* When I look over the presidential candidates, I feel like running myself.

After identifying these categories of feelings, Ryle remarks, "I expect there are plenty more" (p. 276). Nor is it hard to think of some more. Take the director who exhorts her chorus, "Sing it again, this time with feeling!" Ryle himself says that feeling triumphant doesn't fit any of his classes. And it is a little odd that no category in his list encompasses feeling an emotion. A couple of times he mentions emotions (indignation and anger) in connection with feelings of general condition, but it seems wrong to assimilate feeling angry with feeling sleepy or ill or fidgety, or even with feeling depressed. However, in these last two cases we are on the border of intentional states; it is sometimes fitting to ask, "What are you feeling fidgety about?" or "Why are you depressed?" (where we are requesting a reason, and not just a cause).

Ryle's mention of feeling triumphant suggests another kind of feelings that are very close to emotions. Other members of this category would be feeling confident, awkward, ambitious, incompetent, ripped off, excluded. These feelings depend, more than feeling sick or lazy do, on the person's *taking* himself to be in a certain condition or to have a certain property,

[6] "It seems likely that the feelings to be associated with emotions are the subjective registering of the physiological changes." William Lyons, *Emotion* (Cambridge: Cambridge University Press, 1980), p. 212. See Section 2.8 for a discussion of bodily states and their relations with emotions.
[7] "Feelings" in *Collected Papers*, Volume II (London: Hutchinson, 1971), pp. 272–286.

and they depend less on sensory awareness of one's body (when feeling sick or tired, the "condition" one feels oneself to be in is largely a bodily condition, though construal also operates here). Or we might say that these feelings tend to be more thought-dependent than feelings of general condition. While my feeling sick *may* depend heavily on my telling myself I'm sick, it does not necessarily do so; and feeling depressed (in the sense that my world has a dull and pointless look about it) does not depend on thinking of myself as depressed. But I can't feel triumphant, incompetent, or excluded without construing myself in these terms. We might call these *feelings of construed condition*, or feelings of self-estimate.

Perhaps we can get clearer about feelings of construed condition if we look at another kind of experiential construal. Wittgenstein discusses a kind of visual experience that is not a visual sensation. He says, "I contemplate a face, and then suddenly notice its likeness to another. I *see* that it has not changed; and yet I see it differently. I call this experience 'noticing an aspect'."[8] One might see an aspect of a face by construing it in terms of another face, in something like an act of imagination. The analogy with feeling awkward is instructive: Just as one experiences something about the face by letting the other face "inform" it, so in feeling awkward one experiences oneself in certain terms or in a certain connection (perhaps in connection with some paradigm of awkwardness, or in contrast with something graceful). The experience of "seeing-as" is most graphically illustrated with simple drawings like the duck-rabbit that Wittgenstein discusses in this context. Seeing the duck-rabbit as a duck is not merely knowing that it can be seen as a duck, nor merely judging that it is a picture-duck. One can judge that the figure is ducklike while seeing it as rabbitlike; this is most obvious in the case where one makes the judgment on the basis of somebody's testimony, while being unable to see it for oneself. Seeing the duck-rabbit as a duck is a visual experience of it as such, without the experience's being a visual sensation. Similarly, the person who feels triumphant is not merely judging that he is triumphant, but is "perceiving" himself as such, yet without this experience being constituted of any sensory experience of himself. The word "construe" can be so used as to mean nothing more than *interpret*, thus not suggesting the experiential immediacy of perception. But in the somewhat special sense that I am commending, construing is perceptual in this broad sense. I think we must allow for the possibility of unconscious construal (see Section 2.3b). But in the paradigm cases it is a kind of experience that involves having an impression of some aspect – for example, the duckiness of the duck-rabbit or one's triumph.

The kind of construing involved in having a feeling of construed condition is less tied to sensation than seeing the duck-rabbit as a duck, or

---

[8] *Philosophical Investigations*, translated by G. E. M. Anscombe (New York: Macmillan, 1953), Part II, p. 193; italics in the original.

hearing a series of four notes as the opening of "Yankee Doodle." In the latter cases, the description of the construing makes definite reference to a sense experience. But the person who "views" himself as triumphant or awkward does not need to be looking at himself in the mirror, hearing himself speak, or having any particular kinesthetic sensations. No particular sense experience is required for the construal, in the way the visual perception of the figure (or at a minimum a mental image of it) is needed to see the duck in the duck- rabbit.

But construing oneself as triumphant or awkward is not sufficient for feeling triumphant or awkward. Such a construal seems to be necessary to the feeling, but not the whole story. If I am very "philosophical" about my awkwardness in a French conversation – that is, if I have no great stake in speaking graceful French – I may be vividly aware of my awkwardness without feeling awkward. Similarly with triumph: Imagine a jaded old senator who has not been unseated for forty years. He runs once again, this time more out of habit and a mild distaste for retirement than out of enthusiasm for his work or the contest, and wins the election. Upon hearing of his victory he construes himself as triumphant – without feeling triumphant. Lacking in these two cases is a concern about being in the condition one construes oneself to be in. To feel self-righteous, one must want to be (or to be thought to be) morally superior. To feel guilty, one must be concerned not to be guilty.

I suggest that such feelings are very close to the paradigm cases of adult human emotions and can provide the beginnings of a model for understanding the emotions. Such a feeling is an "in-terms-of" experience based in a concern. It is not a sensation that accompanies this "cognition," but it is this concern-imbued "cognition" itself. To feel awkward is not to have a sensation (a twinge, gnaw, curdling, or throb) from which I infer that I am construing myself as awkward, as I sometimes infer from an abdominal burning sensation that I must be anxious. Since the feeling of awkwardness just *is* the conscious concernful construing of oneself as awkward, it is in the strongest sense possible the feeling *of* (one's own) *awkwardness*.

Are feelings of construed condition emotions? It would be fussy to object to calling feelings of triumph, awkwardness, and being ripped off emotions. In fact, most of them can probably be subsumed under one of the standard categories of emotion: Feelings of awkwardness are perhaps often instances of embarrassment or frustration or amusement, while feelings of triumph are probably often instances of pride or joy. But feelings of construed condition have a couple of properties that make them peculiar.

First, they are essentially feelings, whereas emotions are not. People can be episodically angry without feeling so, but no one feels awkward without feeling so. It may seem that the analogue of being angry without feeling so would not be feeling awkward without feeling so but *being* awkward without feeling so. But being awkward is not an intentional state at all; so it cannot be the unconscious complement of the feeling of awkwardness. Though the feeling of awkwardness is essentially a feeling, we have no reason to rule out unfelt episodes of an emotion corresponding to the feeling of awkwardness. On analogy with our verb "to fear," our vocabulary might have contained an emotion term "to awk," the paradigm cases of which would be to feel awkward. In our cultural psychology, awking would be a full-fledged emotion because there could be unconscious instances of this concern-based self-construal. (People might sometimes repress the emotion in much the way we repress shame.) Therapists might undertake to make people conscious of awking about things they don't want to admit awking about. This first difference between emotions and feelings of construed condition, then, is chiefly one of vocabulary. We have no word to apply to the state of mind of concernfully construing *oneself* as awkward even though one is not feeling awkward, whereas we do have analogous vocabulary for the full-fledged emotions. Second, emotions are not directly reflexive, except incidentally, but feelings of construed condition are. One construes *oneself* as triumphant, awkward, guilty, and so forth. If being angry is a construal, what is construed as culpably offensive is not typically oneself but some other person or personalized agency such as the Pentagon or the Republican Party.

If my analysis of feelings of construed condition is correct, there can be intentional feelings – feelings *about* or *of* myself. If so, it is only a small step to "feelings" – that is, conscious concern-based construals – about other things: anger at the government, gratitude to my children, envy of a colleague.

2.3. CONSTRUALS

a. Introduction

Let us take a closer look at the concept of a construal that is crucial to the paradigm of emotion that I am proposing. I begin by offering some examples, with commentary. I hope to convey an impression of the variety of things that count as construals, but also of a set of family resemblances among them. Once the concept of a construal is fairly clear, and we have noticed a number of features of the phenomenon, I will apply the concept to the claim that emotions, in the paradigm cases, are a certain kind of construal.

b. Some Examples

1. A lovely, well-dressed young woman who speaks mid-western English with a university accent says, after a few words, "... they have went...," and your whole impression of her changes. What we call the impression here is a mode of experience: With the *change* of impression, you

now become aware, as you were not before, of the impression you had
of her before.

2. Say "table." Now say it again, thinking of it as a verb. Here you are
    construing the sound in terms of the category or concept *verb*. It
    has a different "sound" when thought of as a verb, in virtue of the
    associations and the readiness to use it in certain ways and not in
    others. A behaviorist analysis of the difference of construal will not
    do: when, in doing this exercise, I construe "table" as a verb, the
    construal does not consist merely in my readiness to use "table" in
    such phrases as 'table the motion' rather than in phrases like 'wipe
    the table'; rather, the word actually sounds (or looks) different when
    variously construed. In the exercise, I am not so much ready to use the
    word in the different ways, as I am experiencing the word in terms of
    the alternate possible usages that with some reflection I can illustrate
    if called upon to so so. In both construals of "table," the purely sensory
    (auditory or visual) input is not changed by the introduction of new
    terms of construal; but the perception of the word – the "feel" of it,
    as we might say – is changed.

3. Consider the well-known old woman/young woman gestalt figure
    (Figure 1). As you see the young woman in the figure, two things
    are clear: (a) This is a perception, not just a belief, judgment, or
    thought that the figure represents a young woman. I believed and
    judged that the figure was of a young woman for quite a long time
    before, with my wife's aid, I became able to "see" the young woman
    in the figure. It is common for people first interacting with the drawing
    to *try* to see one or the other of the women in it; but it makes no sense

FIGURE 1.

to speak of trying to believe or judge that – not even if one doubts it. (b) This perception is not just sensory experience (of lines and shades). It is, instead, an *organization* of the sense-perceptible lines that makes for the picture's being that of an old woman or a young one.

When a viewer sees what is to be seen in the figure, she is making "sense" of it. Some gestalt figures don't make any sense at all to the unaccustomed viewer; the moment of getting the organization right is like a moment of "revelation" in which sense is made of what was meaningless lines and patches. This kind of seeing is akin to understanding.

The fact that the figure can be seen (experienced) in the two very different ways, yet without change of sensory character, suggests that construal is subjective: The organization of the lines is not just in the lines, but is imposed, with the encouragement of the lines, by the viewing subject. Some people, lacking the knack for construing the figure in both ways, are blind to one of the aspects. They can see the lines, but not the required figure. When they become able to see the figure, a subjective change has allowed them to see something. But the two construals are not *sheer* subjectivity; the viewer does not create the figure as she might if she were drawing it. Instead she discovers something that is there in the drawing. Yet it is not as though the old lady is the truth about the picture, while the young lady is not. Different as the construals are, neither is to be preferred to the other, absent some special conventional circumstances.

Notice, too, that when you have sufficient skill at seeing the figure in both ways, the two construals are within the purview of the will. One can respond to the command: See it this way, see it that way.

The "terms" of this construal differ from those of the construal of "table" as a verb or noun. In the background of the ability to see the gestalt figure in the two ways are visual experiences of women of different "looks," but the differential construals of "table" have no analogous auditory experience of verbs and nouns in the background. The background there is supplied, not by sense experience of objects, but by the grammatical concepts of *noun* and *verb* and the speech practices to which these concepts refer.

In virtue of the construal's being an act or event of organization (making something organic out of elements), we have leeway as to which elements we focus on. One can, for example, focus on the two small curved lines that constitute the eye of the old woman and the ear of the young. As one switches between construals, these lines become an eye or an ear, in turn, and as these changes occur, the nature of the surroundings (what physiognomic parts they represent, or the angle from which these parts are viewed) also switches. Other natural foci of the drawing are the line that constitutes the old woman's mouth and the young woman's necklace, and the little protrusion that constitutes the young woman's nose and the old woman's eye-lash. Thus a single gestalt can be seen from a number of "angles."

Since the two views of the drawing are such different organizations of its elements, the one view tends to exclude the other. Thus when the young woman comes into view, the old one disappears, and vice versa. After gaining skill in switching between views, one can see the drawing in such a way that neither of the perceptions is stable but whichever one is in force is constantly threatening to degrade into the other, under the other's influence. But along with this phenomenon comes also the possibility of seeing both figures in the drawing at the same time. The clear switching, the instability, and the ambiguity of the perceptions are all three phenomena familiar to us from the life of emotions. Anger and joy (say, about a small child who has been lost from sight for several minutes in a public place but now is found) are such different construals that they tend to exclude each other; so in some circumstances they are unstable and shifting, vying in a close contest of reciprocal degradation; but sometimes they can coalesce into a single ambiguous perception of the child: One is simultaneously angry and joyful. The last two kinds of case are cases of "emotional ambivalence."

4. Construals are often unconscious. I am reading a journal article in which a quotation appears at the end of one page and extends by three words onto the next. I turn the page and can't find the end of the quotation. I turn back again to see whether the quotation has in fact ended on the preceding page. No. On further examination of the succeeding page I see the three words hanging there isolated at the top, and realize that I have been construing them as a header, with the result that I did not consciously see them at all.

5. An old man is sitting in the bleachers at an auction whittling some wood with his pocket knife. As the auctioneer presents a rocking chair for sale he raises his hand high above his head. You are watching, and you "see the old man bid on the chair." But the truth is that he's paying no attention to the auctioneer, so distracted is he by the bleeding of his finger that he is trying to quell by holding his hand high above his head. Again, your seeing his raised hand as a bid is not just a judgment that he has made a bid (though it is certainly that as well), but a *perceptual experience* of the raised hand *in these terms.* But in this perception, unlike that of the young woman in the gestalt figure, the question of truth is very much to the point, for your perception is false. Our knowledge that it is false invites the language of seeing-as. From our critical, objectifying perspective we say, "You saw the raised hand as a bid." But bedded down comfortably in your ignorance, you would not say, "I saw the raised hand as a bid," but just, "I saw him bid."

So our motive for speaking of construal is not the same here as it is for the old woman/young woman. There it is the optionality of the perceptions and their independence of truth that lead us to speak not of seeing but of seeing-as; here it is the perceived falsehood of the perception, from the "objective" point of view of a third party. In other cases, where we use the language of construal even though truth is at issue and we have no reason to doubt the truth of a perception, it is motivated by an analytical perspective. When in this book I speak of emotions as construals, I am not assuming that the subject of the emotion is in a position to switch his perception, nor am I doubting the truth of his emotional perception; nor am I asserting that the subject of the emotion would describe his own reaction by saying, "I was seeing my rival as. ... " He *might* retrospectively say that, if taking the analytical viewpoint on his own emotion. But as the plain participant subject of an emotion, he will normally report how things look to him in the language of objectivity: "My rival is losing out to me." When I call emotions construals in this book and use the language of seeing-as, I am taking the analytical perspective as a matter of principle; for that is the kind of discussion in which we are engaged.

6. I come into a colloquium at a meeting of the American Philosophical Association, sit down, place my umbrella on the floor a little in front of my chair, plant my feet in front of the umbrella, and put my briefcase on my lap as a writing surface. I do all this without much attention. The briefcase hides the feet and umbrella from view. Throughout the reading of the paper I have the impression that there is something behind my feet that I'd better not step on. But I can't think what it is. My impression is not a sense-impression, but I do feel it in my legs as a sort of inhibition to step back; that is, I have an impression in my legs of something behind them. I wonder what it is, investigate, and see the umbrella. We might call this "kinesthetic impression of the feet as having an obstruction behind them" or (same construal with a different focus) "impression of an unidentified object as behind the feet."

So far, none of our examples of construals is an emotion. The next few examples carry us into increasingly emotional cases.

7. You are watching some chimpanzees. The mother cradles the young one in her arms, and it clings to her as she walks around. She looks at you and gives you a chimpanzee smile (you know that chimpanzee smiles don't have the same meaning as human ones). Suddenly she bounds off and leaps onto a trapeze and swings there, looking at you complacently. You laugh. Why? Note that a chimpanzee expert who interacts with them daily and is intimately acquainted with their behavior probably would not laugh. On one theory of amusement you laugh because her behavior strikes you with a certain incongruity. Because of her humanoid physiognomy and behavior, you tend to see her in human terms, and yet, *as* a human she's very peculiar, in a nontragic way. The chimpanzee

expert does not laugh because the behavior does not strike him as incongruous, and that is because he sees her, not as an incongruous human being, but as just a chimpanzee. Note that it is not enough merely to *note* the ways chimpanzees and humans are similar and different (indeed, noting the differences and similarities rather analytically tends to reduce the amusing effect); to be amused, one must be perceptually struck by the synthetically constructed similarities and differences.

8.   An example yet a step closer to emotion is found in Evelyn Waugh's *Brideshead Revisited.* Charles Ryder is picked up by car at the train station by Julia, the sister of his friend Sebastian. He has never seen Julia before, and Waugh describes Charles's experience as he first gets to know her. The experience is a construal, or a series of construals, inasmuch as Charles is seeing this young woman in terms of her brother.

> She so much resembled Sebastian that, sitting beside her in the gathering dusk, I was confused by the double illusion of familiarity and strangeness. . . . I knew her and she did not know me. Her dark hair was scarcely longer than Sebastian's, and it blew back from her forehead as his did; her eyes on the darkling road were his, but larger, her painted mouth was less friendly to the world. She wore a bangle of charms on her wrist and in her ears little gold rings. Her light coat revealed an inch or two of flowered silk; skirts were short in those days, and her legs, stretched forward to the controls of the car, were spindly, as was also the fashion. Because her sex was the palpable difference between the familiar and the strange, it seemed to fill the space between us, so that I felt her to be especially female as I had felt of no woman before (Book I, Chapter 3).

That Charles construes Julia in terms of her brother means that she has a special look for him, in virtue of Charles's having her brother Sebastian in mind. We will underrate the complexity and depth of experiences like this if we focus too exclusively on the visual aspect. Anyone who had merely seen newspaper pictures of the two siblings might construe the one *face* in terms of the other; Charles's experience is fuller of meaning, and of different meaning, than that. The visual in this case has the depth of history and personality. Julia's look is invested with Charles's entire friend, and not only with his visual appearance, even though the visual aspects are focal here. The construal derives its emotional character from two things: Charles's growing attachment to Sebastian and Julia's sexuality. Both of these count as what I will call "concerns" (Section 2.7). But obviously, sexuality is in the foreground here, with her femaleness striking Charles forcibly because of the maleness in which the resembling features of her brother are embodied. We can easily imagine a similar experience in which Charles sees Julia's sexuality in the same terms as in the present case, but the impression is weaker. This possibility illustrates that two construals with the same content may vary in degree of vivacity, impressiveness, strikingness.

9. Finally, let us return to George, my fictional colleague from Section 2.1. I am very angry at George, and on the account of emotions that I am offering, my anger consists in how George appears to me: I "see" him in terms of his culpable unjust attack on my dignity and the dignity of my discipline and in terms of the punishment that he deserves. Now, a couple of days later, I am at a department social gathering at which various of our members are being "roasted," and I am forced to sit through an 8-mm home movie of George at age nine months. George is lying in his mother's arms, nursing at her breast (which is hidden by a strategically folded diaper). As he suckles, George reaches up his tiny fingers and caresses his mama's face. She beams down at him with pride and pleasure. He shows a little sign of distress, and she turns him onto her shoulder and burps him. Then George turns around and laughs into the camera and waves his little arm.

The movie gives me a new perspective on George. Of course I knew he had been a baby once, but *seeing* him as such is something else, and it threatens to throw a new light on his crime. True, it is not impossible for criminals to have been cute little tykes; it happens all the time. But the two thoughts are incongruous enough to urge that one of them control the other. If those images of George at his mother's breast strongly inform my vision of him, I will find it hard to see him in the terms characteristic of anger, and conversely if my vision of him is strongly informed by the terms of my anger, I will find it difficult to see the lovableness of the little guy in the movie. Perhaps I can do so by telling myself about all the water that's under the bridge: This is not the same person. But the need to distinguish the two Georges makes my point. I may find myself struggling here, resisting the incursion of one of the images and its influence on my vision; or if I am interested in forgiving George, I may struggle to apply the image from the movie and may intentionally bring that image to mind as a mitigator of my anger. Another possibility is that, without any intervention of my will, I find the movie so compelling that my anger at George disappears.

The foregoing examples have illustrated ten or so points about the nature of construals, which can now be summarized:

C1. Construals have an immediacy reminiscent of sense perception. They are impressions, ways things appear to the subject; they are experiences and not just judgments or thoughts or beliefs (see Sections 2.4b–2.4d for distinctions among judgments, beliefs, and construals).

C2. Though they are impressions, they are not, or not merely, sense impressions, that is, impressions of the sort produced by light hitting the retina, air vibrations exciting the ear drum, and so on.

C3. They involve an "in terms of" relationship: one thing is perceived in terms of something else. Construals are "constructive," "synthetic," and "organic," bringing together a variety of elements in some kind of integration.

C4. They are "subjective," that is, highly dependent on special qualifications of the subject; but some of them can be true or false.

C5. They admit of a focus on one or two of the elements, with the rest of the construct in the "background," and the focus can be quite shifty, producing kaleidoscopic variations on a construal.

C6. Opposed construals of something tend to exclude each other, but for an adept it is sometimes possible to engage two opposite construals at the same time.

C7. They need not be states of consciousness.

C8. They often, but not always, have an "emotional" character, and the difference between the two kinds of cases is made by the presence of concerns, personal interests, and attachments of the subject for (to) something in the construed situation.

C9. They come in degrees of depth of impression or impact of strikingness.

C10. They come in varieties of interplay of mental event types.

C11. They are sometimes subject to voluntary control, and they sometimes are not.

C12. The language of construal or seeing-as is not native to the experience except in special cases where the experience is taken to be optional or not to bear on truth, or the speaker is denying, doubting, or analyzing the experience.

c. Emotions as Construals

Let me now make some further general comments about the nature of construals, and apply to the case of emotions a couple of the points about the nature of construals that were not applied in the previous subsection.

Interplay of Mental Event Types C10 was illustrated by some of the examples, but not commented on. A construal is a perceptual event or state in which one thing is grasped in terms of something else. The "in terms of" relation can have as its terms any of the following: a sense perception, a thought, an image, a concept. I can see one face in terms of another, which I am also seeing; or another, of which I am merely thinking; or another, of which I am forming an image; I can see a face in terms of a concept, like *rugged* or *kindly*; I can imagine my living room in terms of furniture in the store, which I am currently looking at; or in terms of either the image or the thought of my parents' living room, or in terms of the concept *grandiose* or *well-coordinated*; or I can think of myself (I have in mind something different from imagining myself or perceiving myself) in respect of likeness to my father, whom I am currently looking at; or in terms of an image, such as coming sweating and triumphant across the finish line; or in terms of a concept, like *intelligent* or *moody*. Most of our experiences, as well as most of our unconscious states of mind, are a hard-to-specify structure of percept, concept, image, and thought.

Focus, Terms, Elements, Objects, Situational Object Thus (by way of further comment on C5) a construal incorporates "terms" that determine how something or other is grasped in an impression. I call what is grasped in those terms the "focus" of the construal. If one perceives a face as rugged, the concept of rugged is the term, and the face is the focus. When Charles Ryder construes Julia Flyte in terms of her brother Sebastian, Julia is the focus and Sebastian is the term. When you hear "table" as a verb, the audible word is the focus; the concept of a verb the term. The terms and focus of a construal are sometimes interchangeable. If I construe my son's face in terms of my own, I may also construe my face in terms of his. To emphasize that the notions of terms and focus are not notions of kinds of furniture of the mind, but instead notions of *roles* that various kinds of mental furniture may shiftingly play, let us call the items that are either the terms or the focus of a construal its "elements." In many emotions we will find that the focus of the construal shifts rapidly and freely so that an element that is at one moment the focus is at another moment one of the terms, with a different element as the focus. Thus a certain fluidity of role among the elements of an emotion is compatible with the emotion's remaining the same emotion despite the shift.

Instances of gratitude, for example, trade on three major interrelated concepts: a benefice, a benefactor, and a beneficiary. If my brother gives me a gift, he is the benefactor, I am the beneficiary, and the gift is the benefice. My gratitude consists in my construing, on the basis of appropriate concerns, (a) MYSELF as recipient of the gift from him, or (b) HIM as the giver of the gift to me, or (c) THE GIFT as something given by him to me. The elements of the construal remain constant in these three cases, but their roles shift, with a different focus in each case. The difference of focus can, again, be accomplished in several ways, all of which involve attention: in sense perception, imagination (particularly memory), and thought. We might be inclined to say that the focus of an emotion is what has been called the emotion's "object," but this is not quite right. In case (a) above, we would not want to say that I am the object of my gratitude, just because I am the focus of the construal. To stay close to ordinary language, we should say that gratitude has two objects, namely, the gift and the benefactor. This is because in propositional characterizations of the emotion, references to the gift and to the benefactor are introduced by prepositions: I am grateful *to* my brother *for* his gift. (The subject of the gratitude is the object of the giving: My brother gives the gift *to* me. But the question here is about the object of the *emotion*.) In this book I usually use the word "object" to refer to things related prepositionally to the emotion. However, an important part of the concept of a construal is that it is a construct or synthesis of multiple elements into an integrated whole; and so I usually speak of the configuration of elements – in the present illustration me, my brother, and the gift in their attributed relationships – as the "situational object" of the emotion. The situational object is the whole thing that the emotion is about.

Construals and Salience The idea that I am trying to convey using the language of construal is sometimes cast in terms of salience. Thus

Emotions involve patterns of salience: if I am angry at you I dwell on special features of what you have done; if what you did instead had made me afraid then I would have dwelt on different features.[9]

This remark is correct but not very precise. The difference between salience and construal can be illustrated with the old woman/young woman figure. If I have been recently preoccupied with hats and scarves, the headdresses of both the old woman and the young woman may be salient to me, but in this case the salience of this feature of the figures is *within* each of the construals. It is not the difference between them. Or some part of the drawing might be salient – say, the black patch in the upper half of the figure that represents the hair of both women. But again, the salience of this part of the drawing does not make the difference between the two ways the drawing can appear. A difference of construal is much more systematic than that of one part of the drawing standing out and others receding into the background. It is, according to C3, a wholistic difference of organization. Whatever in the drawing is salient will look different under one construal than under the other. The difference between fear and anger is similarly not just that one feature of the situation stands out, as opposed to other possible features; it is rather that in fear the situation is of one *kind* (threatening) while in anger it is of another (offensive).

Consider an example. Lem and Mel are going out for a day of fishing on Lake Superior. They have divided the duties of preparation: Mel is to fuel up the boat, and Lem is to pack the lunches. They meet at the dock

9 Allan Gibbard, *Wise Choices, Apt Feelings: A Theory of Normative Judgment* (Cambridge: Harvard University Press, 1990), p. 136. Gibbard attributes the point to Adam Morton. Amélie Rorty also makes much of salience in "Explaining Emotions," Amélie Rorty (ed.), *Explaining Emotions* (Berkeley: University of California Press, 1980), pp. 103–126.

at 10:00 a.m., and Lem assumes that Mel, who arrived an hour ahead of him, has fueled the boat. But unknown to Lem, Mel has just come down from the beachside restaurant where in conversation with some fishermen he packed away three beers, which dimmed the aspect of his fueling duties. They ride three miles out into the lake and are just settling down to some serious fishing when the radio warns all boats off the lake because of an approaching storm. Seeing the thickening sky for themselves, they hightail it toward shore, but after five hundred feet the engine sputters to a stop, its fuel exhausted. In fright and guilt Mel confesses his dereliction. Lem is scared and angry. Lem's fear differs from his anger in that the fear picks out features of the situation that make it threatening: the storm and the boat's inability to get to shore. His anger, by contrast, picks out features of the situation that justify blame: Mel as cause of the boat's inability to get to shore and Mel's having agreed to fuel the boat and neglecting to do so. It is correct to say that Lem's anger and fear are about the same situation but with different features of that situation salient; but that analysis of the difference does not capture the way in which the various features of the situation are grouped and related to one another in the different emotions. In Lem's fear the situation presents itself under the aspect of threat, and all the features of the situation (the approaching storm, the lack of means of getting away, the inadequacy of the boat as protection from the storm) are grouped around, colored, and organized around the concept of threat. But in his anger they are grouped and colored in a quite different way: The whole situation, in its nastiness, is seen as originating from Mel's negligence; the threat is still perceived, but in anger its significance is that it is what Mel is being blamed for. Another way to see the difference is in relation to action: In fear the threat is seen as something *to be escaped*, while in anger it is seen as something *to punish Mel for*. Types of emotions differ from one another not just in patterns of salience, but in structures of significance that determine patterns of salience in a principled way.

Concerns as Terms The multitude and variety of synthetic crossings of percepts, images, thoughts, and concepts in human mental life are countless; only some of these, however, are emotions. My formula is that emotions are *concern*-based construals, that is, construals imbued, flavored, colored, drenched, suffused, laden, informed, or permeated with concern. To be angry is not just to see a person as having culpably offended; the construal must be based on a concern about some dimension of the offense, and possibly a concern about some dimension of the offender. To be afraid of heights is not just to see them as a danger to something or other; it requires that something the subject holds dear appear to him threatened. Grief is not just a construal of something as irrevocably lost; the something lost must be of great importance to the griever. For this reason, concerns, cares, desires, loves, interests, attachments, and enthusiasms are dispositions to emotions;

when we construe circumstances in terms that touch or impinge on our concerns, the construals are emotions.

The concept of a construal also clarifies the idea of the "imbuement" of a construal with a concern, or the "impingement" of a construal on a concern. We can distinguish, in some cases anyway, the construal of an object from the object construed (the ducky-view of the duck-rabbit from the lines constituting the duck-rabbit). Experientially, however, a construal is not an interpretation laid over a neutrally perceived object, but a characterization of the object, a way the *object* presents itself. When one sees the duck-rabbit as a duck, the figure itself takes on a ducky look. Similarly, the case of seeing an interviewer as threatening to me can be analyzed into my construing her as having great power over my life and having contempt for my answers on the one hand, and my being strongly concerned to get a job and esteem myself as a capable person, on the other. But experientially the emotion is not a two-stage process in which I first perceive the interviewer as powerful, contemptuous, and so on, and then add to this perception a concern that is somehow relevant to it. Rather, the concern enters into the perception so as to characterize the appearance of the object. My view of the interviewer as powerful and contemptuous gives her the threatening look characteristic of anxiety only if filtered through my concern to succeed or some other concern on which her looking powerful and contemptuous impinges in that way. Thus the concern is analogous to one of the "terms" of the construal. It is taken up, or synthesized into, the appearance of the situational object and/or its salient elements.

Consciousness According to E1 (Section 2.1), emotions need not be states of consciousness. Many of our emotions pass unfelt, or are felt only on the periphery of consciousness. The present account accommodates this fact, because construals in general have this property. Countless construals that we undergo or perform during any day, in the course of our work or our social interactions, never rise to the level of consciousness. I frequently catch myself calling my younger brother by my son's name, and vice versa, and take this as evidence that I see them in terms of each other. But I do not usually experience this construal; I infer its operation from my linguistic behavior. In a room that I frequent, I construe the arrangement of furniture as normal; I am "ready" for the overstuffed chair to be to the left, the desk at the far end, and so forth. But I am not conscious of this construal until either I have some occasion to reflect about it, or the "normal" arrangement is disrupted and I am jolted into awareness of how normal it looked the other way.

Voluntary Control Fact E9 (Section 2.1) is that the subject of an emotion is sometimes able to exercise voluntary control over it, and sometimes unable to do so. E9 is explained by the present account of emotion, according to which all emotional change is change in the terms in which a subject "sees" the world, including changes in the subject's desires and concerns. I have pointed out (Section 2.3a) how in viewing gestalt figures a person may be aspect blind, able to see the figure in only one way, but then may gain voluntary control over the appearance of the figure to him as he practices his construal repertoire. Even when we have in our repertoire alternative ways of seeing a figure, in the sense that we can sometimes see the figure in these ways, we may not always be able to implement just any of them at will. A person may try for several moments to see something in a figure, and then suddenly he does see it. It "came," as we say (or, even more revealingly, "it came together"); and in such cases we have clearly that mixture of passivity and activity so characteristic of our experience of emotions.

The involvement of concerns in the construals that we call emotions complicates the matter considerably, but still the construal account of emotions explains E9 well. A person at whom I am inclined to be angry may be regarded, quite at will, in various ways: as the scoundrel who did such-and-such to me, as the son of my dear friend so- and-so, as a person who, after all, has had a pretty rough time of it in life, and so forth. If these construals are all in my repertoire, and in addition are not too implausible with respect to the present object, then the emotions that correspond to them, of anger, affection, and pity, are also more or less subject to my will. Emotions are far more complicated than the construals of gestalt figures. Whether an emotion is in our repertoire with respect to a given situation will depend on such factors as the character of the situation in its relation to our system of beliefs, our history of practicing emotional self-control, our personality in the sense of the master concerns of our life as well as our more particular cares and desires, some of which are elicited by passing features of the environment and/or our present state of mind or body (especially mood), our habits of attention, our skills at conceptualization and visualization, our understanding of our own emotions and feelings, and who knows what else. In some situations an emotion may be so compelling that we are (without the help of a friend or therapist, at any rate) virtually helpless in the face of it. The therapist or friend, by suggesting and fostering other possibilities of construal, may be able to liberate us from it by contributing to our emotional repertoire. Or she may not, and the explanation of this resistance to help may be similarly complex. But despite these complexities, the construal account of emotions offers an attractive explanation of the mixture of voluntariness and involuntariness in our emotions.

Besides the direct (though imperfect) control involved in just picking another construal from our repertoire, we have more indirect ways of changing emotion (which are also imperfect). William James comments:

There is no more valuable precept in moral education than this, as all who have experience know: If we wish to conquer undesirable emotional tendencies in ourselves, we must assiduously and in the first instance cold-bloodedly go through the outward motions of those contrary dispositions we prefer to cultivate. ... Soothe the brow, brighten the eye, ... pass the genial compliment, and your heart must be frigid indeed if it does not gradually thaw![10]

Let us say that I have explained to a student, twice in class and thrice in private, the difference between Modus Ponens and Affirming the Consequent, and now once more he asks a question that betrays that he does not get the distinction. Anger begins to well up in me and I want to control it, so I follow James's advice and behave in a way incompatible with anger. Instead of raising my voice, pounding the desk, or becoming sarcastic, I put my hand gently on his shoulder and say calmly, with no expression of exasperation, "you go home and study Chapter 3, and come back tomorrow." And my treating him in a friendly and tolerant manner, rather than punitively, causes my anger to subside.

Why does this sort of strategy work? According to James, it works because an emotion just *is* certain physical sensations that go with certain behavior: Change the behavior, and you change the sensations (emotions) that the behavior causes! On the construal account my anti-anger behavior alters my emotion (when it succeeds) by altering the way my student appears to me. Behaving gently discourages my seeing him as culpably offensive, whereas yelling at him or becoming sarcastic fosters such a perception. An explanation of this phenomenon is near at hand. Our powers of construal are influenced by sense perception. We can see the duck-rabbit as a picture-duck because it resembles a duck. Most people can see it as a picture-pizza, but this is less natural, and they usually succeed only after instructions to think of a rather misshapen pizza with just one tiny anchovy fragment on it, and even then it is not likely to be a very compelling or vivid construal. Further afield still, to my knowledge no one has ever construed the duck-rabbit as a copy of the *Oxford English Dictionary*. Similarly, if I am scowling at the student and voicing sarcasms, it is natural to construe the situation as one of enmity, with me as victim and him as offender. Punitive behavior suggests culpability of the one toward whom the behavior is directed, just as the lines of the duck-rabbit suggest a duck. And seeing as my enemy a person on whose shoulder I am laying my hand affectionately and to whom I am speaking in friendly tones is about as unnatural as seeing the duck-rabbit as

[10] *The Principles of Psychology*, Volume Two (New York: Dover Publications, 1950), p. 463. See the wonderful quotation from Augustine, illustrating essentially the same point, on p. 339 of Rorty's *Explaining Emotions*. And Kant: "When an angry man comes up to you in a room, to say harsh words to you in intense indignation, try politely to make him sit down; if you succeed, his reproaches already become milder, since the comfort of sitting is [a form] of relaxation, which is incompatible with the threatening gestures and shouting one can use when standing." *Anthropology from a Pragmatic Point of View*, translated by Mary J. Gregor (The Hague: Martinus Nijhoff, 1974), p. 120 (Akademie VII, p. 252).

a picture-pizza. Not to speak of the fact that if I become sarcastic, the student is likely to get *his* dander up, and thus to look more like an offender to me.

2.4. JUDGMENTS

a. Introduction

In typical cases of emotions in rational persons, according to E6 (Section 2.1), the subject of an emotion believes most of its propositional content. A rational gardener anxious about her tomato plants because hail is predicted will typically judge her plants to be in some danger from hail. If Sam resents his brother Joe's sneaking efforts to get control of the family fortune, we can usually infer that Sam believes that in Joe's efforts Joe is wronging him or someone whose interests Joe cares about. This fact has prompted some philosophers, both ancient and recent, to think that such beliefs or judgments are essential to emotions. Theories to this effect vary in detail, some claiming that judgments are partially constitutive of emotions,[11] others that judgments are a necessary cause of emotions,[12] and still others that emotions just are a certain kind of evaluative judgment.[13] In the present section I shall focus primarily on the last of these versions, because it is the closest to the model that I am proposing in this book. Martha Nussbaum defends a version of the thesis attributable to the Stoics – in particular, Chrysippus.[14] Being concerned more with substantive questions than with those of historical scholarship, I shall accept without criticism Nussbaum's attributions to the Stoics, and I argue that it is infelicitous to classify emotions as judgments and better to class them with what Chrysippus calls "appearances" (*phantasiai*) that are, in the most standard cases, supported by corresponding judgments. (I take it that what Chrysippus calls *phantasiai* are very much like what I am calling construals.) That discussion will put us in a position to consider briefly (in Section 2.4j) the view that judgment is a necessary constituent of emotions. In Section 2.6 I examine the view that judgments are necessary causes of emotions.

On one plausible reading of "judgment," the thesis that emotions are judgments is vulnerable to several objections. First (Sections 2.4d–2.4f),

---

[11] See Martha Nussbaum, *Love's Knowledge* (New York: Oxford University Press, 1990), pp. 291–293 and *The Therapy of Desire* (Princeton: Princeton University Press, 1994), Chapter 3; Gabriele Taylor, *Pride, Shame, and Guilt: Emotions of Self-Assessment* (Oxford: Clarendon Press, 1985), p. 1; Joel Marks, "A Theory of Emotion," *Philosophical Studies* **42** (1982): 227–242; John Rawls, *A Theory of Justice* (London: Oxford University Press, 1972), pp. 481–483.

[12] See Donald Davidson, "Hume's Cognitive Theory of Pride," in *Essays on Actions and Events* (Oxford: Oxford University Press, 1980), p. 284; Robert M. Gordon, *The Structure of Emotions* (Cambridge: Cambridge University Press, 1987), pp. ix, 49–52.

[13] See Robert C. Solomon, *The Passions* (Garden City, New York: Doubleday, 1977), pp. 185–187.

[14] See *The Therapy of Desire*, Chapters 9 and 10.

the propositional content of some full-fledged emotions is not assented to by the subject of the emotion. Compelling examples are phobic reactions that are understood as such by their subject and typical emotions experienced in reading fictional literature. Second (Section 2.4h), the very same judgment that is supposedly identical with an emotion is sometimes made in the absence of the emotion. A third argument (Section 2.4i) is that emotions are subject to voluntary control in a way they would not be were they judgments. These arguments suppose an understanding of what a judgment is. Let us delineate a concept of a judgment.

b. The Nature of Judgments

J1. *Judgment involves assent.* Judgment is one among several propositional attitudes. Judging that *p* contrasts with hoping that *p*, wishing that *p*, doubting that *p*, wondering whether *p*, denying *p*, construing something in terms of *p*, and so on. To judge that *p* is to assent to *p* with a fairly high degree of confidence or conviction. To assent to *p* is to be disposed to say "yes" to the question "*p*?" or "Is *p* true?" It would be a mistake to analyze assenting to *p* in terms of some feeling about *p* or some inner act of yea-saying to *p* that supposedly always accompanies judgment. Such mental events occur, but to generalize them invites counterexamples that can be fended off only by implausible speculation about unconscious versions of them. A person's being strongly disinclined to say "yes" to *p*, where she is not being disingenuous, is *prima facie* strong evidence that she does not judge that *p*.

J2. *Judging that p requires a more direct presence to mind of p than does believing that p.* I am making plans to conduct a normal day of business at the University tomorrow. I plan to write at the computer, work in my office after dark, and so on. Somebody says, "I see you think there will be electric power in Morrison Hall tomorrow. But the electricians will have the power down all day." And I say, "Yes, I did believe that, though it didn't occur to me." It would not be right, in the same circumstances, to say "I judged that."

J3. *Judgments are sometimes perceptual* – that is, about what is before one's eyes or what one is currently hearing, smelling, or tasting. I judge the recording of the Brandenburg Concerto to which I am listening to be directed by Karl Richter. Judgments are sometimes perceptual in an extended sense, in which the "perceptual" content is supplied by memory or imagination.

J4. *Judgments are not always perceptual.* Sometimes they are made in the absence of what the Stoics call *phantasia*; there is no "appearance" that is judged *of*. For example, somebody asks, "Do you think emotions are identical with a certain range of value judgments?" and I say "No." No sensory or quasi-sensory appearance with the content "*emotions are identical with a certain* *range of value judgments*" presents itself to me to be judged of.[15] To adapt the example from J3, let us say that while listening to the recording, the question of the director did not occur to me, but I am later asked who I think it was. I call certain passages to mind in *phantasia* and make a judgment. But in another case I may just know who the director is, and say "Richter" without calling any passage to mind.

J5. *Judgments are always propositional.* To judge is to judge that *p. Phantasiai* are sometimes propositional and sometimes not. The bent look of the stick in the bucket of water is propositional inasmuch as it inclines one to judge that the stick is bent or wonder whether the stick is bent or deny that the stick is bent. But the mere sound of a Brandenburg Concerto does not press for propositional attitude (wishing that, doubting that, wondering whether) in the way that the look of the stick does. It is possible for the performance to sound like Richter (to somebody), and in that case the *phantasia* is propositional.

J6. *Judgments come in varying degrees of confidence,* that is, of confidence of assent to the proposition – tentative, quite confident, fully confident. At some undefined point in the gradation away from confidence, the subject is no longer willing to assent to the proposition and ceases to make the judgment.[16]

These points orient us to adjudicate the concept of a judgment on which Chrysippus bases his claim that emotions are judgments. According to Nussbaum, the Stoics define a judgment as

an assent to an appearance. In other words, it is a process that has two stages. First, it occurs to Nikidion, or strikes her, that such and such is the case. (Stoic appearances are usually propositional.) It looks to her that way, she sees things that way – but

---

[15] Notice that there is nothing in the merely sensory or pictorial content of any appearance that determines unequivocally what it is an appearance of – that is, the propositional content that it presents for judgment. For any pictorial content, what presents itself to be judged of may be various.

[16] Nancy Sherman seems to identify another characteristic of judgment when, in distinguishing beliefs from construals, she speaks of "evidentiary warrant of the sort that characterizes belief" [*Making a Necessity of Virtue* (New York: Cambridge University Press, 1997), p. 62; see pp. 58–62]. It is not clear whether she thinks that actual warrant by evidence is required for belief, or whether the subject of the belief need only *believe* that he has such warrant. But neither condition is necessary for belief, and both conditions are relevant to construals. Plenty of beliefs are held by people who neither have, nor think they have, adequate evidence for them. And people can both have, and think they have, adequate evidence for their construals. In the last case they will probably, but not necessarily, believe that things are as they construe them. It is just possible that I might construe the silhouette on the evening horizon as my brother, and think that I have evidence that is adequate by normal standards that the figure *is* my brother, and yet not assent to the proposition (perhaps out of an excess of epistemic finickiness, maybe a kind of akrasia engendered by a skeptical upbringing). In other words, believing oneself to have adequate evidence for *p* is not equivalent to assenting to *p*.

so far she hasn't really accepted it. She can now go on to accept or embrace the appearance, commit herself to it; in that case, it has become her judgment. She can also deny or repudiate it: in that case, she is judging the contradictory (*The Therapy of Desire*, p. 374).

Is this a good account of judgment? One might wonder whether judgments always have both stages: appearance + assent. J3 suggests that the account fits some cases of judgment; and J1 agrees with the Stoic stress on assent. But it seems wrong to lay down as a necessary condition either (a) that there be an appearance that p that corresponds to every judgment that p (see J4), or (b) that, in the cases where there is both an appearance and assent to its propositional content, there be a temporal separation between the two – a two-step sequence.

If J4 is right, Nussbaum's characterization of the first stage perhaps runs two concepts together. Is an idea's occurring to Nikidion (or her considering it) the same as an appearance striking her, or a situation's looking to her a certain way? Clearly, if one is to judge a proposition to be true or false, it has to be in some sense in mind; one has to be attending to it (see J2). I cannot come to a judgment about whether it is likely to rain this afternoon without thinking of it raining this afternoon. But surely it does not have to strike me that it's going to rain this afternoon, or look to me as though it's going to rain this afternoon, as a preliminary to my judging so. I may investigate the matter by consulting newspapers, looking at the sky, and so on, with the thought, Is it likely to rain or not? At some point the evidence seems to me to go one way and I judge that it is likely to rain. *Then* it perhaps strikes me that it is going to rain. But even then the striking may not have the character of an appearance. Indeed, I might think, "It does not look like rain; given the sunny appearance of everything, it's hard to imagine it raining. I don't want to think about rain because I'm having such a good time cavorting among the lilies; nevertheless, the evidence adds up: It is likely to rain." In such a case I seem to judge against the appearances, independently of the appearances. I judge that p not because I assent to the appearance that p, but from evidence. Perhaps the Stoic will respond that the weight of the evidence and the logic in favor of *it will rain this afternoon* create a kind of appearance to me that it is going to rain. But in that case it seems we have lost the separation of the judgment from the appearance that is basic to the Stoic account, and also we seem to need to distinguish two kinds of appearance: (a) appearance in a primitive or "look like" sense (the stick in the bucket, the Richter-sound of the Bach performance) and (b) appearances in a less robustly "perceptual," more remote, inferential and indirect sense.

The equivocation on the concept of an appearance is evident in the case in which one denies the appearance. If a judgment is essentially an assent to an appearance, there could be no such thing as *simply* judging the contradictory of an appearance. For such cases the Stoic account appears to require two appearances: the repudiated one (which is probably an appearance in the stronger or "look like" sense) and the "appearance" that is assented to, which is generated by evidence and reasoning. It seems to me that it would be clearer (not requiring the equivocation on "appearance") and less speculative (not requiring us to posit the existence of an appearance with a propositional content corresponding to each inferential judgment that human beings make) to admit J4 and say that some judgments are made in the absence of any *phantasia* with the same propositional content.

c. Attractions of the Judgment Theory

Nussbaum is particularly impressed with the responsiveness of emotions to argument. If emotions are judgments, they depend on assent to their propositional content, and they will disappear if that assent is withdrawn. Since the arguments that all the Hellenistic schools use against troublesome emotions aim to induce us to withdraw assent from the propositions that are central to the offending emotions, the effectiveness of the arguments will encourage us in the thesis that emotions are judgments. Furthermore, if we canvass the propositional attitudes, none seems as universally plausible a candidate as judgment; it is certainly not true, for example, that the person who is angry that p wishes that p, doubts that p, wonders whether p, and so on; but his attitude to p bears at least some resemblance to assenting to p. Some theorists would package the propositional content of human emotions in beliefs, but placing it in judgments is more plausible or more precise, because the episodic character of judgments fits better the relatively event-like character of emotions.

That judgments are sometimes perceptual (J3) suggests that the way situations look is a significant impetus to judge them to be so. The association of the emotions with perception has been often noted. The medievals located the emotions in the sensory appetite.[17] We are more likely to respond emotionally to situations presented audially, pictorially, or in vivid narrative than to situations presented in abstract or unimaginative language; and the judgment theorist's ready explanation will be that the "look" of things normally begets a judgment to the same effect. I am arguing that emotions are a kind of perception, and it is noteworthy that theorists like Nussbaum, Solomon, and Gabriele Taylor who make judgment or belief necessary to emotion often revert to the language of "seeing-as"[18] when

---

[17] See, for example, Thomas Aquinas, *Summa Theologiae*, 1a2ae Questions 22–48. I have discussed this location in "Thomas Aquinas on the Morality of Emotions," *History of Philosophy Quarterly* 9 (1992): 287–304.

[18] In Taylor's discussion (*op.cit.*) of particular emotions, she helps herself generously to the language of construal, to the point that it overshadows the language of belief. In her chapter

characterizing subjects of emotion, as does Aristotle when he characterizes fear as

... a certain sort of pain and disturbance [ταραχή] out of the appearance [φαντασίας] of an impending bad thing, either destructive or painful. . . . It is necessary that those things are fearful that appear to have [φαίνεται ἔχειν] a great power to destroy or to harm in a way that leads to great pain (*Rhetoric* 1382a21-3, 28–30, quoted in Nussbaum, p. 85).

Nussbaum notes, a little uncomfortably, that this passage seems to make fear a "mere impression as to how things are, rather than . . . a real conviction . . . " (p. 85), but comments that Aristotle is just using the language of perception interchangeably with the language of judgment.

The fact that judgments are not always perceptual (J4) does not favor the judgment theory of emotions, but it invites a couple of clarifications. First, emotions can occur in the absence of literal sensory content. I can get angry just thinking about so-and-so. But in the extended sense of "perceptual" perception seems to be required for emotion: Even if the emotion occurs at the end of a lot of inferring, its content strikes a person with an immediacy analogous to that of sense perception (though actual visualizing or auditory *phantasia* need not be very central to the content of the perception). Second, if judgments sometimes occur in the absence of impression, construal, perception, *phantasia*, or whatever you want to call it, this fact perhaps helps us to identify more precisely the *kind* of judgment that judgment theorists take emotions to be or entail. Robert Solomon[19] insists that emotions are a *special* kind of judgment, and Nussbaum, in speaking of the assent characteristic of emotional judgments, writes of "a certain sort of assent or acknowledgment" (p. 381). We have noted the Stoic claim that all judgments have *phantasiai* for their content. Stoics tend to be more interested in emotions than in other kinds of judgments, so we might interpret them as claiming that emotions are a subclass of judgments, one of the features of which is that they take *phantasiai* for their content. (Another special feature is no doubt that they are judgments of value.) None of these writers is explicit about how emotional assent differs from the assent characteristic of other judgments; so my suggestion

on guilt and remorse, for example, she uses the expressions "think of oneself [or something else] as . . . " (pp. 86, 87, 88, 91, 92, 93, 100), an object's "presenting itself as . . . [wrong, etc.]" (pp. 86, 89, 100), the subject's "thinking [or seeing] in terms of . . . " (pp. 87, 101), "seeing as . . . " (pp. 91, 93, 98, 100, 101, 103, 104, 107), "regard as . . . " (p. 98), the subject's "conception of herself as . . . " (p. 98), "the description under which the remorseful agent sees her action" (p. 99, see p. 102), "she takes herself to have brought about . . . " (p. 99), "sees in these terms" (p. 101) "conceive of himself as . . . " (p. 107). By comparison the language of belief occurs as "thinks it wrong" (p. 86, see pp. 91, 92), "accepts [that]" (p. 85), "thinks that . . . " (pp. 88, 89), "belief," "believes" (pp. 100, 103, 104, 105).

19 "On Emotions as Judgments," *American Philosophical Quarterly* **25** (1988): 183–191, 185–186.

that they take *phantasia* to be the special feature of emotional assent is interpretive.

That judgments are always propositional (J5) accords with the plausible supposition that the paradigm emotions always "say" something about a situation (that it contains a severe threat, a benefactor, an offense, a great boon, and so on). That judgments come in varying degrees of confidence of assent (J6) might be construed as explaining (among other factors) varying degrees of emotional intensity. Thus, other things being equal, the degree of a person's fear might vary with the degree of his conviction that *an evil I cannot control is likely to befall me,* and the degree of his joy might vary with the degree of his confidence in the truth of the proposition, *a good has befallen me,* and so on. Other factors determining the intensity of the emotion will presumably interact with this one, on the judgment view. In particular, the judgment that is constitutive of the emotion will include, as part of its content, an assessment of the greatness of the weal or woe that is judged of.

d. Emotions Without Assent

I shall now argue that it is better to think of emotions as a kind of appearance or *phantasia* or construal than as a kind of judgment, because emotions do have the character of appearance and often occur in the absence of assent to that appearance. Let me begin by answering the two points in the last paragraph of the preceding subsection.

Emotions do typically "assert" something about a situation, about its character (what kind of situation it is), and about its importance to the subject. But what the emotion "says" is not always agreed to by the subject of the emotion, and it is *that* agreement that would be required for the emotion to be a judgment *of the subject.* Speaking metaphorically, we might say that the *emotion* makes a judgment (a proposal about reality); but this "judgment" is just the appearance or *phantasia.* The subject's judgment often coincides with the emotion's "judgment," but often it does not. In this way our emotions are like other perceptions: Usually we believe our eyes and ears, but not always. Our perception tells us that the stick in the water is bent (this is how we perceive it), but we judge otherwise, disagreeing with our eyes. Similarly, I may know that my anger is unjustified – not a correct perception of my situation. In that sort of case, it is wrong to say that my anger is *my* judgment. We might say that it "has a mind of its own." Perhaps the inclination to think that emotions are judgments is promoted by taking the emotion's "assertion" for the subject's assent.

The other suggestion in that last paragraph is that the intensity of an emotion might be determined, in part, by the degree of conviction with which the subject of the emotion assents to what the emotion asserts. This proposal is significantly weakened by the fact that one can have an emotion without any conviction at all that its central content is true. But there may be something in the suggestion anyway. On the view that I am proposing – that emotions are concern-based *phantasiai* – emotions are, in the typical case, supported by corresponding judgments. Thus a person is much more likely to be and remain angry if he judges the propositional content of his anger to be true than not true. But if this is so, it seems plausible that the degree of his conviction that, say, so-and-so has insulted him should be *a* factor determining the intensity of his anger at so-and-so.

Consider the acrophobic who denies that *being at the present height is a threat to my well-being* while feeling intense fear of the height. Some psychotherapists conducted an experiment concerning the use of virtual reality in the therapeutic procedure known as systematic desensitization.[20] This therapy for phobias works by generating fear in graded instances of the relevant types of situation while inducing the client to relax. For example, a standard course of systematic desensitization for acrophobia might consist in getting a relaxed client to stand on a four-inch stool until his fear subsides, then on a one-foot stool until he is not afraid, and so on. The experimenters report that systematic desensitization using virtual reality presentation of the feared situation (e.g., giving the client the experience of being on footbridges 7, 50, and 80 meters above water) worked just as well as therapy using *in vivo* presentation. If we assume that the therapy works only if fear is actually induced in the client, and that the clients in the experiment knew perfectly well that they were safely in the therapist's consulting room, then we have a clear case of fear without judgment of fear's propositional content. These clients were subject to the appearance of being seven, fifty, and eighty meters above water, but judged themselves not to be so. The implication seems to be that the emotion is not the subject's judgment of the situation.

The responsiveness of some emotions to a change of judgment does not imply that the emotion was the judgment that one has given up or is the judgment that one now makes. Nor does it follow from such responsiveness that the judgment is a necessary condition for having the emotion. It may be, instead, that the change of judgment tends to carry with it a changed view of things. If we take emotions to be construals rather than judgments, we will hypothesize that the effectiveness of argument against some emotions is due to its effect on our construals. But it is far from the case that all emotions are responsive to changes of conviction about the truth of their propositional contents. It is a commonplace of psychotherapy that merely convincing a client that (for example) it would not be catastrophic if she flunked out of

[20] "Effectiveness of Computer-Generated (Virtual Reality) Graded Exposure in the Treatment of Acrophobia," by Barbara Olasov Rothbaum, Larry F. Hodges, Rob Kooper, Dan Opdyke, James S. Williford, and Max North, *American Journal of Psychiatry* **152** (1995): 626–628.

law school may not be enough to dispel her anxiety about this. In addition to such "rational" therapy, she may need to do various exercises of action and imagination (homework) that will gradually transform her construal of herself and her world. The technique of systematic desensitization clearly works by shaping construals otherwise than via arguments.

Nussbaum reports a response by Seneca to purported cases of emotions without assent to their propositional content.

> Sometimes, he says, the presence of an appearance might evoke a reaction even when the appearance itself is not accepted or taken in, but, so to speak, just strikes against your surface. Sudden pallor, a leap of the heart, sexual excitation – all of these bodily movements may be caused by the appearance alone, without assent or judgment. But these are not passions: these are mere bodily movements (p. 381).

Again, the explanation fits some cases. Startle caused by a sudden loud sound is arguably not an emotion but just a bodily reaction (see Section 3.16c). Although it has a phenomenology, it does not seem to have an evaluative proposition such as the paradigm cases of emotions have. But Seneca's explanation does not fit the cases that are most challenging to the judgment theory. The reaction of the snake-phobic to a closely presented four-foot bullsnake that he judges to be harmless on the basis of careful consideration of the evidence is not a mere bodily movement but a full-fledged emotion. And what makes it such is that the snake looks threatening to him despite his present judgment to the contrary. The very same content might be assented to by the subject but in this case is not.

e. The Helm Objection

According to Bennett Helm,[21] my proposal that we think of emotions as concern-based construals rather than as judgments does not do justice to the irrationality of emotions in the kind of cases that I have mostly appealed to. He notes that after we get used to optical illusions like the stick in the bucket, we do not regard the co-occurrence of the visual impression with the judgment that the stick is not bent as a contradictory state of mind; but we do regard the knowing phobic's state of mind as irrational. Helm then distinguishes two kinds of assent: active assent, which is characteristic of judgments proper, and passive assent, characteristic of emotions. Helm is convinced by cases like the knowing phobic that emotions are not *standard* judgments; but he still thinks they are more like judgments than mere construals: Involving passive assent, they are passive, not active judgments.

---

[21] "Emotions and Depth of Judgment," a colloquium paper read at the Eastern Division Meeting of the American Philosophical Association, December 1998.

I used to describe emotions as "verisimilar concern-based construals." I wanted to say that in the emotion the situation looks to the subject as if it is actually as he is construing it, whether or not he assents to that look.[22] I dropped "verisimilar" several years ago, because it seemed redundant. I include in the notion of construal the idea of verisimilitude, but I want the notion to remain neutral about whether the subject assents to the impression. Helm's objection is insightful, and I think that answering it will help to clarify how the verisimilitude of emotions differs from that of simple visual impressions.

Why is the knowing phobic's state of mind irrational, but not that of the knowing subject of an optical illusion? I say it is because the knowing phobic feels torn between his judgment and his emotion in a way that the knowing stick-viewer does not feel torn between his judgment and his visual experience. The latter is complacent and normal, taking the illusion in stride; the former is in trouble and goes to a therapist. Where does the trouble come from? It comes from the fact that, unlike the impression of the stick, the impression of the phobic object is a *concern*-based construal. The fear has a personal depth and life-disrupting motivational power that the illusion lacks. The bent stick is, at most, puzzling; the fear is personally compelling. This means that when the subject dissociates from his fear by denying its propositional content, it is like denying a part of himself, whereas denying his visual impression is not. This explanation does not reduce the difference between the two cases to pure motivation (a mere behavioral tendency to recoil from the phobic object). The power and trouble of the fear resides also and necessarily in its perceptual or affective character: that the phobic object is personally upsetting because it *appears threatening*. The fear is no less an impression of a threat than the illusion is the impression of a bent stick.

What shall we say about the proposal to call the compelling, personally involving character of the dissociated emotion passive assent? When I say that the knowing phobic's fear is not a judgment because he dissents from its propositional content, I mean that it is not *his* judgment. I have admitted the metaphorical sense in which it is the *emotion's* judgment, because of the verisimilitude. We can say, in similar metaphor, that the eyes assent to the bentness of the stick, while the knowing subject dissents from it. Since the "assent" in each of these cases is an automatic reaction that the knowing subject cannot immediately avoid, we might say that the knowing subject is passive with respect to this sort of "assent." But note three things here: First, passivity, in this sense, does not distinguish emotions from other kinds of "cognitions." Many of our non-emotional judgments are spontaneous and automatic. Second, in neither case is the "assent" the subject's assent. In

[22] "What An Emotion Is: A Sketch," *The Philosophical Review* **97** (1988): 183–209, 191.

both cases it is a part of the person that "assents," but not the person. The difference between the cases is that the part of the person that "assents" to the content of the emotion is more like a whole person than the eyes are, because this content touches and involves the person's concerns. But it is not, finally, the whole person, but a dissociated part. If you ask the phobic subject of the virtual reality experiment what *he* believes about the danger, he will say that he knows there is none. Third, when a subject does assent to his emotion's content, the assent is not always passive. Emotions are often the result of active, deliberate inquiry. I try to figure out whether a friend has betrayed me; and when the results are in, I get angry.

f. An Objection from Linguistic Usage

My first argument against the claim that any emotion is or entails a judgment that *p*, where *p* is the central propositional content of the emotion, has been that subjects of emotions frequently withhold assent from parts of the central propositional content of their emotions. Thus my counterexamples have the form: S is angry that *p*, but S does not believe that *p*; S feels guilty that *p*, but S judges that not-*p*; and so on. An objection to my counterexamples is that people don't talk this way. We do not say "Ben is proud that his son won the 440-meter race, but he knows in fact that he lost it." Nor do we say, "Ben is afraid that he will fall seven meters to his death, but he knows he is safe in the consulting room."

Because of this linguistic fact, I have sometimes formulated my counterexamples objectively, avoiding a "that" clause. Thus I have said that Ben fears *the snake* without believing that it may harm him. Or I have pointed to an unbelieved part of the propositional content that is not normally expressed in the 'that' clause: Ben is angry, though he does not believe that anyone is to blame for his son's being prevented from running the 440. Or Ben is proud that his son won the race, even though he knows that he has no claim to association with his son, having disowned him as a baby and not having acknowledged him since, until the day of the race. Or I mix the two strategies and say that Frank feels guilty for going to the theater, though he does not believe there is anything wrong with going to the theater. I think my strategies are legitimate, and the oddness of the ruled-out formulations is not much of an objection to my counterexamples. To think my counterexamples lack purchase because they cannot be formulated in sentences with that-clauses places too heavy a reliance on linguistic usage, and it depends on a too-simple conception of the propositional content of emotions. That the rebuttal relies too much on linguistic usage and oversimplifies content will become clearer when we consider how construals can be propositional (see Section 2.5b).

That the strategy of relying heavily on simple linguistic formulations is mistaken can be shown by the absurd consequences of doing so.

Donald Davidson, relying on the fact that we do not say "Ben is proud that his son won the 440" unless we suppose ourselves to know that Ben's son won the 440, says that "an attribution of propositional pride is false unless the corresponding belief is true."[23] The reasoning behind this supposed principle is made clearer by Robert Gordon, who claims that most emotions (including anger, pride, and regret), are *factive*, in contrast with a few (fear and its variants, and hope) that are *epistemic*. The difference is the relation to knowledge:

[I]f a person is glad or unhappy that *p* then he knows that *p*, whereas a person hopes or fears that *p* only if he does not know that *p*.[24]

If Ben is proud that his son won the 440, then he knows that his son won the 440. But Ben knows this only if it is true. So if Ben is proud that his son won the 440, then his son did win the 440! It follows (absurdly) that if Ben's emotion of pride is a response to false information about who won the race, then what Ben feels while under this misapprehension is not pride. But why suppose that if Ben is proud that his son won the 440, then he knows that his son won the 440? Gordon's answer is that *we* cannot properly *say* that Ben is proud that his son won the 440 unless we suppose that Ben knows that his son won the 440 (p. 37). Gordon does not think there is any device in English by which we can ascribe this emotion to Ben without presupposing the truth of the propositional content of the emotion we ascribe to Ben. In this Gordon errs. We can say, for example, "Ben is proud that (as he thinks) his son won the 440."

But what if Gordon were right about the resources of English? Should we conclude, on the basis of such a limitation, that Ben cannot be proud that his son won the 440, in case he believes falsely that his son won the 440? We should not, for to do so would be to let some facts about the language about emotions blind us to some facts about emotions. And the objection that people cannot disbelieve any of the propositional content of their emotions, because it is hard to ascribe such states of mind using "that" clauses to identify the propositional content of these emotions, is similarly weak.

g. Emotional Responses to Fiction

Another context in which people feel emotions without believing the propositions that form them is that of novels, movies, and theatre presentations. For simplicity, let us call the consumers of such representations "readers."

---

[23] "Hume's Cognitive Theory of Pride" in *Essays on Actions and Events* (Oxford: Oxford University Press, 1980), p. 279.

[24] *The Structure of Emotions: Investigations in Cognitive Philosophy* (New York: Cambridge University Press, 1987), p. 26.

Readers experience pretty much the whole range of emotions – anger, hope, pity, horror, sadness, regret, relief, joy, and so on – in response to the presented situations. Readers quickly become so attached to certain fictional characters that the depiction of their vicissitudes can be quite exciting, satisfying, or upsetting. I found George Eliot's *The Mill on the Floss* distressing because of the way Maggie Tulliver is treated by her brother Tom and by the circumstances of her life. In fact, I became so attached to her, and found her sufferings so painful, that I aborted a second reading of the book after about 100 pages. And yet there was never a moment in my reading in which I believed that Maggie Tulliver was a living person who was actually undergoing these sufferings.

Unlike emotional responses to music (see Sections 2.5g–2.5j), emotions in response to fiction are highly propositional. If asked what he is afraid of, what he feels sorry about, or why he is so glad, the reader can normally pick out with precision the (fictional) states of affairs to which he is responding, identifying those states of affairs in language. But all propositions about Maggie's and Tom's interactions are bracketed, by the normal reader, with a proposition to the effect that *this is fiction.* This proposition is believed, with the result that all the other propositions, which determine the content of the emotions, are not. They present a world of characters and actions that are judged not to exist, a series of richly articulated states of affairs that the reader judges not to obtain.

Such emotions present an obvious problem for judgment theorists. Kendall Walton[25] has responded to the problem by suggesting that the emotions we feel in response to fictional presentations are not real, but only "quasi"-emotions; we are "making believe" that we are distressed, afraid, joyful, and so on. But a judgment theory is the primary motivation for such a conclusion; the notion that emotions are concern-based construals presents no barrier to recognizing responses to fiction as full-fledged emotions. This is because fiction evokes perceptions, in the relevant sense, that impinge on our concerns (some of which, as in my response to Maggie Tulliver's adventures, are generated by the fiction).

One reason sometimes given for supposing that responses to fiction are not full-fledged emotions is that we are not inclined to act on them. If, in real life, I see a boy treating his sister the way Tom treats Maggie, my distress and anger may move me to take him aside and have a talk with him (and if it does not so move me, we have some reason to think that the emotion is not genuine; see Section 4.5); but no such thing happens as I read the novel or attend a stage presentation. On my account, what prevents action in the case of emotional responses to fictional presentations is that extra proposition that brackets the content of the emotions: *This did not*

[25] "Fearing Fictions," *The Journal of Philosophy* **75** (1978): 5–27.

happen or *This is not happening.*[26] This proposition also enters into the construal and alters it: One sees the presentation as fiction. But the withholding
of assent to the propositional content of the emotion is not the only way that
action can be forestalled. Consider a reader who believes *The Mill on the Floss*
to be a minutely veridical account of events that actually occurred in the
early 19th century. Such a reader will have as little inclination to take action
against Tom as one who reads the book as fiction. In his case, the belief
that prevents action is not *This did not happen,* but *This happened a long time
ago.* When we read emotionally gripping narrative, fictional or otherwise,
we follow the story as though it is unfolding before us. This is so even if the
story is in the past tense. Thus we can be in suspense about what is "going"
to happen, can refer to what has "already" happened by page 300, and so
on. Whether we read a narrative as fiction or as history, we believe that what
is being presented is not *currently* happening, and thus is not a situation
calling for action.

   In general, I do not think that our emotional responses to realistic fictional narratives are significantly different from our responses to narratives
we take to be historical. I say "in general," because there are exceptions.
A traditional American Southerner would not have the same emotional
response to the stories about Robert E. Lee if she came to believe them fictional. Nor would a traditional Christian respond to the narratives of Jesus'
crucifixion and resurrection in her wonted way if she thought them historically untrue. In both cases, the subject is already personally involved with
the figure in a way that differs from our relationship to most individuals in
fiction and history, individuals like Tom and Maggie Tulliver or King Louis
XVI. The Southerner is proud of Lee and her connection to him in a way
that would be undermined if it turned out that he never existed or didn't
do the central deeds that make for his claim to fame. The traditional Christian has an ongoing personal relationship of mutual love with Jesus and
trust in what he has accomplished in his crucifixion and resurrection that
cannot be had with a fictional character. We have seen that many irrational
emotions are such just because the subject disbelieves something crucial
in the emotion's propositional content, and perhaps there are eccentric
cases of Southern pride in Robert E. Lee or faith in Jesus in which the relevant figure is believed to be fictional. A person who was deeply formed
in childhood and adolescence by a traditional Christian understanding of
his relationship with Jesus Christ, and then comes to believe that the Jesus
of faith is a fictional character yet without giving up the practices of Christian worship, might well have some irrational emotions of this sort before
he makes the full transition to a symbolic or mythological understanding

---

[26] We do distinguish true from false beliefs *within* the fictional narrative, and this difference
   makes an emotional difference. I will be more anxious about Maggie if I "believe" she is
   about to drown than if I "think" she probably won't.

of Jesus. Their irrationality would consist in his believing Jesus is fictional while construing Jesus as in an actual ongoing relationship with himself.

Yet another possible reason for thinking that responses to fiction are not real emotions is that we often enjoy, in a fictional context, emotions that would be intolerable in real life. If we pay good money and spend our leisure time to be made angry, anxious, and horrified, surely these cannot be real anger, anxiety, and horror. Our ability to tolerate or even enjoy sadness, pity, and disgust better in the theater than in real life is no doubt due, in significant part, to the bracketing proposition, *This is fiction.* But the argument exaggerates the difference between emotional responses to fiction and responses to the actual situations of life. First, we do sometimes enjoy negative emotions in real life. Self-pity can be enormously pleasant. The anxiety associated with the vicissitudes of one's ball team seems to be part of the pleasure of spectator sports. Anger can be delicious. Romantic melancholy is a form of joy (see Section 3.6h). Second, negative emotions in response to fiction are sometimes intensely unpleasant, even to the point of being intolerable. For me, the sadness, pity, and anger evoked by Tom's abuse of Maggie Tulliver outweighed the very real pleasures of reading the novel, and moved me to put the book down the second time around. Third, even when we gladly subject ourselves to negative emotions in response to fiction, the emotions themselves may be quite unpleasant and may be tolerated only because they are part of an experience that is, on the whole, pleasant, or at least positively valued. The first time I read the novel, I tolerated my feelings about Maggie and Tom because the novel is beautiful and because I wanted to see how things would work out for Maggie. The pleasures of the narrative, the hopes and expectations and fascinations and joys of it, kept me going; the second time through I knew things would just go from bad to worse for her and didn't want to see that again. Often, the negative emotions are unpleasant in themselves but essential to intense involvement in the narrative.

I conclude that while emotions in response to fiction differ in some ways from our responses to real life, we lack sufficient reason to deny that they are real emotions. They differ in the following ways: They are in response to presentations that are not normally believed by their subject to obtain or to have obtained; we are little inclined to act on them; and we are more inclined to subject ourselves to negative versions of them than we are to subject ourselves to negative emotional responses to real life. But none of these is a clean difference from emotional responses to real life.

h. Judgments Detached from Their Emotions

Let us now pursue what Robert Solomon calls "the standard objection" to his judgment theory, namely the argument that emotions cannot be judgments because a subject can assent to the full propositional content of a possible emotion, yet without being in the relevant emotional state.[27] Solomon's response is that the objection fails to appreciate the special character of emotional judgments and their complexity. He does not deny that a person might make a judgment similar in some ways to a given emotion without having the emotion, but he insists that one cannot make a judgment that (a) judges that content in the special *way* that emotions do and (b) has *all* the content of the emotion, without having the emotion.

Solomon does not distinguish, as Chrysippus and Nussbaum and I do, between judgment and appearance. Instead he distinguishes the mental act of judgment from its propositional contents.[28] Initially, this distinction seems irrelevant because the standard objection is not that one can entertain, without emotion, the free-floating propositional content of some possible emotion, but that one can *assent* to this content – that is, perform the "mental act" of judgment – without emotion. We might suspect that what Solomon is calling the mental act is in fact not judgment proper but the construal or impression or *phantasia* of the situation that is characteristic of emotions. Maybe construal just is the special "way" that the content of an emotion is "judged," on Solomon's theory. (Solomon once wrote me a note saying that he meant by "judgment" what I mean by "construal.") Construal is certainly different from the propositional content of construal, but it seems wrong to call a construal or *phantasia* a judgment, for reasons that I have detailed and that Chrysippus and Nussbaum recognize. It seems confusing or eccentric simply to stipulate that emotional *phantasiai* or concern-based construals be called "judgments." We need a narrative example to help us adjudicate both responses (a) and (b).

Nussbaum, expounding Chrysippus, addresses the standard objection using both the (a) and (b) responses. Let us adapt Nussbaum's example. Nikidion's lover has just died. According to Chrysippus, her wrenching grief is a judgment to the effect that she has irrevocably lost him who is of very great importance in her life. After a while her grief subsides, but, deploying the standard objection, let us say that her judgment does not change: She still assents to the proposition that he is gone and very important, but she is not stricken as she was before. The evidence that she still judges this way is straightforward: When asked whether he is gone and whether he is very important to her, she responds in the affirmative. If we ask her how convinced she is of these things, she claims to have no doubt about them, to believe them with the fullest conviction. Furthermore, she can give evidence for both propositions: (1) He hasn't been seen since his funeral; and (2) in her recent dreams that he has returned from the grave, she is pictured as ecstatically glad. From these pieces of evidence she infers,

[27] See Michael Stocker and Elizabeth Hegeman, *Valuing Emotions*, pp. 43–44.
[28] "On Emotions as Judgments," pp. 185–186.

and thus assents to the proposition, that he is gone and still very important to her. Because her beliefs have not changed in any relevant way, it seems that what has changed is her "impression" of him, the way he "strikes" her. Indeed, Nussbaum quotes Chrysippus as saying about cases like this, "Things don't present the same appearances" (p. 382), and in a related context Nussbaum describes such differences as a matter of "perspective," "view," "vision," "picture," "appearance," "seeing as," and "how to imagine the world" (pp. 384–385). But this sort of mental state varies somewhat independently of judgment, as we have seen.

However, Chrysippus and Nussbaum do not officially characterize the difference between Nikidion's states of mind as a difference in the appearances, but hold that the *judgment* changes in some way whenever emotion changes. Chrysippus stipulates, reminiscently of Solomon's (a) response, that "the judgment, to be equivalent to a passion, must be *prosphaton*: not yet spoiled or digested, 'fresh'" (p. 381). Nikidion's judgment about her loss is not an emotion because it is not "fresh."

We might suppose that freshness in judgments just is the being struck with an evaluative propositional appearance. But to admit this understanding of freshness is to concede that the difference in Nikidion's mental states is not after all a difference of judgment proper. So Nussbaum looks for ways fresh judgments differ *propositionally* from unfresh ones. Her interpretation of freshness is reminiscent of Solomon's (b) response. She offers two such modes of differentiation.

First, she says that when Nikidion's belief that she has lost something precious is fresh, it "assaults" others of her beliefs, but when it is unfresh, it "sits alongside of them" (p. 382). For example, its being fresh may consist in there being other beliefs, such as "that [her lover] will be with her tonight" and that she will "see his face when she opens the door" (p. 382), that are contradicted by the belief that he is gone forever. After a while, though, she stops believing she'll see him, so the judgment that she has lost something precious finds less in her mind to assault. This explanation of freshness is nifty for purposes of the judgment theory because it identifies a propositional difference between fresh and unfresh judgments while preserving the internal propositional identity of the judgment.

But the explanation fails, at least in the present case, because, to feel grief at her lover's absence, Nikidion need not believe any such propositions as Nussbaum mentions. If she is normally rational, she will give up believing he will be with her tonight long before her grief goes away. A more plausible explanation is that his absence no longer strikes her in the light of those former patterns of interaction – that the difference is not a difference in belief, but in appearance.

It is possible that the difference between a judgment that is an emotion and one with exactly the same propositional content that is not an emotion is always made by the judgment's relation to other beliefs, but that Nussbaum

has not correctly identified those other beliefs in the present case. The
claim is speculative and not likely to be borne out in every case. But even if
it were, it seems odd to identify the emotion with the judgment that does
the assaulting. It would seem more accurate to identify the emotion with
the *whole* mental state, namely the judgment in question *plus* the beliefs that
it assaults. If some such conjunction were proposed as the propositional
content of some emotion, we would want to examine it, to see whether
there could be a non-emotional judgment with exactly *that* content. But if
"assault" means *contradict*, then the conjunction would be a contradiction,
with the result that "fresh" grief (and other emotions as well?) would be
irrational in a very strong sense.

Distinctions among grades of freshness are hard to make sense of when
applied to judgments. The most plausible interpretation is in terms of degrees of conviction, but conviction is not only poorly described as freshness;
it seems quite inapplicable to the present case. Nikidion does not become
less convinced that she has lost something of great importance to her. She
does not, for example, get evidence to the conclusion that her lover was less
wonderful than she thought, nor does her conviction that he is gone forever
increase (or decrease). Construals, however, do come in varying degrees of
vivacity or strikingness, and concerns come in varying degrees of intensity;
these variations account for much in variations of emotional intensity.

In a second kind of attempt to find judgmental differences corresponding
to emotional differences, Nussbaum notes that Nikidion's change of attitude
may be due to a change in her judgment's "eudaimonistic content" (p. 383).
Thus she retains the proposition that the beloved is dead, but revises the one
about his importance to her: He is no longer as important as he was. This is
indeed one kind of case. But in other cases the conviction of his importance
remains undiminished, while the emotion fades. I mentioned such a case
earlier: She infers from the content of her dreams that he is very important
to her but does not, while consciously judging this to be true of herself,
feel her former grief. Again, the judgment of his importance is separable
from her sense of it; and it is the sense (perception, construal, impression,
appearance, *phantasia*) of this, and not the judgment, that is essential to the
emotion. Nussbaum herself seems to withdraw the claim that freshness is a
predicate of judgment proper when she says that Nikidion may "eventually
stop grieving altogether, but . . . continue to retain the very same judgment"
(p. 385). On Chrysippus' view, by contrast, unfreshness somehow changes
the identity of the judgment as a judgment, and thus provides a strategy of
defense against the standard objection.

Solomon has responded (in personal communication) that the standard
objection is just as deadly against the view that emotions are concern-
based construals as it is against the view that emotions are evaluative
judgments. That is, just as, given any emotion, one can conceive the evaluative judgment that is supposedly identical with the emotion being made

without the emotion's occurring, so, given any emotion, one can conceive the concern-based construal that is supposedly identical with the emotion being performed or undergone without the emotion's occurring. I think that Solomon's claim fails to reckon with what is meant by "concern-based construal." For in my somewhat special use of "construal," to construe a situation in certain terms is for the situation to strike one, or impress one, or appear to one, as having that character. I have noted (Section 2.3b) that many construals are not emotions; emotions are a subclass of construals, the ones in which an active concern of the subject is impinged upon by the other dimensions of the construal and thus the active concern is one of the terms of the construal. Thus fear, for example, is not just construing one's present situation as involving a threat to one's well-being or someone else's well-being (*that* construal can be performed or undergone without emotion); it is, rather, construing one's present situation as involving a threat to something (oneself or someone or something one cares about) in such a way that an active concern for one's own or someone else's well-being is impinged on by the impression of threat and thus that the concern for what is threatened enters into the construal as one of its terms. I do not see how such a construal can be performed or undergone without emotion. By contrast, evaluative judgments can be made without their corresponding emotions because judgments can be made without impression (see J4, Section 2.4b) and without active concern for what is evaluatively judged of.

At one point, like Nussbaum, Solomon admits that an emotion's judgment may be separable from it. He says, "the judgments that make up the emotion cannot be separated from the emotion except in the most unusual pathological cases" (p. 189). No doubt, some pathological conditions involve a separation of emotion and judgment,[29] but sometimes such separation is eminently healthy. The virtue of forgivingness, for example, involves the ability to retain the judgment that someone has culpably offended you in a matter of significance, while giving up the emotion of anger at the offender, with the vindictive view of him that it involves. It is indeed one of the many advantages of the view that emotions are appearances and not judgments that it explains phenomena like forgiveness.[30]

Nussbaum pictures Nikidion, in her grief, trying with intermittent success to become a Stoic. She tells herself, in the words of Seneca, that her lover is after all not irreplaceable, and her grief subsides.

[29] See Antonio Damasio's account of his patient "Elliot," who because of a brain tumor had suffered a certain kind of frontal lobe damage. On tests Elliot showed normal ability to make judgments about options for action, consequences of actions, means-end problem solving, prediction of social consequences of actions, and the morality of actions, and yet was severely limited in his ability to respond with appropriate emotion. *Descartes' Error*, Chapter 3. I discuss Elliot in Section 2.7e.

[30] I have elaborated this point in "Forgivingness," *American Philosophical Quarterly* **32** (1995): 289–306.

Then the thought of her lover, with his particular eyes, his ways of moving and talking, overwhelms her, and she assents, once again, to the thought that something has gone from her life that she can never replace (p. 384).

Admittedly, it is possible that Nikidion is undecided about whether to assent to the Stoic proposition or to the proposition involved in her grief, and she finds herself actually assenting to and denying these propositions in rapid succession. But more likely, if she is a Stoic pupil, she is committed to the Stoic proposition and finds herself akratically subject to appearances contrary to that proposition. She succeeds intermittently in perceiving the world in accordance with her beliefs.[31]

i. Argument from Emotional Self-Control

The fact that a rational person can control his emotions to an extent, and in a way, that it would be unfitting or impossible to control his judgments, shows that emotions are not judgments. I am standing on a wobbly ladder, doing something important enough to warrant the risk to my bodily well-being. My judgment regarding the danger I am in is rational. And my fear is intense enough to impede me doing the job I am on the ladder to do; so that, other things being equal, it is rational for me to try to mitigate my fear. On the judgment theory, to mitigate my fear is to change my judgment about the situation, in one of two ways: I might replace it with another, incompatible judgment, thus denying it; or I might cease to make it without denying it (letting the judgment sink to a dispositional belief by putting it out of my mind). In the situation I have described, it will be epistemically irrational for me to deny that the situation is dangerous or to start judging it to be less dangerous than I now judge it to be (for I know that it is just this dangerous). But equally, it will be practically irrational to put the danger out of my mind; I must keep the danger in mind so as to avoid it as far as possible. If my judgment is rational and importantly relevant to the situation, rationality usually requires that I keep it as is. However, it is not irrational to try to mitigate my fear so as to be better able to do the task that needs to be done.

To cease feeling afraid, I do not need to cease judging the situation to be dangerous. To cease feeling afraid (or start feeling less afraid), I need to refocus the situation in some appropriate way, to get a different impression of the situation. If, for example, my task on that wobbly ladder is to rescue my little daughter from the third-story window of our burning home, I need to focus on getting her safely to the ground. Instead of construing the situation

---

[31] In her response to some of the remarks I have made here, Nussbaum seems to want to explain the possibility of cases like the knowing phobic by reference to the possibility of straightforwardly contradictory beliefs. See "Reply to Papers in Symposium on Nussbaum, *The Therapy of Desire*," *Philosophy and Phenomenological Research* **59** (1999): 811–819, 814.

as *a threat to my well-being* – say, in terms of an image of myself plummeting 25 feet to the pavement – I construe it as a rescue task – say, in terms of an image of walking down that ladder with my daughter safely in my arms. The former construal is a form of fear, while the latter is not; both are compatible with the judgment that my daughter and I are severely endangered. It may be within my psychological repertoire as a rational chooser to construe the situation in these two, and an indefinite number of other, ways: If I take an athletic view of situations calling for courage, I may construe this one as an opportunity to test my mettle; as a religious believer, I may construe the situation as being in the hands of God; if I have a flair for the dramatic aspects of things, I may see myself in heroic terms; and so on. It is largely in virtue of this optionality of construal that one has emotional options. It is far less often within one's repertoire as a rational chooser to decide to modify one's judgments or even just to abandon them; to be a rational person is to be subject to a kind of evidential and logical compulsion regarding most of one's judgments.

j. Emotions as Requiring Judgments

I have directed my arguments chiefly against the thesis that emotions are a certain kind of judgment. A weaker thesis is that a belief or judgment with the emotion's propositional content is a necessary ingredient of the emotion, but that other ingredients are necessary too – say, desires to act or physiological changes or the sensations of such changes. The "standard objection" that the judgment corresponding to an emotion can be made without the emotion's occurring is no objection to this weaker thesis, but my argument that significant portions of the propositional content of many emotions are not believed by the subjects of those emotions is just as powerful here as it is against the Chrysippus–Solomon thesis, if assent is essential to judgment (see Section 2.4b). Let us look at the responses of a couple of authors who hold the weaker thesis, when they are confronted with the kind of case on which my argument turns.

John Rawls has commented:

> . . . a person raised in a strict religious sect may have been taught that going to the theater is wrong. While he no longer believes this, he tells us that he still feels guilty when attending the theater. But these are not proper guilt feelings, since he is not about to apologize to anyone, or to resolve not to see another play, and so on. Indeed, he should say rather that he has certain sensations and feelings of uneasiness, which resemble those which he has when he feels guilty.[32]

We see here a resource of response to my objection that may not be as readily available to the stronger version of the judgment theory. If judgments

---

[32] *A Theory of Justice* (New York: Oxford University Press, 1971), p. 482.

are only one element among others that go to constitute emotion, then there may be phenomena of behavior and feeling that resemble emotions because they contain these other elements, yet are not strictly speaking emotions inasmuch as they lack the necessary judgmental element. Rawls fixes on sensations and feelings characteristic of the emotion of guilt as the elements that may be present in the absence of the emotion, and thus may lead a person to think falsely that he feels genuine guilt. This is not a very realistic supposition. It is not typical of the person with irrational guilt that he experiences only "certain sensations and feelings of uneasiness" that resemble those that accompany guilt; it is much more characteristic of such a person that he appears to himself to be in violation of some morally important standard.[33] Rawls also suggests that guilt feelings not accompanied by belief in real guilt will not motivate action. But this also is not generally true. Some people may be moved by irrational guilt to resolve not to see another play, if the emotion is strong enough; just as the behavior of phobics who understand the harmlessness of what they fear may be indistinguishable from that of people who believe the same objects to be harmful. And guilt feelings with judgment of guilt may not issue in confession, apology, or amendment of life, for a variety of reasons, including both rational considerations and akrasia.

Gabriele Taylor holds that anyone experiencing humiliation, shame, or guilt "believes of herself that she has deviated from some norm and that in doing so she has altered her standing in the world."[34] Yet later, discussing irrational guilt, she seems almost to adopt the construal view when she says,

Just as a person is guilty if he breaks the law whether or not that law is just or justified, so he feels guilty if what he does *presents itself* as a wrong, whether or not what he is doing can in fact be regarded as a wrong, and *whether or not he himself thinks it wrong when he views the matter from a more rational point of view* (p. 86, italics added).

But this is not in fact the construal view. It employs two devices for interpreting irrational guilt in terms of beliefs. The first is to posit shifting beliefs like the ones by which Nussbaum explains Nikidion's vacillations about Stoicism. The person suffering irrational guilt vacillates between "a more rational point of view" in which he believes that his action is not wrong (he presumably does not feel guilty at that moment), but feels guilty "if what he does presents itself as a wrong" (at this moment he believes that it is wrong). The other device distinguishes two senses of "is wrong," which can mean either "breaks a law" or "breaks a justified law." Thus when a person is

---

[33] However, in Sections 4.3–4.5 I show how people may have false feelings of emotions like guilt that are triggered by the kind of sensations of which Rawls writes.
[34] *Pride, Shame, and Guilt,* p. 1.

feeling irrationally guilty she believes that her action is wrong in the sense that it breaks a law (a "taboo" as Taylor says a few lines later) but not in the sense that it breaks a justified law.

Neither of these devices works. The first fails because what needs to be explained is how a person can feel guilty and *at the very same moment* judge that he is not guilty of what he feels guilty about. The second fails because believing that one's action breaks a taboo or unjustified law does not explain one's feeling guilty about it. Consider the law, "Thou shalt not step on the crack, for it will break thy mother's back." I step on the crack, believing that my action violates this prohibition and that the law is unjustified. Of course I can do this without feeling guilty, but let us say that I feel guilty. What is the explanation of this? Is it my believing that there is such a law? If I come to think there is no such law, will I necessarily stop feeling guilty? What if I accept the theory that there is not sufficient communal backing and historical precedent for this to count as a genuine unjustified law? It is nothing but a children's game. I don't think this change of belief is likely to affect my emotions, if they are already irrational. I feel guilty not because I believe there is a genuine unjustified law that I have violated, but because I construe myself (contrary to my belief) as having violated a justified law.

So far, our examples of emotions whose propositional content is disbelieved by the subject at the moment of having the emotion are either responses to fiction or irrational emotions. But these are not the only cases. We do not think a person who sees a mirage is being irrational, just because his judgment deviates from his perception; it is better, in this case, for his beliefs to conflict with his perception than for them to coincide. Nor does having the visual experience characteristic of seeing a mirage indicate any malfunction of one's visual apparatus. A person unable to see mirages might even count as visually defective. Since emotions are characteristically spontaneous responses to situations, a similar nonirrational discrepancy between emotion and belief may also arise. The disposition to get angry at the misbehavior of children under the age of accountability seems to be just about as natural to human beings as the disposition to have of-water-like visual experiences in mirage situations. Furthermore, it can be defended as appropriate in terms of its importance to the moral development of children, for it is an ascription of responsibility that (in an otherwise proper setting of parent-child relationships) helps to generate a responsibility that was not there. But the ascription of responsibility that is involved in anger[35] is

---

[35] I am assuming that one of the propositions in terms of which an angry person construes the offending agent (A) is something like *A is morally responsible for x*. The evidence for this is twofold. First, anger generates the desire to punish A. Angry behavior is punitive; and among rational people, people are punished only for what they are morally responsible for. Second, a fully rational person who is angry can be, in the central cases, disabused of his anger by

not true (let us suppose) when directed at a two-year-old child. So the fully rational and virtuous parent who is well-informed about child development is one who in appropriate circumstances of misbehavior feels anger at his child, while disbelieving at least one of the propositions in terms of which he construes his child when angry at her.

k. Conclusion

I have argued that judgment without the appropriate construal is not emotion, even if the propositional content of the judgment is that of the (possible but absent) construal, and that construal can be emotion in the absence of the corresponding judgment. So even if, as I acknowledge, many or most emotions in fact involve judgments over their propositional content, the judgment is neither necessary nor sufficient for the emotion. It is better to think of emotions as a kind of appearance or impression that is, in the normal case, supported by judgment than to think of emotions as judgments or as requiring judgment.

2.5. PROPOSITIONS

a. Introduction

As the fish are formed and suspended in the sea, human emotions are formed and suspended in a medium of language – of narrative formations and explanations to which beings lacking syntactic language have no access. Many of the "terms" of many of our emotions are the possession, uniquely, of communities in which language is spoken and understood. In the present section I try to get clear on the role, and the limits of the role, of language in our emotions. I first sketch an account of how we identify our emotions propositionally, and then I look at a couple of fields of emotion in which propositions have only a small, if any, role, namely the emotions of nonlinguistic animals and emotions that we feel in response to purely instrumental music. Juxtaposing the linguistic and the nonlinguistic aspects of the field of emotion will, I hope, help us to a balanced and nuanced view of the question. In speaking of the content of a human emotion that both defines it as to type (say, joy versus anger) and establishes what the particular emotion is about (say, joy about the healthy birth of a child versus joy about having been released from prison), one might speak about either propositions or thoughts. A proposition is either a declarative sentence or what that sentence declares; a thought is a mental content that is or might

being shown that A is not morally responsible for x (A may be instrumentally responsible for x without being morally responsible for x). For more discussion of the structure of anger, see Section 3.3a.

be expressed in such a sentence; an utterance is either a written or spoken proposition, or the clear occurrence of the corresponding thought to a subject.

In the preceding section we examined the recently popular view that emotions are judgments or necessarily entail judgments. Because a judgment is minimally an assent to a proposition, all such views are committed to the propositional character of all emotions.[36] The model I am proposing treats the paradigm cases of human emotions as having a propositional structure, but does not entail that emotions are all propositional. It treats emotions as a kind of perception, but perceptions may or may not be propositional. Thus the model seems more likely to handle animal emotions and emotional responses to textless music. Let us begin by considering the variety of ways that construals can be related to propositions or thoughts.

b. Propositions and Construals

A construal can be related to propositions in a number of distinct ways. Consider Figure 2 and its various propositional interpretations.

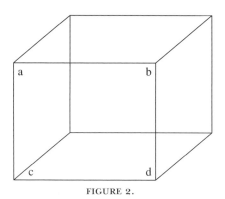

FIGURE 2.

    1.   "Figure 2 is two-dimensional."
    2.   "Figure 2 is three-dimensional."
       a. "Plane abcd is in the back."
       b. "Plane abcd is in the front."

---

[36] Patricia Greenspan makes propositions essential to emotions without being a judgment theorist. On her view an emotion is an array of evaluative propositions or thoughts held in place by comfortable or uncomfortable affects that take the propositions as their intentional objects. See her *Emotions and Reasons* (London: Routledge and Kegan Paul, 1988), pp. 3–9.

It seems to me that the three-dimensional construal of Figure 2 comes most naturally or spontaneously. One can imagine an unprompted very young child recognizing the figure as "a box." On the other hand, construals 2.a and 2.b seem equally natural, though some individual might see one of the two and not the other and might have to be told that the other is a possibility. Then, having been directed using something like proposition 2.a or 2.b, the subject tries and succeeds in making the less natural construal. This less "natural" or less "immediate" construal is, we might say, more *utterance-dependent* than the construal of the figure as a box. By comparison with recognizing the figure as a box, it is much less visually natural to construe the figure two-dimensionally, and so this construal will require even more linguistic prompting.[37] So we have a graded range of construals along the dimension of naturalness or spontaneity, which follows the principle: The more natural the construal, the less utterance dependent it is. We can transfer the notion of utterance dependency to an educational context such as microscopy, in which a great deal of prompting in the form of linguistically directed training in "seeing" is presupposed by the most expert construals. So we must also distinguish secondary spontaneity from primary. The thoroughly trained microscopist does not require linguistic prompting to see what she sees on the slide, even though without lots of such prompting in her educational history she would not be able to see what she now sees spontaneously; but the student microscopist may require actual present prompting to see the same thing.

But if the construals corresponding to propositions 1, 2.a, and 2.b differ in their degree of causal dependency on utterance, all of them are equally describable in their corresponding propositions: Even the construals that do not in any sense require an uttered characterization as a prompt – because they are formed with primary spontaneity in response to the figure – can in retrospect be quite precisely described or expressed in a proposition. So we can distinguish two kinds of relations between construals and propositions: causal dependency on utterance and utterance expressibility.

On the other hand, it seems in principle possible for a linguistically non-capable animal to construe Figure 2 or some real-life analogue of it in any of the three ways. But we must qualify this observation. Such an animal would not so construe it in response to linguistic characterizations and would be very unlikely to be aware of alternative construals or to "switch" construal at will, since these last-mentioned abilities depend so heavily on the linguistic identification of the various construals. Nor would the concepts that play central roles in the various propositions – concepts like *figure, dimension, plane, back,* and *front* – inform the construal in the sense that the animal would see the figure in terms of the concepts. An animal that cannot

---

[37] Perhaps this is because, unlike the case of the box, there is nothing familiar in our visible environment that Figure 2, construed two-dimensionally, looks like.

understand the words for these concepts, or their counterparts in some language other than English, will not experience the figure in exactly the way a person will construe it in accordance with the propositions. Even the human being with the concepts in his repertoire who spontaneously sees the figure in one of the ways will see the figure somewhat differently upon bringing the propositions explicitly to bear. For example, the notion of a plane typically has associations with the practice of geometry; if it does not have these associations, it is bound to have others for any language speaker. These associations inform the construal in subtle ways. So when we say that a nonlinguistic animal might construe Figure 2 in the three ways specified by the propositions, we mean that the animal is capable of construals that are *strongly analogous* to the three that a master of the concepts would have. And language will vary in its associations from speaker to speaker, depending on such factors as the speaker's depth of geometrical sophistication, and so speakers will also differ from one another in the subtler dimensions of their construals of the figure.

So we can add a third way that construals can be propositional: Not only may they depend causally on utterance and be expressible in utterance, but they may also be internally structured by language-dependent concepts. A clearer case is my earlier example of hearing (or seeing) "table" as a verb. Here the experience of the sound is internally structured by the (linguistic) concept of a verb, and so the construal has no analogue in the experience of any nonlinguistic animal. Noticing this third relation of construal to propositions leads us to qualify the second: The expressibility of a construal is approximate only, because the concepts in terms of which it is expressed give it further, and sometimes significantly different, definition. When, for example, we put into language a construal that we attribute to a nonlinguistic animal, we must realize that the animal's construal lacks any features that would be contributed by the specifically linguistic concepts in terms of which we describe the animal's construal.

c. Propositional Content of Emotions

For many human emotions, a propositional expression of the character of the construal is compelling. A person who is anxious about an upcoming job interview construes the interview in some such terms as

Bad things, I'm not sure what, are significantly probable in connection with the interview.

or

There is a good chance I will somehow mess up the interview.

Though these words may not be the ones the subject will utter in explaining his anxiety, they express thoughts that have a form definitive of the emotion type, a form that distinguishes anxiety from hope, panic, gratitude, and so on. If the proposition is actually to express an emotion, the evaluative terms such as "bad," "threaten," and "mess up" have to express a concern of the subject. A sentence expressive of an instance of emotion and referring to the particular items in the emotion's situational object I will call the emotion's *material proposition*. The various material propositions expressive of instances of a given type of emotion (say, resentment or nostalgia) should have a form in common. A sentence expressing this form I will call an emotion's *defining proposition*. The defining proposition for anxiety might be

X vaguely presents an aversive possibility of some degree of probability; may X or its aversive consequences, whatever they may be, be avoided.

See Section 3.2c for discussion of anxiety. Human emotions come in a variety of more or less named types, such as indignation, regret, gratitude, and hope, and these are distinguished from one another by their defining propositions. In Chapter 3 I offer discussions of the defining propositions for a wide range of emotion types.

Let us pursue the case of anxiety. Evidence that such material and defining propositions shape the subject's construal of his situation is easy to see in cases where the onset of the anxiety coincides with receipt of threatening news (e.g., a report about how roughly the interviewer has handled other candidates), or where it increases as one ruminates about the threatening features of the situation. Here we have a case of causal dependence on utterance. To think that such propositions are determining the individual's construal of the prospective interview, we need not hold that he explicitly contemplates them or rehearses them to himself. They are the propositions he *would* utter were he to *explain* his anxiety. His anxiety (construal) is expressible in such propositions. Perhaps he is initially inarticulate about them; they need to be drawn from him artfully, as in psychotherapy. But the following considerations suggest that even in such a case some propositions or thoughts determine the character of his experience: In inquiry about his emotion, they can be drawn from him, or could be drawn from him with the right prompting. The formulation of some such propositions as these may accurately characterize the subject's emotion, and without knowledge of some such propositions it may be impossible to know what the emotion is and is about. If, as in cognitive psychotherapy, one can get the subject to stop thinking of the interview in these terms, and think of it in other terms that are less threatening to him, he may cease to be anxious. Because the subject in this case is a user of the language to which these sentences belong, and thus has mastery of the concepts of which the sentences make use, it is plausible that the construal is not just expressible in terms of these sentences, but is actually internally structured by its central concepts. Our assumption is that our conceptual powers sometimes operate in our perception even when we are neither uttering nor capable of coming up with these propositions unaided, as is the case with some emotions met with in psychotherapy. Admittedly some propositional explanations of emotions are rationalizations (false reinterpretations). But not all are.

Another reason for thinking that emotions can have a propositional character even in the absence of utterance is the existence of irrational instances of them. David Pugmire, arguing for a feeling theory of emotions against even such a mildly "cognitive" account as mine, says

With some quite familiar aversions, it is hard to locate any type of thought, even a construal. For irreligious and unsuperstitious people to shrink from corpses . . . need not be for them to be prey to any thoughts . . . of supernatural danger. . . . Wayward emotions such as phobic fear reveal that some emotions, at least, can occur independently of the sorts of thought that could give them grounds, and this includes non-assertional thought. They can arise even in the teeth of thoughts that should preclude them.[38]

If we take irrationality in an emotion to be the emotion's conflicting with what the subject believes, then Pugmire's argument from irrational emotions backfires. A mental state cannot contradict a thought if it does not itself have at all a character that can be expressed in thoughts.

Two kinds of things are expressed in an emotion's material proposition: claims about what we might call the situation's "layout" features, and claims about what we might call its "value" features. Thus in a proposition like

There is a good chance I will somehow mess up the interview.

the reference to the interview and the degree of probability ascribe layout features, while the term "mess up" ascribes a negative value to the situation (as well as the layout feature of the involvement of my agency). The two kinds of features are inextricably intertwined, both in the proposition and in the construal that incorporates its full meaning. So, for example, the fairly high probability is bad by virtue of being a probability of messing up. And the interview is laden with value in virtue of being a means to a (good) end. As a concern-based construal, every emotion will refer, in its material proposition, to some value of the situation that the proposition depicts. But the emotion is not merely the ascription of layout and value features of the situation, in their situational integration. In other words, merely construing a situation in these terms does not amount to an emotion because it is possible for the evaluation to be ascribed without concern. Insofar as the material proposition is that of an *emotion*, its value elements must express a concern of the subject, and this concern has to connect with or enter into the rest of the construal as one of its terms. For example, to be anxious in the above case I must be actually concerned to avoid messing up the interview, and then my construal of myself as fairly likely to perform substandardly must actually synthesize with that concern – not just

---

[38] *Rediscovering Emotion*, p. 31.

coolly construing the situation as having a pretty good chance of turning out badly.

Let us turn now to cases of emotion or emotion-like states in which propositions do not play the kind of roles I have been talking about. I shall address first the case of moods, then of emotions in nonlinguistic animals, and finally emotions in response to nonlinguistic music.

d. Mood and Emotion

Moods can occur without being propositional in any of the three senses I have distinguished – that is, without being either elicited, structured by, or articulable in any declarative sentences. A person can be depressed or melancholy, cheerful or elated, or fidgety or agitated without having any reasons for his state of mind, without being elated or depressed or agitated *about* anything, and without construing himself or his world in terms of any such reasons. It is typical of moods that they have causes rather than reasons: They are brought on by fatigue, depressive or elative drugs, sensory input such as certain kinds of noise or music or tactile irritation or pleasures, a psychodevelopmental history of a certain sort, the weather, dark lighting or the opposite, squalid environment or the opposite, intense and/or sustained or repeated emotions, sustained physical pain, and the like. We can also be depressed or elated about some state of affairs, but in that case the depression is not just a mood but an emotion. If one is elated *about* something, "elated" belongs among emotion terms such as "joyful," "glad," "hopeful," and "grateful."

So moods are not differentiated, like the paradigm cases of human emotion, by their propositional content. How then are they differentiated from one another? What makes cheerfulness one mood and makes depression another? I suggest, on a clue from O. K. Bouwsma, that they have a character:

The zig-zag line has character and the wavy line has character. Each letter of the alphabet is a character, but also has character. The number tokens, 1 2 3 4 5 6 7 8 9 – each has its character. In the same way sounds have character. . . . You might say that if some dancing master were to arrange a dance for each of the numbers, you might see how a dance for the number one would not do at all for number five. Or again if the numbers were to be dressed in scarfs, again a certain color and a certain flimsy material would do for six but would not suit five at all. [39]

In specifying what an emotion is about, one refers to some state of affairs. "I am sad about . . . ," "I am glad that . . . ," "I am fearful of. . . . " But in characterizing a mood, one punts to metaphors (shades of light and colors, degrees of weight, height, and depth): He was gloomy, his mood was gray, blue, dark;

[39] "The Expression Theory of Art," in *Philosophical Essays* (Lincoln, Nebraska: University of Nebraska Press, 1965), p. 47.

she was lighthearted all evening, floating on a cloud. When I got up this morning, I had a bright outlook. She is depressed (pushed down) or elated (lifted up). Wittgenstein says,

When we're asked "What do 'red', 'blue', 'black', 'white', mean?" we can, of course, immediately point to things which have these colours – but that's all we can do: our ability to explain their meaning goes no further.[40]

Wordlike sounds have a character too. Bouwsma offers the following:

Hi diddle diddle!
Fee! fi, fo, fum!
Intery, mintery.
Abra ca da bra.

And he says about these, "But to ask now 'What is its character or what does it express?' is to fall into the pit."[41] How does coffee smell or sherry taste? They have a distinctive character, but no "logic." The most straightforward way to characterize them is to present them: Take a sniff, a sip, if you want to know what they're like. It also helps to juxtapose them with similar and contrasting things: Sniff some coffee and then sniff some tea, and you'll learn something about the character of the coffee smell. But we can also talk about them: Coffee smells more blunt than tea (but Italian coffee is as sharp as some tea). Tea tastes more transparent, coffee more opaque. Coffee is heavier (even when it's sharp) than tea and is deeper. Coffee has a yellowish or reddish flavor, while tea is toward blue and green and gray. But this will not take us far with someone who has never smelled coffee herself.

Something similar is true of moods. The metaphors in which we talk about them are no substitute for direct acquaintance, though fluency with the metaphors can enrich our ability to recognize, experience, and discriminate moods. The fact that one can characterize emotions quite without recourse to metaphor, by reference to their reasons, makes them articulable in a way that moods are not. In fairly large measure, emotions can be explicated in prose, but moods need "poetry."

So far I have noted differences between emotions and moods, but they are connected as well. First, emotions have moods: joy is bright and cheerful and has a light character (in both senses of "light"), while grief is heavy and dark and slow. The mood or color of an emotion may be what is sometimes referred to as its "affect," and is sometimes (mistakenly) taken to be its essential core, to which the reasons for the emotion play an incidental or ornamental role. In discussing feelings, Wittgenstein says,

[40] G. E. M. Anscombe, (ed.), *Remarks on Colour*, translated by Linda L. McAlister and Margarete Schättle (Berkeley: University of California Press, 1977), Part III, Section 102.
[41] *Op. cit.*, pp. 47ff.

But it is surely important that all these paraphrases exist. That care can be described in such words as: 'the descent of a permanent cloud'. I have perhaps never stressed the importance of this paraphrasing enough. [42]

Why is such paraphrasing important? Why not just account for the character of an emotion by giving the reasons that define it? Because an important aspect of the "feel" of an emotion is its mood, and when we describe our emotions by speaking of clouds, rain, gloom, sunshine, blue skies, dark colors, bright colors, muted shades, and the like, we articulate the mood. In giving the propositional content of an emotion, we tell much about it, but not everything; the paraphrases tell us more. And of course even then we will not be able to *communicate* about the emotion with someone who has not experienced a range of moods.

The moods that characterize emotions can detach from them. So a second connection is that an emotion can beget a mood that remains after the departure of the emotion. We have already noted that moods are generalized. You win the lottery and are glad. So you have this emotion of gladness, with its reason: having won the lottery. It is not generalized, but focused on a particular state of affairs. But now you notice that all sorts of other "objects" have taken on the color of gladness: People you meet look more worthy of beneficence, assigned tasks appear more feasible and the work seems more attractive, and colleagues' jokes seem funnier. That a mood is operating here is shown by the fact that you do not have reasons for regarding your acquaintances as more worthy of beneficence than before, your tasks more feasible, or your colleagues funnier. This gladness seems to color everything more or less indiscriminately. A nice literary example of this can be found in Chapter 20 of Jane Austen's *Persuasion*.

Thus a third connection is that moods predispose emotions. It seems clear that these particular responses – of brotherly affection for one's acquaintances, of hope in one's work, and of amusement at colleagues' jokes – are emotions or something very similar to them and not mere moods. As such, you can give some reasons for them: the friendly responsiveness of the acquaintances, say, or the good prospects of the work, or the particular incongruity that the jokes put on display (though you may catch yourself exaggerating the reasons). But despite the reasons, we know that the mood was operating by knowing that on another day, in the absence of the mood, you would not have responded with these emotions, or at any rate not with the same intensity, despite having the same reasons for having the emotion (roughly, the same beliefs and concerns) as you have today. (On that other day, the reasons would not have been pushed into operation.) So the connection between emotion and mood here seems to be that mood

---

[42] G. E. M. Anscombe and G. H. von Wright (eds.), *Zettel*, translated by G. E. M. Anscombe (Oxford: Basil Blackwell, 1967), Section 517.

helps the reasons to obtrude, thus fostering the emotions. Some days we find ourselves thinking gloomy thoughts of what we regret, of what we are ashamed, or of losses and disappointments. A natural explanation for an otherwise unexplained preponderance of such emotions is that we are in a down mood.[43]

Can we say anything about *how* mood predisposes emotion? Depression and elation color the objects of our experience in hues of value. Depression, the dark, heavy, down mood, colors everything bad; while gaiety, the bright, light, up mood, colors things in the welcoming hues of goodness. Analogously, emotions are usually "positive" or "negative," which is to say they are perceptions of states of affairs as good or bad. The perception of value that characterizes emotions comes from their nature as concern-based construals. In the negative emotions, the terms of the construal impinge inauspiciously on the concern that is at the base of the emotion. Thus, in fear the concern that something (perhaps oneself) (S) be safe or well is impinged on inauspiciously (frustrated) by some such thought as *X may very well damage S*. In the positive emotions, the impingement is auspicious. Thus, in parental joy, the concern (love) for one's child is auspiciously impinged on (satisfied) by the construal of the child as thriving. Because frustrating situations are experienced as bad and satisfying ones are experienced as good, these perceptions can be advanced or hindered by the coloration that moods supply. If we are cheerful, what is reason for joy will seem the more so, and what is fearsome will tend to seem the less so. Our depression will tend to hamper our perception of satisfactions and facilitate our perception of frustrations.

e. Animal Emotions

The rabbit jumps in fright at the sight of a snake, the dog wags its tail joyfully at its master's return, the she-bear angrily attacks people who come too close to her cubs. Animals seem to have a range of distinguishable emotions that parallel the main types of human emotions, while not having the kind of language necessary to formulate the material and defining propositions that elicit, express, and structure the human emotions. Typical "cognitivist" theories, which make judgments, or at any rate propositions, essential to emotions, do not handle very well the emotions of nonlinguistic animals.[44] One of the strengths of the construal account is that it makes neither judgments nor propositions essential to emotions, though propositions structure most post-infantile human emotions. Construals, as we have

---

[43] "When good things happen to someone whose general mood is dysphoric, they may remain unappreciated; and when bad things happen to someone whose general mood is euphoric, they may fail to produce the expected distress." R. S. Lazarus, *Emotion and Adaptation* (New York: Oxford University Press, 1991), 266.

[44] See John Deigh, "Cognitivism in the Theory of Emotions," *Ethics* **104** (1994): 824–854.

begun to see, may or may not be structured propositionally. The construal account of emotion admits that in being nonpropositional, animal emotions differ significantly from their human counterparts. But since construals are not necessarily propositional, it leaves room for animal analogues of many human emotions. All that is needed for emotion, on this account, is a power of perception that is not merely sense perception, but some organization of sense perception that can impinge on and incorporate some concern (perhaps instinctual, perhaps learned) of the animal. If this organization is similar enough to the organization that is achieved partly through propositions in the case of the animal emotion's human analogue, we are justified in ascribing something like the standard human emotions to animals. We have seen that construals that are not structured by propositions may nevertheless be characterized or expressed in propositions, and it seems to me that this is what happens when we ascribe emotions to nonlinguistic animals, as when we say, "The she-bear is angry because she thinks you're too close to her cubs" or "Fido is happy that his master is home" or "The rabbit feels threatened by the presence of a snake."

When the rabbit reacts with fear to the snake, it does not see the snake as *dangerous*, because it doesn't have any of the human concepts of danger – concepts that presumably no animal can have unless it is able to understand sentences using "danger" or some other-language counterpart. It does, however, see the snake in a different way than it sees a stick that has much the same sensory properties as the snake (color, elongation, smoothness, taper, curve). The difference between its perception of the snake and its perception of the snakelike stick to which it does not react with fear seems to be not just one of sensory properties, but a difference of construal. The difference in sensory properties may be slight, but the difference in "meaning" is considerable. A slight difference of sensory input triggers a qualitatively different perception, and this is a difference in the way the sensory input is organized – where "organized" denotes the kind of thing that has happened in the perception of the old woman/young woman figure when a subject sees one of the figures in the lines. Rabbits come hard-wired for this construal of things with just the sensory properties of snakes, and this construal impinges on, or is formed (in part) out of, the survival instinct (the animal analogue of a human concern). Thus while it is wrong to say that the rabbit has any thoughts about snakes or sees snakes in terms of propositions about the dangers they involve, it is plausible to think that the rabbit's emotion, like human fear, is a construal of the emotion's object in certain "terms," including a concern.

That animal emotion is something like adult human construal becomes particularly clear when we consider animals from whose experience this organizing perceptual element can be trained away. The horse initially reacts with something like human panic to the sensation of having a rider on its back; when later it does not so perceive the rider, this is surely not due to a difference in the sheer sensory properties that the rider has for the horse. Or take the human case, for we too have emotional responses that are not structured propositionally. It seems instinctual in us that when, unused to the experience, we look down from a precipice, we recoil with something analogous to fear. As human beings, we probably also see the precipice as dangerous (we "think of what might happen to us were we to fall"), but the experience precedes and seems to be largely independent of the concept of danger, and so it is natural to suppose that it is something like the animal reactions involving sense perceptions that we have been discussing. But with experience some people overcome this perception when looking precipitously down; rock climbers and roofers learn to see the precipitous drop differently. Since it is not plausible to think that the sensory input differs significantly from what it was when they did so react, the instinctual–emotional experience must be something like a construal, a "seeing" of the precipitous drop *in some aspect* – in particular, as touching an instinctual concern for safety. In human beings, learning not to fear heights is no doubt partially propositional: We think about the protective railings, or remind ourselves of our successes at dealing with heights. But the change is also in part nonpropositional: Through our habituation to certain sense impressions, they cease to be organized in the way characteristic of this primitive fear.

The vast majority of post-infantile human emotions are propositional in the sense that the view they take of things could not be taken by a being unable to understand certain sentences, which have to be articulated in any adequate characterization of the view in question. This is not to deny that the construal constitutive of many emotions is determined in part nonpropositionally, by animal disposition (e.g., biologically fixed sexual and spatial perception) or habit (think of the "comfortable" feel of familiar surroundings). Many, perhaps most, post-infantile emotions are determined by both propositional and nonpropositional factors.

f. Human and Animal Emotions Compared

I now note, through some illustrations, how animal emotions differ cognitively from their human analogs. We can compare human and animal emotions with respect to both material and defining propositions.

The material propositions informing human emotions often identify objects that animal emotions cannot take. Dogs do not fear disease, war, a painful death, a fall of the stock market, food shortages, contempt of peers, or the judgment of God, though they are subject to harm from some of these things. Propositional language gives us access to these objects, and so puts us in a position to fear them. Thus while we construe the prospect of a painful death analogously to the way the small dog construes a doberman, and so we and the small dog have emotions both of which can be called fear, they have quite different diagnostic and therapeutic implications. Pippy's fear of the doberman may be caused by a memory of being mauled by a large black dog, and it may be curable by "desensitization" – that is, by (gradually) habituating Pippy to the perception of the doberman in circumstances that are otherwise nonthreatening. A human patient who fears a painful death may, by contrast, be instantly cured of this fear by being convinced that anaesthetics capable of handling the pain characteristic of her disease will be available. (Of course the fear of pain may not be her only fear, so even after she gets rid of this fear she may still be afraid.) Since human emotions are often structured in part nonpropositionally, some may be modified by nonpropositional techniques like desensitization; but animal emotions are never subject to modification by argument.

The capacity to use language makes human emotions much less dependent than animal emotions are on sense perception and features of the subject's immediate environment. I have noted that the gestalt figures set fairly definite limits to how they can be seen. The old woman/young woman figure can be seen in the two prescribed ways, but it cannot (I think) be seen as a bowl of flowers because the lines do not lend themselves to this construal. By contrast, because of human emotions' independence of sense experience, the very same situation may be construed, by different people, or by the same person at different times, in such a variety of ways as to yield virtually any of the whole range of emotions. A person may take delight in his own degradation (see the opening sections of Dostoevsky's *Notes from the Underground*), may be angered by proffered kindnesses, may fear success, or may be relieved to discover that he has a terminal illness. This indeterminacy of emotion vis-à-vis the situation it is about derives from the great diversity of terms in which the situations can be construed, and this diversity derives, in turn, from the power of speech and thought.

The defining propositions for some major types of human emotions exclude nonlinguistic animals from having emotions of these types, even though animals have emotions that go by the same names – say, "anger" and "pity." A proposition that is defining for a central form of mature human anger is

S has culpably offended in the important matter of X (action or omission) and is bad (is to some extent an enemy of what is good); I am in a moral position to condemn; S deserves (ought) to be hurt for X; may S be hurt for X.

For analysis of anger, see Section 3.3a. That *S is culpable for X* is defining for this kind of anger is evident from the fact that a rational person experiencing this kind of anger ceases to be angry upon being convinced that the offender is not culpable for what she did or omitted. If someone continues to be angry at a person for an offense, after being convinced that the "offender" was guilty of neither malicious intention nor negligence in performing the offense, we regard the anger as irrational. The angry she-bear construes the intruder upon her domestic life in some terms analogous to offense, but has no access to the concept *culpable*, constituted, as it is, by complex conceptual links with other moral concepts such as *responsible* and *just*, all of which concepts are available only to language users. Thus her anger is not just limited in the objects to which it can be directed, as in the case of the dog's inability to fear a free-falling stock market; it is limited in its essence: The bear is incapable of this central *type* of human anger.

Let us turn to another context in which non-propositional emotions abound, that of human response to instrumental music.

g. Emotional Responses to Music

Emotions often figure in explanations of the power and importance of music.[45] Music is frequently said to express emotions, such as joy, sadness, and love, and it is also said to evoke emotions in listeners. Evocation of emotion by music is clearly different from expression of emotion in music. Music that sounds joyful (thus expressing joy) may on occasion cheer you up, but it may just as well evoke other emotions, such as annoyance (especially if it's not very good). Sad music is not so likely to make you sad, as it is to impress and delight you with its beauty; indeed, I doubt that sad music would ever make anyone, who did not already have something else to be sad about, sad. Angry music, like angry people, is sometimes amusing; and unlike angry people, it is seldom infuriating. Since my interest here is primarily the nature of emotions, and only secondarily the nature of music, I shall concentrate on emotions as evoked in human beings by music. Music can evoke emotions in a number of ways, only one of which is relevant to our present question about the role of propositions in emotions. Consider the following three:

Music may figure in an emotion-evoking situation. According to the film *Amadeus*, Mozart's music evoked envy in Antonio Salieri, and perhaps it evoked a counterpart invidious pride in Mozart, vis-à-vis Salieri. The sound of music coming, after midnight, from the room of his thirteen-year-old daughter can evoke anger in a father, no matter how lovely the music. In such cases the music is one item in a life situation, the concern-based construal of which is the emotion. Such emotions are of the standard types, and they are propositional in the ordinary ways.

An emotion may be based on a concern for music. You go to the concert hall with high expectations of an excellent evening of classic guitar, and the performance is mediocre because the famous player is half drunk. You are disappointed about the music, or perhaps angry. Or, dragged by your friends, you go to hear this same player, expecting a soggy performance, and are pleasantly surprised that he is sober tonight and plays very well. Your disappointment or pleasant surprise about the music presuppose the possibility

[45] For a survey and ruthless critique of the theories, see Malcolm Budd, *Music and the Emotions: The Philosophical Theories* (London: Routledge and Kegan Paul, 1985).

of the more direct responses to the music that people have in mind when they speak about the emotions in which the importance and power of music reside. Your disappointment, anger, or pleasant surprise are based on your concern to experience some of these fundamentally musical emotions. The disappointment, and so on, are straightforward examples of propositional concern-based construals.

Music may be associated with an emotion-evoking situation or something one cares about. If you were fifteen in 1957, the strains of "Heartbreak Hotel" from your car radio in 2003 may bring on a rush of nostalgia; at the sound of "The Stars and Stripes Forever," the hearts of many an American swell with patriotic pride. Here the music serves to trigger thoughts or images of the good old days or the fatherland, and these thoughts are no doubt colored by the music and the music by the thoughts. The character of the music (that it is this particular melodic, harmonic, and rhythmic configuration, with its particular auditory effects), being a term of the construal, is more intrinsic to the emotion in these cases than in the earlier examples; but still the emotion is less about the music itself in its musical character than about the situation with which the music is associated.

Emotions evoked in these three ways by music may belong to virtually any of the standard emotion types: hope, resentment, gratitude, indignation, regret, and so forth. Notice that in the first two kinds of case the emotions are naturally connected to music using the prepositions that standardly connect emotions to the situations they are construals of: Salieri is envious *of* Mozart's music; the father is angry *about* his daughter's music; you are disappointed *in* the performance; but as we will see, the musical emotions proper are not naturally connected to music using such prepositions. When people speak of the emotions whose evocation by music explains the power and importance of music, they do not have anything like such examples in mind, but rather the emotions *directly* evoked by music as *music*, emotions whose primary or only content is purely musical sounds. To examine these, we do best to work with pieces that have no text and no strong associations with extra-musical situations (for example, tone poems).

h. Music as a Cause of Mood

One way music affects us emotionally is by causing moods. Two pieces that I find particularly affecting in this way are Samuel Barber's Adagio for Strings and the second movement of J. S. Bach's second Brandenburg Concerto. Each of these pieces expresses a mood – in the first case (as I hear it) serenity or calm; in the second, cheerfulness. We are not interested here in what the music expresses, as such, but rather its effect on the listener; but it seems to me that the effect in these cases tends to parallel the expressed mood.

I used to listen to the Brandenburg Concerti when driving, and I re-member that the movement in question would sometimes put me almost into a "high," a sort of ecstatic cheerfulness. This mood interacted with my emotions in the standard way (see Section 2.5d): If I was already in some positive state of emotion, such as joy, gratitude, or hopefulness, that state would tend to be enhanced by the mood in the sense that I would feel the emotion more intensely. If I was feeling some negative emotion, such as anger, regret, or sadness, then either the mood would take the edge off the feeling of the negative emotion or the negative emotion would prevent the mood from coming over me. But this does not always work. As I listened to the movement again just now, so as to write this paragraph, it happened that I was sad and apprehensive because of some news in a letter from a family member that I had received earlier in the afternoon. The music did not detectably lighten the sadness, though I had no trouble at all hearing the cheerfulness expressed in the music.

Instrumental music, simply in its character as music, does not elicit any paradigm emotion – say, joy, gratitude, relief, or hopefulness – except indirectly, via the mood that it elicits, because it is incapable of presenting anything (see E3 in Section 2.1) to be joyful, grateful, relieved, or hopeful *about* (excluding the modes of presentation reviewed in the previous subsection). This point can be brought out by comparing an instrumental musical performance with a stage presentation or piece of literature. Because these other art forms present situations of human life that impinge on our concerns, with all their propositionality in all the three senses that I delineated in Section 2.5b, the art form can quite directly elicit joy, relief, hope, and many other paradigm emotions, and these emotions are easily and confidently identified by their subject, by his knowing how he is viewing the depicted situation under the influence of the concerns he has about it (see Section 2.4j).

The Barber Adagio sometimes puts me in a mood that I might call calm serenity. The mood of calm could fit, and thus enhance, several paradigm human emotions, such as quiet regret, calm sadness, [46] or poignant nostalgia. Since the music does not and cannot present anything for us to regret or be sad or nostalgic about (except in the senses identified in the previous subsection), it does not determine any such emotion on its own. If it is to contribute to some real emotion, the emotion's identifying content (what it is about) must be supplied from elsewhere – perhaps by a movie to which the music plays background, or by the personal history of the individual listener.

I have been thinking globally about the Bach movement and the Barber Adagio, in terms of the overall impression the pieces make; and I have contrasted them, in their emotional power, with discursive works like

---

[46] Again, it seems to me that the mood of the music is more likely to contribute to the calmness of the regret or sadness than to the negative character of the emotion. I offer a speculative explanation of this supposed fact toward the end of Section 2.5j.

plays and novels. But musical works (including the ones I just mentioned) do have a quasi-narrative character: They contain what musicians call "ideas" or "themes," which undergo "development"; these themes are "stated" in "phrases," which have definite beginnings and ends. When written music is performed ("read"), something like the syntax of the phrases needs to be respected; performers who do not get this right are as immediately recognized as are oral readers of texts who read badly. The conclusion of many pieces is more than just the end; it is a kind of consummation. No stage presentation would be appreciated for its emotional impact if we looked only at the overall impression it makes. Our experience in the theater is one of emotional ups and downs – of anxieties and joys, of terror and relief, of anger and forgiveness. So perhaps we can find in our responses to music something closer to the paradigm case emotions if we look inside a couple of pieces, following our responses to the various things that happen as they are performed.

i. Some Narrative Auditions

Let me give you an emotional self-report on some keyboard pieces. As I describe the pieces and my response to them, I will place the emotion terms (including some terms describing the music that correlate with the emotional responses) in small capitals for easy identification. The first is the C Minor Fugue in J. S. Bach's *Well-Tempered Clavier*.

The fugal subject DELIGHTS me. It is sprightly, in a quiet sort of way, but that is not a sufficient explanation of why or how it delights me (other melodies that are sprightly in a quiet sort of way don't delight me as this one does). It delights me because of its *character* – because of the particular series of notes and their time values that constitute it, because of anticipating how it will be deployed in the rest of the piece (I have heard the whole piece before), and because of the finesse with which it is executed (I am listening to the London compact disc recorded by Andras Schiff). The best way to indicate what delights me about the subject is to play it for you. I can tell no *story* about this delight, analogous to the one I might tell in explaining how I felt about being admitted to Yale many years ago. The latter story goes something like this: I wanted badly to study at Yale because ..., and then the news came that I was accepted. I can hardly imagine trying to convey the Yale delight to you without using words, but here the *best* I can do is done without words, by presenting the subject in performance.

In the third measure the subject is reintroduced, slightly modified, in G Minor, against a descending scale that recurs throughout the piece. At this point the delight shifts to EXCITEMENT, but it is a DELIGHTED EXCITEMENT (not, for example, a nervous or angry excitement). The occurrence of the subject against the second voice (and elsewhere against both the second and third voices) produces HARMONIC PLEASURES, not the least of which result from some IMPRESSIVE and BEAUTIFUL dissonances. Throughout the piece the subject recurs, in various keys and registers, typically against some variant of that descending scale. Each time it enters it delights, but in these instances the delight can be specified a bit more: Because each subsequent hearing of the subject is against the background of the previous statements of it, I now DELIGHT in the combination of variety and familiarity of this melody (every hearing of the subject after the first is obviously a construal). In the fifth and sixth measures a fragment of the subject is presented three times in stepwise ascending imitation, against an ascending scale in the second voice. This imitation is INTERESTING in itself and as reminiscent of the subject, but it also serves as a momentary respite from the full fugal subject, a respite that renders the subject's recurrence in C Minor in the bass, in the seventh measure, even more DELIGHTFUL. In measures thirteen and fourteen occurs a two-step imitation in a generally ascending scale. The first scale lands on the B flat two octaves above middle C, and the second scale lands on the C two octaves above middle C.

The high c gives me a feeling I might call UPLIFT, and this moment in the piece is ESPECIALLY EXCITING inasmuch as the next beat after the climactic high note begins the descending scale that typically accompanies the full fugal subject, which is here DRAMATICALLY introduced in G Minor high in the middle voice. Two measures later, Bach gives us again the fragment in imitation, now with the fragment in the base and the ascending scale in the middle voice, with just a piece of the fragment sounding a tenth above the base in the top voice. This figure is repeated in the next measure and a half a fifth lower but with the fragment in the middle voice and the ascending scale figure in the base. In these three measures, notes of the ascending scale produce six times a seventh or a ninth with a note from the subject fragment, with the notes struck together on a stressed beat. The DRAMA of the ascending imitation, the BEAUTIFUL counterpoint, and these STRIKING dissonances are very MOVING. I must keep my account brief, skipping over much of emotional power in this beautiful piece, but I would mention, finally, as especially STRIKING, the next to the last introduction of the subject, five measures from the end, in C Minor. Nowhere else in the Fugue does the subject occur in so low a register (here one octave below middle C), and this difference lends DRAMA to this moment.

The second piece is Frédéric Chopin's Nocturne in E Flat, Opus 9, Number 2. One would not, I think, call the theme of the C Minor Fugue gorgeous, though it is certainly delightful and EXQUISITE. The theme of the Nocturne, by contrast, is GORGEOUS and LUSCIOUS. These words convey nothing but the abstractest difference between the themes, and the only way really to "communicate" this difference is to present the two aurally in succession. The Chopin piece makes an entirely different EMOTIONAL IMPRESSION: It is "WARMER," more "PASSIONATE," more "LYRICAL." This impression is created by the melodic leaps (there are many sixths, octaves, and tenths), frequent seventh chords, chromaticism, strong dynamic variation, and lavish use of rubato. I found myself especially MOVED in measure two by the turn on C followed by an octave leap from which the melody then descends stepwise. The power of this measure to MOVE one is lent in significant part by the fact that it is an imitation of the first measure, with the principal notes after the first note a fourth higher. (Again we meet the phenomenon of construal: The second measure would make nothing like the same IMPRESSION were it not heard against the background of the first.) Another EMOTIONAL moment is the cadence of the theme in the fourth measure, which is very lyrical with its leap of a tenth and descent of a sixth in the context of the first sixteenth notes to occur in the piece, which give a bit of a SENSE OF RUSH. This four-measure theme occurs three more times, with different (and generally increasingly elaborate) ornamentation. The grace notes, the trills, and the increasingly chromatic and crowded cadences deepen, or at least maintain, the EMOTIONAL IMPRESSION. The Nocturne ends with a long and MOVING coda that employs a number of the DRAMATIC effects found in the body of the piece.

I would also mention a couple of "negative" emotions in response to passages in Chopin. The middle section of the Étude Number 3 in E Major grows in AGITATION culminating in measures 38–52, in which the sense of melody is virtually lost and the tritone (diminished fifth or augmented fourth) dominates both harmonically and melodically. Measures 38–41 consist in chromatically descending tritones in the left hand, against a jaggedly ascending figure of tritones in the right. So each sixteenth beat, executed at a fairly animated pace, consists in a diminished seventh chord tonally unrelated to its predecessor and/or successor. Another figure, found in measures 46–52, exploits the tritone melodically. Right and left hands execute oppositely undulating sixths and sevenths between which about half the melodic intervals are tritones. This passage not only sounds agitated (expresses agitation), but gives me a feeling of agitation. This impression is created by the tempo, the intervals, and the relative atonality of the passage, and it is enhanced by the contrast of this passage's character with the moderately slow and lyrical main theme of the piece, solidly in E Major. This agitation, like the feeling I get from passages in the Bach Fugue, is a kind of EXCITEMENT, but there is something tense, a little UNPLEASANT or UPSETTING, almost akin to ANXIETY, in this excitement, a kind of TENSION from which it is SWEET to get RELIEF; so it differs markedly from that other excitement.

In the second section of the Waltz in A Flat Major, Opus 69, Number 1, there is a two-measure melody that in itself is DELIGHTFUL if not profound, but it is immediately repeated twice verbatim (with only slight variation in the left hand) and then the whole eight-measure phrase is repeated verbatim, after which we get sixteen measures of different but related material, and then the whole 32-measure section is repeated again! My emotional response to this repetition is IMPATIENCE. Whereas I have no reason to doubt that Chopin intended the listener to feel agitated in the middle of the Étude (this response is integral to the overall logic of the piece), I don't think he intended us to feel impatient in the middle of the Waltz because this seems to indicate a defect in the music.[47] But this impatience is clearly an emotion, and it is clearly in direct response to the music as music (in contrast with the emotions discussed in Section 2.5g).

j. Musical Emotions and the Paradigm Cases

I shall now comment on similarities and differences between (a) the emotions I have noted in my responses to these pieces of music and (b) the paradigm emotions.

As I listened to these pieces, I felt some changes in my mid- section and on my skin analogous to ones that often accompany strong instances of the paradigm emotions (see E2 in Section 2.1). Also, I sometimes found myself moving my head or arms or fingers in a way that "followed" or "directed" the music. These particular movements are not characteristic of any of the standard emotions, but they are analogous to the muscular tensions, gestures, and facial expressions expressive of many emotions (see E8).

The musical emotions, like the standard ones, are in response to something we might call an "object" (E3). Just as the standard emotions are responses to situations with various features that are gathered together and read in a construal, so the musical emotions are responses to configurations of sound and rhythm, melodic, harmonic, contrapuntal, and so forth. In many cases of the most powerful emotional impressions, the phenomenon of construal is very clearly at work – for example, in the hearing of the fugal subject or the theme of the Nocturne or the various imitations. Within the themes of both pieces, imitation occurs, so that even intelligent hearing of the theme by itself depends on hearing parts of it in terms of what has gone before. Analogously to the differentiation of focus and background terms of construal in the standard emotions (E4), certain features of the music tend to stand out – in particular, the melodies and certain stressed notes in those melodies, which are then heard against the background of less salient features of the music that nevertheless contribute their essential function to the musical impression. The listener can shift focus and background to some extent at will, by focusing attention on a certain voice or chord progression

---

[47] Though it could indicate a defect in the listener, or perhaps even in the performer: If I were a more cultivated one, perhaps I would hear the sense or musical point in the repetition, and thus enjoy it; if the performer could vary the repeated phrase, or bring out the musical point in the repetition, the listener might enjoy it. But I doubt it, and I notice that Artur Rubenstein's recording of the Waltz omits the repetition of the 32-measure section.

or rhythmic pattern. The emotional impact of the music depends on the listener's success in construing the sounds at least approximately as they were intended to be construed by the composer and/or performer. This is because the music has "sense" analogous to the "sense" of the situations to which the paradigm emotions respond. A person's emotional sense of a situation may be a right or wrong reading of the situation; and, analogously, a person's emotional sense of a piece of music may be a right or wrong reading of the music; or, more likely, if one doesn't "follow" the music (i.e., construe it in a way that makes sense of it), one will not feel much emotional impact at all.

But the musical emotions seem to be somewhat more strictly tied to sense perception than the standard cases. In this respect, the musical emotions are more like the emotions of animals (Sections 2.5e and 2.5f). While human emotions are a kind of perception, they are pretty independent of the *sense* perception of their objects, and their objects have some aspects (say, culpability in the case of anger) that are not sense-perceptible at all. By contrast, the musical emotions are rarely experienced by people in whose ears music is not actually sounding; or if they are experienced (as a tune goes through one's head), it is usually in a degraded form. The exceptions would be among very talented and very musically cultured individuals who can "hear" complex musical configurations (counterpoint, harmony) in their imagination. Along with the independence of the standard emotions from sense experience goes the situational indeterminacy of the human emotions that I noted in Section 2.5f: Humans can hope for disasters, rejoice in their sufferings, hate their good fortune, and be angered by favors. Such indeterminacy is much less evident in the musical emotions: It is virtually impossible to hear the third occurrence of the theme in Chopin's Nocturne in the same way one hears the second introduction of the subject in Bach's Fugue; just as it is virtually impossible to construe the old woman/young woman figure as a bowl of flowers.

It follows that the musical emotions are varied. The feeling that I called "uplift" on that high C at the center of the Fugue is quite different from the feeling of delight that the opening subject gives one, and these both differ from the excitement of hearing the second statement of the subject, and all these are quite different from the feeling of the lyrical evoked by the theme of Chopin's Nocturne. It is decidedly not the case that there is an emotion that all music evokes.

The emotions of everyday life also show considerable variety, as reflected in the rather highly articulated vocabulary in which we distinguish *types* of emotion. In Chapter 3 we will see that the types are quite definite and can be explicated with some precision in terms of their defining propositions. Because we experience in the theatre the same types of emotion as in everyday life, a theatre-goer is emotionally articulate: "I was anxious about Helen at that point," "I so hoped they would get together in the end," "Didn't you just want to strangle the uncle?" and so on. By contrast, I found myself straining for words, sometimes desperately, to identify just what I was feeling at different junctures in my auditions. And the words I did come up with were either improvised and metaphoric, like "uplift" and "sense of rush," or rather generic, like "emotion," "delight," "excitement," "interest," "moved," "impression," "struck," and "agitated." Characterizations of the music itself were somewhat more definite, but not by much: "interesting," "warm," "sprightly," "lyrical," "dramatic," "delightful," "luscious," "gorgeous." We do not have a clear and firm conceptual framework for discussing the musical emotions. Instead, we have generic terms and more or less improvised metaphors.

The paradigm emotions can usually, with a little thought, be identified as to category (what kind of thing they are about and how, the defining proposition) and further identified as to their particular content (what they are about in particular, the material proposition). This type-individual distinction applies in the following way to the musical emotions: The "negative" feeling of agitation that one gets from passages like the middle of the Chopin Étude is obviously a different type of emotion than the delight one feels in the sprightly subject of the Bach Fugue. But the delight in the fugal subject is also rather different from the delight in the luscious lyrical passages of the Nocturne. Perhaps these two delights differ as hope and gratitude, among the paradigm emotions, differ from one another – both positively hedonically toned, yet with different kinds of objects. Within any of these categories of response, different emotions are still possible, just as anger differs from anger and hope from hope, depending on what one is angry about and whom at, or what one hopes for and on what grounds. Different sprightly figures might give one delights that are similar enough to count as belonging to one category of musical emotion, yet because they are responses to different particular musical phrases, they would also count as different particular emotions.

Does our poverty of vocabulary for these similarities and differences among musical emotions suggest that we should get busy and develop one, so as to be just as articulate about them as we are about our prides and resentments and hopes and regrets? I think not. The things the standard emotions are about – the ordinary situations of life – *lend themselves* to linguistic representation, so that propositions naturally structure the standard emotions, while it is unnatural to represent musical phrases linguistically. Or rather, we *can* represent them linguistically, but no such representation captures them for us as linguistic representations capture the ordinary circumstances of life. Novels can be as interesting and moving as life itself, or more so; but no collection of sentences about Barber's Adagio will do for us what the Adagio does.

The propositions that structure the paradigm emotions are propositions about what the emotions are about, and we have an analogous vocabulary for talking about the sounds that elicit the musical emotions. The vocabulary includes such words as "fugal subject," "measure," "ascending scale," "treble voice," "tritone," and the like. Notice two facts. First, propositions about the situational object of the standard emotions convey to us quite precisely the emotional state of the subject. Someone says, "It was terribly important that we quickly find a doctor knowledgeable about spinal injuries, and after several dead ends we got a phone call saying that an expert was on her way." From this bit of language about the situation of these people, as they saw it, we can judge with high confidence that they were hopeful, even if the word "hope" does not figure in the report. Second, where the listener to such a proposition shares the standpoint of the speaker, the proposition tends to elicit in the listener the same emotion as the speaker is expressing. A husband tells his wife, who has been out of touch, that their daughter has been missing for two days. The husband has only to depict the situational object of his emotion in this proposition, and the wife goes into the same emotional state. Neither of these observations is true of the speaker of the language about music.

My narrative auditions could no doubt be expressed more precisely by someone better trained in the vocabulary of musical objects. But I venture to say that even the most fluent speaker of this language would not be able, by describing melodic sequences of notes, chord progressions, rhythmic patterns, and so on, to convey to us what he felt when listening to the music, much less to make us (who, let us assume, share his standpoint in the sense that we are as sensitive to music as he is) feel the same emotions ourselves. You may be as moved by the sounds of Chopin's Nocturne as the narrator, but when he tells you the "story" about the Nocturne you are not in the least moved, even if you are a fluent user of this vocabulary. I propose that the explanation of these two facts is that propositions do not structure the musical emotions. That musical emotions are not structured by propositions is also indicated by the way we speak of them. We say, "I was delighted by the music" but not, "I was delighted *about* the music." We might say, "I felt relief when we got back to the sweet theme of the Étude," but not, "I felt relieved *that* we were back in the sweet theme of the Étude." We can, indeed, use "about" and "that" and other expressions introducing propositions and their stand-ins in describing emotions in response to music; but when we do, we are talking not about the distinctively musical emotions, but about standard emotions that involve music in some way (the father is angry about the music coming from his daughter's room; see Section 2.5g).

In a way, music evokes these emotions much as a cacophony causes irritation and a cool breeze on a summer day causes pellicular pleasure, or perhaps even as a cup of coffee can cause one's mood to brighten up. In each of these cases, too, we do not use certain prepositions – like "about," "at," and "of " – that are characteristic for the propositional emotions. We do not say we are irritated at or *about* the noise, but *by* it; we do not say we are pleased at or about the cool breeze, but that it delights or that we take pleasure in it; we do not say that we are feeling cheerful about the cup of coffee, but that it makes us feel more cheerful. These differences of linguistic expression mark differences between emotions proper and other hedonically toned states of mind. The prepositional phrases used in describing emotional states are shorthand for the propositions that structure the emotions. Thus to be afraid of the bear is to be in a state of mind structured by some proposition like *the bear is dangerous to me*; to be irritated about the noise is to be in a state of mind structured by *the noise is a nuisance or the noise is preventing my getting my work done*; to be pleased about the cool breeze is to be in a state of mind structured by *the cool breeze will be a good thing for us*, or some such proposition; to feel cheerful about the cup of coffee is to be in a state of mind structured by some such proposition as *it is good that we were able to get this Sudanese coffee for the occasion*. We might say that the nonpropositional forms of irritation, pleasure, and cheerfulness are caused without the immediate [48] intervention of thought, while the paradigm cases of human emotion are defined in terms of their constitutive thoughts.

In not being structured by propositions, the musical emotions are even farther from the paradigm cases than the animal emotions are. It is true that animal emotions are not typically structured *by* language, but they are ways of perceiving situations in the world that are analogous to the ways situations are perceived, with the refinements of language, by human beings. But in another way connected with language, the musical emotions are closer to the paradigm cases than most animal emotions are. I have noted that musical phrases are reminiscent of language. Like sentences, they come to completion (classically, in a cadence), and they have parts that correspond to clauses and words and syllables. We naturally speak of the content of musical phrases as "ideas." Like spoken sentences, phrases of music have stress points and often internal pauses corresponding to commas and semicolons. In natural speech, the human voice has a "musical" character, with stresses, rhythms, and changes of pitch. We follow music, understand it, hear one phrase in terms of another, and the like. In experiencing pleasure from a cool breeze, one may need to attend to the sensation just a little bit, but one does not need to "follow" the breeze as one needs to follow a musical phrase to appreciate it. The musical emotions, then, are peculiar in their intentionality: They are intelligent responses to sounds, even if the kind of sense they make of those sounds is not propositional, like the sense the paradigm emotions make of the situations of life. Our tendency to interpret our deeper experiences of music as emotions (despite

---

[48] Thoughts may have some more remote effects even here; for example, lots of propositional thoughts occur in the course of hearing a set of lectures on music appreciation, and these may enhance one's ability to experience musical emotions. That is why I insert the qualifier "immediate." For more on such remote causes of emotions, see Section 2.6.

the rather striking differences we have noted) is due in part to these similarities between music and the utterances that so often mediate the paradigm emotions.

My model for the paradigm emotions is that they are concern-based construals. We have seen that nonpropositional construals abound in our hearing of music; the musical emotions are perceptual (mostly sense-auditory) states in which notes are heard as having a distinctively musical kind of "meaning." What about the other part of the model? Are the musical emotions based on concerns? The concept of a concern does not throw much light on the musical emotions, but concerns do have an analog here. Music of one sort or another is attractive for the vast majority of human beings. We like it, or love it; we are attached to it. Some people like it more than others, and music loved by some people only irritates others. People respond with the distinctively musical emotions to the music they love; they respond with negative emotions, like annoyance and boredom, to music they do not love, especially if it is loud or persistent. In these respects, the love of music parallels other concerns, which also take the form of loves, likings, and attachments that vary considerably from person to person (see Section 2.7).

But the musical emotions are not *based on* concerns in the same way as the paradigm emotions. If I rejoice upon receiving an acceptance letter from a leading professional journal, it is because I care about or desire something rather particular: confirmation of the value of my work, a means of getting my work before a particular public, or increased luster of reputation. My construal of myself as having had a paper accepted becomes the emotion of joy as it impinges on some such concern. The same concern can be the basis of many different emotions, both negative and positive, depending on what construal impinges on it.

But my audition of the theme from the Chopin Nocturne does not become a delight in virtue of impinging in a particular way on some preexisting desire for a musical phrase of that kind. Rather, it delights me in virtue of a rather general susceptibility to music of certain kinds. The "concern" for the music (my liking of it, or attachment to it) does not seem to be separable from my delight in particular pieces, in the way that my desire for professional status is separable from disappointment or delight, as the case may be; rather, my "concern" for music seems simply to *consist in* my delighting in certain passages of music. When I feel the negative emotion of agitation in the middle of the Étude, it is not because the passage frustrates my love of music (as anxiety over a repeatedly rejected paper results from frustration of my concern to publish). It is rather that my auditory mind is just set up (through basic neurology and the influence of education) to respond with agitation to a rapid deployment of tonally unrelated diminished seventh chords. It seems to me that the response here is more like the tasting of sweet and sour upon putting sugar and lemon juice, respectively, on the taste buds of a neurologically normal person than it is like the satisfaction or frustration of a previously existing concern. The sweet is pleasant and the sour unpleasant; but the pleasantness of the sweet is not due to the satisfaction of a previously existing desire for sweets, and the unpleasantness of the sour is not due to a frustration of that same previously existing desire. We can speak of concerns here because there is a liking of sweet and a disliking of unmitigated sour. But the likes and the dislikes do not create the sensations; the character of the sensations constitutes the likes and dislikes. Having said that the musical emotions are more like responses to flavors than they are like the mental satisfactions of previously existing concerns, we must also remember our remarks about music's "syntactical" character and the listener's need to "follow" it intelligently; I am not saying that musical emotions are just unintelligent sensations.

I have said that I don't think people are made sad by sad instrumental music nearly as often as they are made cheerful by cheerful instrumental music. Why is this so? One possible answer is related to the remark I just made about the natural human love of music. Music does not get very far with us if it is not beautiful.[49] But if the music that moves us is nearly always beautiful, in addition to whatever mood it expresses, then its effect on us is always more likely, on the whole, to be agreeable or pleasant than it is to be disagreeable or unpleasant. As an agreeable state of mind, cheerfulness corresponds to the agreeableness of beauty, but sadness is disagreeable, and so it is counteracted to some extent by what is beautiful.

What shall we say, then? Are our experiences in response to music, excluding the kinds discussed in Section 2.5g, emotions? Or are they some other kind of experience? The question of what to call these experiences is not very interesting. More interesting is how these experiences are like and unlike the paradigm cases of emotions, and I have offered some answers to that question: Like the paradigm emotions, the musical sometimes involves physiological changes and characteristic gestures; they are hedonically toned, take objects, and are varied (different kinds of delight, agitation, sense of uplift, darkness, drama, etc.). But the distinctively musical emotions are not among the standard ones. Our vocabulary for the paradigm emotions is rich and definite; the vocabulary for the musical emotions tends to be generic or improvisatory. The musical emotions are more tied to sense experience and more determinate with respect to what evokes them than are the paradigm emotions. Whereas the standard emotions are reportable in language about their objects and evocable in the same language, the musical emotions are not; certain prepositions, such as "about," "at," and "of," are

---

[49] I know that some 20th century music attempts to be interesting rather than beautiful, but I think most people insist on beauty; few other than academic composers and theoreticians can be satisfied with being interested, or indeed can even *get* interested or stay interested very long in nonbeautiful music.

used in reports of the standard emotions but not of the musical. Musical emotions, unlike the standard ones, are caused by music without the intervention of linguistically renderable thoughts, yet music sounds like language in some ways. Just as the standard emotions are not just sensations, but intelligent responses to the situations of life, so the musical emotions are not just auditory sensations, but intelligent responses to sounds; but the kind of sense they make of those sounds is not, like the sense that the paradigm emotions make of the situations of life, propositional. The attractiveness of music to most human beings corresponds to the concerns on which the paradigm emotions are based, but the musical emotions are not based on this concern in the same way. Throughout the discussion I have referred to these experiences as emotions because that seems to be the drift of our ordinary thought and language about musical experiences. I see no reason to legislate against ordinary usage, and we have noted enough similarities between musical emotions and the paradigm cases to warrant it.

k. Conclusion

Our question has been about the role of propositional thought in emotion. I have suggested that the content of the standard or paradigm emotions is, in important part, propositional in three senses: In explaining our emotions we naturally identify them in propositions; they are often a response to propositions representing the situations they are about; and they are, in large part, ways of viewing those situations that are internally structured by propositional thought. I have not said that the content of the standard human emotions is entirely propositional. My basic paradigm is that emotions are a kind of perception, and perceptions in the relevant sense may, but need not, be propositional. The paradigm accommodates the emotions of nonlinguistic animals better than any theory that makes emotions strictly propositional. The emotions of animals lacking syntactic language are something like concern-based perceptions of the situations of their lives that are strongly analogous to those concern-based perceptual states in human beings that are significantly shaped by propositional thought. The emotions that humans experience in response to purely instrumental music likewise fit the model better than they fit proposition based theories, for the reasons I have detailed.

2.6. CAUSES

a. Introduction: Analytic and Exogenous Causes

The explanation of emotions is a ubiquitous activity of everyday life. Why is Jimmy depressed when everything seems to be going so well for him? Why does Dora feel guilty about taking a vacation (after all, she hasn't had one for five years)? Why did Beth fly into a rage just at that moment (Andy has often made similar remarks to her without getting a reaction like that!)? Such explanations figure in moral reasoning aimed at ascribing motives and assessing blame, in understanding actions and characters, and in ascribing traits to people.

On the view of emotions that I am proposing, many such explanations take the form of clarifying the internal structure of the construal that constitutes the emotion, either by highlighting the terms in which the subject is "seeing" the situation or by clarifying the nature of the subject's concerns. Jimmy is depressed, despite his present success, because he's been preoccupied with death ever since he began his meteoric rise in the world, and he does not care very much about success. Dora feels guilty about taking a vacation, even though one is long overdue, because she sees vacations as decadent and irresponsible behavior and is very concerned to be responsible in all she does. It is natural to call such explanations "reasons." The explanations given are Jimmy's and Dora's reasons for feeling the way they do. These ascriptions could be correct without being known by Jimmy or Dora. Perhaps they come to realize later how they were thinking about their situations, with the help of reflection or conversation with a friend or therapist, but at the time were unable to explain their own emotions. Or perhaps they never come to see the truth; still it may be the truth about their emotions. Our assumption is that, whether or not they were aware of it, the kind of thinking and caring that is ascribed to them in the explanation was actually characteristic of their construal of their situation; that is, they actually thought and cared in those ways, in the sense that this is how they were reading their situation.

The kind of explanation that appeals to internal features of the thing to be explained can be thought of as a kind of causal explanation, but it is a special kind that we might call "analytical." In explaining why I am currently seeing the young woman in the old woman/young woman figure, I may simply analyze my experience: I am seeing this little blotch as the nose, this line as the ear, and so on. It does make sense to say that I am seeing the young woman *because* I am allowing this to represent x and allowing that to represent y. So the seeing of this blotch as the nose can be said to be one of the causes of seeing the whole thing as a young woman. This kind of explanation differs from appeal to causes outside the thing to be explained, which we might call "exogenous." An exogenous cause of my seeing the young woman in the picture is my wife's teaching me how to do so in 1992. Another is those parts of my visual history that have made me able to recognize young women by sight. The causes appealed to in analytical causal explanation are definitive of the very thing they explain, while those appealed to in exogenous causal explanations are not: It is not definitive of my seeing the young woman in the figure that Elizabeth taught me to do it, even though I might not be able to do it now if she hadn't. While it is hard to imagine my being able to do it without having had a visual history that includes recognizing young women, nevertheless that history is not definitive of the experience. We might say that visual experiences of actual young women are *behind* my seeing of the young woman in the figure, but they are not *in* that seeing.

If we explain Beth's unusual rage at Andy by saying she hasn't slept well for the last three nights, or that it's just that time in her monthly cycle, or that she's been taking a medicine that makes her irritable, then we are offering exogenous causal explanations of her emotion. Such factors as fatigue or unusual chemicals in the bloodstream are not terms in which she sees Andy and the other features of the situation that her anger is about. They do not figure *in* her anger, though they certainly have their influence *on* how she sees her situation. Such explanations point to the fact that for all our emotions a background of normal neurochemical functioning is presupposed, without which we would not be able to construe the world as we do in our various emotional states. In references to menstrual cycles and sleeplessness the ordinary explainer touches crudely on this physical background.

Another kind of causal explanation, which may be either analytic or exogenous depending on how we conceive of it, is psychohistorical explanation. Traumatic incidents in one's past, even if not consciously remembered, may help to explain present fears; early childhood patterns of interaction with one's parents may throw light on one's reactions to social rejection or frustrated ambition. The incidents referred to in such explanations are ones to which an emotional response similar to the one to be explained was experienced; and the patterns referred to in such explanations are patterns of emotional interaction. If I'm edgy around the neighbors' friendly boxer because I was mauled by a pitbull when I was four, that memory, even if unconscious, might be a term of my present view of the boxer; perhaps I am in some sense seeing the friendly boxer *as*, or in light of, the remembered pitbull. On the other hand, maybe the causal mechanism makes the pitbull experience more external to the boxer experience than that: Perhaps the pitbull experience is followed closely by seeing other dogs in terms of the pitbull, but then a generalized perceptual set of dogs-as-hazardous sets in, and it is this set that determines my later view of the boxer, rather than directly the memory of the pitbull. The analytic reading of the pitbull's effect on my response to the boxer is more psychoanalytic, while the exogenous explanation of it (which makes it result from a kind of perceptual habit) is in a more cognitive-behavioral style. My own view of emotions as concern-based construals does not favor one or the other of these styles of psychohistorical explanation of emotions. My present concern is just to point out that we use both analytic and exogenous kinds of explanation of our emotions. It seems to me natural to reserve the word "reasons" for factors referred to in analytic explanations. For example, on the analytic interpretation of the pitbull experience, the person (after psychoanalysis has made the explanation available to him) might offer as a reason for his fear of the boxer that it looked like that pitbull. But on the cognitive-behavioral interpretation, the client would be more likely to say simply that the pitbull experience caused him to fear the boxer.

Environmental factors influence our emotions, and here again the status of the causes is subject to interpretation. A person's anxiety may be intensified by the anxiety of those around him; one's sense of the comical may be heightened by others' laughter; the anger of a crowd can be infectious; the weeping of others enhances one's grief. In each case the emotion of the others augments the appearance of whatever one is anxious, amused, or in grief about, yet without giving one any new *reasons* for the emotion in question. Irritating noise (vacuum cleaner, crying infants, people yelling at or interrupting one another, rock-and-roll music), physical overcrowding and restriction of movement, bodily discomforts such as being too hot or too cold, itching, clothes that are too tight, and the like, can augment anger without being what the anger is about. Or, contrariwise, beautiful surroundings, unusual comforts, and the friendliness and calm of one's associates can increase one's joy, gratitude, or hope without being what any such emotion is about. All these factors have their effect, it seems, by contributing to one's impression of the character of the situation.

Are such causes analytic or exogenous? They are analytic insofar as the causal factor becomes part of the very experience of the emotion: Clothes that are too tight become part of an overall impression of being offended against, which is central to the analysis of anger. Anxiety in the face and gestures of one's associates becomes an element in one's impression of being in a situation of threat, which is central to the analysis of anxiety. But such causes are likely often to be regarded, by rational people, as exogenous – that is, as merely causal influences – inasmuch as they do not constitute reasons that a person *would own* as reasons for his emotion. By its very nature, the analytic/exogenous distinction depends on a judgment about what is and is not internal to an emotion. People who insist on fairly high standards of rationality for their emotions will tend to keep the admissible content of their emotions fairly close to their propositional content and so will tend to see environmental factors that they cannot interpret in terms of that content as exogenous.

b. Causal Theories of Emotion

Hume's theory of the "indirect passions"[50] seems to run analytic and exogenous causal explanations together. One of his chief examples is the kind of

---

[50] *A Treatise of Human Nature*, Book II: *Of the Passions.*

pride one feels in being, or being closely related to, something excellent and admirable. He distinguishes the causes from the object of such pride. Consider his example of a man who feels pride in his beautiful house. Hume says that the cause of this emotion is the idea of this house as belonging to himself and as being beautiful. A sensation of pleasure accompanies the consideration of a beautiful house independently of whom it belongs to, but the idea of the house as belonging to him causes him to think of himself as admirable or praiseworthy too, and so his idea of himself gives him a sensation of pleasure corresponding to the one that the idea of the beautiful house gives off; and this pleasure in the idea of himself is pride. The idea of himself is the object of pride, Hume says.

To various requests for explanation of the man's state of mind, we can imagine various explanations being offered. Why is he feeling so good about himself? – He's thinking about his house. Why is he proud of his *house?* – It seems very beautiful to him. Why is he feeling so good about *this* beautiful house? – It's his very own. Why is he especially proud of his house *right now?* – Everybody's making so much fuss about it. Why is *he* proud of *his* house? – There aren't many people who own such a beautiful house. On one interpretation all these explanations are analytical. Even if some of them (say, the last two) seem to refer to events or states of affairs outside the man's mind, they in fact make reference only to his impressions and ideas: He feels proud because he *thinks* there are few people who own such a house; because he *notices* that people are making such a fuss over his house. The explanations do not refer to events outside the state of mind of pride that bring about the pride, but all just point out features of the construal that is pride.

This much Hume agrees with: The causal explanations are analytical of the man's mind. But Hume seems committed to denying that the explanations can be analytical of the man's emotion. The referents of the explanations of the emotion are mental entities other than the emotion – in particular, events (impressions and ideas) that precede the emotion, give rise to it, and in this sense explain it. In this sense, Hume's causal explanations are exogenous, and his language for causation suggests this interpretation: "reflective impressions . . . *proceed from* . . . original ones" (p. 275); an idea "*excites* the passion, connected with it" (p. 278), some qualities "*produc[e]* the sensation of pain and pleasure" (p. 285), "the present impression gives a vivacity to the fancy, and the relation *conveys* this vivacity, by an easy *transition,* to the related idea" (p. 290), "an association of ideas . . . is not alone sufficient to *give rise to* any passion" (p. 305; italics added throughout). A casual survey suggests that "produce" is the dominant word, with "excite" coming in second. On the other hand, Hume's analysis does purport to be analytical of the emotion: to tell us what emotions are like, and to tell us what fits an emotion for inclusion in a particular category, such as *pride* or *hatred.*

It does sometimes happen that a man *starts* thinking about his house, and that *leads* him to reflect how beautiful it is, and that *brings* him to think especially of its belonging to him, and this *results in* his thinking that he's a pretty important person. Sometimes it happens so, and sometimes not. Sometimes the emotion supervenes all of a sudden, without any such mental antecedents. But when such an exogenous causal sequence does occur, it does not define pride as an emotion; at most it *reflects* the structure of pride, and thus it offers *clues* as to what emotion the man is feeling. Pride as an emotion is defined, rather, by its defining proposition (see Section 2.5c), which contains, in a syntactically locked configuration, the various terms that shape or determine the construal. All of the material that Hume relegates to the supposed status of exogenous cause is in fact contained *in* the emotional state as a construal.

The idea of self, which Hume makes to be exogenously caused by the passion of pride, is just as much an analytical cause of pride as any of the other terms of the construal, and several of the other terms have every bit as much right to be called the objects of pride as the self. (One is proud of one's *house* because of its beauty, or proud of the *beauty* of one's house, just as one is proud to *be the owner* of this house.). It is true that the emotion of pride is defined in part by the reference to self, but self is not always the focus of pride (see Section 3.12). We have seen (Section 2.3c) how the focus of an emotion may shift among its terms. If I am feeling very proud of my daughter's piano performance, I *may* focus especially on MYSELF as the one whose status is enhanced by this beautiful child's wonderful playing. But the passion may remain pride at the same time as my focus shifts to HER or to THE PERFORMANCE (in such cases, my self as a term of the construal remains in force but recedes into the background, informing the construal of the focus). In extreme cases, pride can be almost self-forgetful in the intensity of the focus on what one is proud of.

In the preceding interpretation of Hume's theory, I have supposed that Hume posits, at least confusedly, a structure of analytical causes of pride such that pride is a complex though unified state of mind something like what I call a construal. My criticism has been that he tries to analyze such an internal structure by reference to a selected few of its supposed external causes. A rather different kind of causal theory is suggested by the comment with which Hume opens his discussion of pride and humility:

The passions of PRIDE and HUMILITY being simple and uniform impressions, 'tis impossible we can ever, by a multitude of words, give a just definition of them or indeed of any of the passions. The utmost we can pretend to is a description of them, by an enumeration of such circumstances, as attend them (p. 277).

And a little later he says:

The first idea, that is presented to the mind, is that of the cause or productive principle. This excites the passion, connected with it; and that passion, when excited, turns our view to another idea, which is that of self. Here then is a passion plac'd betwixt two ideas, of which the one produces it, and the other is produc'd by it (p. 278).

In the first quotation, Hume seems to say that the passions are unanalyzable in themselves because they lack aspects or parts in terms of which they might be described or analyzed. He may even be saying that, in themselves, pride and humility are indistinguishable. Given the simplicity and in-themselves indistinguishability of the passions, the only way they can be identified is in terms of their setting. In the present case the relevant setting is "betwixt two ideas, of which the one produces [the passion], and the other is produc'd by it." In a functionalist spirit we might call every emotion in itself X, and then say, When X is caused by the idea of a subject that is closely related to oneself and has an admirable quality, and causes the idea of oneself as being admirable, then the X is pride; when X is caused by the idea of a subject that is closely related to oneself and has a shameful quality, and causes the idea of oneself as being shameful, then the X is humility. This would be a forthrightly exogenous causal analysis, without the ambiguities and complications of the first view I have read into Hume, but it does not seem very promising as a theory of emotion, since emotions are neither logically simple nor indistinguishable in themselves, but have, despite their unitary character, the kind of complexity that any construal has and are distinguishable from one another in precisely those terms. Furthermore, analysis of the emotions can be carried out in terms of analytic causes, and it does not strictly require any reference to emotions' causal antecedents and consequences. (I admit, obviously, that the historical setting of an emotion – say, the events that provoked it and the actions that issued from it – often provides vital clues for deciding its correct analysis.)

Donald Davidson has written an updated version of Hume's causal theory of emotion that differs from both of the versions I have considered.[51] Davidson converts Hume's ideas into beliefs, drops out impressions altogether, and interprets the causal relations among ideas as relations of logical implication. Thus the causal sequence of pride in one's beautiful house is represented as a syllogism:

All owners of beautiful houses are, as owners of such, praiseworthy.
I am the owner of a beautiful house.
So I am, as the owner of a beautiful house, praiseworthy.[52]

---

[51] Donald Davidson, "Hume's Cognitive Theory of Pride" in *Essays on Actions and Events* (Oxford: Oxford University Press, 1980), pp. 277–290.

[52] Annette Baier has pointed out that as written, the syllogism is not valid; and that it is very difficult to figure out how to make it valid while preserving the needed notion, in the conclusion (the emotion) of *praiseworthy as...* "Hume's Theory of Pride," *The Journal of Philosophy* **22** (1979): 27–40.

The conclusion, according to Davidson, is the emotion of pride. Thus Davidson's interpretation of Hume belongs among the judgment theories, and so it is vulnerable to the criticisms raised against such theories in Sections 2.4d–2.4f. But one wonders what contribution is added, beyond the other versions of judgment theory, by including in the analysis the premises from which such a judgment *might* be derived. I italicize "might" because, psychologically, it does not seem plausible to suppose that people always derive their emotions from such premises. And does Davidson wish to suggest that, in cases where such a judgment just pops into someone's head without the aid of, say, the generalizing first premise, the judgment then does not constitute an emotion because the canonical causal sequence is missing? And the argument of the preceding paragraph seems to apply here, too: The judgment by itself (at least if put in sufficiently elaborate form) seems to contain all the conceptual content necessary for the emotion. The second premise adds nothing to that content, and the distinctive content of the first premise – the reference to "all owners" – does not seem to be required for pride. The premises do not seem to enrich, in any strictly required way, the judgment that Davidson identifies with the emotion.

Causal theorists who admit my distinction between analytic and exogenous causation of emotions will no doubt point to the special status of exogenous beliefs and desires as causes of emotions. Prior to plunking herself down on a Bahamian beach, where Dora starts feeling guilty about being there, she has, let us say, a general belief that vacationing is irresponsible behavior, which somehow[53] causes her to see her own vacation in this light. The prior belief and the present seeing in terms of the proposition

Vacationing is irresponsible behavior

are not the same mental states; so when the one causes the other, it does so exogenously. But the present seeing is so closely related, logically, to the prior belief that gives rise to it that we make no distinction between them when we say that Dora is feeling guilty because she thinks that vacationing is irresponsible behavior. It is as though that prior belief were an element in the emotion, and the distinction between analytic and exogenous causation disappears in the practice of such explanations. Perhaps this is so. My point is not to deny that emotions have exogenous causes, among which are prior beliefs and desires; it is to point out that the identity of an emotion is given *in* the emotion and does not depend logically on its causal history.

c. Construals as Causes?

A response sometimes made to my account of emotions is that while emotions clearly have something to do with construals, it is wrong to *identify* any

---

53 The causal mechanism does not seem to be inference in every case.

emotion with a construal. Dora's emotion of guilt is not her self-perception as having morally transgressed in going on vacation, but it is something else that is *caused* by seeing herself in this way.

Perhaps I can clarify my claim by acknowledging that an emotion may have all sorts of causally contributing mental antecedents, in the form of perceptions, judgments, desires, thoughts, and so on. Dora's episode of guilt-feeling may have been triggered by a mental image of her mother at work in the strawberry fields in the heat of the day, or by a passage in a book that she is reading while lying on the beach, or by the sight of a billboard advertising cigarettes by picturing a couple enjoying decadent leisure. Such thoughts and perceptions often are, or involve, construals, and these are to be counted among the causal antecedents of Dora's emotion. Or, to nod to Davidson, Dora's emotion may result from an inference:

People who lie on beaches are being unproductive.
I am lying on a beach, so I am being unproductive.
To be unproductive is to be decadent.
So I am being decadent.

Any of these mental events and countless others may be causal antecedents of Dora's emotion. But none of this goes to show that the sense of guilt itself is not a construal, different from any of its exogenous causes.

But let us suppose that Dora's emotion is not the concern-based construal of herself as having morally transgressed in going on vacation, but instead this construal is the cause of her emotion. What would the emotion then be? It cannot be the behavior that issues from her emotion, because whatever behavior the emotion may generate could be performed without the emotion. We might suppose that it is the autonomic arousal that goes with her episode of guilt (increased heart rate and blood pressure, muscle tension, perspiration, etc.). But even if all sense of guilt is accompanied by such arousal, the arousal cannot *be* the sense of guilt, because it does not have, in itself, the meaning that guilt has in itself, the meaning that is expressed in the propositional content of the sense of guilt. And William James's view, that the emotion is the *sensation* of those physical perturbations, is implausible for the same reason. Or perhaps it will be proposed that the sense of guilt is to be identified with the desire to confess and make atonement, this desire being caused by the construal that I identify with Dora's sense of guilt. But a desire to confess and make amends is not itself a sense of guilt, for a person might desire to confess and make amends without having any sense of guilt (she might desire this because she desires to keep her puritanical mother from disowning her). My argument is not conclusive because there may be something else, which I haven't thought of, to identify the emotion with that can be thought to be caused by the construal that I identify as the emotion. But I think the burden of proof is on the challenger who says that an emotion is an effect of its characteristic construal, and not the construal itself, to identify this effect.

I have not denied, but strongly affirmed, that emotions have exogenous causes, some of which are "intentional" (beliefs, thoughts, perceptions, desires) and others not (brain structure, neurochemical conditions). One such cause, to which I have referred repeatedly in these pages without yet clarifying very much, is the concerns on which the construals that are emotions are based.

2.7. CONCERNS

a. Introduction

Allan Gibbard puzzles over the fact that

what shames one person leaves another untouched. One person might be ashamed of his shabby clothes, while for me, say, shabby clothes matter not at all. Must we have different beliefs about clothes? ... Each of us might well know his clothes are shabby, and each of us might have like beliefs about what sorts of people have shabby clothes and who will disdain us for it and who will not. Our difference seems to be just that he finds shabby clothes shameful and I do not – and it is not clear what that amounts to apart from the fact that he feels ashamed of it and I do not.[54]

On the account of emotions as concern-based construals, a natural answer to the puzzle is that the one person is *concerned* about his clothes in a way that the other is not – say, concerned to make a good impression on social equals by way of his clothes. If this is a difference in beliefs, we might characterize it by saying that the one person believes something to be *important* that the other does not. But this formula does not capture the difference, either, because two persons might be equally convinced that *it is important to make a good impression on social equals by way of one's clothes,* and agree on the reasons for this belief, yet differ emotionally in the way Gibbard describes. The difference between them is that in the one person a concern to make a good impression, corresponding to the evaluative belief, is taken up in his construal of his clothes and social situation, thus making his experience of the situation quite different from that of someone who lacks that concern, or in whose construal that concern is not taken up. Furthermore, a person might sincerely state, and even have excellent arguments on hand, that it is *not* very important to make a good impression on social equals by way of his clothes and yet be concerned to make a good impression this way, with all the emotional consequences. But though a

---

54 *Wise Choices, Apt Feelings*, p.137. In a footnote, Gibbard appears to move in the direction of the explanation that I elaborate in this section.

concern for X is not the same as a belief that X is important, most concerns for X are supported by and support, in rational people, beliefs that X is important.

Gibbard's observation suggests that differences of emotional response mark differences of personality or character; and his question is about how to explain such markings. Reference to concerns is an explanation of the differences, and not just another and redundant way of saying that people differ in emotional response; to explain an emotion by reference to a concern is to make the concern a principle of prediction of a range of widely various emotional responses. The concern to make a good impression on social equals by means of one's clothes could be the basis of pride for someone who construes his clothes as favorably impressing his social equals, or of hope if he sees this eventuality as having good prospects, or of anxiety if it looks to him as though the prospects are in jeopardy; and someone who lacked this concern can be predicted to be analogously untouched. A personality is an exceedingly complicated configuration of concerns, beliefs, powers of self-understanding and self-management, repertoire of construal dispositions, and so forth. All these factors are relevant to the question when and why a person responds with a given emotion, so reference to concerns in particular yields only a rough and informal principle of prediction. Nevertheless, concerns are central to personality and to the explanation of emotions, and they will figure prominently in the analysis of virtues that I will present in Volume 2 of this work.

b. Kinds of Concerns

I use "concern" to denote desires and aversions, along with the attachments and interests from which many of our desires and aversions derive. Concerns can be biological ("instinctive") or learned, general or specific, ultimate or derivative, and dispositional or occurrent. The aversion to bodily damage and death is presumably biological and thus virtually universal, as is a concern to be estimable, though no doubt the *meaning* of bodily damage, death, and the esteem of one's fellows is culturally variable; by contrast, the concerns to avoid cancer and to be esteemed for one's philosophical works are culture-relative and learned. A concern to be a success in business is general, compared with the specificity of a concern to succeed in a particular business deal. My attachment to my daughter may be ultimate in that it can be given as a reason for other concerns, while no other can be given as a reason for it. Concerns for which it can be given as a reason (e.g., a desire to have the house fire-safe) are derivative from it, but it derives from no other concern, not even from a concern for my own happiness, if I am willing to give it up for her sake. If I am concerned to have the house fire-safe without having it actively in mind, my concern is dispositional; if I have it in mind, it is occurrent. (Concerns can be occurrent without being conscious, however, in which case their active operation is inferred on the basis of linguistic and other behavioral evidence.) Concerns from all the above categories can ground emotions. But some dispositional concerns are so deeply covered up as to be inaccessible, and thus emotions will not be constructed on their basis unless the covering is broken through (see the discussion of François Mauriac's *The Viper's Tangle* in Section 4.6).

The word "concern" captures better what I want to get at here than do alternatives like "desire" or "wish." Certainly, many of the concerns on which emotions are based are desires. If I am training hard with the aim of winning an upcoming foot race, my concern to win it is a desire. At some moments in my day the desire will be occurrent (I'll be thinking about winning it), and at other moments it will be merely dispositional (though I am not currently attending to the goal, my state will be such that I will start occurrently wanting to win it immediately upon beginning to think about it). If, then, I do poorly in the race, I experience an emotion (disappointment) that is based on my desire to win the race. Whether occurrent or dispositional, the desire is quite definitely focused on a goal: winning the race. R. S. Lazarus tends to see emotions as based on desires, or what he calls "goal commitments."

There would be no emotion if people did not arrive on the scene of an encounter with a desire, want, wish, need, or goal commitment that could be advanced or thwarted. The stronger or more important the goal, the more intense is the emotion, other things being equal. ... to understand a person's emotional response fully it would seem important to know which narrow goals people think are at stake in an encounter (horizontal) and how they think these are related to more global goals within the goal hierarchy (vertical).[55]

But many emotions are based, not on goal commitments, but on personal attachments or carings. The answer to the question, "Why do you feel so *E*?" is often not, "Because I want G," but "Because I care about her (him, it)" or "Because it means so much to me." My attachment to my daughter or to my own health is not a desire or wish. One can of course say that I wish to be healthy and that I wish my daughter to thrive, but these "wishes" have only the most diffuse goals, and it seems to me that the correct reading of this use of "wish" is: I *would* have wishes about her health *if* it were seriously called into question. In any case, my attachment to my daughter is not identical with my having any particular goal or set of goals with respect to her. So I prefer not to call such attachments wishes, but instead to call them concerns and to allow that, via emotions, these concerns that are not desires may issue in desires: If my daughter is threatened, then in my fear for her (based on my attachment to her) I begin to desire

---

[55] *Emotion and Adaptation* (New York: Oxford University Press, 1991), pp.94, 95.

her safety; if I go for a medical check-up, then in my anxiety (based on my concern for my health) I want the doctor to give me a clean bill of health.

The last examples call for a distinction between the concerns on which an emotion is based and the concerns generated by or in an emotion – that is, between *basic* concerns and *consequent* concerns. Returning to an earlier example, let us say that my daughter is in her upstairs room and I realize that the house is on fire. I am stricken with intense fear for her safety. My fear is based on my concern for her – my attachment to her, my love for her. It explains my fear: She *whom I love* is endangered. Thus the character of the construal is affected by my concern; I do not react with the same emotion if, say, all that is at stake is the house and its contents, even though other elements of the construal are quite similar: I construe the house as just about to be destroyed by fire. So, prior to the construal, as a feature of my personality, is my concern for (attachment to) my daughter; at this point it is dispositional and is not doing any particular work. Then I see the fire and realize that Beth is in the house, and my concern for her is taken up into the construal of the situation in such a way that the construal is intense fear. Before the onset of the emotion, the concern was dormant or dispositional; in the emotion it becomes active; the concern is there *in the form of* the emotion. The emotion is not the same as my love for Beth; it is an effect of it. But an aspect of the emotion (or perhaps a consequence of it) is a fairly definite, focused goal orientation (desire), namely the desire to get Beth to safety. This I call the consequent concern. Many emotions have consequent concerns that are determined in the type of object the concerns take by the nature of the emotion in question. Envy, for example, involves a consequent concern that one's rival be "put down," anger involves a concern that the offender be punished, and gratitude involves a concern to return a favor to one's benefactor. Not all emotions have consequent concerns.

Another distinction, which will come in handy later, is that between bipolar concerns, like the ones we have been discussing, and unipolar concerns. Desires and attachments are bipolar in the sense that if someone desires that p, then he is necessarily averse to not-p. It is because bipolar concerns have this characteristic that they can ground both positive and negative emotions. Some emotion types (if one wants so to class them), such as amusement (at comical representations) and surprise, are not based on bipolar concerns but involve, in a somewhat different way from the based-on relation, *interests*. Interests seem to be a kind of concern, but they may lack bipolarity. For example, some people find basketball games interesting enough to give them surprises and perhaps amuse them, without caring which way the game goes. Thus they do not experience the joys and disappointments typical of the true fan. For the applications of this distinction, see the discussions of surprise and amusement in Sections 3.16a and 3.16b.

c. "Based On," "Taken Up In"

At the end of Section 2.6 I said that (basic) concerns are exogenous causes of emotions – that is, causes that are not parts or aspects of the emotions they cause, but outside them. But the metaphors in which I describe the relation between such causes and the emotions to which they contribute causally suggest that the basic concern is not really, or not wholly, outside the emotion it causes. The word "basic" might suggest a base (like that of a lamp) or a foundation (say, of a house), both of which seem to be part of the things they are bases of. And when I say that the basic concern is "taken up in" the emotion that is based on it, again I seem to be saying that the concern is an element of the emotion.

In the previous subsection, I have already begun to suggest that I want to have it both ways. The basic concern is an exogenous cause of the emotion, and yet in some sense it also becomes an element of the emotion, though in a different form. At various points in this book I have suggested that the basic concern becomes a "term" of the construal, along with aspects of the situation as the emotion pictures it. This notion of *becoming a term* should help to explain how I can have it both ways. Imagine the old woman/young woman figure drawn as in Section 2.3b with one exception: The little blotch that constitutes the young woman's nose is missing. This image is being projected on a screen by a computer that is capable of adding the blotch. You watch the screen and see the old woman in the figure, but are unable to see the young woman. Then the projectionist adds the blotch, and suddenly the whole image of the young woman comes together for you. The blotch is an exogenous cause of your seeing the young woman insofar as it comes from outside the figure to be added in, and insofar as, considered by itself, it is not a nose. The blotch becomes a nose (this particular nose, pointing away as it does from the viewer) only by being placed in a certain setting in the drawing, by its playing a role in the whole. And by appearing on the scene, it changes the whole, giving rise to the image of the young woman. But once it is in the figure and is playing its crucial role, then it is an analytic cause of the construal; it is "taken up" in the image.

In a similar way, the concern basic to an emotion has a dual aspect: Prior to its role in the construal, it is a different concern from the one it becomes once the construal impinges on it and takes it up. In this sense it comes from outside the emotion, and is not in itself a basis of intense fear. But once it is integrated into the construal of *Beth as in danger of burning*, it becomes an integral or analytic cause of the emotion: The construal is now of *Beth* WHOM I LOVE *as in danger of burning.* Thus it is a different concern, yet it is the same concern, just as the blotch constituting the nose is both the same and different when constituting the nose and when not.

d. Worries About the Concept of a Concern

Emotions are distinguished from other construals, on the account offered in this book, by being based on concerns in the way I have just described. If my analysis is to be explanatory or enlightening, concerns must be something other than emotions, but some[56] have worried that concerns are themselves emotions. In this subsection I address this worry by distinguishing emotions from concerns.

Let me begin with a linguistic point. The range of things that I take to be the paradigm cases of emotions (and I hope to be following ordinary English usage in this) have names that divide them into categories: "hope," "envy," "resentment," "nostalgia," "regret," and so forth. I have already suggested (Section 2.5c) that these classes of emotion are defined by their defining propositions, and I will explore this proposal in greater detail in Chapter 3. If we are told, for example, that somebody is in a state of regret, we know a great deal about his emotion without being told *what* he regrets because we know what the defining proposition for regret is. (I am not saying that just any of us can *formulate* it with precision, but even the most unlettered know that a person who is in a state of regret is looking to some event or omission of his past, that he takes this to be a bad thing, that he thinks of it in terms of better alternatives, that he would, if he could, change the past in respect of what he regrets, and so forth.) But the words for concerns, such as "interest," "enthusiasm," "desire," "wish," "attachment," and "caring," do not define categories of concerns in the same way and thus do not carry much internal information beyond the fact that the subject of the concern somehow positively values what he is concerned about. If we wish to identify a concern more particularly, we get little help from our concern vocabulary and must be told what the concern is about. Thus it is far less informative to say "Bob is experiencing desire" than it is to say "Bob is angry." In fact, nobody would say it, but would instead say, "Bob wants a piece of inner tube" or "Bob wants more attention from his mother." In general, concern language is empty without reference to the objects of the concerns.

But why might one think that concerns are emotions? One reason could be that some emotions contain or beget concerns – what I have called the consequent concern – and a theorist might think that this concern is the very center or essence of the emotion. Aristotle, for example, defines anger as a desire (ὄρεξις) for conspicuous revenge (*Rhetoric* 1378a30); and in a somewhat similar way, Nico Frijda defines emotions as tendencies to act. I will offer criticisms of Frijda's proposal in Section 2.9e.

Another possible reason for thinking that emotions are concerns is that some words that refer to emotions may also refer to concerns. The premier

---

[56] In particular, Steve Evans and Linda Zagzebski, whom I thank for discussions of this matter.

examples are "love" and "hate" and "concern" itself. "Love" sometimes refers
to an emotion, and sometimes to a concern, and when love is an emotion
it seems to deviate somewhat from the model I am offering in this book
(see Section 3.15). But it does not follow from the fact that the same term
can refer both to emotions and to concerns that emotions do not differ
from concerns. "Concern," too, is sometimes a synonym for emotion words
such as "worry," "anxiety," and "fear"; but this does not show that what I
am calling concerns are emotions. Note that in the noun form, when used
for an emotion, "concern" does not take an article, while when used for
a concern, it does; for example, "we were wracked with concern for those
who were traveling in the ice storm," but "we have a concern for public
safety."

Another worry stems from the fact that some desires are concern-based
construals; if so, how do these concerns differ from emotions? Take, for
example, my concern to get a piece of inner tube to make myself a slingshot.
Because I have no desire for a piece of inner tube other than as a slingshot
part, my desire is clearly a case of wanting-as: I want the piece of inner tube
as a slingshot part. Furthermore, my desire for the inner tube is *based on*
my desire to make a slingshot. Thus the desire is a concern-based construal.
Why, on my account, does this desire not count (counterintuitively) as an
emotion? The answer lies in the perceptual character of emotions that I
have been stressing throughout this chapter. John Searle distinguishes the
intentionality of desires from that of perceptions (and beliefs) in terms of
the "direction of fit" that the mental states bear to the world.[57] Perceptions
have mind-to-world direction of fit; for example, one's perception of a yellow
station wagon before one is veridical only if there is a yellow station wagon
before one (that is, the mental state conforms to the world). But desires
have world-to-mind direction of fit; my desire for a piece of inner tube
is satisfied only if I acquire an appropriate piece of inner tube (that is,
the world conforms to my mental state). It seems clear that emotions have
mind-to-world direction of fit. In anger one has a perception[58] of a culpable
injustice, in fear a perception of a threat, in compassion a perception of a
sufferer; in each case, as I have pointed out, the perception is also of some
kind of importance or worthiness that is lent the object by the concern on
which the emotion is based. In emotions, as in sense perceptions, qualities
are attributed to "the world," qualities that the world may or may not have.
And it is largely in virtue of these attributions that we judge emotions to be
appropriate or inappropriate. Emotions can succeed in fitting the world, or
fail to fit it, in much the way that visual and auditory experiences can. So

---

[57] See his *Intentionality: An Essay in the Philosophy of Mind* (Cambridge: Cambridge University
Press, 1983). The notion of direction of fit goes back to Elizabeth Anscombe's *Intention*
(Oxford: Blackwell, 1957).

[58] In the sense expounded in Section 2.3.

while it is true that many desires are concern-based construals, they are not the kind of construals that emotions are.

I have noted that for every concern there is a range of possible emotions that may be based on it, depending on the construal that impinges on the concern or takes it up into itself. Among this range are mutually contrary emotions such as joy and sadness, hope and regret, and so on. I have also noted that emotions give rise to concerns, namely the ones that I call consequent concerns. But the way emotions give rise to concerns differs from the way concerns give rise to emotions. The consequent concerns of an emotion like anger or fear are all of a particular type dictated by the structure of the emotion – a desire for punishment in the case of anger, a desire to avoid a threat in the case of fear, and so on – not of a variety of contrary types, as are the emotions that arise out of a concern. Thus anger gives rise to or involves the concern to punish the offender, but it does not equally give rise to the concern to give the offender pleasure.

An emotion can in a sense be based on another emotion, but it is based on the consequent concern of the first emotion. For example, a person might take joy in getting revenge on a person he was angry with, or might feel relief upon escaping a danger that he feared. Both emotions and desires can also be the objects of both emotions and desires. Thus one can fear getting angry; one can regret one's desire for fame; one can desire to feel more joy in one's brother-in-law's successes; one can desire to desire money less. But these relations of mental state to mental state as object differ from the based-on relation that holds between the paradigm emotions and their basic concerns.

e. A Neurological Basis for Concerns?

Antonio Damasio reports[59] that patients with damage to the ventro-medial sector of both frontal lobes of their brains consistently show a dual loss. On the one hand, they do not experience emotions, except fleetingly and in response to immediate stimuli; on the other hand, their capacity to make practically rational decisions and take actions that foster their well being is deeply impaired. Yet if the brain damage is limited to just this area, they show no loss of *intellectual* functioning. The coincidence of just these two losses, along with their independence of intellectual functioning, seem to me to be further confirmation of my proposal to consider concerns a distinct phenomenon and one basic to emotions.

Damasio gives an extended account of one patient, whom he calls "Elliot":

Consider the beginning of his day: He needed prompting to get started in the morning and prepare to go to work. Once at work he was unable to manage his time

59 *Descartes' Error.*

properly; he could not be trusted with a schedule. When the job called for interrupting an activity and turning to another, he might persist nonetheless, seemingly
losing sight of his main goal. Or he might interrupt the activity he had engaged, to
turn to something he found more captivating at that particular moment. Imagine a
task involving reading and classifying documents of a given client. Elliot would read
and fully understand the significance of the material, and he certainly knew how to
sort out the documents according to the similarity or disparity of their content. The
problem was that he was likely, all of a sudden, to turn from the sorting task he had
initiated to reading one of those papers, carefully and intelligently, and to spend an
entire day doing so. Or he might spend a whole afternoon deliberating on which
principle of categorization should be applied: Should it be date, size of document,
pertinence to the case, or another? The flow of work was stopped. One might say
that the particular step of the task at which Elliot balked was actually being carried
out too well, and at the expense of the overall purpose. One might say that Elliot
had become irrational concerning the larger frame of behavior, which pertained to
his main priority, while within the smaller frames of behavior, which pertained to
subsidiary tasks, his actions were unnecessarily detailed. His knowledge base seemed
to survive, and he could perform many separate actions as well as before. But he
could not be counted on to perform an appropriate action when it was expected
(pp. 36–37).

Along with the inability to make moment-by-moment rational choices, he
was deeply deprived of emotional responsiveness:

Elliot was able to recount the tragedy of his life with a detachment that was out of
step with the magnitude of the events . . . , always describing scenes as a dispassionate,
uninvolved spectator. Nowhere was there a sense of his own suffering, even though
he was the protagonist. . . . Elliot was exerting no restraint whatsoever on his affect.
He was calm. He was relaxed. His narratives flowed effortlessly. . . . I never saw a tinge
of emotion in my many hours of conversation with him: no sadness, no impatience,
no frustration with my incessant and repetitious questioning. . . . He tended not to
display anger, and on the rare occasions when he did, the outburst was swift; in no
time he would be his usual new self, calm and without grudges (pp. 44–45).

On the other hand, he showed normal on a number of tests: His IQ
was in the superior range, as was his immediate memory for digits, words,
and geometric designs. His language production and comprehension tested
normal.

In short, perceptual ability, past memory, short-term memory, new learning, language, and the ability to do arithmetic were intact. Attention, the ability to focus on
a particular mental content to the exclusion of others, was also intact; and so was
working memory, which is the ability to hold information in mind over a period of
many seconds and to operate on it mentally (p. 41).

Elliot was normal in his ability to make estimates on the basis of incom-
plete knowledge. The Minnesota Multiphasic Personality Inventory rated
him normal. He showed normal in his ability to solve investment problems.
He performed well on a social problem-solving test: A man has just broken

his wife's favorite flower pot; what does he do to avoid her anger? He scored normal or superior on tests for the abilities to anticipate the consequences of actions, identify actions that lead to a given outcome, and predict the social consequences of events. Elliot scored stage 4/5 on the Kohlberg moral reasoning scale.

Consider how the notion of a concern, and of emotions as concern-based construals, might explain Elliot's configuration of abilities and disabilities. His poor performance in staying on task is not due to a lack of attention, memory, or understanding of the task, but it might well be explained by a lack of ongoing concern to complete it. A normal person in Elliot's job and possessing Elliot's understanding of the task will, at each separate stage of the task, be concerned to complete it. This "larger," "framing" concern will transcend and organize the particular episodic desires that arise in the course of the task – a desire to get started, a desire to settle on a principle of organizing the documents, a desire to read a particular document, a desire to reread a passage that was unclear, a desire to know which category a particular document belongs in, and so on. In the course of a day's work one might run across a document that strikes one's fancy and feel an urge to keep reading beyond what was necessary to get the job done; but the concern to accomplish the task within the day would motivate one to overrule this urge, and so one would stay on task. The larger concern will also set limits to deliberation that are not set in Elliot's case. A normal person will weight the merits of various principles of organization under pressure from the concern to get the job done; so if after weighing three principles two seem better than the third but neither of the two is decisively better than the other, a normal person will simply settle on one, so as to get on with the job. In this way a larger concern generates desires appropriate to the various stages of the job, eliminates inappropriate ones, and precipitates decisions where smaller desires by themselves would not do so. We should note that Elliot is not entirely without concerns. That he can be "captivated" by a distraction suggests otherwise, as does the fact that with prompting he can get started in the morning and prepare to go to work. He is not entirely bereft of motivation, but the only ones to which he is susceptible are momentary urges that do not belong in any significant sense to a larger framework.

We see the same pattern in Elliot's emotional responsiveness. Damasio found that patients like Elliot, when tested with a polygraph, showed normal skin conductance changes in response to startling auditory and visual impressions, but not in response to disturbing pictures (e.g., of a homicide); while neurologically normal people show skin conductance changes in response to both kinds of stimulus (p. 209). And he notes that on the occasions when Elliot displayed anger, it quickly dissipated. Damasio does not tell us what sort of stimulus elicited Elliot's rare flashes of anger, but we can guess that it was some obvious, perhaps even bodily, momentary irritation rather than some consideration that would have to touch a larger ongoing concern (say, an insult to his family). Elliot showed no emotional response at all to the disaster that his life had become. But a concern that one's life go well is precisely one of those "larger" organizing concerns that give to a normal person's behavior the kind of coherence and practical rationality that Elliot's so conspicuously lacks.

Thus if we assume that emotions are concern-based construals, the hypothesis that damage to the ventromedial sector of both frontal lobes deprives a person of the capacity for larger, nonimpulsive concerns would explain the deficits in both Elliot's behavior and his emotions. According to Damasio, the prefrontal cortices are "convergence zones" (p. 182) mediating between, among other things, the kind of higher processing required for sophisticated (language-dependent) construals and the drive- and interest-formation supplied by the evolutionarily older parts of the brain such as the amygdala, hypothalamus, and brain stem. Such convergence suggests how the prefrontal cortices might be necessary both to the formation of sophisticated, nonimpulsive concerns and to the taking up of such concerns into episodic situational construals. Damasio's own explanation of the deficits does not involve reference to concerns, nor does he use the word "construals"; his explanation is that frontal lobe damage reduces one's capacity to generate "somatic markers," which are both feelings of emotions and guides to practical decision making. I discuss the somatic marker hypothesis in Section 2.8c.

2.8. BODILY STATES

a. Introduction

E2 (Section 2.1) states that physiological changes often accompany emotions; sometimes they are felt; and the feeling of them is not the feeling of the emotion, though it is characteristically an aspect of that feeling. Thus heart rate, blood pressure, respiration, activity of sweat glands, tension of muscles (e.g., in hands, neck, and face), constriction and dilation of facial blood vessels (producing pallor and blushing, respectively), activity of tear glands, variation in salivation, and trembling of the extremities, to mention just some of the more overt and obvious changes, occur with fair regularity in association with the more intense forms of anger, fear, embarrassment, sadness, and the like. These changes are sometimes felt, and the feeling of some of them can be an aspect of the feeling of the emotion.

Such changes appear to vary, in predictable if somewhat loose patterns, among particular types of emotions. Anger increases diastolic blood pressure, especially if the anger is expressed, while systolic blood pressure increases whether anger is expressed or not. Anxiety such as occurs prior to taking an examination or when one's blood pressure is being taken also tends to increase blood pressure, but the shock that occurs in response to tragic news produces a facial pallor that seems to be due to constriction of facial blood vessels combined with a drop in blood pressure. The blushing characteristic of embarrassment is due to dilation of facial blood vessels. Heart rate tends to accelerate during fear and anxiety, and also during joyful expectation; but it characteristically decelerates with surprise, if the object is nonthreatening. Electrodermal response, which is the electrical conductance of the skin and is strongly correlated with perspiration, rises with both fear and anger, but tends to rise more with anger. It also rises in response to a wide variety of exciting or interesting objects, such as erotic or novel images. Fear, grief, and depression tend to inhibit gastrointestinal activity (secretion of gastric acid) and suppress appetite, whereas anger, resentment, and impatience (but also sometimes fear) tend to increase gastric activity. The flow of saliva tends to decrease with anger, fear, and grief but increase with eager expectation of food.[60]

A view of emotions that seems to be widely held by laypeople and was until recently a major option among scientific psychologists is that emotions just *are* these bodily states, or perhaps (in William James's view) the sensations generated by these. Sylvan Tomkins, for example, says,

> affects are sets of muscular and glandular responses located in the face and also widely distributed throughout the body, which generate sensory feedback that is either inherently "acceptable" or "unacceptable."[61]

I shall offer some arguments to the conclusion that emotions cannot be either such bodily states or the awareness of them, and that the "acceptableness" and "unacceptableness" is not an attribute of sensory feedback, but of the construal of the situations that we call the "objects" of emotions.

b. Why Emotions Are Not Bodily States

E3 (Section 2.1) is that emotions take objects: They are about something or other. Let us suppose, with Tomkins, that my anger *at* George *for* insulting me and my discipline consists in a configuration of bodily states: a little sweating in the armpits and the palms, an accelerated heart rate, an increase in gastric acid secretion, and so on. One difficulty with Tomkins's theory is that sweating armpits and a 90 bpm heart rate are not, in themselves, *about* anything. If we think they are, it is because we confuse them with

---

[60] For a summary of research on the physiology of emotion, see Nico Frijda, *The Emotions* (Cambridge, England: Cambridge University Press, 1986), Chapter 3, from which the information in this paragraph derives.

[61] "Affect as Amplification: Some Modifications in Theory," in *Emotion: Theory, Research, and Experience*, edited by R. Plutchik and H. Kellerman (New York: Academic Press, 1980), p. 142.

the emotion, which *is* about something. But the theory is that the emotion just is those bodily states; so they themselves have to be able to be about things like George's insulting me. The insight that emotions are about things like George's having insulted me has led people to postulate that emotions are beliefs, judgments, thoughts, construals, perceptions, and the like; for such states of mind are "intentional" – about states of affairs. A related point is that human emotions can and typically do have a propositional structure (Section 2.5c), whereas the action of sweat glands and the like does not.

The sort of bodily states that accompany emotions do not have the kind of significance in human life that emotions have. My anger at George constitutes a certain relationship with him – in particular, an alienation from him, in which at least one of us needs to be in the wrong. If my anger is justified, then he is in the wrong; if he is fully justified in what he says, then I am in the wrong in my anger. But such states as increased gastrointestinal activity and sweaty armpits do not constitute a personal relationship; they cannot be either morally justified or unjustified, as my anger can be.

Anger moves its subject to a particular kind of action, namely, punishing action (E8). But if we put together the whole configuration of bodily states that, on Tomkins's theory, constitute my anger, the most we could suppose in the way of motivation is that some of the aspects of this configuration would be uncomfortable, and would thus motivate me to try to alter them. It is impossible to see how these could motivate me to the particular action of insulting George or trying to get him fired.

Any theory of emotion needs to account for how the different types of emotion differ from one another. It needs to be able to show how envy differs from anger, resentment from pride, hope from gratitude, and so on. Chapter 3 of this book is dedicated to an analysis of about sixty-five different emotion types by which to test the account of emotions as concern-based construals. Tomkins's view can meet this theoretical demand only if it can specify the differences in configuration of physiological response that, on this theory, constitute the differences among the emotion types. Frijda summarizes:

Judging from the available evidence, different emotions tend to differ in their physiological response patterns; they do not differ, however, to such a degree and with such consistency that the response patterns could serve to define or identify the respective emotions (p. 162).

Furthermore, it seems that emotions can occur in the absence of the bodily states that in Tomkins's theory are identical with them. As Frijda remarks,

Sometimes, to all evidence, there are no signs of autonomic arousal while subjects say they are, or feel, happy or anxious or angry. It is as well to take such subjects at their word, as long as their behavior does not contradict them. Emotion can be there, it appears, without physiological upset of any note, according to the criteria of subjective experience and expressive behavior (pp. 172–173).

William James's idea that emotions might be sensations of these bodily states is implausible for similar reasons and other reasons. For one thing, emotions are about the items that are mentioned in their propositional content (e.g., my anger is about George and his insult and the violation of my dignity that it involves). Emotions are not about events going on in my body, but the sensation of trembling or sweating is of something going on in the body. Second, just as the sweating of armpits does not have the kind of significance in human life that emotions have, neither does the sensation of sweating in one's armpits. Nor does the sensation have the kind of focused motivational power that an emotion like anger has. Nor does it seem very likely that enough differences among the various sensations generated by these bodily changes can be discriminated to account for the very fine-grained and easy discriminations we make among our emotional states. Tomkins, evidently trying to account for the hedonic tone of emotions (their being positive or negative), says that "the sensory feedback" from the bodily states "is either inherently 'acceptable' or 'unacceptable'." But the unpleasantness of anxiety or envy is not an unpleasantness of bodily sensation, like the unpleasantness of sweaty armpits and stomach cramps; it is the unpleasantness of the meaning of the situation as the subject of emotion sees it. And finally, if Frijda is right that emotions can occur without there being any particular bodily disturbance associated with them, it follows that the emotion cannot be the sensations of that (missing) bodily disturbance.[62]

Why are people inclined to identify emotions with physical states and their sensations? Experimental psychologists no doubt find bodily states attractive because they are more susceptible of empirical observation and quantification than other factors. Machines have been devised that can measure them quite accurately (it is hard even to imagine a machine that could identify and analyze concern-based construals). But the mistake is not just a professional liability; ordinary people can be easily induced, with a few leading questions, to think they feel their emotions in their bodies. The reason, I think, is that these sensations are conceptually simpler and easier to identify than the emotions themselves. This

---

[62] Damasio agrees with Frijda's observation that emotions can occur without any special bodily state and answers my objection by distinguishing, as I do in a rather different way (see Chapter 4), between emotions and feelings of emotions. According to Damasio, *feelings* of emotions are *impressions* of bodily states, and the brain is constructed with a "feeling as-if" loop so that a normal subject can have an impression similar to that of the bodily state characteristic of an emotion without actually being in that bodily state. See *Descartes' Error*, pp. 155ff. This was discussed in Section 1.4c.

homely theory is just an instance of our pre-reflective tendency to alight on the simple and obvious, even the mechanical. Like James, we introspect and immediately start searching for sensations. Introspection is not a particularly bad method of research into the emotions, but to practice it one needs to know what kind of thing one is looking for. One needs to know that one is not looking for sensations – subjective states in that sense – but for "views" of things, syntactically organized "pictures" of the situations of our life, structures of self-involved (that is, concern-based) "meaning."

c. Emotional Pleasure and Pain

I have referred to emotions as "negative" or "positive," and it seems that most emotions belong in one or the other of these categories. Emotions like joy, relief, hopefulness, and gratitude are pleasant; ones like grief, impatience, disappointment, fear, and envy are uncomfortable. Some emotions are perhaps both pleasant and uncomfortable (Aristotle says that anger is always like this; see *Rhetoric* 1378a30-b9), and some instances of surprise, amazement and wonder seem to be hedonically neutral, but most emotions have at least one definite hedonic value.

How shall we analyze this? Damasio, following in the tradition of William James, proposes that we understand this feature of emotions in terms of the bodily sensations that characterize strong emotions, and he builds an account of practical reason on this theory of emotions' hedonic values. When stimuli cause certain "images" in the brain, certain parts of the brain generate somatic states that in turn are signaled to other parts of the brain, where they become conscious. The resulting complex sensation of a state of the body, which may include feelings of agitation in the stomach, palpitation of the heart, prickling of the skin, and tension of facial and skeletal muscles, is either pleasant or unpleasant. To feel an emotion, in Damasio's view, is to have a sensation of such a complex body state while having a cognition of the stimulus situation that gave rise to it:

> That process of continuous monitoring, that experience of what your body is doing *while* thoughts about specific contents roll by, is the essence of what I call a feeling. If an emotion is a collection of changes in body state connected to particular mental images that have activated a specific brain system, *the essence of feeling an emotion is the experience of such changes in juxtaposition to the mental images that initiated the cycle* (p. 145, Damasio's italics).

Some such feelings are "in the positive and pleasant band of the spectrum," whereas others are "toward the painful band" (p. xv); negative emotions are felt as "painful body states" (p. 180). The pleasures and pains one experiences in feeling emotions are thus analogous, one must suppose, to other pleasures and pains in the body – pleasures of eating and drinking and sexual stimulation and release, of having one's back rubbed but not too hard, of warming up when too cold and cooling down when too hot; and pains and discomforts of burns and blows and abrasions, of pangs of hunger, of stomachache and backache and being too cold or too hot.

Are the pleasure and pain of joy and sorrow really pleasures and pains of the body? Is the discomfort of terror that of one's heart beating wildly and one's muscles tensing up? Is the pleasure of joy at reunion with a loved one the pleasure of one's heart beating strongly and one's facial skin and muscles configuring in a smile? Three considerations suggest a negative answer. First, the sensations characteristic of emotions are typically neither *especially* pleasant nor *especially* painful. The sensations associated with ecstatic joy are not pleasant enough to account for the extreme pleasantness of the state of mind; nor are those associated with a panic attack before an exam unpleasant enough to account for the great discomfort of the emotion. Second, the sensations don't divide in the way the theory requires: To my mind, no bodily sensation associated with an emotion is particularly pleasant. All sensations associated with strong emotions, taken simply *as sensations*, are mildly *un*pleasant, whether the emotion is pleasant or not. It is mildly unpleasant to have your heart racing as it does when you are pleasantly excited by your team making the winning basket with two seconds to play. The prickly sensation in your skin when you read of Levin's proposal to Kitty Shcherbatsky (*Anna Karenina*, Part Four, Chapter 13) is hardly pleasant, taken as a sensation, yet it is part of your feeling of joy that they are finally to be united after so many troubles. And third, whatever pleasures or discomforts are characteristic of sensations, those of emotions are of a different kind: They are pleasures taken in, and pains suffered from, situations because of the situations' meaning for the subject of the emotion. Sensations, taken simply as such, do not derive their hedonic value from meanings.

It is true that sensations can be pleasant or painful by virtue of their meanings: The pain of sore muscles can be pleasant if taken as a sign of bodily vigor and growing strength; the pleasure of sexual intercourse can be painful if its meaning is an odious betrayal of one's spouse. The pain of toothache can be made more painful if it presages an expensive and inconvenient operation; the pleasure of a good meal can be enhanced by a cook's pride in a work well done. But these are special cases in that emotions react on the awareness of bodily states; they are not paradigms of the relation between sensation and emotion. And even in such cases, the distinction between the hedonic character of the body state and that of the emotion is easy to maintain: Despite its pleasure, the muscular pain is still recognizable as physical discomfort; despite their painful aspect, the sensations of treacherous venery are still recognizable as pleasures of the body. These facts of interaction of the hedonic values of sensations and emotions is no comfort for Damasio's supposition that the hedonic values of emotions *are* those of sensations.

On the account of emotions that I offer in this book, the pleasure or discomfort of a paradigm case emotion is the perceived satisfaction or frustration of a concern by a situation. Among the more obvious examples are relief (a kind of joy) and disappointment. A student has had a demanding semester, and in the tenth week he begins to desire intensely that it be over. The pleasure in this relief, when the semester is over, is that involved in perceiving the object of a desire as attained. On the other hand, he strongly desired, and even half expected, to get an "A" in chemistry. When the report says "B" he is disappointed. The displeasure in this emotion is that involved in perceiving the object of his desire as failing to be attained. The pleasure in hope is not in perceiving the object as actually attained, but in anticipating its attainment; the discomfort in fear is not in perceiving the desired safety or well-being as actually lost, but in perceiving the real possibility of this. In general, emotional pleasure is the perception of a situation as satisfying, whereas emotional pain or discomfort is the perception of a situation as frustrating. The mixture of pleasure and pain that Aristotle discerns in anger depends on special circumstances. Anger is based on a concern for something (e.g., to be treated with respect), and it is the perception of an object (an offense, an offending situation, an offending agent) as contravening that concern; the displeasure in anger is the sense of frustration involved in this perception. But anger also generates a consequent concern – to punish, to get rectificatory justice. Aristotle assumes the special circumstance that the subject perceives his prospects of getting revenge as good (perhaps he does not believe they are good, but sees them as good only by fantasizing). Thus the pleasure in anger resides in something like the hope of revenge (anticipatory satisfaction). Not every angry person enjoys good perceived prospects of revenge, and so, contrary to Aristotle, not every instance of anger has a pleasant side.

I have argued that emotions are not plausibly identified with the bodily states that accompany many of them, nor with the sensations of these states, and that the pleasure and pain characteristic of emotions is not an attribute of such bodily sensations. The sensations that accompany many emotions are, however, an important aspect of our feelings of emotions. They often function as a sort of anchor for our emotional interpretations of ourselves. I will return to this topic in the more extended discussion of emotional feelings of Chapter 4.

2.9. ACTIONS

a. Introduction

E8 (Section 2.1) says that many emotion types are motivational in the sense that they beget or include a desire to perform characteristic types of action; but not all emotions are motivational in this sense. Thus a person's action can sometimes be explained by reference to the emotional state he was in. The envier may want to "put down" the envied one, the angry person to punish the offender, the grateful person to say "thank you" and return favors, and the fearful person to do something to get clear of the perceived danger. The desires to perform actions of these types compose a subset of what I call consequent concerns (Section 2.7b) – a subset, because such concerns are not always desires to *do* something oneself; an angry person, for example, may desire that his offender be punished, without wanting to do it himself. In the present section I argue for a certain interpretation of this motivation to act. Before I do that, however, I must clarify the concept of an action, as it figures in our question. In the fourth subsection I consider the chief rival of my interpretation of the emotional motivation of actions, a view that has been put forth by Patricia Greenspan. I end this section by considering a recent theory of emotion that places the notion of an action at the center of the definition of emotion – Nico Frijda's proposal that emotions are, most basically, tendencies to act.

b. Actions and Behavior

Charles Darwin's *The Expression of the Emotions in Man and Animals*[63] is the *locus classicus* of a strand of emotion theory that has made much of the fact that emotions are often expressed in overt behavior. This emphasis is associated with the biologization of psychology, in that psychological traits are explained as adapting our ancestors for physical survival. Behavioral expression becomes the most important dimension of emotion because it mediates the relation to the environment that both threatens and succors the organism and thus calls upon it to avoid the threats and grasp the aid. Emotions, then, are dispositions to behave in ways that "adapt" the organism to its environment. Whatever the possible merits of biological explanation in psychology, it is beyond question that the generation of characteristic kinds of behavior is one of the most important and striking features of human emotions. The concept of *behavior* is very broad, covering both intentional action and nonvoluntary movement. Behavioral expressions of emotion can be divided into two kinds: *actions proper* and *mere behaviors*. I begin with the notion of behaviors.

Behavioral expressions differ from the kind of bodily changes that we looked at in Section 2.8, though the line between the two concepts is gray in places. Heart rate increase, stomach contractions, perspiration, blushing, and tightening of shoulder muscles are not usually called behaviors, though they are, in a somewhat stretched sense, "expressions" of emotions, whereas smiles, tears, slumped shoulders, and a raise clenched fist, are clearly behaviors. But cases like blushing or tears can straddle the categories. Generally,

---

[63] Chicago: University of Chicago Press, 1965; originally published in 1872.

more visible changes are more likely to be thought of as behaviors; but changes that are closely tied to the circulatory system or glands tend not to be so thought of. Also, the possibility of voluntary control tends to make for behavior; but this, too, is only a loose criterion, because some people can control their blood pressure voluntarily, but no one, I think, would call a drop in blood pressure behavior.

Behavioral expressions seem to fall into four categories: (1) *Facial expressions:* Smiles come in a variety of kinds – smiles of contempt, of compassion, of anger, of embarrassment, of anxiety, of joy, of gratitude, and so on. (If given only a picture of a face, without narrative or situational setting, even the most sensitive people cannot reliably discriminate all these kinds of smiles; and yet it is commonly believed that there are subtle differences among them.) Frowns vary similarly: There are frowns of anger, resentment, vexation, disgust, and more. Some facial expressions do not fit in the smile or frown categories – expressions of curiosity, puzzlement, interrogativity, embarrassment, contempt, anger, and other emotions. (2) *Vocal expressions:* Our voices express emotion by pitch and changes in pitch, vocalizing speed, loudness, emphasis, cadence. (3) *Postural expressions:* The carriage of the head, the shoulders, the stomach, whether the arms hang down at the side of the body or are folded across the chest or are held in some readiness position, the placement of the legs and feet (spread apart, one planted forward, or together relaxed), whether the body is reclining or inclining, and so on, can be or be part of the expression of one emotion or another. (4) *Gestural expressions:* Arms held out, palms up, palms down, palms forward, arms held out in incipient embrace, fists clenched and pounding, stamping feet on the ground, kicking objects, and so on. This last category verges more strongly on actions than do the others.

Actions do not by definition involve bodily change. Devising a plan for revenge on one's offender is an action that might involve no constitutive bodily movement (no vocal sounds, no handwriting, etc.). But my examples will be actions that do involve constitutive bodily movements, since such actions are far more common, and they overlap better with "behaviors."

An action, as contrasted with a mere behavior, is undertaken by the agent for a purpose of his own. For example, smiling in response to good news is behavior, but not an action unless the agent has some purpose in so behaving. A smile might just be a coordinated set of spontaneous muscular contractions associated with joy or amusement. If, on the other hand, the agent smiles *in order* to express his joy or *so as* to appear friendly to the good herald, then the very same muscular contractions constitute the *action* of smiling. I believe that any of the body movements that I have identified as behaviors can in principle be performed as actions, and some of the body changes that are not (usually) behaviors can be, as well.

Typically when a person weeps in grief, he does not do so to any end, in which case his weeping is a behavior but not an action; but if he weeps intentionally, his behavior is an action. However, when behaviors that are not typically actions become actions their relation to the emotion seems to change: A person who weeps intentionally usually does not weep *out of* grief (does not by weeping "express" grief) but weeps either to simulate or stimulate grief. If he succeeds in working it up, then while the grief is not the initial cause of his weeping, it is possible that he *now* weeps out of grief. Similarly, a smile as an action is likely not to express what it would express as a mere behavior; a slouch as an action is likely not to express what it would express as a mere behavior; and so on. If one wants to know what emotion is expressed by an action, one must ask to what *end* it was performed; and this, along with other information about the state of mind of the subject, should provide an answer. The fact that a behavior typical of an emotion can be undertaken when it does not express the emotion, and that this expression has a tendency to bring the emotion on, is an important basis of our ability to control emotions. If other things are in place, weeping can bring on the feeling of grief because weeping fosters the person's construing the situation in grief-terms.

c. How Emotions Generate Actions

Of the three kinds of "expression" of emotion, only actional expressions are understandable in terms of the "logic" of the emotions, their nature as concern-based construals with a propositional structure. Let me anticipate the analysis I will offer with an abstract statement of my account of emotional motivation.

Concerns that are consequent on emotions are frequently desires to act, and it is such a desire that is normally[64] the proximate explanation of the action that may be taken. But that desire is itself a product or aspect of the emotion, and it arises out of the concern(s) on which the emotion is based. The concern or concerns on which the emotion is based are shaped, focused, actualized (in case the basic concern was purely dispositional), and mixed (in case there is more than one basic concern), in the construal, into the desire for a certain kind of action or a particular action. The terms of the construal that is the emotion supply reasons to want to act.

The production, via emotion, of desires to act is very much like the transformation of concerns in general, via judgments and perceptions, into desires to act. The wish to sharpen a pencil, for example, can be transformed into the wish to use this particular pencil sharpener, via the knowledge that pencil sharpeners are an excellent way to sharpen pencils along with a perception of the pencil sharpener mounted on the north wall.

Let us start with an example of fear that seems to have just one basic concern, and that one dispositional. I am walking in downtown Chicago

---

[64] For a discussion of this qualification, see Section 2.9d.

and without thinking much about where I am I take a shortcut and halfway down the block realize that the street I'm on is not safe for solo middle-class walkers. I start to be afraid, and at that moment I want more than anything else to be off that street. The desire to be off the street, which will no doubt motivate some actions such as looking for the quickest way out and then taking it, is a fairly specific desire. It is a consequence of a construal of myself as in danger that is based on a much more general concern not to be harmed. The more general or basic concern is not, prior to the occurrence of the emotion, an active desire; it is dispositional. So the consequent concern, the specific desire to get off that street, is a specification and actualization of the more general concern to be safe, generated by the construal of myself as in a particular kind of danger. It is a specification because the concern *to be safe* has now been specified into the concern *to be safe from the dangers of this street*; and it is an actualization because the dispositional concern to be safe is now active. The desire, as part or product of the synthetic unity of the construal, contains within it, as it were, the terms of the emotion. If asked, "Why do you want to get off that street?" I answer in the terms of my fear: "That's a dangerous street; I could be mugged; I'm bait there; I don't want to be robbed, maimed, or killed."

Most of the concerns prior to most emotions are, I think, nonoccurrent, but they need not all be so. Take a case of gratitude, which will illustrate both the possibility of an active basic concern and the mixing of basic concerns. I actively desire to go to lunch with a particular prominent philosopher of my acquaintance, and just as I'm thinking how nice that would be, she steps up and invites me to lunch. I'm grateful and feel a desire to make some gracious return – to please her with my expressions of gratitude, to supply her with information she may find useful, or whatnot. The prior concern that I have mentioned – to be invited to lunch by that philosopher – is already pretty specific, and the desire to make some return is not a *specification* of the desire to be taken out to lunch by this philosopher. But it is a consequence of construing myself as in her gracious debt and her, thus, as one to whom I "owe" some responding grace. We can see that the desire to be taken out to lunch by this philosopher is not by itself a sufficient basis for the emotion of gratitude because it will not generate the desire to return grace upon construing myself as taken out to lunch by this philosopher. There is also, behind gratitude, a concern for a special kind of justice that operates in gratitude. A signal difference between people who are merely *glad* to receive favors from others and people who are grateful is the presence in the latter group of this concern for "justice" – the concern that favors be returned. The concern to return this particular philosopher some grace because of her grace to me is a specification of that more general concern for "justice." This concern, it seems to me, is in its prior state virtually always nonoccurrent; and thus it not only gets specified, but also actualized, in the emotion. We can see, too, that in typical cases of gratitude this concern has to be combined with some other one, like the desire to go out to lunch, or some more general and probably dispositional concern for some kind of well-being that the benefactor may bestow. A more thoroughgoing analysis of gratitude will reveal an even more complex structure of underlying concerns, which mix in the formation of episodes of gratitude and a consequent desire to make a gracious return.

My general view, then, of how an emotion moves us to action is that it serves as a sort of lens in which general concerns are focused into more specific desires, and as a sort of rational stimulus by which dispositional concerns become occurrent desires, and as a sort of womb in which diverse concerns mingle to produce desires, which may be satisfied by action. Thus my account depends on the common-sensical, and not further to be explained, principle that people perform actions of one or another type because they want to perform actions of that type. We may highlight this view by comparing it with an account proposed by Patricia Greenspan.

d. Escaping Discomfort

In Greenspan's view,[65] an emotion is an array of evaluative propositions or thoughts held in place by comfortable or uncomfortable affects that take the propositions as their intentional objects. Thus if A is angry at B for publishing without acknowledgment an idea in one of A's circulating typescripts, then A is uncomfortable about

B (wrongly) published my idea without acknowledgment.

In addition, he may be comfortable about

I may (rightly) get revenge on A for his crime.

In the case of motivating emotions, like anger, there will also be some ought proposition such as

I ought to perform some action of revenge on B.

Prior to taking such action, A must conjoin the above proposition with

I have not yet performed the required action.

On Greenspan's account it is part of the analysis of *emotion*, as contrasted with merely holding evaluative propositions coolly in mind, that the propositions are objects of comfort or discomfort. So if these last two propositions are conjoined in A's anger, the conjunction will be an object of discomfort for him. Because the discomfort is about the unfulfilled action requirement, performing the vengeful action is the most direct way to escape the discomfort.

[65] See *Emotions and Reasons* (New York: Routledge, 1988).

Greenspan calls her theory the "escape from discomfort" view (p. 153), because in it the discomfort at the conjunction of the ought proposition in an emotion with the proposition that the agent has not yet obeyed this ought proposition provides the psychological pressure, characteristic of emotions, to perform actions. When the agent acts out of emotion, the prospect of relief from this discomfort moves him to obey the ought proposition. Apart from this pressure of discomfort, the emotion provides only "a desire in the philosopher's sense" (p. 7) – that is, a proposition to the effect that such-and-such ought to be done – but no proper or compulsive motivation. As Greenspan points out, her account makes the central mechanism of emotional motivation self-regarding (see pp. 10–11).

In my view, emotions motivate actions by generating active desires for instances of safety (fear), revenge (anger), return for favor (gratitude), compensation for fault (guilt), disappearance from view (embarrassment), and so on. Thus, they are garden variety human desires, their distinction as *emotional* motivation deriving from the fact that they have been shaped and actualized by emotions. Thus the desire to hit a home run *might* be an emotional motive, in case the hit was desired as a form of revenge or perhaps as a salve for wounded pride. But the desire might be for a lark, or a win, a desire that is not the consequence of any emotion. I do not think that the way emotion- generated desires generate actions differs in kind from the way other desires do, and I have no explanation of how desires motivate. Explanations – at least mine – come to an end here.

Is it true that the compulsive or tractive element in motivation is provided by the prospect of a relief from discomfort? If a man wants his sick daughter to get well, what he *seems* to want, at any rate, is not relief for himself of the discomfort involved in wanting his daughter to get well, conjoined with the fact that she is not yet well; he wants *his daughter to be well.* If someone wants a computer, she seems to want *the computer*, not relief from the discomfort of wanting a computer and not having one yet. If, in these cases, the urge to escape from discomfort is providing the basic motivation, the true character of the motivation is hidden; experientially, the "pull" or "push" of the motivation is from the thing wanted. No doubt, discomfort is often involved in wanting things, a discomfort that may be brought to an end when the wanted thing is attained. But in paradigm cases the wanting explains the discomfort, not the discomfort the wanting. I cannot feel discomfort about not yet having a computer, unless I already want the computer (or something that the computer can secure). Similarly, a person whose mind holds the proposition

I ought to perform some action of revenge on B

and the proposition

I have not yet performed the required action

will not feel discomfort about this conjunction unless the first proposition expresses some concern to get revenge on B. A person who merely acknowledges that he ought to do something, but does not at all care about whether he does it, will not feel discomfort about not yet having done it. While discomfort is certainly involved in many emotions and in motivation, this is not the most basic explanation of the push or pull of motivation, since there would be no motivation by the kind of discomfort that Greenspan identifies if there were not, more basically, another kind of motivation, which is manifested actively in desires.

I once objected that Greenspan's account makes emotions "dishonest." The consequent concern native to anger is the desire for revenge, and one who has taken revenge in anger will naturally think he did the action "to get even," or "because the bastard deserved it." But on Greenspan's account the explanation of his action – insofar as it is motivated by the emotion – is not that he wants revenge, but that he wants to escape a discomfort created in him by the emotion. If the angry one who wants revenge comes to see himself as motivated by the desire to escape the discomfort of his anger, he has stepped outside his anger; he has started treating his anger not as an honest viewpoint to be occupied but as a malaise to be overcome.

Greenspan's account correctly describes some instances of motivation by emotion. We may give to Oxfam to reduce the discomfort of our guilt for using more than our share of the world's resources. We might even act punitively to get relief from the discomfort of our anger or remove ourselves to more secure circumstances with a view to reducing the discomfort that anxiety causes us. We can imagine a psychotherapist prescribing such actions as a way of escape from emotional distress. In such cases we are moved by the emotion, all right, but not – or not primarily – by the consequent concern given in the special logic of the emotion. In this way, psychotherapy – in some forms more than in others – threatens to alienate us from our emotions. It encourages us to dissociate from them, to become "reflective" and "clinical" about them, treating them as symptoms to be manipulated or suppressed or endured, rather than as perspectives potentially expressive of our very identity. For example, people may be encouraged to think of grief as a process to be gotten through, a distress to be escaped – in a certain prescribed "healthy" way – rather than as an expression of oneself and one's love for the grieved one.

Greenspan responded to my comments by stressing that on her view the "reasoning" that goes

I am uncomfortable at the thought, *I ought to get revenge on X;*
I can get relief from this discomfort by getting revenge on X;
So let me get revenge on X;

is *subliminal* (see Greenspan, pp. 153–157). She seems to accept that, to the extent that one consciously owns this reasoning, one has dissociated from the standpoint of one's anger. But since it is subliminal in the normal cases, she holds, this reasoning does not generally make one's emotions dishonest or alienate one from them. It is on a par with other processes of subliminal monitoring that do not undermine our conscious activities though they would do so if they became the center of our attention. Thus a soccer player subliminally monitors his foot movements as he moves the ball forward for a goal; a philosopher reading a paper at a meeting monitors muscle contractions in lip and tongue, though if she paid them much attention she would probably impede her reading.

But the analogy is not strong enough. There is nothing contrary to the soccer player's natural self-understanding in the claim that he gets to the goal by moving his feet. He does not feel disabused of an illusion upon being given a muscular account of his activity. But to the angry person it comes as a disillusioning and demoralizing shock to learn that when, out of anger, he wants to get revenge on his offender, he really wants, in the motivational sense, only to escape the discomfort of his anger. Perhaps an even more compelling example is that of contrition. The contrite person desires to make some atonement for his moral fault – to right a wrong. The revelation that what he really wants is to escape from the discomfort of his contrition is thus a deep revision of his self-understanding: not just a shift in perspective, but a shift in world view. If Greenspan's account is correct, then emotions in general are sources of wholesale deception.

Indeed, Greenspan entitled her written response to my objection "Fooling the Motivational Meter"[66] because in her view, emotions are a strategy for turning egoistic motivation to altruistic purposes. You desire in the philosopher's sense to promote your friends' and neighbors' well-being, but since on the level of push–pull motivation you are only concerned about yourself you (or better, nature) must find a way to get something for yourself out of the altruistic action. Emotions supply the egoistic motive for altruism by providing us with discomforts associated with altruistic ought-propositions. Thus in seeking escape from the discomfort we feel in our anger at a racial slur directed at a colleague, for example, we may take a kind of action that on purely egoistic principles is irrational (say, telling off the boss), yet on a subliminal level we act egoistically. Because the real, egoistic motivation is hidden, its inconsistency with our altruism does not become evident to us, and we are prevented from becoming out-and-out conscious egoists.

I wonder, though, what happens to someone who comes to accept Greenspan's account and not only accepts it but takes it enough to heart to begin experiencing his own emotions in its terms. It seems that we can fool the emotional meter, and retain the sense that our emotions are honest,

---

[66] Paper presented at the Central Division meetings of the American Philosophical Association in April 1991.

only to the extent that we are ignorant of, or manage to disregard, Greenspan's theory of emotional motivation. If Greenspan is right, her theory blows the whistle on our emotions; if she is wrong, it is one more potential source of false feelings (see Chapter 4) – in this case a tendency to feel our emotions as about ourselves in a way that they are not. But these troubles are artificial by-products of a theory. We need not suppose that emotional motivation is always at root egoistic. Sometimes, when we intensely want to say "thank you," or see justice done to others, that is what we want – not just in a philosopher's sense, but in the sense of real desire. The motivation is just as the meter reads it.

A chief argument for Greenspan's theory is that we do often respond to our emotions in ways other than seeking to achieve their proper aim. Instead of seeking revenge on X,

I might do a number of things for which my anger counts as a motivating reason, though I know that they will not achieve revenge. I might mutter a few inaudible curses; or entertain fantasies of wringing X's neck; or kick Fido; or make an angry face; or simply attempt to work off anger by removing myself from X's presence and engaging in vigorous exercise (p. 156).

If one does these things in full consciousness that they will not satisfy the proper aim of anger, and yet derives some emotional satisfaction from them, it follows (so goes the argument) that what one wants must be something other than the proper aim of anger. It is plausible that this other thing one wants is relief from emotional discomfort.

Consider someone concerned that justice be done to native South Africans. He is angered by a TV report that includes a portion of an Afrikaner leader's racist speech. He would like to hit the speaker in the mouth, or at least insult him, but in the impotence of his living room has to make do with completely ineffective gestures such as snarls and a raised fist. Assuming that our subject does not believe in voodoo and is basically rational, we cannot explain these gestures, thinks Greenspan, by reference to his desire to punish the Afrikaner; the best explanation of this kind of action is that he performs it to relieve his emotional discomfort. She notes, though, that such gestures' power to relieve discomfort "is typically greater as they resemble the proper aim" (156) – that is, because they *seem like* punishing behavior to the agent.

That substitute gestures, and so on, derive their power to satisfy from their resemblance to punishment suggests that our TV viewer really wants not escape from the discomfort of his anger, but the punishment of the Afrikaner. Substitutes are precisely *substitutes*. But I wonder whether "escape from discomfort" is the best description of what the agent derives from these punitively ineffectual gestures. If I want a new Maserati and know I can't possibly afford it, I may still get considerable satisfaction from visiting the Maserati showroom and displaying pictures of gleaming Maseratis on my bedroom walls. It seems introspectively inaccurate to describe my satisfaction as "escape from the discomfort of not being able to buy a Maserati." I'm not escaping from a discomfort here, but taking fantasy pleasure in an unattainable object. Similarly, it seems to me that our snarling TV viewer may not be escaping a discomfort so much as indulging himself in a pleasurable fantasy – pleasurable because he sees the punishment of the Afrikaner itself as a motivating good.

e. Defining Emotions as Tendencies to Act

Theories of emotion have been constructed on the basis of just about every phenomenon that is associated with emotion. One theory has it that emotions are attitudes toward propositions. Another says that emotions are the bodily changes that accompany some emotions, and yet another that emotions are the sensations of those changes. Another says that emotions are the neural processes that underlie the experiences we call emotions, and yet another that emotions are judgments. Some theorists, resisting the reductionist strategy, have proposed that emotions are syndromes of the above, and other, items. We have noted the proposal, in a Darwinian spirit, that emotions are tendencies to act or behave in certain ways – that the most essential thing about an emotion is its overt expression, whatever other elements it may have being in the service of this.

Nico Frijda[67] is impressed with the functions of overt expressions of emotion in enabling organisms to survive and reproduce by changing the organisms' relations to their environments. Some expressive behavior can be understood as activity that establishes, weakens, or negates the physical and cognitive relations of the organism with the environment, by means of locomotion and modifications of bodily and sensory exposure. Thus in fear, freezing or running away from the frightening object changes one's relation to it advantageously; the wide openness of the eyes in surprise makes the animal better able to see dangers; body posture expressive of anger is a readiness to attack; in disgust (at olfactory sensation), spitting gets rid of the offensive substance. The "vertical frown" expressive of fear "may well result from an impulse to protectively close the eyes while simultaneously forcing oneself to keep them open, in order to keep track of the fearful object" (p. 16). Some expressive behavior can be understood as action that influences the behavior of other individuals. The crying of the baby brings the mother; baring the teeth in anger frightens the intruder away; expressions of love (courting activities, calling to young) bring the potential mate or young. "Joyful [exuberant] behavior entraps the other in an interaction" (p. 27). "Smiling serves as a sign of friendliness and inoffensiveness" (p. 28). Some expressive behavior can be understood as the manifestation of behavior activation as such, or of decrease in behavior activation. The tensed muscles

---

[67] *The Emotions.*

and alert body posture in fear or anger constitute increased readiness to flee or attack. Some expressive behavior can be understood as the result of inhibition of expressive behavior falling under the previous principles. Part of the body posture of fear may be explained by reference to the effort *not* to run away; part of the facial expression of sadness may result from the effort *not* to cry; and so on. "[T]he foot stamping of impatient horses [is] the closest substitute to the blocked intended behavior" (p. 36). Frijda concludes:

> *Emotions, then, can be defined as modes of relational action readiness, either in the form of tendencies to establish, maintain, or disrupt a relationship with the environment or in the form or mode of relational readiness as such* (p. 71, Frijda's italics; see pp. 12, 56, and 466 for somewhat different formulations).

Let us examine this thesis, interpreting "action" first in the strict sense, and then in the sense that includes also what I have called mere behavior (Section 2.9b; Frijda does not distinguish these).

As I noted in my criticism of the theory that emotions are bodily states (Section 2.8b), an adequate account of emotion must provide the conceptual wherewithal to distinguish one type of emotion from another (say, anger from fear or resentment). I noted, with support from Frijda, that the correlation of emotion types with types of bodily states is too loose to allow such discrimination; so emotions cannot be defined as bodily states. A similar argument shows that emotions cannot be defined as action tendencies.

Let us suppose that anger can be defined by the kind of action to which it tends to give rise. I have said that anger's consequent concern is that the offender be punished. So we might define anger as a tendency to punitive action. But what kind of action is that? Take the case with which I began this chapter, my anger at George for proposing that I get last choice of upper-division course assignment because I'm nothing but a white protestant male and ethics isn't real philosophy anyway. What will my action be? I might give him a dirty look, or smile at him contemptuously; I might shoulder him into the gutter, or boycott his birthday party; or go to the party and tell embarrassing stories about him; or, following a biblical directive, I might treat him kindly in an effort to scorch the remnants of fluff on the periphery of his shining pate. What do all these actions have in common? Only, as far as I can see, that they are ways of punishing him. But notice that none of them needs to be an act of punishment. I might give him the same dirty look out of disgust, rather than anger; or the same contemptuous smile out of contempt, rather than anger; I might shoulder him into the gutter because I adore him and think he's in imminent danger of being beaned by falling crockery.

So the idea that anger is defined by the action to which it is a tendency seems to be under threat from two directions: Any number of highly diverse actions can count as expressions of anger, and any action that is an expression of anger might be an expression of some other emotion, or of no emotion at all. Something like this situation seems to prevail with regard to all actional expressions of human emotions. The emotions of simpler animals, or at any rate animals with stereotyped expressions, seem to fit Frijda's definition better. Anger in wasps, for example, might be plausibly defined as a readiness to sting. One might think that wasps sting only and always when angry. But, Frijda might respond, the actional expressions of human anger have in a way just as much consistency as those of wasp anger. After all, that diversity of things I might have done in anger at George are all forms of punishment. So we can say that anger is definable as a readiness to take punitive action.

But this response admits that we cannot identify the emotion in terms of the action it motivates, unless that action is already defined as a way of punishing somebody; but that is tantamount to identifying the action in terms of the emotion of which it is an expression. It is to identify the action in terms of its meaning to the agent; but its meaning, as punishment of an offender, is supplied by the emotion. The action of shouldering George into the gutter out of anger derives its punitive character from the situation-construal that I am claiming to be the emotion. But in that case the emotion can be defined in terms of the expression only if the expression is first defined in terms of the emotion. If all we know is that I shouldered George into the gutter, then for purposes of emotion expression we do not yet know what action I performed. It might have been punitive, but it might also have been protective, or mercenary, or defensive, or motivated by a yearning to be a hero. Only if we know how the agent was concernfully construing the situation do we know, with the kind of precision necessary for identifying actions as expressions of emotion, what he was doing. The proposal to define emotions as readinesses for actions seems to reverse the conceptual priorities, at least for human emotions.

What about the kind of expression I have called merely behavioral, as in contrast with actions? Perhaps spontaneously clenched fists, smiles, scowls, a lightness in one's gait, and the like differentiate emotions with enough precision to do the job that the action readiness theory needs overt expressions to do. Early in his book, Frijda puts an odd qualifier on emotional expression: "*Emotional phenomena* are noninstrumental behaviors and noninstrumental features of behavior ... " (p. 4; Frijda's italics). Why noninstrumental? we might ask. When a man picks up a stone to hurl at his attacker, does his picking up the stone not express anger? Perhaps Frijda sees the argument of the preceding paragraph looming, and thinks he had better restrict defining emotional expression to the more stereotyped and automatic responses. After all, the theory works better with wasps than with people, and we may take the stereotyped behavioral expressions to be the sort of thing we share with the wasps.[68] The problem with this suggestion is that merely behavioral expressions, too, lack the precise coordination with emotions that is needed if emotions are to be defined as states of readiness to perform them. Frijda himself notes that,

The relationship, in fact, is not simple. A given emotion does not invariably manifest itself in a given expression; we saw this in the preceding, where different manifestations of fear, anger and joy were discussed. Also, a given expression does not invariably manifest a given emotion. Weeping occurs in anger, frustration, and happiness as well as in grief and distress; laughter may spring from nervousness as well as from joy, and smiling from embarrassment as well as from amusement or friendliness. . . . Furthermore, whereas recognition accuracy, in expression recognition experiments, usually is far above chance, it also usually is far from perfect; and the same holds for consensus among observers. Differentiation between emotions on the basis of expressions alone, and when unselected samples of expressions are used, appears to be rather crude and unstable. There is, moreover, an experimental finding not mentioned so far. If subjects are given large sets of labels to choose from (or are left free to choose their own labels), the range of interpretations given to any one expression almost always is very large (p. 66).

I conclude that emotions cannot be defined as action tendencies, even if we broaden the concept of *action* to include mere behaviors.[69]

The suggestion that emotions are concern-based construals is superior to the action tendency theory in giving us the wherewithal to identify emotion types with some precision and to distinguish both them and their tokens from one another. If we want to know the difference between anger and fear, we look at how the subject of each of these emotions "reads" his situation – what are the terms of the construal.

f. Emotions and Merely Behavioral Expressions

Elaborating the view that emotions are concern-based construals, I have sketched an account of emotional expression in action (Section 2.9c). The

[68] The wasp's sting is certainly instrumental for the genetic survival of wasps, but the wasp does not employ it *with the intention* of gene survival, or even individual survival, any more than a baby (initially) uses a smile as a way of ingratiating herself with her parents. Perhaps Frijda should have referred to nonintentional behaviors rather than noninstrumental ones.

[69] Frijda shows awareness of the weakness of his theory at various points in the book, and he tries to adjust for it. He says, for example, that "emotions may be defined either by mode of action readiness change or by the nature of the emotional object" (p. 73), and in Chapter 4 he develops an account of emotional experience that resembles, in some ways, the model that I am advocating for emotions as such. Portions of that account potentially enable him to define emotions by reference to their objects, and thus define the actions (but not the merely behavioral expressions) for which some emotions are a readiness in terms of their corresponding emotions. If he did this, the account in Chapter 4 would become not just an account of emotional experience but an account of emotion as such, and action readiness could be given its proper, subordinate place in the account.

logic of my account is to explain the expressive action in terms of the emotion, rather than the emotion in terms of the expression. On the proposed view, the action is motivated by a desire that I call the consequent concern of the emotion, and which is a specification, actualization, and/or mingling, via the construal, of the concern(s) on which the emotion is based. The action makes sense, given the internal logic of the emotion as a concern-based construal. Can we give any analogous account of merely behavioral expressions? No.

No such logic is to be discerned in the relation between emotions and their merely behavioral expressions, as important as these are. Why does that particular smile express joy, or that particular scowl express anger? Why do we weep when we are very sad or greatly relieved? Why do we laugh when we see or hear something funny? Why do we dance when glad and slump when sad? Couldn't it have been the other way around, that those particular chest convulsions and muscular contractions of the face that we call laughter expressed the direst torment, while the sobbing and tears that we associate with deep grief expressed our response to hilarious comedy? Couldn't a slumping posture, with eyes averted, express joy? Merely behavioral expressions seem to be, not logical consequences of our emotions, like their actional counterparts, but biological facts about them. Historical physiology may offer more or less plausible explanations of these facts. I summarize one such explanation, by way of illustration.

In a chapter entitled "Low Spirits, Anxiety, Grief, Dejection, Despair,"[70] Charles Darwin offers an explanation why these emotions are expressed by an elevation of the inner ends of the eyebrows, producing a somewhat pyramidal shape, and horizontal straight creases in the forehead.

The eyebrows assume this position owing to the contraction of certain muscles (namely, the orbiculars, corrugators, and pyramidals of the nose, which together tend to lower and contract the eyebrows) being partially checked by the more powerful action of the central fasciae of the frontal muscle.[71] These latter fasciae by their contraction raise the inner ends alone of the eyebrows; and as the corrugators at the same time draw the eyebrows together, their inner ends become puckered into a fold or lump (p. 178).

When children cry out, says Darwin, they contract the orbicular, corrugator, and pyramidal muscles, because this squeezes their eyes, thus protecting

---

[70] *The Expression of the Emotions in Man and Animals*, pp. 176–195. Notice the rather great diversity of emotions that are expressed with this one configuration of facial features.

[71] The orbiculars are the muscles around the eyeball, used for opening and closing the eye and squinting; the corrugators are at the inner ends of the eyebrows, used for lowering the eyebrows and furrowing the brow, as in a frown; the pyramidals, which Darwin notes are less under voluntary control than the other three kinds of muscle, are at the top of the nose; the frontal muscle extends across the forehead, and it is used for lifting the skin on the forehead and thus the eyebrows.

the eyes from being gorged with blood. Thus people have developed the automatic habit of contracting these muscles in preparation for crying out. So when a person feels an urge to cry but wants *not* to, he or she contracts the central fasciae of the frontal muscle, which work against the other three muscles, and this combination produces the facial expression in question. Thus,

In all cases of distress, whether great or small, our brains tend through long habit to send an order to certain mucles to contract, as if we were still infants on the point of screaming out; but this order we, by the wondrous power of the will, and through habit, are able partially to counteract; although this is effected unconsciously, as far as the means of counteraction are concerned (p. 191).

This is a speculative explanation, which might be disputed in several respects, yet admired for its ingenuity. I report it not to commend or criticize it, but to show the kind of explanation that *can* be offered for typical merely behavioral expressions of emotion. It differs in kind from the explanations we offer of our own and other people's actions, when we explain them by reference to the emotions that motivate them. Explanation of expressive action, unlike explanation of expressive behavior, arises independently of scientific theory and speculation and plays, as such, an integral role in everyday practical reasoning. We do not need a theory to mediate our understanding of why one man insulted another in anger, or burned the other's house down, or socked him in the jaw, as we do to explain the particular contraction of his facial muscles in the same episode of anger. The former is transparent by virtue of the "logic" of anger, as it has been recognized, more or less clearly, by such diverse thinkers as Aristotle, the Hebrew psalmists, the Apostle Paul, Mohammed, the Ilongots, the Ifaluk, Descartes, and Hume, and appears to be recognized in all cultures. I have offered a conceptualization of this ordinary explanatory framework in Section 2.9c, on the basis of the model of emotions as concern-based construals. The kind of explanation that Darwin offers, by contrast, is theory relative, speculative, and contestable in a way that explanations in the ordinary framework are not.

How do these two kinds of explanations differ? When I say that the ordinary framework for explaining action-expressions of emotions is not theoretical, I am not referring to the explanation of this mode of explanation that I offered in Section 2.9c. That is indeed theory-like and contestable (Greenspan's theory contests it). I am referring not to an interpretation of a mode of explanation, but to the following mode of explanation itself: In answer to the question, "Why did S do A?" one says, "S was angry," and one may specify this further by saying something like, "S wanted to punish (or get revenge on) O for X and thought he could do so by doing A." It is this mode of explanation, reflective of the logic of anger, that seems to arise universally among human beings, without aid of philosophy or science; it is this mode of explanation that is explained by contestable, theory-like constructions such as Greenspan's and mine. Key terms in this mode of explanation are "angry," "person," "do," "want," "punish," "revenge," and so on. Concepts like these, or close counterparts of them, arise naturally in human cultures and are explained in various theories (they are part of what Wittgenstein calls "our natural history"[72]). A fuller argument for the universality that I am claiming will have to await Section 3.3. No analogous framework explains why people smile when glad, scowl when angry, and get that pyramidal eyebrow configuration when grief-stricken. Within the moral life, the life of ordinary human intercourse and folk-psychological explanation, it is just a "given" that these behaviors betoken roughly these emotional states. If we wish to explain the connections, we must go to scientific inquiry, with its contestable hypotheses and rival frameworks.

Such explanations, when plausible, are to be welcomed as possible supplements to our understanding of the emotions and our allied behavior; the details, however, seem unlikely to be of any very direct relevance to moral psychology and may perhaps be left to students of physiology and biological history. For our purposes, patterns of merely behavioral expression seem to be important primarily as givens. But taken as given, they can help to explain the feeling and generation of emotions. For example, the fact that a certain posture is a typical expression of sadness explains why a person may feel sadder if in that posture than if in some other: The posture inclines him to construe himself as in a situation fit to elicit sadness, and thus to feel sad. Whistling in the dark can help overcome feelings of fear because whistling expresses attitudes incompatible with fear, and so the impression of oneself as under threat may be mitigated by whistling. Smiling in a certain way and speaking in a certain tone of voice can reduce the feeling of anger, and by consequence, in many cases, the anger. (We will take up the issues about such generation of emotions and feelings, and the relation between these, in Chapter 4.)

g. Accumulation of Pressure

We sometimes speak of "bursting" with joy, or being unable to "contain" our anger. In a layman's "theory" of mind, as well as in that of some psychologists, when one "expresses" an emotion, one is letting *it* out. Thus results the familiar hydraulic model of emotions as creating, like urine, internal pressure that needs to be relieved. The context for metaphors of pressure is obviously that in which some natural expression, such as tears, vengeful action, or smiling and dancing about, is for the moment frustrated. Circumstances make it improper to cry or take revenge, and so one "holds the

---

[72] *Philosophical Investigations*, Part I, Sections 25 and 415.

emotion in." On this model, holding in the anger repeatedly and consistently over a period of time augurs an explosion.

Evidence for this view is found not only in our emotion language – "letting off steam," "boiling with anger" – but also in our experience. We do sometimes feel a discomfort with being joyful but unable to smile, angry but kept from giving our offender an ear full, grief-stricken but unwilling to cry, and then a corresponding relief from that discomfort in the expression of the emotion. And sometimes we even experience release *from the emotion*: When one has acted in revenge, one may feel angry no longer. It is also true that with the expression – either behavioral or actional – the feeling of the emotion often increases, giving the impression that the emotion is getting out through the expression. All this seems to suggest that what comes out in the "expression" is the emotion.

Not everyone who talks about emotional expression has in mind this quasi-theory. In Darwin's discussion, for example, nothing hydraulic is suggested. There, expression belongs not to a world of pressures, but to a world of devices and especially messages, and thus follows more a model of linguistic expression. It is not a matter of expelling something, but of effecting, and especially of articulating, something. And the general purpose of expression is not relief, but environmental influence.

On the account of emotion offered in this book, what we are bursting with is not the emotion, but its natural expression. Thus the discomfort involved in not being able to express the emotion is not a discomfort with having the emotion in one (being full of joy is not uncomfortable), but with being impeded in the natural expression of it. It is natural, when joyful, to smile and walk about with a lilt in one's gait; and the discomfort of unexpressed joy comes from going against the natural inclinations here. This explanation seems to account for much of the discomfort generated by frustrated inclinations to behavioral expression. The hydraulic model predicts that expression of emotion is followed by its cessation or mitigation of the emotion, while my model predicts that expression is followed by cessation of the discomfort of withholding the expression of it. The hydraulic theory's prediction is not borne out in expressions of joy. Smiling and walking about with a lilt in one's gait does not rid one of joy but even tends to intensify the present feeling and increase the emotion over the longer haul.

The hydraulic theory's prediction is borne out in other cases, and I must explain why such cases do not confirm the model. In Section 2.9c we saw that some emotions involve or generate a consequent concern to take action of a certain sort. The perceptual synthesis of terms, including concern, that constitutes the emotion provides a logically transparent explanation why the agent would want to take that kind of action. Anger and fear are typical. In each case the desired action, if successful, satisfies the consequent concern and thus transforms the situation, as construed by the subject, into one that no longer calls for the emotion. For example, anger is a construal of a situation as unjust in such a way as to call for the punishment of the offender; fear is a construal of a situation as threatening in such a way as to call for rendering the situation safe. But if the offender is satisfactorily punished or the situation is rendered safe, in the eyes of the subject, then the emotion subsides. It is easy to see, then, how successful actional expressions sometimes do away with the emotions they express. They do not dispel the emotion by providing a conduit for its exit, but instead dispel it by satisfying the demand native to its structure as a concern-based construal. We can reinforce this point by noting that such satisfaction is sometimes provided without any expression: Some other agent, or just the vicissitudes of circumstance, may dispel the fear or anger by satisfying the emotion's demand for safety or punishment.

An expression of anger need not actually rectify the injustice to mitigate or dispel the anger; since emotions are construals, it need only give the subject the impression – not even necessarily the belief – that some rectification has occurred. So all sorts of silly expressions *may* calm an angry person down: Yelling, glowering, stamping one's feet, and pounding the table may all give one the impression that some real punishment has been meted out. But we should note, too, that expression of anger does not always mitigate it; very often expression intensifies anger. My explanation of this intensification is that the expression makes more vivid the subject's sense that he has been culpably offended, and the intensified feeling intensifies the emotion.

Grief may seem to be a counterexample to the principle that merely behavioral expressions do not dissipate the emotions they express. Does not a grief-stricken person feel better for giving free rein to weeping and wailing? I would say two things. First, that a person feels better for weeping, and wailing does not show that he *grieves* less. As we have seen, a special discomfort may arise from suppressing the behavioral expression of emotion; the relief of this discomfort is not the same as a relief from grief. Second, grieving does naturally diminish over time, and it seems that this diminishment can be facilitated by forthright grieving – by abandoning oneself to the emotion. Grief is a concern-based impression of oneself as in loss, or a construal of one's world as lacking the loved one. Perhaps letting that sense of loss be vivid, as weeping and wailing tend to make it, gradually wears it out because, like other intense experiences, it cannot be repeated indefinitely without some loss of vividness. Thus the behavioral expression of grief can contribute to its diminishment, but it does so indirectly, rather than literally providing an "outlet."

A corollary of the hydraulic theory is that anger can build up over time if not expressed. A wife suffers in silence, time after time, her husband's unfair verbal assaults. She is angry each time (or, more precisely, resentful), but out of fear refrains from giving voice to her anger. Then she explodes and murders him. The hydraulic theorist says that if she had let off her steam a bit at a time, the anger would never have built to such an intensity, and disaster would have been averted. But other explanations of how expression along the way might have averted disaster are more plausible. Expressions of anger serve to alert the offender to the subject's attitude and to give the offender an impression of the subject's readiness to defend herself. Such a show of "courage" will often put a stop to, or mitigate, the offenses, thus providing the subject less reason to be angry. From the subject's point of view, the expressions of anger may provide a certain satisfaction of the anger, giving her a sense that the injustice has been rectified, at least partially. But if she does not take small revenges, then the husband's offenses pile up, the injustice becomes greater and greater, and so her anger becomes more intense. It is not that anger flows in upon anger like beer into an already bursting bladder, but rather that anger intensifies because the offenses are accumulating.

2.10. STRENGTH

a. Four Dimensions of Strength

Emotions vary in strength along at least four dimensions: felt intensity, action determination, behavior and autonomic determination, and depth of personality ingress. These dimensions are somewhat independent.

By introspection we know that, like bodily pains and pleasures, emotions vary in how intense they feel. At one end of the continuum, they can be unfelt or only faintly felt; on the other, they dominate consciousness. We can find ourselves acting and behaving anxiously or angrily without feeling the emotion, or feeling it much less intensely than our action or behavior would suggest. In the other direction, in the theater we sometimes feel intense anxiety or joy or anger, but without its determining any action at all. It may cause a rise in blood pressure and some merely behavioral responses like facial expressions and laughter or a tightened grip on our seats, but we do nothing to avoid danger, celebrate good fortune, or redress injustice. Furthermore, such emotions may show rather little about our personality. Not only does this episode of emotion result in no action, but we might tend not to feel the same emotions, or to feel them less intensely, in the analogous situations of real life. (We suspect that this failure is due to the absence, in real life, of background music, beautiful heroes and heroines, carefully calculated dramatic buildup, and rhetorically well-crafted lines.) Once we are out of the theatre, the emotions we intensely felt there may seem to belong to another world or another person. But a similar pattern can sometimes be observed in real life: A person feels intense compassion for a sufferer, but undertakes no action even though avenues of action are available, and in a couple of hours has forgotten the episode. In the other direction, even our action on a given occasion may be strongly affected by an emotion that does not arise from deep in our personality. We may be carried away by the anger of a crowd, or the mesmerizing speech of an orator, or the spirit of a revival meeting, to do things that in a sober moment of self-possession we would never do. Emotions that are strong in the sense that they arise from what is solidest and belongs to the central core of our personality may be weakly felt or unfelt and weak in determination of our action or behavior for long stretches of our lives. This possibility is illustrated by Louis, the central character of François Mauriac's *Viper's Tangle*, discussed in Section 4.6. Such emotions can be called strong because they are manifestations and embodiments of what is most real in the personality.

b. Analysis of Strength of Emotions

Let me now offer briefly an account of the strength of emotions in the first three dimensions, that of felt intensity and action and behavior determination. (I leave the discussion of depth of personality ingress for Chapter 4 and the second volume of this work.) If emotions are concern-based construals, their strength in these three dimensions will be determined by the strength of the underlying concern, the vivacity of the construal, and the rate of impingement of the other terms of the construal on the concern. A case will illustrate this pattern of explanation.

Consider Pietro, who is anxious about the outcome of his friend's surgical operation. According to the formula, Pietro's anxiety will be stronger, other things being equal, the more he cares about Luigi. If Luigi is just an acquaintance, Pietro may not be anxious at all; if Luigi is Pietro's best buddy from the war, and they've been bosom pals and inseparable all these years, then Pietro's anxiety may be intense. But not necessarily, because the other parts of his construal of Luigi's (and his) situation also affect the intensity of his anxiety. If the operation is just an appendectomy, Pietro may not be very anxious because, although he construes his friend as in a little danger, it's not very great in his view. If the surgery is for colon cancer (and Pietro has commonly held views on the degree of danger involved in this), then he may be pretty anxious; if it is lung cancer, he may be beside himself with anxiety. The formula calls this variable the *rate of impingement* on the concern. Thus, given a certain strength of concern, the different assessments of danger impinge on that concern at different rates, the appendectomy rate being lower than the colon cancer rate, and so on. These rates may be irrational: If Pietro had a bad experience with an uncle's appendectomy when he was a child, his construal of the danger from appendectomy may impinge on his concern for Luigi at a higher rate than a construal of some more serious danger (and Pietro may even know that his construal is out of line with reality).

The third factor determining strength of emotion is *vivacity of construal*. If we imagine strength of concern and rate of impingement at some given levels, the emotion may still vary in degree of either felt intensity or action and behavior determination depending on how vividly Luigi's situation strikes Pietro. This may vary from moment to moment during the day of Luigi's operation. When Pietro turns his attention to the operation, he gets more intensely anxious; when his attention is absorbed by other things, his anxiety drops to a lower level of intensity. Not only may he become virtually unaware of it, it also affects his action and demeanor much less. When, in the afternoon, he walks into the hospital and sees convalescing surgery patients in their beds and wheelchairs, his anxiety may reach an unprecedented pitch of intensity.

As to action and behavior determination, more intense anxiety is marked by Pietro's more frequent and effortful actions and greater readiness to undertake to secure Luigi's safety and greater frequency and vehemence of behavioral expressions like pacing and nail-biting. Such action and behavior may occur at levels incommensurate with the intensity of feeling of anxiety, sometimes even in the absence of such feeling. In such cases, vivacity of construal may seem no longer part of the explanation of intensity, but I do not think that such a conclusion is necessary. I do not intend vivacity to be the same as consciousness. We saw in Section 2.3b that construals are not necessarily states of consciousness. The possibility of unconscious construals may encourage us to posit variable degrees of vivacity of construal in the absence of conscious awareness of construal.

Responses to earlier formulations of the account of emotions offered in this chapter have often characterized the view, rather casually, as another "cognitive theory" of emotions. I hope the present presentation has dispelled that urge. 'Cognitive' seems to lack any agreed-on definition in the literature, though in particular authors it may suggest judgment, knowledge, consciousness, and propositionality; and opposition to feeling, concern, motivation, and biological givenness. Construals may seem to some to be cognitions, in some sense, even if they are not judgments, do not constitute knowledge, are not conscious states, and lack a propositional character, as my view allows to be true of some emotions. But the construals that I take to be paradigm cases of emotions are concern-based, and in Section 2.7c I take pains to point out that I am not saying that an emotion is a construal plus a concern, but that the concern is a constitutive term of the construal. (The phrase "concern-based construal" may obscure this point a little.) So an emotion, in my view, is fully as "conative" as it is "cognitive," and these two aspects (if one wants to think of the matter this way) are fully synthesized in the emotion.

In this chapter I have sketched an account of emotions, and have illustrated my points by reference to a variety of emotion types and limned instances of some of these types. This has given us a quick look, along the way, at various particular emotion types. But to test the account, to discern its limits, to investigate the extent to which emotions are specific to cultures and worldviews, and to come to a deeper understanding of the types of emotion in their similarities and dissimilarities with one another, we must undertake a more systematic and detailed study of the various types of emotions, as well as of some borderline cases as diverse as vanity and the startle response. That is the agenda of Chapter 3.

3

The Variety of Emotions

3.1. INTRODUCTION

a. The Varieties of Emotions

A remarkable fact about natural languages is their high articulation about emotions. In speaking about people's beliefs, we always mention or assume a particular content: Amos believes *that the pliers are in the toolbox*. It is virtually uninformative to say simply that Amos believes, unless the context supplies implicit reference to what is believed; and the same goes for the variants of belief: doubt, conjecture, strong conviction, and so on. Desire is in a like case. To speak significantly of desire is to designate some more or less particular desired thing, action, or state of affairs, or to exploit a context that makes this clear. Amos wants (desires, wishes for) *a pair of pliers*. It is almost uninformative about Amos's state of mind to say simply, "Amos desires." By contrast, to hear that Amos is angry, afraid, or contrite is to receive significant information about his state of mind, quite apart from knowing what Amos is angry about or afraid of. By the account given in Section 2.5c, this informativeness can be explained in terms of the two kinds of propositional content of relatively mature human beings' paradigm emotions. Even if we do not know the material proposition forming Amos's emotion – *that Jeremy has maliciously hidden my pliers just when I need them* – if we know his emotion is anger, we know a great deal about his state of mind because we know anger's defining proposition. We know that Amos construes himself or someone he cares about as *offended* in some important way, that he construes the offender as a *responsible agent* who is *culpable* for the offense and *deserving of some kind of harm*; we know that he would *like to see such harm meted out* to the offender. If we know his emotion is fear or contrition, we know similarly structural things about his state of mind, in virtue of knowing the defining propositions for those emotion types.

To understand the name of an emotion is to have at least a rough and intuitive grasp of its defining proposition, and human languages have, as I say, a rather articulate emotion vocabulary. The following 160 English nouns, for example, represent, in the practices of social intercourse and self-understanding, an enormously rich and subtle grasp of states of mind: Fear, alarm, apprehension, spook,[1] concern, anxiety, buck fever, fretfulness, dither, agitation, solicitude, diffidence, fright, trepidation, dread, terror, panic, consternation, horror, distress, intimidation, calm, confidence, assurance, contentment, relief, anger, ire, resentment, disgruntlement, dudgeon, indignation, rage, outrage, wrath, animosity, spleen, fury, hostility, annoyance, displeasure, exasperation, vexation, umbrage, upset, discontent, dissatisfaction, irk, frustration, respect, admiration, reverence, veneration, deference, awe, wonderment, contempt, disdain, smugness, scorn, hate, aversion, antipathy, disgust, revulsion, abhorrence, rancor, loathing, envy, spite, schadenfreude, jealousy, grief, anguish, sadness, sorrow, repining, despondency, glumness, rue, bitterness, gloom, dejection, forlornness, loneliness, resignation, despair, depression, discouragement, melancholy, boredom, ennui, regret, chagrin, self-recrimination, remorse, disappointment, guilt, compunction, contrition, uneasiness, qualms, discomposure, discomfort, hurt, shame, humiliation, mortification, embarrassment, abashment, bashfulness, thrill, excitement, interest, enthusiasm, joy, delight, elation, gladness, buoyancy, exultation, rapture, pleasure, amusement, cheerfulness, gaiety, exuberance, jubilation, nostalgia, wistfulness, serenity, fidgetiness, expectancy, eagerness, longing, homesickness, missing, pride, triumph, hope, optimism, love, attachment, affection, benevolence, fondness, gratitude, compassion, pity, empathy, sympathy, surprise, dismay, puzzlement, misgiving, incredulity, mystification, bewilderment, astonishment, shock.

Some of these words, like "contentment," "diffidence," and "optimism," may be more often used as trait terms than as emotion terms, but they can be used for episodic concern-based construals of self and situation. Several pairs of words in the list are synonyms or come close to being so, yet a sensitive English speaker may distinguish more of them, especially on careful reflection, than we might at first expect. These differences, often slight, can sometimes be elaborated as differences of concern-based construal. That is, a careful analysis of the emotion type in terms of its defining proposition will reveal that it is distinct from several or all of its neighbors. Some emotion terms, like "excitement," "thrill," and "discomposure," are quite generic, but could be analyzed.

The 160 words seem to me ones that in at least one of their senses actually refer to emotions. Many other words, not included in the above list, are sometimes included in other philosophers' and psychologists' lists. Examples are

---

[1] It seems I have invented the nominal name of this emotion; one usually speaks of being spooked.

"ambition," "vanity," "courage," "fascination," "curiosity," "greed," "apathy," "indifference," "faith," "desire," "weakness," "tiredness," "listlessness," and "startle" (for others, see Section 2.1). As I pointed out in Section 2.2, virtually any quality that a person can care about having attributed to himself can be (part of) the content of an emotion type; one can speak of feeling ambitious, vain, courageous, or greedy. This fact may be what leads some thinkers to include such items in lists of emotions. To avoid prejudicial selectivity as much as possible, I shall examine a representative sample of these more dubious and borderline concepts, as well as the samples that seem to me closer to the center of the concept of emotion.

The main business of this chapter is to look at a representative selection of these types of emotion, with a view to (1) understanding them as types, (2) testing against particular kinds of emotion the proposal that we think of emotions as concern-based construals, and (3) getting a tolerably clear view of the various relationships that emotion types can bear to one another. In connection with the third question, we will be interested in adjudicating the rather polar views represented, on the one hand, by cultural anthropologists who hold that the number of possible emotion types is virtually unlimited because emotions are "socially constructed" and vary with cultures and, on the other hand, the view held by many philosophers and psychologists, and recently especially by biologically oriented psychologists, that we can identify a set of well-defined "basic" emotions that are universal and from which, in some sense, all the "nonbasic" emotions derive. Finally, (4) much of the psychological and moral interest of emotions lies in the particularities of their structures, so that the present chapter is an important preparation for the discussion of the broadly moral import of emotions that will be pursued in Chapter 4 and the succeeding volume of this work.

Some items belonging indisputably in the class of emotions do not fit perfectly the concern-based construal model that forms the backbone of this volume. For that reason I have eschewed the name of "theory" for what I am doing. I think that most of the central cases fit the model, and for the ones that do not, the model provides a baseline for comparison that is conceptually instructive. Philosophy, as I see it and practice it, is a discipline of conceptual exploration that aims less at theory than at understanding. To suppose that theory – or even the pursuit of it – is the only way to understand philosophically seems to me a mistake. Careful comparisons can produce understanding even in the absence of the exceptionless generalizations that theoretical philosophers seek. And the compulsion to theorize often leads to a procrustean and reductivist denial of facts and a conceptual artificiality that serve obfuscation as much as understanding.

b. Culture and Emotions

Many anthropologists stress the cultural and historical variability and "social construction" of emotions. On their view, my 160 words should not be taken as names of so many (or fewer, considering synonyms) universal human emotion types, but instead as a list of types that prevail in North America and/or Europe, or perhaps better as a list of words with meanings that vary from one subculture to another within roughly that geographical compass. We should not expect to find the same emotions among some isolated group of stone-age headhunters as we find in a present-day seminar room of graduate students at the University of Chicago or in a monastery of medieval Spain. The anthropologists' supposition is congruent with thinking of emotions as concern based construals, inasmuch as both concerns and construals seem to be highly variable and culture-dependent.

Yet the notion that some human emotions are universal hangs on. It is remarkable how acceptable Aristotle's account of the defining proposition for anger (*Rhetoric*, Book II, Chapter 2) is to that of the medieval Christian Thomas Aquinas (*Summa Theologiae*, 1a2ae, Question 46), and how similar it is to an analysis that might be offered by a 20th-century American who is neither Aristotelian nor Christian. An emotion structurally similar to what we call envy was well known to Dante[2] and can be discerned among the Ilongots of the Philippine province of Nueva Viscaya.[3] And to some extent the notion that some emotions are universal is even unintentionally abetted by the work of the anthropologists. For example, Catherine Lutz strains to show how different Ifaluk emotions are from those of North America and Europe,[4] but her central three chapters on Ifaluk emotion types are about emotions that unmistakably call for description in terms very reminiscent of love, anger, and fear, three items that persistently recur in Western lists of "basic emotions" (though love occurs less than anger and fear). And Lutz's efforts to show strong dissimilarities between Ifaluk emotions and their Euramerican counterparts depend heavily, as we will see, on ideological caricatures of the latter.

I shall argue that Lutz and other anthropologists need a more powerful set of concepts than they use for analyzing similarities and differences among emotion types. They need, for example, to distinguish differences

---

[2] *The Divine Comedy*, Purgatorio XVII, pp. 115–120:

> There is, who through his neighbour's overthrow
> Hopes to excel, and only for that cause
> Longs that he may from greatness be brought low.

> There is, who fears power, favour, fame to lose
> Because another mounts; wherefore his lot
> So irks, he loves the opposite to choose.

Translated by Laurence Binyon in *The Portable Dante* (New York: Viking, 1947), p. 276.

[3] See Michelle Z. Rosaldo, *Knowledge and Passion: Ilongot Notions of Self and Social Life* (Cambridge: Cambridge University Press, 1980), pp. 88, 126–28.

[4] *Unnatural Emotions: Everyday Sentiments on a Micronesian Atoll and Their Challenge to Western Theory* (Chicago: University of Chicago Press, 1988).

of emotion *type* as determined by defining propositions, from differences of cultural *evaluation* of emotions of a given type, from differences of *object range* of some type of emotion, from differences of *association* created by emotion vocabulary, from differences of *theory* about such things as where emotions come from, what they are made of, and where (e.g., in the body) they occur. Such distinctions among distinctions would facilitate much more refined assessments of the similarities and differences among emotions across cultures.

If we make defining propositions central to the determination of emotion type, we will find that it is a matter of judgment just how much to build into the defining proposition of an emotion. If we *want* to identify a culturally distinctive emotion, we will sometimes be able to find some distinctive propositional content definitive of the emotion for that particular culture. For example, Christian contrition can be taken to have, in its defining proposition, a reference to the grace of God in Jesus Christ; if this thought is not informing a person's contrition, then his emotion is not the distinctively Christian one. But we may wish to stress what is common in the structure of contrition as it is found in several cultures or outlooks, and on this agenda we will build into the defining proposition just enough distinctiveness to differentiate contrition from some of its neighbors like compunction, shame, and embarrassment but little enough to keep to cultural commonalities.

These judgment calls may seem arbitrary and confusing, but they are not so if kept aboveboard. The business of defining emotions by type is a human enterprise with human purposes, and thus the precise line between material and defining propositional content is likewise determinable by human purposes. Arbitrariness and confusion enter when the agenda – say, the conservative protection of a moral tradition, or the desire to stress commonalities for purposes of dialogue and reconciliation, or the biologization of psychology – is not acknowledged, and the analysis is undertaken on the assumption that the inquiry is guided by steel rails like Platonic forms or features of the human genome. This is not to say that just anything can be placed in the defining proposition for an emotion; limits are set by the notion of a type. For example, it would make no sense, on any agenda, to say it is definitive of Christian contrition that it make reference to Tom Sawyer's disobeying his Aunt Polly.

The studies of emotion types that follow will not be consistently either strictly indexed to a culture or of the more ecumenical type. I will be doing both types of analysis, as occasion presents. Usually I will write out of a North American context, but I attempt to do so in such a way as to encompass some other cultures as well. On occasion I will study an emotion type as indexed to a fairly well-defined subculture such as Christianity or a fairly enclosed culture about which I have anthropological information such as that of the Ifaluk or the Ilongots. These methodological comments make clear that this chapter cannot pretend to be a comprehensive summary of all emotion types. Instead, it is a sampling that I hope will be representative enough to show the variety of things that count as emotions, the broad aptness of the concern-based construal paradigm, and the fruitfulness of the method of analysis suggested by the paradigm.

Another limitation on the present endeavor is the precision and the determinateness of the analyses of individual emotion types. I will be specifying differences of a grain fine enough to make some of my attributions of emotion types to particular items of emotion vocabulary controversial among accomplished speakers of English. Such disagreement about vocabulary does not trouble me if I can garner agreement that my analysis has identified *some* distinct type of human emotion. In everyday usage, emotion vocabulary is not as discriminating as I try to be in the analyses of this chapter. But I have tried to follow real discriminations embedded in English as it is spoken by its most sensitive speakers, or to discern the subtleties of usage, as well as I can, of non-English vocabularies.

I noted that it seems indisputable that some broad basic categories of emotion are universal or nearly so. Something recognizably like what we call anger, fear, love, joy, hope, sadness, envy, pride, shame, disappointment, and regret seem to transcend cultural differences and to be found universally among human beings. If something in the neighborhood of this claim were not true, it is hard to imagine how the people of one culture could understand those of another, in the sense of understanding why, as agents, they do what they do and why, as behavers, they react as they react. People in widely different cultures fairly reliably recognize one another's emotional states, in a general sort of way, by facial expressions,[5] and even more reliably if other behavioral data are added. If we came across a human group whose members never exhibited any emotion that we would call by any of the 160 names, their minds and actions would be very opaque to us. But in fact even the most isolated human groups are not opaque to us in quite this way. Of course there *are* difficulties of understanding alien cultures, and some of these are traceable to differences of emotional response; yet we understand the plays of Sophocles, the novels of Jane Austen, and anthropologists' narrative accounts of very foreign people. This is one of the reasons for the recurrent efforts to identify a set of "basic" emotions.

c. Basic Emotions

The idea that some emotions are basic or primary while others are derivative or secondary is a little bit like the idea in chemistry of a small number of elements of which a much larger variety of other things can be compounded. Or it is like the biological idea of a relatively small number of species (dogs,

[5] See Paul Ekman and Willard Friesen, "A New Pan-Cultural Facial Expression of Emotion" *Motivation and Emotion* **10** (1986): 159–168.

finches), of which there are a much larger number of varieties (wolf, coyote, fox; bunting, cardinal, sparrow). Or sometimes it is like the culinary idea of a basic soup or bread or sauce, which can be varied by adding different ingredients that are not themselves soups or breads or sauces. Let me review a sampling of such theories, including some older and newer ones.

Diogenes Laertius reports that the Stoics held the emotions to be divided into four classes, distress (λύπη), fear (φόβος), desire (ἐπιθυμία), and pleasure (ἡδονή). The more particular emotions are species or forms of these four. For example, pity (ἔλεος) is distress at another's undeserved suffering; envy (φθόνος) is distress at others' prosperity; rivalry (ζηλοτυπία) is distress at the possession by another of what one has oneself; dejection (ἄχθος) is distress that weighs one down; fretfulness (ἀνία) is distress coming from obsessive or intensifying self-talk; confusion (σύγχυσις) is irrational distress; shame (αἰσχύνη) is fear of disgrace; panic (θόρυβος) is fear with pressure exercised by sound; enchantment (κήλησις) is pleasure that charms the ear; malevolent joy (ἐπιχαιρεκακία) is pleasure at another's ills; and so on.[6]

Thomas Aquinas lists eleven emotions (*passiones*), five pairs of two opposites and a single, which belong to two different parts of the sensory (nonintellectual) appetite, the concupiscible or desiring appetite, and the irascible or striving appetite. He seems to regard this as a complete list of the emotions: love (*amor*) and hatred (*odium*), desire (*desiderium*) and aversion (*fuga*), and joy (*gaudium*) and sadness (*tristitia*) belong to the concupiscible appetite, while fear (*timor*) and courage (*audacia*), hope (*spes*) and despair (*desperatio*), and anger (*ira*) belong to the irascible (see *Summa Theologiae*, first part of the second part, Question 25, Article 3, Reply). He thinks of some of these emotions – joy, sadness, hope, and fear – as principal; but unlike later theorists, Thomas does not speak of nonprincipal emotions as mixtures or kinds of principal ones. Instead, an emotion is principal relative to other emotions if it is in some sense the *goal* of the other emotions:

> Joy and sadness are called principal emotions because in them all the others have their end and fulfilment. . . . Fear and hope are called principal, not in the sense that one says, *tout court*, that all the others find fulfilment in them, but in the sense that they are the last stage of appetitive movement towards some objective: for where the objective is some good, appetitive movement begins with love, passes into desire and ends in hope; where it is some evil, it begins with hatred, passes into aversion, and ends in fear (Question 25, Article 4, Reply).[7]

Thomas Hobbes enumerates seven "simple passions," namely "*appetite, desire, love, aversion, hate, joy, and grief*" (*Leviathan*, Part I, Chapter VI; Hobbes's italics). These take different names depending on different "considerations"

[6] See Diogenes Laertius, *Lives of the Eminent Philosophers*, Book VII, pp. 111–115.
[7] Blackfriars edition, Volume 19, translated by Eric D'Arcy (New York: McGraw-Hill, 1967), translation slightly altered.

such as how likely the subject thinks it is that his desire will be satisfied, what kind of object is loved or hated, how these simple passions are compounded, and the order in which they change into one another and succeed one another. For example, *appetite* is called "hope" when the subject thinks his appetite will be satisfied, but it is called "despair" when he thinks not. *Aversion* is called "fear" when the subject thinks the object of aversion will harm him but "courage" when he thinks he can avoid the harm by resisting it. *Desire* is called "ambition" when it is for office or precedence, "covetousness" when it is for riches, and "curiosity" when it is for knowledge. *Grief* is called "dejection" when the subject feels it upon considering that he lacks power, and it is called "shame" when the consideration is that he is dishonorable because lacking in some ability. When appetite, aversion, hope, and fear succeed one another, the succession is called "deliberation." When such a succession comes to an end, the last passion in the series is called "will." And so on.

René Descartes distinguishes the principal passions from all others, commenting that,

I speak only of the principal [passions], because many other more particular ones could be distinguished besides, and their number is indefinite. . . . But the number of those which are simple and primitive is not very large. For by carrying out a review of all those I have enumerated, one can discover with ease that only six of them are of this kind—namely Wonder [*l'admiration*], Love [*l'amour*], Hatred [*la haine*], Desire [*le désir*], Joy [*la joie*], and Sadness [*la tristesse*] – and that all the others are composed of some of these six or are species of them.[8]

The emotions Esteem and Scorn "are only species of Wonder" (article 150), while Hope is "Joy and Desire mingled together" (article 165), and Envy is "a species of Sadness mingled with Hatred" (article 182).

Robert Plutchik discerns eight primary emotions forming four pairs of polar opposites, which correspond to eight patterns of biologically adaptive behavior that he finds in organisms at every evolutionary level. The eight behavior patterns are incorporation (e.g., of food), rejection (e.g., of feces), destruction (e.g., of enemies), protection (e.g., against enemies), reproduction, deprivation (e.g., of something loved), orientation (e.g., to a new or strange object), and exploration. The corresponding emotion pairs are acceptance–disgust, anger–fear, joy–grief, and surprise–expectation. "All other emotions are mixed; that is, they can be synthesized by various combinations of the primary emotions."[9]

Carroll Izard considers anger, contempt, disgust, distress, fear, guilt, interest, joy, shame, and surprise basic, though he sometimes prefers not to

---

[8] René Descartes, *The Passions of the Soul*, translated by Stephen H. Voss (Indianapolis: Hackett, 1989), articles 68–69.

[9] *The Emotions: Facts, Theories, and a New Model* (New York: Random House, 1962), p. 41. See also Plutchik (1984) "Emotions: A General Psychoevolutionary Theory," in K. R. Scherer and P. Ekman (eds.), *Approaches to Emotion* (Hillsdale, New Jersey: Erlbaum), pp. 197–219.

call them emotions but instead "feeling-motivational states." He thinks these are basic because they can occur without cognitive mediation and "because each of them has (a) a specific innately determined neural substrate, (b) a characteristic facial expression or neuromuscular-expressive pattern, and (c) a distinct subjective or phenomenological quality."[10] These basic states generate nonbasic emotions (though Izard calls them "affective-cognitive structures") when they interact with cognitions. The very small infant is capable of the feeling-motivational state of joy, for example, without this being connected with the thought or perception of any object; at this point it is just a feeling with a particular neurological realization and a characteristic facial expression. But as the child grows, this state gains cognitive accretions. For example, joy becomes a response first to faces, then to Mother's face in particular, and later, when the child can conceptualize *Mother*, to the whole individual that Mother is. At that point joy is transmuted into *love*, a nonbasic emotion, or as Izard calls it, "complex affective-cognitive network." A similar story can be told about the whole range of adult human emotions. So the basic emotions are noncognitive, and all other emotions (thus the vast majority of what we call emotions in human life) are constituted by adding cognitions of various kinds to one or another of the basic emotions.

Keith Oatley tentatively proposes a list of five basic emotions: happiness, sadness, fear, anger, and disgust.[11] He thinks these five types are basic because each type meets all three of the following criteria: (1) It has eliciting conditions that are well-defined and shared with birds and nonhuman mammals. The condition for fear is dangers, for sadness losses, for happiness successes, and so on. (2) It has distinctive physiological accompaniments. Thus anger, fear, and sadness have a higher heart rate than happiness and disgust, while anger has a higher skin temperature than fear and sadness, while sadness involves greater decreases in skin conductance than disgust, anger, and fear (p. 58). (3) It has a cross-culturally consistent facial expression.[12] Oatley seems to follow the rather standard pattern of reducing "nonbasic" emotions to variants of basic ones. Thus, while disgust is properly elicited by contaminated food, the same feeling, if elicited by viewing a person of greatly inferior rank, is called contempt (p. 60); and "'embarrassment'

---

[10] *Human Emotions* (New York: Plenum Press, 1977), p. 83. See also his *Patterns of Emotions: A New Analysis of Anxiety and Depression* (San Diego: Academic Press, 1972), and "Basic Emotions, Relations Among Emotions, and Emotion-Cognition Relations" *Psychological Review* **99** (1992): 561–565.

[11] Keith Oatley, *Best Laid Schemes: The Psychology of Emotions* (Cambridge, England: Cambridge University Press, 1992), p. 55.

[12] Oatley cites evidence from P. Ekman and W. V. Friesen, "Constants Across Cultures in the Face and Emotion," *Journal of Personality and Social Psychology*, **17** (1971): 124–129; and P. Ekman, "Cross-Cultural Studies of Facial Expression," in P. Ekman (ed.), *Darwin and Facial Expression: A Century of Research in Review* (New York: Academic Press, 1973).

means fear with the semantic content of being an object of unwelcome attention" (p. 63).

It is instructive to compare the enterprise of finding basic emotions with the chemical project of finding elements and with the biological project of classifying animals and plants in species. Whereas the table of elements and the classification of species are quite well agreed upon by the experts in these fields, experts on the emotions exhibit no such agreement about which ones are basic. None of the seven lists that I have reviewed is identical with any other, and this situation would not be helped by extending our review to other proposed lists. Andrew Ortony and Terence Turner[13] present a table of fourteen authors or sets of collaborators since 1884 who have proposed lists of basic emotions, including eleven beyond the ones that I have reviewed. None of these lists maps perfectly onto any other. Why do we not find agreement among the experts on emotions such as we find among their colleagues in chemistry and biology?

James Averill[14] points out that basicality is relative to human interests; and Turner and Ortony, in a response to the critics of their criticism of basic emotions, show nicely how the differing lists of Ekman, Panksepp, and Izard are conditioned by the different research interests of the three men. "The problem, as we see it, is that each theorist has his own preferred approach to understanding emotions – Ekman's is the face, Izard's are biosocial considerations, and Panksepp's is the brain."[15] But, different as these three foci are, they are relatively similar compared to other approaches that might be taken; Ekman, Izard, and Panksepp all research the emotions along broadly biological lines. The emotions are, however, by no means narrowly biological phenomena. They are strongly influenced by culture, interacting with culturally variable norms of ethical and spiritual character, social organization, and individual and social well being. It is plausible to suppose that an expertly composed list of chemical elements or taxonomy of animal species is not relative to variable cultural standards in the way that lists of basic emotions are, because they can be kept free of such contestable norms. But separation of emotions from their ethical, social, and psychological contexts is impossible, or at best highly artificial.

The very criteria of basicality that tend to guide biologically oriented psychologists – namely, evolutionary usefulness in a remote ancestral past, homology with related species, and distinctive ANS and CNS patterns – are called into question by recognizing the variety of functions of emotions in human life. Given the role that culture plays in our emotions, why should

---

[13] "What's Basic About Basic Emotions?" *Psychological Review* **97** (1990): 315–331.

[14] "In the Eyes of the Beholder," in Paul Ekman and Richard J. Davidson (eds.), *The Nature of Emotion: Fundamental Questions* (New York: Oxford University Press, 1994), pp. 7–14.

[15] "Basic Emotions: Can Conflicting Criteria Converge?" *Psychological Review* **99** (1992): 566–571; 570.

we suppose that the same emotions that would be basic for toads and rabbits would be basic for us? Human emotions are not tied to biologically relevant situation types in the way that nonhuman emotions are. People get angry not just about invasions of their nests and assaults on their persons, but also about injustices in far-away countries and situations depicted in novels. They fear not just predators and natural calamities, but the moral degeneration of themselves and their children and their communities.

A list of basic emotions guided by questions of human fulfilment and health and social well-being, the kind of thing that the Greeks called *eudaimonia* and which is not so very far from what our personality theorists think about and our psychotherapists try to help people attain, will surely need to include emotions that are not *biologically* basic. The remote historical past can be crucial in human lives in a way that it is not in any other species. Thus an emotion-tinged historical memory – perhaps something like nostalgia or pride or respect – might well be considered a basic emotion (I am thinking of the Hebrews). Because shame and pride and envy depend heavily on a concept of self, they don't extend very far down the evolutionary "hierarchy" and will thus probably not be included in biologically oriented lists of basic emotions. But they are likely to be very basic to an educator or psychotherapist, who is concerned with distinctively human development and well-being.

Most of the 20th-century lists of basic emotions contain fear and anger, emotions that are arguably both biologically and eudaimonistically basic. In the table of Ortony and Turner's 1990 article (p. 316), only the lists of Frijda, Mowrer, and Weiner & Graham lack anger and fear. But none of the lists contains pride or envy and only two (Tomkins and Izard) contain shame. But pride, envy, and shame seem much more basic to the formation of human personality than surprise, which shows up in five of the lists in the chart (Ekman, Frijda, Izard, Plutchik, and Tomkins). Surprise shows up in none of the older lists that I reviewed, which tended to be driven more by interests in moral and personality formation than biology. Similarly, disgust appears in six of the lists in the chart (Ekman, Izard, McDougall, Oatley of Johnson-Laird, Plutchik, and Tomkins), but in none of the older lists I reviewed.

Another explanation of the wild disagreements among the lists of basic emotions proposed by experts is the complexity and variety of the relationships among the emotion types. The lists of basic emotions that we reviewed from the Stoics, Aquinas, Hobbes, Descartes, Plutchik, Izard, and Oatley illustrate that schemes of basic emotions tend to be proposals of systematic connections among emotions. They aim to highlight certain connections and disconnections, and they predispose the visibility of some connections and the invisibility of others. Thus the differences among the lists can be explained in part by a prejudicial selectivity among the possible relationships. One of the chief aims of the present chapter is to explore such relationships, but I suggest that these are more fruitfully explored if we do not presuppose some view about which emotions are most basic. Accordingly I shall propose no such list of my own. Lists of basic emotions, while they highlight some relationships among emotion types, hide others – both similarities and dissimilarities. If we resist the temptation to make a particular set of emotions basic, we will be freer to see the *variety* of ways in which emotion types are similar to and contrast with one another, are forms of one another, and share common elements. I believe our survey will show that the variety of these interrelationships is too complex to be captured by any schema of basic emotions.

Let me preview some of the kinds of relationships that we will explore. (1) As I suggested in Chapter 2, emotions may be connected to one another by the concerns on which they may be based. A concern for a loved one, for example, can give rise to a wide range of emotion types, depending on how the loved one is construed. Instances of diverse types of emotions, then, can be family members in virtue of a common basic concern. (2) We will find that some pairs of emotion types have strongly symmetrical defining propositions, even if they are "opposites" in some respect. Envy and a certain kind of pride are like this, as are anger and gratitude, hope and fear. (3) An even broader similarity among groups of emotions is their hedonic value, since so many emotions seem to be either pleasant or unpleasant (or in some cases a combination thereof). (4) Some kinds of emotions share a conceptual element. For example, envy and jealousy both involve the concept of a rival, while pride, shame, and envy all involve some kind of evaluative self-reference. (5) Lists of basic emotions are often motivated by the fact that some emotion types can be seen as versions of other ones. Thus anxiety, panic, and terror seem pretty clearly to be versions of fear; or we might say that fear functions as a paradigm or prototype for this family of emotions. The version-of relationship is easy to abuse, and it is often abused when we traffic in basic emotions. Are grief, sorrow, despair, and boredom all versions of sadness? Are jealousy and embarrassment forms of fear? To try to make them such would incline us to gloss over some crucial dissimilarities among them.

d. The Character of the Present Chapter

The account of emotions as concern-based construals divides emotion types most fundamentally along the lines of concern-based ways of "seeing" situations, not of physiological indicators or observable behaviors. It is a conception of emotion designed to throw light especially on *human* emotions – that is, to distinguish among them in a fine-grained way, but at the same time to throw fairly precise light on their similarities. I want to steer a way between two extremes: on the one hand, the tendency to oversystematize and so reduce and falsify the diversity of emotions, as the lists of basic emotions are prone to do; on the other, a tendency to exaggerate diversity among emotion types as some cultural anthropologists tend to do.

As I limn each of these many emotion types in terms of the construal that is constitutive of each and the concern(s) on which it is based, I shall try to avoid describing one emotion in terms of another (jealousy is fear of losing one's beloved to a rival, envy is coveting what belongs to another combined with hating the other for possessing it, etc.). That is, I shall shun as much as I can the language of emotion in characterizing the various emotions as concern-based construals.

An error that haunts the neighborhood of basic emotions is a kind of Platonism, though today's Forms reside in DNA molecules rather than in abstract entities beyond the realm of empirical particulars. The error is the supposition that certain English words, like "anger" and "fear," have a single genuine meaning that is given with human nature. But an analogous and opposite error, a kind of radical nominalism that haunts anthropologists' thinking, is that virtually *any* difference in the consistent usage of an emotion term constitutes a difference of emotion type. Perhaps neither of these schools would affirm these doctrines, were they clearly posed for assent; nevertheless, the doctrines seem to operate in the work of these scholars. Though I eschew Platonism, I see remarkable agreement, across centuries and across cultures, in the identity of certain types of emotion, such as anger and fear, hope and envy; and I do not think that all consistent differences of usage of emotion terms provide evidence of difference of emotion type. For example, emotion terms, like any other terms, can have more than one established usage. In one usage the Ilongot term *"liget"* may be very similar to one of the North American usages of the term "anger"; and if so, we should not be misled by the fact that *"liget"* has *other* usages to which "anger" is never put, into thinking that the Ilongots do not have an emotion type that we could designate as "anger." Even the fact that an emotion is not particularly lexicalized in a given society does not imply that people in that culture are not subject to that emotion. And even within a society, ordinary language is not, by itself, a very reliable guide to emotion types, because emotion terms may be used more or less loosely. Some speakers will hardly know the difference between anger and frustration; and even the best spea-kers *sometimes* use these terms interchangeably. For precision we must go to the more competent speakers of English and then press them for precision.

Given the ingenuity and perspicacity of philosophers, I am sure that some of my proposed defining propositions will be found wanting. I am happy to receive corrections. My point, however, is not so much to get perfectly exceptionless formulations of defining propositions as to show, at least in a rough way, the complexity and variety of human emotions and to show a way of analyzing them that is potentially more precise than people are initially inclined to think an analysis of emotions can be.

3.2. BAD PROSPECTS

a. Defining Fear

Let me begin by mentioning two kinds of "fear" that I will not be talking about. We sometimes ascribe dispositional fears. If we say that Richard fears being rejected in social situations, we do not suggest that he is currently in a state of fear; we mean that, when the occasion arises, or he thinks about a social situation in which it seems to him that he might be rejected, he tends to experience fear or, if he does not actually feel it, at least he tends to be in a state of (unconscious) fear. Another use of "S fears..." that I will not discuss is in conventional expressions that make no real reference to any emotion: "He built the engine with great care, for fear it wouldn't last long otherwise." By contrast with these two kinds of case, I am interested in the actual occurrence of the emotion. An analogous proviso applies to some of the other emotions discussed in this chapter.

It might seem that the object of fear is always construed as a danger of some sort, but this would define fear too narrowly. We do fear dangers – auto accidents, AIDS, slippery sidewalks – but we also fear being rejected by Yale and looking foolish to our colleagues, and these need not be exactly dangers. So let us say instead that the object of fear must be construed as *aversive* (where this adjective encompasses undesirable as well as harmful or dangerous). The aversive "look" of the object depends on some concern or concerns of the subject: to be safe from harm, to get into Yale, to look good to one's colleagues.

Often we construe what we fear as lying in the future, but this too is not quite general. A man might fear that his mother was on an airplane that he knows to have crashed a couple of hours earlier. What seems to be essential about fear is that the aversive object is construed, not as in the future but as still *a possibility*. It is of course in fact now settled, and no longer merely possible, whether the man's mother was on the plane. But he, not knowing whether it is so or not, construes the event as a possibility: It is possible that she was on the plane, and it is possible that she was not.[16] Once he knows that his mother has died in the crash, he does not fear that she died in the crash. Instead he grieves over her, or is angry at the airline – or he may fear something else, say, that his father, who is now in declining years, will not survive for long without his wife.

But the aversive state of affairs is not, in fear, construed as *merely* possible; our man might construe it as remotely or logically possible that his mother

---

[16] Note again the inadequacy of a view of emotions that makes their propositional content generally a matter of belief or judgment. A perfectly rational person who knows that either she was or she was not in the plane still construes the situation in terms of the proposition: *It is [only] possible that she was in the plane.* A person would have to be quite disoriented to believe that it is really still only a possibility whether his mother was in the plane or not.

was on a plane that he knows to have crashed, without fearing that she was on it. If he fears this, it seems that he construes the event as *significantly* possible, or *probable* in some degree. It would be wrong to try to quantify the construed probability more narrowly than with the vague quantifiers "significantly" and "in some degree."

David Hume stresses fear's ascription of probability to the aversive object, but he seems to go wrong in characterizing fear as a "direct passion" in contrast with such emotions as pride and shame, love and hatred. What makes pride, for example, an "indirect" passion? Pride is a pleasurable view of oneself that has a certain kind of "cause" – what we would call a reason. Thus if I am proud of my house I take a pleasurable view of myself *because that* (fine) *house is mine.* Hume thinks that fear does not have a "cause" in this sense and, thus, is a direct passion. But this seems incorrect. If someone fears a slippery sidewalk, it makes perfectly good sense to specify his reason(s) for fearing it: He needs to traverse it, his shoes do not have good traction on ice, he is unskilled at remaining upright on slippery surfaces – in short, the conditions are such that the slippery sidewalk may well occasion an injurious fall. Apart from some such reasons, it may be as hard to see why a slippery sidewalk would be an object of fear as it is to see why, apart from reasons, a self would be an object of pride.

To defend Hume's thesis that fear is direct, one might reply that no one fears slippery sidewalks anyway; instead, people fear the harm that slippery sidewalks can do. But this reply goes against our ordinary way of talking and thinking about fear. We do speak of fearing slippery sidewalks, and it seems, experientially, that such objects as snakes, precipices, the ridicule of others, and so forth are typically what is feared, and not just the harmful consequences or properties of these things. Sometimes we fear things without knowing why we fear them, and some objects of fear are in fact direct: It makes no sense to ask a person why he fears excruciating pain, when he construes it as probable that he will suffer some. In most cases, however, reasons can be given for fearing what we fear, even if we do not fear what we fear merely for the reasons we might give. The notion of a construal nicely accounts for this fact: The slippery sidewalk is (in an imaginable case) *itself* feared, *under the aspect* of a more or less articulable set of reasons. The construal integrates the reason into the object, yet we remain able, upon reflection, to separate the two.

But if we do fear slippery sidewalks, charging bulls, and the like, it might seem that our analysis of fear as involving attribution of possibility cannot be correct. This is because such objects are actualities, not possibilities. The solution here, as elsewhere, is to see that fear is a construal. To fear the charging bull is not merely to perceive the actuality of a bull accelerating toward me with head down, but to perceive this as *fraught with aversive possibility.* The fact that this construal is, in the normal case, highly spontaneous and that the "reason" for the fear is so locked into the perception as to be separable only in reflective analysis does nothing to undermine the reference to possibility.

Let us consider fear's consequent concern. Depending on how clear the subject is about his reasons for fearing something, or how well he can distinguish his reasons for fearing something from what he fears, the subject will either want to avoid the feared thing or want to avoid its consequences, or both. Thus if he is not very clear about his reasons for fearing the slippery sidewalk, he will simply want to avoid slippery sidewalks; but if he is clear (as is normally the case) that the slippery sidewalk has its aversive look under the aspect of the probability of its occasioning a nasty fall, and that the fall is made more probable by his having shoes without proper traction, then he may wish to have some shoes with proper traction, or wish for something else that will allow him to avoid the nasty fall. Fear's consequent concern, then, is either a desire to avoid the thing feared or a desire to avoid the consequences that figure in the subject's reasons for his fear. The consequent concern is sometimes, but not always, a desire to act so as to avoid either the object or its consequences. Thus the subject may want to walk on the snow to avoid the sidewalk, or he may want to get out his golf shoes so as to be able to navigate the sidewalk. But in other cases the consequent concern may not be a desire to *act* at all:

A fan conscientiously umpiring a Yankees game may be afraid that Jackson will strike out without wishing to bring it about that he won't, and without wishing to bring it about that the Yankees will not lose if Jackson does strike out.[17]

The defining proposition for fear, then, will be something like the following: *X presents an aversive possibility of a significant degree of probability; may X or its aversive consequences be avoided.*[18]

b. Is Ifaluk *Metagu* Fear?

Catherine Lutz has an account of a couple of fear-like emotion concepts in use on the coral atoll of Ifaluk (about 1200 miles southeast of the Philippines).[19] She tentatively translates "metagu" as "fear/anxiety," and

---

[17] Wayne Davis, "The Varieties of Fear" *Philosophical Studies* **51** (1987): 287–310; 296.

[18] Just as "aversive" is to be read, not just as an evaluative term, but as expressing the *concern* to avoid things *like* X or its consequences (thus the basic concern), so "may" is to be taken "personally," as expressing a desire (thus the consequent concern) to avoid X or its consequences. This formulation, like all the formulations of defining propositions in this chapter, is to be interpreted in light of the discussion that precedes it. It would be a mistake to think that we can actually pack the logic of an emotion type into an unaided formula. The formula is merely a guide and an approximation, a summary of the preceding discussion. I have found that the discipline of trying to formulate defining propositions raises questions and forces precision in the discussion of an emotion type's logic.

[19] *Unnatural Emotions*, Chapter 7.

"rus" with "panic/fright/surprise," but the general strategy of her book is to point out how different Ifaluk emotions are from those of North America and Europe. Because the use of "*metagu*" seems to be closer than that of "*rus*" to our concept of fear, I propose to use Lutz's account to adjudicate the question, Is *metagu* fear?

Lutz entitles her chapter "The Cultural Construction of Danger" and consistently refers to the things and situations that evoke *metagu* in the Ifaluk as "dangers." Since I have suggested that "danger" does not categorize well the things that are feared, we might look here for a difference between *metagu* and fear. In careful English, dangers threaten fairly severe physical, social, or psychological harm. Situations that threaten drowning, loss of crucial food supplies, sickness, and blows to the body constitute dangers, but the angry disapproval of others, if it does not threaten such eventualities, is not properly a danger, nor is some situation that only threatens to embarrass us. But Lutz appears to be using "danger" loosely. On her account, *metagu* is like fear in being a response to this whole range of things, and not just the ones that we would call dangers. Representative situations that evoke *metagu* in the Ifaluk are typhoons that threaten drowning and the loss of food supplies, fishing in shark-infested waters, climbing tall coconut trees, being beaten up by drunks, being visited by ancestral spirits who threaten physical harm, being the object of justified anger, especially of authority figures, and being ridiculed, gossiped about, and placed in uncomfortable social situations. This appears to be just the range of kinds of things that North Americans fear, namely, dangers and *other* aversive eventualities.

The particularities of the list differentiate Americans somewhat from Ifaluk. Most North Americans, I venture, do not fear the spirits of their dead ancestors; but if we believed, like the Ifaluk, that offended dead mothers-in-law are fairly likely to visit their sons' houses and gouge out the eyes of their wives and children (p. 192), we would fear them too. A difference in that degree of particularity does not differentiate one emotion type from another. If we run into somebody in our culture who fears the spirit of her dead mother-in-law, we are not inclined to think that the type of emotion she is feeling is different from what we normally call fear; so finding such a thing in another culture is not a reason to suppose that we have encountered a different type of emotion.

What about the possibility/probability ascription in fear's defining proposition? *Metagu* does not seem to differ from fear in this respect. *Metagu* is about *possible* death, illness, embarrassment, anger of others, and so on, and we have no reason to doubt that the Ifaluk experience *metagu* in situations involving these things only when the construed probability of the aversive eventuality reaches a certain degree.

Nor does *metagu* differ from fear by involving reasons or consequent concerns in a different way. The Ifaluk can tell you why they fear fishing in shark-infested waters and why they fear sleeping alone (it's because of the spirits). *And metagu's* consequent concern, just like fear's, is to avoid the aversive object or its consequences. *Metagu* motivates Ifaluk to climb coconut palms *carefully*, as well as to avoid sleeping alone.

So it looks as though *metagu* has the same defining proposition as fear. Or, if there are differences, they are subtle enough not to be identifiable using Lutz's examples and generalizations. But she points out another way *metagu* differs from American fear: The Ifaluk prize *metagu* in a way that Americans do not prize fear. She recounts the self-report of an older and highly ranked man who is complacent, or even a little prideful, about his fear. Some ruffians from a neighboring island arrived one day by canoe and wrought a bit of havoc on Ifaluk. Eventually they came to Gatachimang's house and loudly demanded liquor.

He was extremely afraid, he said, as he told them in a small voice that he had none, and he imitated the cowering and fearful posture he took then in the course of his storytelling (p. 184).

Lutz points out that an emotion that would probably embarrass most Americans or Europeans occasions self-congratulation in this Ifaluk elder.

A person who declares her or his fear – either *rus* (panic/fright/surprise) or *metagu* (fear/anxiety) – can be seen as saying to others, "I am harmless, and because I am harmless, I am a good person and worthy of your respect" (p. 185).

The Ifaluk also use fear liberally in moral education. When a child has misbehaved, a woman of the household may slip away and dress up as a special bush-dwelling spirit, the *tarita*; then she appears in the bushes motioning the child toward her and making eating gestures, for she is a child-eating spirit.

At this, the child usually leaps in panic into the arms of the nearest adult who, after calling the *tarita* to "come get this child who has misbehaved," often ends up holding the child in amused approval of its reaction (p. 206).

This evaluation of fear does seem to distinguish Ifaluk culture, in a pretty general way, from Western cultures. Gentleness is regarded as a virtue by many Westerners, but it is not usually associated with fear as it is among the Ifaluk. It does not seem to the reflective among us that boldness and gentleness are incompatible.

And yet Ifaluk approval of fear is not unqualified. Fear must be overcome or managed when it stands in the way of gathering fish and coconuts (p. 198). People often refuse offers of food from others they do not know well, and "a lack of *metagu* and a corresponding readiness to accept offers of food is considered to be a positive sign of intimacy and mutuality" (p. 189). Perhaps we can generalize that the North American evaluation of fear is nuanced and mixed: Sometimes fear is regarded as praiseworthy, as when someone fears for the safety of his child or fears doing an injustice; sometimes it is regarded as disabling (stagefright) or craven (a fear of the authorities that prevents the doing of justice). The Ifaluk evaluation is also nuanced and mixed, but the mix seems to include a greater proportion of approval than the American mix, and the reasons for approval differ somewhat.

How shall we characterize the difference between Americans and Ifaluk with respect to fear? Because *metagu* and fear seem to have the same defining proposition, let us say that they are "essentially" the same emotion. Lutz points out some differences in object range between *metagu* and fear – for example, that dead ancestors are a common object of *metagu* but much less commonly an object of fear. I have argued that *such* differences of object range do not imply difference of emotion type. Lutz also points out both similarities and differences of evaluation between *metagu* and fear. So I propose that we leave the matter thus: *Metagu* and fear are the same emotion, partially differentially evaluated[20] and with a partially different object range.

c. Anxiety, Fright, Dread, Terror, Panic, Horror, and Spook

Let us now take a briefer look at some emotions that are related, closely or more distantly, to fear.

Anxiety is sometimes said to differ from fear in being "objectless" or "free floating," but if we go by ordinary usage of the term "anxiety," we are sometimes anxious about particular aversive possibilities, just as we fear particular ones. No very clear line distinguishes fearing that one's mother has died in a plane crash from being anxious about the possibility, but a difference of shading is real for careful users of English. Fear is about *more* defined and *more* probable possibilities. If one construes the situation as vaguely threatening, then one speaks of anxiety. For example, if our man has heard of no plane crash but just has a vague premonition of disaster connected with his mother's flight, he will not speak of fearing that she has died or of fearing the possibility of her death; he speaks instead about anxiety and probably does not identify the relevant state of affairs so definitely as "her death" but leaves open the description of the possible evil. Or, if he knows that the plane has crashed but construes the likelihood of her having been on it as only remote, he will incline more to speak of anxiety than of fear.

Because the aversive possible state of affairs is less well defined in anxiety, anxiety will generate a less definite consequent desire. Not knowing very precisely what the state of affairs is that is threatening, one will not know what it takes to avoid that state of affairs, and thus will not form a desire to

---

[20] Martha Nussbaum once asked me, Why should we not include evaluations of the emotion in the emotion's defining proposition? I have pointed out that, both on Ifaluk and in America, fear receives differential evaluation depending on context. This is probably true of most emotion types. Thus the evaluation of an emotion seems context dependent in a way that the type of the emotion is not. When we approve of someone's fear of doing injustice and disapprove of his fear of social disapproval, we do not for this reason have a sense of dealing with different emotion types.

take some definite course of action; or not thinking that it is very probable that evil will come from it, the desire to avoid the object or its consequences will be less urgent. If anxiety generates a consequent desire to act, it will be just a desire to do "something," and consequently the behavior may not be very logically connected with the emotion. One may pace or bite one's nails. (We should say, though, that fear may generate this kind of behavior too, if the subject does not see a course of action by which he can avoid the aversive possible state of affairs.) We might venture the following as anxiety's defining proposition: *X vaguely presents an aversive possibility of some degree of probability; may X or its aversive consequences, whatever they may be, be avoided.*

If the construal in terms of aversive possibility is less definite in anxiety than in fear, it is less definite in fear than in fright. Paradigm cases of being frightened are ones in which the subject sees (e.g., a bear) or hears (e.g., a rattle as of a snake) or smells (e.g., smoke) something that one construes in terms of dramatic aversive possibility (that the bear will maul me, that the snake will bite me, that the smoke indicates a fire in my house). But fright does not *necessarily* involve an object of sense perception, and cases of fear shade into cases of fright. We would probably not say that someone was frightened by the news that a plane that his mother might have been on had crashed. But it would be quite natural to say that we were frightened of a tornado that we had not perceived but only heard reported on the radio. On the other hand, I think we would not say that we were frightened by the tornado unless we saw it, or at least perceived some of the telltale signs of its coming. Perhaps the expression "frightened of..." indicates a sort of cross between fear and fright. More paradigmatically we say "afraid of..." without any commitment to the perceptible presence of the object of fear, and we say "frightened by..." with commitment to some sense perceptual immediacy of the object. "Frightened of..." would then be used in cases that may lack perception of the object but where it is construed as very concrete and imminent – as though it were *virtually* perceptible. In any case it is clear that fear and fright are close relatives, and both involve the construal of something as presenting an aversive possibility. Speaking somewhat loosely, we might say that the defining proposition for fright is *X presents an immediate and definite aversive possibility of a high degree of probability; may X or its aversive consequences be avoided right away.*

In dread the subject sees the aversive object not as present, but as inevitably[21] approaching. "I dread the progress of my disease." "I'm dreading the news, because I know it will be bad." "I dread next week's examination." (Of course one can do something to avoid an examination – just not take

---

[21] I am expounding here what I take to be the force of "dread" at the beginning of the 21st century. A look at the many earlier examples in the *Oxford English Dictionary* suggests that dread did not always differ in this way from fear, anxiety, and fright. I thank John Hare for calling my attention to this fact.

it, for example; and a normal subject of dread will know this. Nevertheless, in dread the subject construes the aversive state of affairs as more or less unavoidable.) Thus, though he may be taking measures to avoid the threatening possible state of affairs, or actively bracing himself for its arrival, he construes himself as relatively passive with respect to the threat. For this reason – since the dreaded state of affairs is construed as virtually fated – dread verges on jumping out of the fear family altogether and becoming a form of simple aversion to what is in the offing. Still, it is essential that the object be in the offing, and not fully present, and in this respect it is like a possibility. Unlike anxiety's object, dread's is definite enough; if the dread is conscious, the subject knows pretty well what he is dreading. Fear shades into dread along the avoidability dimension: The more the aversive eventuality or its consequences are seen as inevitable, the closer the emotion is to the dread end of the continuum; to the extent that the eventuality looks somewhat avoidable, dread shades into fear. Because the evil is construed as inevitable, the consequent desire is not, in pure dread, a desire to *do* anything; still, dread may have a consequent *wish* that what is dreaded should be avoided. If the subject of dread does take measures to avoid what he dreads, then either his dread is not pure, being somewhere on the continuum toward fear, or the action is desperate, just "something to do." So we might write the defining proposition for dread as follows: *X is an unavoidable aversive future eventuality; if only X or its aversive consequences could be avoided!*

Terror and panic are both very intense variants of fear or fright. They differ from each other (if they do differ) in the character of their behavioral consequences, which tend to be irrational. Terror is a more or less paralyzing kind of fear or fright, while panic begets precipitous, undeliberated activity, such as aimless running, struggling, or shrieking. We are talking here about linguistic usage, and our characterization of it must be sensitive to its roughness. My claim is only about *tendencies* in the usage of these words; we certainly do sometimes say that somebody who shrieks is experiencing terror. By the same token, panic may be relatively behaviorless, as when a person is inserted in an MRI testing machine. Here the subject, because of self-control, is not actualizing his claustrophobic tendency to try to struggle out of the tube; but he knows his emotion is panic or near panic because he knows what behavior he feels *urges* toward. Because of these behavioral consequences, however they may divide between terror and panic, we may reckon panic and terror, unlike fear, as emotions that contribute little to the good life. One might think it a mark of the courageous person that she is never in a state of panic or terror, though she may well feel fear or be frightened.

I said in Section 2.10b that emotions' intensity is a function of the strength of the underlying concern, the vivacity of the construal, and the rate of impingement of the construal on the concern. Let us use this formula to explain the greater intensity of terror and panic, in comparison with fear and fright. Paradigmatic instances of panic and terror are based on very strong human concerns, such as the concern to continue living or the concern for one's children's well-being. (When a person says she's in a panic because she's probably going to be late to the office, or because she's about to miss her plane, she is probably using the word to comic effect.) Similarly, the propositional content that informs panic impinges at a high rate on the concern in question: One's child is about to be terribly injured, one's own life is threatened by fire, one's livelihood has been taken away, and so on. In other words, the basic concern appears as under *high* probability of being *greatly* contravened. And last, panic is not just a dim premonition or a vague "sense" that something very important is under threat, much less a mere judgment, but a very vivid impression, either to the senses or to the imagination, of this threat: The bear is charging; the child is on the railroad tracks with the train bearing down on her; I have lost my job. I hazard the following defining propositions for these emotions. Terror: *X vividly presents an extremely aversive possibility of a very high degree of probability; and I don't know what to do. Panic: X vividly presents an extremely aversive possibility of a very high degree of probability; let me do something, just anything.*

Horror perceives something as aversive, but unlike fear, not necessarily as possible/probable, and unlike dread not necessarily as in the future. Furthermore, the object is aversive in a special way. Horror is a concern-based construal of something as aversive *partly on account of being grotesquely abnormal, disfigured, or disfiguring.* To be horrified by what occurred in the Nazi death camps differs from being afraid that it happened or fearing that it will happen again; in being horrified, one's focus is on the disfigurement of humanity that occurred there – the grotesqueness of the moral aberration as well as the physical and social disfigurement of the victims. Monsters – grotesquely abnormal appearing beings, whether human, insect, animal, plant, extraterrestrial, and so on – are the normal fare of horror films and novels. It is true that in the horror literature what is horrible is often presented in contexts where it is also frightening (the monster appears suddenly out of the dark cellar to attack the heroine), and the horror enhances the fear and the fear the horror. Still, they are distinguishable emotions. If one concentrates on cases of what Noël Carroll calls "art-horror"[22] – that is, the emotional response to presentations of the horror genre of book and film – one may think that horror necessarily includes an element of fascinated enjoyment. Such pleasant fascination is often involved in the experience of horror, even of the nonliterary type (think of the practice of gaping at gory highway accidents), but apart from the special case of art-horror, it is not a necessary aspect. A sensitive person may experience horror at a strip-mined mountainside in Kentucky. The horror depends on a sense of

---

[22] See *The Philosophy of Horror* (New York: Routledge, 1990), pp. 27–35.

what normal Kentucky mountainsides look like and a concern for them, which makes the strip-mined one look horrible. A wastebasket of human fetuses, some whole and some in parts, is horrifying to most people (including most who condone abortion – as indicated by their resistance to seeing them or seeing pictures of them); it is even more horrifying if one of them is still moving. One is not afraid of them, nor is one afraid for them (not, at least, for the dead ones); but one is horrified by them. The abnormality in this case is that of babies being dead and in a wastebasket; and the horror is no doubt in part also of the procedure, in the background, by which they got there. The horror is all tied up with a natural valuation of babies in their normal state. Horror's consequent concern is a desire to escape from the horrific thing or a desire that it be restored to a state of normalcy. Horror's defining proposition, then, is something like this: *X is strongly aversive because it is grotesquely abnormal; may I escape from X or may X be restored to normalcy.*

Finally, let us look at the emotion that I have called spook. This one, too, seems to belong in the family of fear, inasmuch as the subject construes himself as under threat – an aversive possibility with a certain degree of probability. But the threat is rather undefined, being presented in the form of the strange, the mysterious, the unknown. In the indefiniteness of the construed threat, spook is like anxiety. One might call it a form of anxiety, but if so, this is a specialized form: Anxiety does not in general get the indefiniteness of its object from mystery and strangeness. You're alone in the forest, sitting at your campfire just about ready to crawl into your tent for the night and you hear a grunting, seemingly in the middle distance, that sounds half human. You cannot identify it as either animal or human. You don't believe in ghosts or goblins, but the strangeness of the sound calls to mind some of the superstitions of the people local to this part of the Canadian wilderness, and you begin to get spooked, in spite of yourself. You feel an urge to pack up your tent and get out of the woods. But it's twelve miles to the nearest village, and the only way to get there is on foot through the forest, and the night sky is black. Spook's defining proposition seems to be something like this: *By its sinister mysteriousness, X vaguely presents an aversive possibility of some degree of probability; may X or its aversive consequences, whatever they may be, be avoided.*

3.3. OFFENSE

a. Defining Anger

Günther and Karla share a flat in Stuttgart with another couple, Johann and Elfrieda. It's Thursday afternoon, cleaning time for the household. When Karla gets home from work, the other three have already divided the chores, so it falls to her to clean the loo. Günther is to clean their bedroom.

Wanting to get her task over with, she gets right to work. Twenty minutes later she emerges, perspiring, to find Günther sitting at the table with his cigarette and beer, making cracks about what a busy beaver she is. She turns angrily and goes into their bedroom and starts tidying up, where the piles of Günther's car magazines and tennis equipment and dirty clothes remind her of an important letter that got lost in this chaos last week and still hasn't been found. She strides back into the kitchen and starts yelling at him, "You're always making the whole mess and then not cleaning up!" She screams and pounds on the countertop, so that it's quite a spectacle for Johann and Elfrieda.[23]

How does Karla construe Günther at this moment? She sees him in terms of his offenses against her: That he is not doing his fair share of the work, and then, rather than respecting her for doing hers, makes fun of her for doing it; that by his untidiness he has caused her an important inconvenience. But the attribution of offense is of a special moral kind: He has not just hurt and inconvenienced her but has done so as a responsible agent. If she came to see the unfairness and mischief he has occasioned as arising from a pathology that completely bypassed his responsible agency (say, a brain tumor of just the right kind), then her emotion might be irritation, frustration, or disappointment, but it would not be anger.

I see all the while how folks could say he was queer, but that was the very reason couldn't nobody hold it personal. It was like he was outside of it too, same as you, and getting mad at it would be kind of like getting mad at a mud-puddle that splashed you when you stepped in it (William Faulkner, *As I Lay Dying*, Chapter 53).

In her anger, Karla construes Günther as culpable and blameworthy. In construing *him* as blame*worthy* for his actions and omissions she does not "separate the sin [completely] from the sinner." He, as a whole person, looks bad to her (which is not to say that he looks completely bad to her). But again, this badness is of a special kind, because it is connected with his offense: He has, in her eyes, the character of an enemy, one who opposes what she values.

None of the terms of this construal – of Günther as culpably originating these offenses and being her enemy – would constitute anger if they did not impinge on such real concerns as Karla's desires to be treated fairly, to be respected, and to be helped with the housework. If we generalize too hastily from the present example, we might think that the basic concern has to be self-directed, but anger is not limited in this way. Elfrieda and Johann may be angry at Günther on Karla's behalf and without construing themselves as the brunt of any of Günther's offenses.

---

[23] The story is a fictionalized adaptation of one collected during an empirical study. See Klaus R. Scherer (ed.), *Facets of Emotion: Recent Research* (Hillsdale, New Jersey: Lawrence Erlbaum and Associates, 1988), p. 234.

But the self of the angered person does seem to get referred to, in anger, in a way that is not always noticed. If an angry person can be induced to see herself as the culpable originator of some offense that strongly resembles that of the person she is angry at, her anger disappears. For example, Karla suddenly remembers, in moral terms and with perceptual immediacy, that she has sometimes treated her own sister in the way she is being treated by Günther. This suggests that one of the terms of the anger-construal is oneself as in a moral position to judge (in the sense of condemn) the offender; anger dims as this aspect of the construal is withdrawn.

Anger's consequent concern is also pretty clearly illustrated in Karla's anger. When she finds Günther sitting at the table kibitzing about her industriousness, she first goes into the bedroom and starts cleaning up. She seems to intend to shame Günther by casting herself in a martyrial role. Then she changes strategy, taking the more direct approach of yelling and creating an embarrassing spectacle in front of their flatmates. Common to these two approaches is the intention to punish, to give deserved pain, to pay Günther back for his offenses. This is perhaps not quite generalizable because in some cases the angry person does not wish to do the punishing herself; so we should say that anger's consequent concern is a desire that the offender be punished. The defining proposition for anger will thus be something like the following: *S has culpably offended in the important matter of X (action or omission) and is bad (is to some extent an enemy of what is good); I am in a moral position to condemn; S deserves (ought) to be hurt for X; may S be hurt for X.*[24]

b. Is Ifaluk *Song* Anger?

In an effort to draw lines of contrast between anger and its Ifaluk counterpart, *song*, Catherine Lutz (*Unnatural Emotions*, Chapter 6) stresses the "moral appeal" characteristic of *song* and translates *"song"* as "justifiable anger."

Unlike "anger," [*song*] is not used to talk about frustrating events which are simply personally disliked, rather than socially condemned. While the uses to which "anger" is put may often involve the kind of moral appeal that *song* does, the former concept is seen as referring, in the main, to the restraint of individual desire (p. 156).

In other words, most of what we call anger in Europe and America does not attribute blameworthy offense and moral badness to an offender, or worthiness to judge to its subject. Perhaps Lutz is thinking

[24] The word "important" in this and many of my formulations of defining propositions is intended to express the subject's concern, in this case for whatever is offended against.

about cases like these:

    A. A woman waiting in line for a long time starts to get angry.

    B. A man whose motorcycle will not start gets angry at it (curses it and kicks the tire).

    C. Someone trying to thread a needle without success may get "angry."

In case A the woman probably has no real moral claim on the line's moving faster, but she may still see the situation in moral terms. She looks for somebody to blame, somebody bad behind her inconvenience. She is inclined to say things like, "Don't they have any consideration for their customers?" "Why don't they hire enough clerks to get the job done?" And she would like to punish "them" by scolding, embarrassing, smacking, or getting them fired. So Lutz's judgment about the frequency with which "anger" is used to refer, nonmorally, to a sense of "restraint of individual desire" may depend on confusing the character of the objective situation (which in many cases does not in fact contain a moral issue) with that of the subject's viewpoint on it.

In case B it is even clearer that there is no issue of justice in the situation; at least the motorcycle, as the object of the man's "punishment," cannot be culpably unjust. But his behavior is unmistakably punitive. The fact that he acts punitively toward the motorcycle suggests that, however irrationally, he does see its failing to start in moral terms; he wants to give it a "payback" (p. 174). We think it irrational to behave this way toward a machine. A plausible explanation of why we ascribe irrationality is that the behavior and attitude are moral and *as if* directed to a moral agent, while the motorcycle fails, in everybody's considered opinion, to qualify as such.

In case C we do not have punitive behavior. It is still possible, of course, that the person is seeing the recalcitrant thread and needle in moral terms, but let us say he isn't. This person is just frustrated, annoyed, irked, fed up, or vexed. I admit that people in this state, speaking modern English, sometimes say they're angry. If you interview some people about their use of the word "anger," you will find this out. People are sometimes not very reliable witnesses to the real usage of their own language. They often use words loosely, unless challenged with the right questions. For example, instead of asking, "What sort of situations make you angry?" the social scientist might ask, "Which of the following situations anger you, *rather than* annoy, disappoint, frustrate, or irritate you?" Here you're pressing the subject to use "anger" more carefully, though still only consulting her or his own sense for how the word is used. My guess is that most intelligent native speakers of English, confronted with case C and asked the more discriminating question about usage, will prefer one of the other words, rather than "anger." Lutz gives evidence that, in parallel with anger as characterized in Section 3.3a, *song* involves the moral condemnation of the offender (p. 174), the ascription of badness to him or her (p. 162), and the desire that in recompense for the offense he or she should be hurt or deprived in one way or another (p. 174).

Lutz points out that on Ifaluk "justifiable anger" is often declared when the important Ifaluk value of sharing is contravened (this includes the sharing of work, thus paralleling our example from Germany). "Justifiable anger," especially when expressed by people in authority, evokes fear in offenders and thus constitutes an important means of social control. North American anger functions similarly in social control by parents, teachers, bosses, elder brothers and sisters, friends, and so on; but it is equally clear that the Ifaluk value of sharing differs in particulars from the generality of American values. For example, most North Americans will not get angry at a woman for not sharing her cigarettes, but on Ifaluk this is regarded as a moral offense (pp. 160, 179) calling for *song*. But the fact that situations anger Ifaluk that would not anger Americans does not imply that *song* is a different emotion from anger. After all, different offenses push different Americans' buttons. One American gets very upset about Afrikaner manipulations but is undisturbed by the government's raising his taxes (though if pressed he admits it's not fair). Another American greets with equanimity reports of Afrikaner manipulations (though he admits they're immoral), but gets very upset about raised taxes. These people have different moral outlooks, or we might say different moral characters, or again different sets of moral concerns. The differences of moral character explain why they respond differentially to moral situations. But, different as are the objects or occasions of these individuals' anger, we don't say that one is experiencing anger and the other some other emotion. So differences in anger responses based in difference of particular values between Ifaluk and North America do not imply that anger and *song* are different emotions.

The term "justifiable" in Lutz's translation for *"song"* suggests a possible difference in the logic of the two concepts. In the defining proposition of anger as I have formulated it (Section 3.3a), we might find two kinds of claims to justification. Karla construes Günther's action and omission as *un*justified, and so her anger implicitly claims to be a just perception; and she construes herself as justified, in the sense of being in a moral position to condemn Günther. We have seen that the *subject* of anger does not necessarily claim to be justified in her anger (a person can feel anger while knowing or suspecting that her anger is not justified), but that there is a kind of "claim" that is made by the anger itself, like the "claim" of a sense perception to which its subject may assent or not (see Section 2.4d). Neither of these kinds of justifiability would distinguish anger from *song*.

But in translating *"song"* as "justifiable anger," Lutz seems to be defining *song* as justifiable. This would indeed distinguish *song* from anger, because anger is not by definition justifiable, but has *both* justifiable and unjustifiable instances. The implication is that if an Ifaluk elder becomes *song* about what he takes to be the unequal sharing of a catch of fish, but it turns out that his *song* was based on an overestimate of the number of fish that was caught, then the Ifaluk will judge that the elder's emotion was not *song* after all because it lacked the property of being justifiable. Thus the defining proposition for *song* might be this: *S has culpably offended in the important matter of X (action or omission), and is bad (is to some extent an enemy); I am in a moral position to condemn; S deserves (ought) to be hurt for X; may S be hurt for X;* **and all the moral claims made by this emotion are correct.** This formulation is not quite correct because defining propositions, as I define them in this book, are subjective (that is, they are the internal form of a construal and thus need not be true of the states of affairs whose form they identify), while the clause in boldface is objective in the sense that it makes the correctness of the emotion as a representation of an objective state of affairs a criterion of the emotion type. But this deficiency can be corrected by our reading the boldface not just as a device of emphasis, but also as indicating this special logical status not characteristic of other clauses of defining propositions. The boldface clause is not part of the defining proposition of anger[25]; in other words, in North America, when we adjudicate someone's anger to see whether it is justified, we are not trying to determine whether he is angry but whether he is *right* to be angry. If the defining proposition of *song* includes the clause in boldface, then *song* is not anger.

Is the boldface clause in the defining proposition of *song*? When Lutz writes of the negotiations by which *song* is adjudicated among the Ifaluk, she speaks of "negotiating over the emotion term to be used" (p. 172), and "negotiation over the right to use the concept of *song*" (p. 173), seeming to suggest that the Ifaluk would withdraw or deny the ascription of *song* to someone who thought she felt *song* but turned out to be unjustified in her ascription of wrongdoing, or was not in the right social position to feel *song*. But she also seems to suggest that the justification of instances of *song* can be questioned, when she says that negotiations occur "over the aptness of, or justification for, someone's justifiable anger, in other words, over the meaning to be assigned to an event" (p. 162), and she reports that,

Several women told me . . . that the men are always justifiably angry at the women when the interisland steamer comes, because the women do not make food. But, they said, the women do not listen to the men and just continue in their happiness/excitement (*ker*), visiting with the new arrivals and gathering the news from other atolls (p. 174).

If the women agree that the men are *justifiably* angry, why do they disregard the obvious moral implication of this? Are they being openly defiant of the moral right? Or do they think that the men's "justifiable anger" is not really

---

[25] Robert Gordon's claim that anger is a "factive" emotion amounts to the claim that the expression in boldface is included in the defining proposition for anger. See Section 2.4f for my objections to this proposal.

justified (perhaps because it is not so important that food be made right now)? But if the clause in boldface is part of the defining proposition of *song*, and they think that the men's "*song*" is not justified, should they not have told Lutz, skeptically, that "the men always *think* they are *song* at the women . . ."? I suspect that the women, while recognizing the men's emotion as *song*, did not take it very seriously, because they did not regard it as justified. If so, then *song* is like anger in having both justified and unjustified instances, and it is misleading to translate "*song*" as "justified anger." It would be more accurate to translate it simply as "anger."

c. Is Ilongot *Liget* Anger?

Michelle Rosaldo has studied a complex emotion concept – *liget* – that is central to the moral psychology of the Ilongots, a headhunting group who live in the uplands of Luzon in the Philippines.[26] In some contexts "*liget*" seems renderable as "anger," but in others the word is better translated as "passion," "energy," "drive," "impetuosity," "aspiration," "vitality," "firmness," "intensity," "enthusiasm," "desire," "dissatisfaction," "inspiration," "competitiveness," "ambition," "perseverance," "mettle," "force," or "valor." Chili peppers, ginger, violent storms, fire, liquor, and illness all have *liget*. Semen is a concentrated form of it. *Liget* is expressed in the intense activities of a woman in her garden, a man on a hunt or climbing vigorously in the treetops to chop away the foliage that shields the garden from sunlight, or a suitor who approaches boldly the house of the maiden he wishes for a bride. It is expressed, too, in the "hard time" that the girl's brothers may give the suitor. Very old people lack *liget*, and young unmarried men have it in the greatest abundance. *Liget* is begotten of the "envy" that one gardener has for another whose crop is more abundant, as well as the "envy" that a young bachelor may feel toward successful headhunters of his own age, if he himself has never killed anyone. It is begotten likewise by the grief that ensues upon the death of close kin. And above all, perhaps, *liget* is what drives Ilongots to take human heads, even when they do not do so in revenge.

An aspect of *liget* that is strongly reminiscent of anger – that its consequent concern is a desire for revenge – sometimes enters into Ilongot killings. But holding the severed head of a victim and throwing it on the ground need not have the meaning of punishing or getting even. Even when revenge is involved, most acts of beheading seem primarily to express vitality that is very important to the Ilongot sense of self and community. As performed (as it usually is) by young bachelors, beheading is an act of personal and communal fulfillment, perhaps distantly analogous to the suburban American act of learning to drive: It is an affirmation of life, a ritual of passage marking

[26] *Knowledge and Passion.*

independence and full adulthood, generating respect and self-respect. But heads taken by the young gratify Ilongot elders, who usually make the arrangements, in a way that teenage drivers' licenses do not gratify suburbanite elders: According to Rosaldo, Ilongot elders perceive in the *liget* expressed in their sons' headhunting the continuation of life (vitality) that they see fading in themselves, while they supply the moderating and channeling "knowledge" (*béya*) that is lacking in young bachelors. Thus success in head-hunting demonstrates not just individual valor, but the continuing vitality of the community.

Clearly, *liget* encompasses far more than our concept *anger*. But one distinguishable usage of "*liget*" is similar to the usage of "anger" that I identified in Section 3.3a. Let us call this sense of *liget* "*liget* in the anger sense"; I will now try to determine just how close *liget* in the anger sense is to anger. In this part of its usage, "*liget*" denotes a response to perceived insults, slights, and offenses against oneself and one's kin (see p. 139). Vengeance against the offender or the offender's kin "satisfies" such *liget*, as will payment (say, in tools or weapons) from the offender to the offended, as deemed appropriate by the offended one and (sometimes, when the offender and the offended are not regarded as kin) as adjudicated in an elaborate debate forum called "*purung*." Another similarity is that Ilongots are interested in questions of subjective responsibility for offenses evoking *liget*. For example, when Burur, in a fit of youthful violence, endangered the life of his aunt by slashing a footbridge she frequented, elders decided that her *liget* should be dropped because, being immature, Burur lacked "knowledge" (*béya*).

Burur's lack of *béya* meant that his threatening deed lacked "focus," permitting senior kin to treat his violence much as they might the wild actions of a man whose heart "relaxes" (*ringring*) under liquor – but who, when sober, is assumed to "come to know" that he offended kinsmen and to feel "ashamed." Such a man is rarely faulted for his acts (p. 95).

We regard knowledge of proprieties, consequences, and relationships as relevant to the adjudication of the culpability that anger ascribes to the offender. It appears that some status very similar to culpability is being adjudicated in asking whether an Ilongot offender knew what he was doing in committing the offense. The Ilongot word that Rosaldo translates "shame" – "*bétang*" – indicates something like humble acknowledgment or respect; thus, it seems, in this kind of case, an admission of the offensiveness of the offense.

But Rosaldo tells a story, bearing on acknowledgment, which might indicate a difference between *liget* in the anger sense and anger.

Punlan, who infuriated me by spending two months at a distant sawmill when he had agreed to help me translate texts, never excused himself or said that he was sorry; rather than satisfy my desire that he admit his violation, he appeared smiling at our house as if nothing had happened, and handed me something he knew I wanted: a beautifully carved and decorated wooden spoon.... Whereas acceptance of a gift implies a willingness to forget the *liget* that was its occasion, the absence of exchanges (especially after killings) indicates that tensions remain vital be-neath quotidian surfaces and external calm. In fact, for Ilongots, it was unintelligible that American soldiers could befriend the Japanese with whom they fought in World War II without indemnatory exchanges – and equally peculiar that, after accepting the spoon that Punlan gave me, I remained unsatisfied and acted moody and annoyed (p. 94).

Rosaldo feels that Punlan owes her a verbal acknowledgment of his dereliction, while he (seemingly) feels that he only owes her a rather nice gift. Does this indicate a difference in their understandings of *liget*/anger, or merely a difference of some customs surrounding the emotion(s)? And where does one draw the line between these two kinds of difference? We might guess that Rosaldo and Punlan assess differently the severity of his offense. Perhaps he thinks that translating texts is not a very urgent business and that, while Rosaldo has a right to be mildly annoyed, translating can wait a couple of months without any great harm. Thus a smiling presentation of a nice gift should suffice. Or maybe, among Ilongots, in the appropriate context, gifts *mean* an acknowledgment of wrongdoing and, thus, do not need to be accompanied with verbal admissions and lugubrious countenance. Rosaldo's account does seem to show that gift-giving is a much more important expedient of reconciliation after *liget* in the anger sense than it is among us after anger. But if we distinguish at all between emotions and the practices with which they are interwoven (and my suggestion that emotions are concern-based construals whose types are determined by their defining propositions does promote such a distinction), it seems reasonable to allow that particular practices of reconciliation after anger may differ without affecting the identity of the emotion type. We can imagine families within our own culture who vary in this way: In the one family, verbal acknowledgment of wrongdoing is required for reconciliation after anger, while in another it is enough to give nonverbal tokens of reconciliation. We do not suppose that such differences imply that in the two families emotions of different types are in play.

We are reminded of our concept of anger also by the fact that *liget* is often dissolved or averted by the consideration that the offender is kin to the offended (and thus cannot be an enemy). Just as the angry person construes the offender as an enemy of what he cares about (see Section 3.3a), among the Ilongots, *liget* (as demanding either vengeance or payment) is not tolerable among close kin and, if it persists, can actually undermine kin status; thus when offenses occur among kin, an effort is made to ignore them or "abide" them or rationalize them as in the case of Burur's offense. And when warring groups of Ilongots get reconciled to one another through *purung* and exchange of goods, they find ways of construing themselves as kin. Among the Ilongots, kinship is the complement of enmity in a way that it is not among us. But the similarity between anger and *liget* remains: Both are construals of the offender as in some degree an enemy.

Rosaldo's account of *liget* suggests that in one of its aspects, *liget* has most of the main semantic features of anger – construal of someone as a responsible offender, in some matter of importance, and thus an enemy to whom retribution is "owed." What about the feature expressed in the phrase "I am in a moral position to condemn"? Our evidence for this clause in the defining proposition of anger is that when an angry person comes actually to see himself as guilty of an offense sufficiently similar to the one that angers him, his anger dissipates. That this feature of anger is also a feature of *liget* is suggested by what happened when two groups of Ilongots held a peace meeting, or *béyaw*, intended to arrange for the elimination of *liget* between them by some payment of the offended by the offenders. But during the preliminaries to the meeting "it was established that men of *each* place had killed relations of the other, offenses that – as 'siblings' – they could 'rub away' (*redred*) immediately with a mere exchange of knives" (p. 190, Rosaldo's emphasis).

But despite the profound similarity of *liget* in the anger sense to anger, the typical experience of *liget* would seem to differ significantly from the typical experience of anger because *liget* associates markedly different things via language and cultural practice. We can understand, as a metaphor, the suggestion that chili peppers and storms are "angry," and perhaps we can see how the energy of a person who wants revenge against an offender is like the energy of someone cultivating a garden in intense competition with neighbors or singing a song or courting a maiden or finding his adulthood and manliness in the act of severing and tossing another human being's head. But it appears that to the Ilongots the connections between these (to us) diverse thoughts and practices are not quite metaphorical. Nor do these various applications of "*liget*" in the Ilongot moral psychology amount to homonymously designated different concepts. Instead, they are different applications of the same concept. And this is to say, roughly, that the Ilongots *experience* chilies – and excellent gardeners and headhunters (both those who are seeking revenge and those who are not) and courtship – as exemplifying this *one* thing that they call "*liget*."

I use the word "roughly" for a couple of reasons. First, a reflective Ilongot will, I think, be able (with prompting) to distinguish *liget* in the anger sense (as focusing on an offense and offender and implying the responsibility of the offender and a disposition to revenge and as being "satisfiable" by gifts) from the *liget* of a competitive gardener or a shot of semen or a chili pepper. I say this because it is *liget* in this particular sense that is the subject of the important Ilongot practice of oratorical peace negotiation (*purung* or more specifically *béyaw*); it is *liget* in this sense that raises all the questions about the severity of offenses, the balance or mutuality of offenses, the closeness of kinship or the distance of enmity, the "knowledge" of the offender, and the propriety of propitiatory gifts. By contrast, the *liget* of semen and chilies and women working their fields does not need to be negotiated in such terms because it does not have such rationales. In other words, the distinction between *liget* in the sense of energy and aspiration and *liget* in the anger sense is implicit in Ilongot practices. As far as I know, Ilongots do not explicitly distinguish senses of "*liget*" any more than ordinary users of English distinguish explicitly among the "is" of identity, the "is" of predication, and the existential "is." But since such distinctions are embedded in usage, we can say that, in the same way that English speakers have an implicit or latent knowledge of these distinctions, so the Ilongot have an implicit or latent knowledge of the distinction between these senses of "*liget*." The salience, in Ilongot life, of peace negotiations, whose main terms are the terms of *liget* in the anger sense (see Chapter 6), gives the distinction even greater salience or potential salience. *Liget* in the form of the youthful yearning to go head-hunting bridges between the broader *liget* and *liget* in the anger sense. On the one hand, it may involve vengeance or it may be just youthful energy and aspiration; on the other, it is clear enough to everybody that headtaking is an offense against the victims and will arouse *liget* in the anger sense in their kin, and reprisals that in their turn will be offenses against those who are now forming the intention to take heads.

Second, the associations of semen, chili peppers, energetic gardening, and vengeful responses to offenses form a concept in a looser sense than the sense in which *liget* in the anger sense is a concept. Associations are, after all, precisely that: associations. The aspects of the construal that is *liget* in the anger sense – offense, offender, responsibility, and revenge/payment – belong together not just by association but by a kind of logical implication, while the potency of semen and the energy of a woman in her garden belong together, and belong with *liget* in the anger sense, by a more accidental relatedness.

My proposal in this book, that emotions are concern-based construals, helps to make sense of the observation that "*liget*" is not just an ambiguous word – a word with a number of senses – but designates a distinct Ilongot concept, to which corresponds an Ilongot emotional experience that is different from North American experiences of anger. Even when *liget* is what we would call anger (because the emotion has the same defining proposition as anger), it is still, typically, colored by associations that are gathered to it by the wide-ranging use of "*liget*." Thus some of the headhunters on a mission that involves revenge will usually experience what we call anger, but the feeling of anger will be distinctively Ilongot in virtue of the offense, the offender, the desire for revenge, and so on, being construed in terms of the sting of ginger that they rub on their bodies during the hunt and in terms of Ilongot ideals of valor and manhood and communal continuity that are tied up in the Ilongot usage of "*liget*." The associations with gardening, dancing, hunting, courtship, storms, and whatever else has *liget* will tend to color the experience of anger, just as the experience of anger will color one's experience of *liget* in the garden and in the treetops[27] and in courtship. It will be typical for an Ilongot to gain a sense of heroism and human fulfillment in taking revenge on an offender, or demanding payments from him, a sense of fulfillment that comes from the association of *liget* with headhunting and its celebration of vitality, well-being, and manly maturity. By contrast, a European or American experiencing anger might feel somewhat embarrassed or guilty because in his culture, vengeance is associated with immaturity and lack of self-control.

In Section 3.2b, I distinguished three ways that emotions may vary from culture to culture. First, they may differ in their defining proposition, and I proposed this as the most fundamental way in which emotion types differ from one another. In this respect, *liget* in the anger sense does not seem to differ from anger, although there are other senses of "*liget*" – enthusiasm, aspiration, valor, intensity, and so on – that differ vastly from anger. Second, emotions may differ in object range. In the case of *liget*/anger, different kinds of actions might be taken as insults by Americans than are taken as insults by Ilongots. If we take *failing to share game with kin after a hunt* to be a type of action, then this is an action that is more likely to anger Ilongots than Americans. But it seems as though broader categories of action – like *insult* or even more broadly *offense* – are needed to define emotion types. Third, emotions may be evaluated differently from culture to culture. The Ilongots do seem to value what we would call anger more highly than Americans do.

In connection with *liget* we have uncovered a couple of more ways in which emotions may differ from culture to culture – in their associations, established by vocabulary and cultural practices, and in the practices that are associated with them. Thus even if we say, as I have proposed, that Ilongots have an emotion that is identical in type with our anger, we must acknowledge that their experience of that emotion is not the same as our experience of anger, because our word "anger" does not cover such things as intensity of work in the garden and intensity of pursuit of a mate. This fourth kind of difference overlaps with the third, since the cultural evaluation of emotions also affects how they are experienced. The difference between an emotion and the experience of the emotion, along with the relations between these, is the subject of Chapter 4 of this book. A fifth kind of difference is illustrated by the divergence between Rosaldo, who expected that someone seeking reconciliation with an angered person will make verbal apologies to her, and Punlan, who thought that a nice gift would suffice. Let us now turn to a brief discussion of some distinguishable types of emotion that are similar to anger or prone to be confused with it.

---

[27] When a man is hacking off the leaves of trees over the garden, he may boast that he is beheading the forest (p. 126).

d. Resentment, Indignation, Rage, Frustration, and Annoyance

Resentment is a "smoldering," as contrasted with a "flaming," anger. The subject construes himself or ones he closely identifies with as offended by a culpable offender, and yet in such a way or by such a person that he construes himself as impeded from getting frank, direct retribution. Thus "resentment" tends to be preferred where the offender is significantly more powerful than the offended, and intimidating as well as offensive. To say that a teenager resents his father's control over him, rather than to say simply that he is angry about it, suggests that the boy sees himself as in a position of weakness vis-á-vis his father's policies and actions. It is likely to suggest a fear of the father and a fear of the consequences of taking frank revenge. This is no doubt why the retribution is likely to come out in devious and unacknowledged ways, and it is probably why resentment has a reputation for being "repressed." The teenager's vengeful actions, if there are such, tend to be "passive aggressive" or devious in some other way. Typically, parents are angry at their small children, rather than resentful of them; but they can resent them too, if the parents feel constrained, by ongoing circumstances or timidity, to forego punishment. Resentment also differs from anger in being directed at offenses against oneself or persons close to one – say, one's family, or in wartime one's compatriots. A Christian suburbanite American might be angry or indignant about Serbian policies toward Muslims, but it seems improper to say that she resents those policies; but if she is married to a Bosnian Muslim, she could resent them. So we might write the defining proposition for resentment as follows : *S has culpably offended in the important matter of X (action or omission) that touches me quite personally and is bad (is to some extent my enemy); I am in a moral position to condemn; I wish I could hurt S for X, but I am impeded from doing so directly.*

I have analyzed resentment as directed toward a person or personified agency. Albert Borgman[28] diagnoses contemporary Americans as suffering from a kind of sullen resentment that is not directed against any person or persons, but against pain. Speaking of such people, he says that

victims do not as a rule feel resentment toward those who were the cause of the suffering. Nor are large settlements sought from individuals and intended to pain them in return. The payments are exacted from insurance companies and ultimately provided by all policyholders (p. 12).

Borgman's observation does seem to identify a usage of the word "resentment" and thus illustrates the ambiguity or flexibility in our use of emotion terms. The "resentment" that Borgman identifies is as closely related to self-pity as to anger. In feeling this emotion, the subject construes himself as a poor and passive victim, needing and deserving succor. Yet in

[28] *Crossing the Postmodern Divide* (Chicago: University of Chicago Press, 1992).

the sense of entitlement that it involves, the emotion touches on the issues of justice that help to define anger and resentment. This kind of resentment picks up on the sense of injury and passive constraint that classic resentment involves, changes culpable offense into anonymous injury, and replaces the desire for revenge with a sense of entitlement to compensation. And it seeks compensation not from personal agents but from impersonal agencies. This appears to be an emotion type that is, unlike anger, strongly local, culturally and historically. It would appear to depend on the existence of impersonal agencies like insurance companies and a correlative generalized sense of entitlement that is very far from being a cultural universal. Perhaps because the emotion does not have a very long history, and thus lacks an established name of its own, it tends to adopt the name of an emotion that has some similar defining features – in this case, resentment. Linguistic conservatives may seek another word for it than "resentment" – perhaps "victim entitlement" or "entitled self-pity" – but efforts to regiment emotion vocabulary neatly are hopeless. For purposes of present exposition, however, we need a way to distinguish this resentment from the more classic kind. Just to have a name for it, let us call it "impersonal resentment." Its defining proposition will run something like this: *I have been victimized and injured by forces beyond my control, and so am entitled to succor in the form of compensation from the System; may I be so compensated.* Like all defining propositions for emotions, this one must be read as expressing, in words like "victim," "injured," and "entitled," a caring about things – in this case, chiefly a caring about oneself.

The indignant person construes the wrong done to him or to persons or things he cares about as especially grotesque, blameworthy, or morally shocking. He does not, like the resenter, necessarily construe himself or someone close to him as the sufferer of the wrong, but may be indignant about wrongs suffered by rather distant others, and the others need not be persons (somebody might be indignant about the dumping of trash in a virgin forest). In fact, one of the nuances suggested by the word "indignation" is the "generosity" of this kind of anger – that it may be about offenses *not* directly touching the subject. Indignation, like any of the variants of anger, does, however, require that the indignant person care about the issue (say, of fouling forests or respecting rights) and regard the issue as moral. "Indignant" suggests a rather strong sense of one's own rightness, along with confidence of being in a moral position to condemn. The word also suggests a strong sense of the need for retribution. These factors make indignation an especially "judgmental" or condemnatory form of anger, marked by a sense of rather great moral distance between the "judge" and the offender. We might write the defining proposition for indignation thus: *S has very culpably and shockingly offended in the important matter of X (action or omission) and is bad (is an enemy of what is good); I am very confident of being in a moral position to condemn; and S deserves (ought) to be hurt for X.* Note that this defining proposition differs from that of anger only in what we might call "stress."

In my analysis, resentment differs from anger in a qualitative, if somewhat minor, way: Its defining proposition contains a clause that is absent from the defining proposition of anger: *I am impeded from directly hurting S for X*. Still, it makes sense to regard resentment as a kind of anger because so much of its defining proposition is shared with that of anger. Indignation does not differ from anger in an analogous way. The difference is only in such words and phrases as "very culpably and shockingly" and "I am very confident of being in a position to judge." Another difference between indignation and anger is indicated by our tendency to say "indignant about" (name the offense) rather than "indignant at" (name the offender). Thus the focus (see Sections 2.3 and 2.3c) of indignation tends to be a little different from that of anger; but as I remarked in my discussion of focus, variation of focus does not change the identity of an emotion as to type. Outrage is, as far as I can see, just unusually intense indignation (on intensity, see Section 2.10).

Rage is intense anger marked by proneness to violent action. Actions characteristic of rage are typically performed in an intense and violent behavioral style – for example, with loud voice, reddened visage, tightly tensed muscles, perspiration, wild swinging of the arms, and so on. Like any adult human emotion, rage is a construal of the situation in terms, some of which are propositional (I do not notice any difference from anger in the defining proposition); but rage, bordering as it typically does on the irrational, is likely to be a blurry kind of construal in which one's consciousness seems to be overlaid by nonpropositional forces. For example, the desire to destroy may get detached from its anchor in the concern for justice, and the question of the culpability of the recipient of the punitive behavior may become irrelevant to the action. It is typical for rage (as it is not for plain anger) that, for the duration of the emotion, the subject is blind to "reason"; that is, that rage is not penetrable by considerations contrary to its propositional content. The enraged person may need to cool off before he can listen to reason. "Rage" suggests a state in which the desire for retribution is so intense that it is at best only barely within behavioral control and may be out of control.

In Section 2.8c I pointed out that frustration is a general form of negative emotions: The distinctively emotional kind of pain is not that of a sensation, but of a concern contravened or, more precisely, the perception of one's situation as contravening some one or more of one's concerns. Thus anger has the form of frustration in this sense, inasmuch as one's concern for respect, or justice, or the well-being of something, is frustrated by the offense about which one is angry. Fear, envy, disappointment, regret, and indeed all the paradigm negative emotions share the form of frustration. But in most cases of negative emotions, it will not do to speak of feeling frustrated. The emotion that we typically call "frustration" is a distinct one, with a defining proposition all its own. Here are some situations in which one typically speaks of feeling frustrated: I have not played the guitar for years, and when I pick it up I find I can make none of the delicate sounds I used to make: I feel frustrated. Or I try to read with inadequate glasses and am frustrated. But if I am trying to find the base form of an irregular Greek verb that I came across in a past perfect form, and my first guess is unsuccessful, I will probably not feel frustrated: I feel a momentary disappointment and then try another approach. It will probably be only after repeated unsuccessful attempts, as the impression dawns on me that I may simply not find this word, that I begin to feel frustrated. Thus frustration, in this sense of a distinct emotion, seems to involve the construal of one's desire as opposed by a significant, if not insuperable, obstacle. Of course, some people get frustrated more easily than others; this is to say that it takes less opposition and failure to elicit from them a perception of being up against a significant obstacle than more patient or persevering people require. Unlike most other emotions, which do not require desires on which to be based, but only concerns (see Section 2.7b), frustration seems to be desire based. The frustrated person must have a goal that appears to him to be frustrated. The consequent concern is redundant, given that it is just the same as the basic concern. Let us try, then, to write the defining proposition for frustration: *I strongly desire X and am meeting high resistance if not insuperable obstacles to achieving or acquiring X; if only I could achieve or acquire X!*

Annoyance or irritation, like frustration, is not properly a form of anger, but it may be discussed here because it, too, frequently shades into anger and the terms are not always distinguished, for example, "I am very annoyed (irritated) with you," spoken in unmistakably angry tones. Annoyance ranges from something like unpleasant sensation such as may hardly be counted an emotion, to a propositionally definite concern-based construction of our situation. On the former end of the continuum, we may be annoyed (irritated) by a beard clipping caught in our T-shirt, a fly buzzing around our head, a jackhammer operating outside the window of our study carrell, a baby screaming in the next room, or someone playing a violin out of tune. Such instances of annoyance conform only remotely to the model of emotions being presented in this book because they seem neither to involve construal nor to be based on any independently discriminable concern. If there is a "concern" involved, it is just a disposition to find these experiences unpleasant. They seem to be just sensory irritations, on a level with having our skin scraped or our hair pulled or a bright light shone in our eyes. I think most people would not be inclined to call the unpleasantness of having one's skin abraded an emotion, but some responses to the above-mentioned jackhammer, screaming baby, and dystonal violin playing probably would count, in most people's estimation, as emotions. Why? The account of emotions offered in Chapter 2 supplies an explanation. In the jackhammer case, the person is probably trying to study, and so the sound is more than a physical irritation; it is an impediment to study. Via the physical irritation, the source of irritation is construed as impeding the activity that the subject is concerned to pursue. Being distracted is unpleasant not just physically, but also because it impinges negatively on the concern to understand, to make progress in the work, and so on. The baby's screams, similarly, grate not only on the ear but on the heart; they grate, in part, by meaning: I am busy, but the poor thing needs attention; so I am torn. The badly intoned violin irritates the *educated* ear – that is to say, the ear that demands proper intonation. In other words, these are cases of emotion because they are cases of concern-based construal.

So far, the cases I have cited all involve physical irritation. But that is not a necessary condition for annoyance. When I am studying, I am annoyed by excellent music as well as by unpleasant sounds; in fact, excellent music is annoying in part because of its very excellence, which makes it the more distracting. The displeasure, in this case, is that of being torn from my primary object of attention, the object that I am concerned to attend to at this moment. Another kind of case that does not involve sensory discomfort is the wife who is annoyed at her husband for telling corny jokes at parties. She is not distracted from an object of concern, nor do his jokes occasion an unpleasant motivational conflict. She just finds the jokes distasteful – but without being angry, for she does not regard the jokes as a moral offense, nor wish him to be punished for them. It is clear that *annoyance* is a rangy emotion concept, one that is not very "defined," and no doubt I have missed some of its applications. But given the preceding discussion, it appears that the defining proposition for annoyance, when it is an emotion, is roughly as follows: *X impinges unpleasantly on some concern of mine, either by contravening the standards implicit in that concern, or by distracting me from the activity that the concern moves me to, or by appealing to some other concern that is in competition with it, thus creating a motivational conflict; may such impingement cease.*

e. Anger's Nastiness

In the preceding analysis, a significant difference between anger and such close relatives as indignation and resentment, on the one hand, and more distant ones like annoyance, irritation, vexation, and frustration on the other, is that the defining propositions of the former group contain clauses that are socially nasty. Thus in anger we have clauses like "S is bad," "S deserves to be hurt for X," and "may S be hurt for X" – clauses without counterparts in the defining propositions of the emotions in the other group. To these aspects of my analysis of anger I have encountered repeated resistance. People often respond that anger is *sometimes* nasty in the way these clauses suggest, but not always or necessarily.

Several reasons come to mind why people might resist the analysis. First, as I noted in my discussion of Catherine Lutz (Section 3.3b), people do sometimes say they are angry when they are really only frustrated or annoyed. Second, this linguistic tendency is encouraged by the fact that frustration and annoyance often evolve into anger: In the middle of a plumbing job we find we lack the right wrench, we feel tense, and when the kids make an innocent pitch for attention we snap at them. A third encouragement to run these emotion types together is that when we are angry but do not want to admit it we can often exploit the imprecision of everyday English and get away with speaking of ourselves as annoyed, frustrated, or irritated. Fourth, we want to downgrade our anger to irritation because we know that anger is socially nasty: If anger has the defining proposition I have ascribed to it, then to admit we are angry is to imply that we see somebody as bad and as deserving hurt, that we take ourselves to be in a position to judge, and that we would like him to suffer some hurt or discomfort. To bring such material out into the full light may be an open declaration of estrangement too dramatic for our taste. A fifth reason for thinking that anger does not always have the nasty dimensions is that we are sometimes angry with people we love. And a sixth is that some anger is morally good, but it is never morally good to will the hurt of anyone. The last three of these points can be made into arguments, which I shall now address.

The first is a pragmatic argument. People with psychotherapeutic interests are especially uncomfortable with admitting anger's essential nastiness. An important part of therapy, for many clinicians, is to help clients to an awareness of unconscious or displaced anger, and full candor about anger's nastiness may seem likely to reduce the prospects of success. Therapists want to create an emotionally safe environment, and so it is in their interest to tell the client, in word and gesture, that "feelings are neither good nor bad, but it is important to express them." But to teach clients that their anger is morally neutral when in fact it contains an alienated and condemning view of its object, along with destructive impulses toward him or her, seems to perpetuate just the kind of unhealthy self-opacity that the therapy aims to dispel. Fortunately, a therapist can achieve her ends without teaching clients that anger is morally indifferent. First, she can convey an openness to hear of the client's anger without saying that anger is morally neutral. Not all aspects of anger need be addressed at every stage of therapy, and anger's nastiness may be addressed after the client has come to terms with his anger and begun to get some distance on it. Second, though anger is nasty, it is not always wrong; in some moral traditions, at any rate, it is sometimes right to see somebody as bad, in some limited way, and deserving to be hurt, and one may be justified in wanting to hurt him or her. Third, in some therapeutic traditions, forgiveness is an attitude that can be applied both to the offender and to the subject of anger; that is, the client may mitigate his anger through a process of forgiving the offender, and he may receive forgiveness for his anger, insofar as it is wrong. Fourth, a doctrine that the client's anger, even if wrong, does not necessarily express the client's most basic or truest self may serve a therapeutic purpose similar to that of the doctrine that anger is morally neutral. For example, a Christian in therapy might be told that his anger, though it is wrong, belongs to his old self and not to the new one that has been created for good works through Jesus Christ.

How can anger be always nasty, when the object of our anger is so often someone we love? Are not cases of anger at loved ones counterexamples to the universality of anger's nastiness? Jonathan Edwards has argued in this vein:

> . . . a father may be angry with his child, that is, he may find in himself an earnestness and opposition of spirit to the bad conduct of his child, and his spirit may be engaged and stirred in opposition to that conduct, and to his child while continuing in it; and yet, at the same time, he will not have any proper ill-will to the child, but, on the contrary, a real good-will; and so far from desiring its injury, he may have the very highest desire for its true welfare, and his very anger be but his opposition to that which he thinks will be of injury to it. And this shews that anger, in its general nature, rather consists in the opposition of the spirit to evil than in a desire of revenge.[29]

But it does not follow from the fact that the father has good will toward the child that he does not have ill will toward the child. The good will may be dispositional, the ill will episodic. Consider a father whose eight-year-old has just defiantly disobeyed him in foolishly subjecting herself to an unnecessary danger. Angry, he wants to subject her to a discomfort because she deserves it, in which he will take a fleeting pleasure. At that moment the earth under their Los Angeles dwelling begins to shake and the walls start cracking. He scoops her into his arms and just manages to escape the house as it collapses. In the yard he falls on his knees in thanksgiving to God for her deliverance and hugs her passionately. It is clear that his episodic ill will toward her is compatible with an intense dispositional good will. Furthermore, the ill will may be based on the good will: Because the father loves the child, he wishes the child to do what is in her interest, to be obedient, and so on. Edwards seems to be of two minds about whether anger is essentially only an "opposition of spirit" to the evil done, or whether it is also an opposition to the doer of the evil. For he allows that the father's opposition may be "to his child," and it is hard to see what an *emotional* opposition to the child herself would be if it were not ill will toward the child. In my example, the father takes pleasure in a small pain of the child, perhaps only a passing discomfort. In this connection, Edwards prejudices the conclusion by speaking of "injury." "Injury" suggests some real physical or psychological damage to the child, or some momentous loss. And surely a desire that the child be significantly damaged *is* incompatible with the love of a rational and mature father. The "revenge" that a loving father desires in his anger may be only a sting on her posterior, or the sting of disapproval, or the discomfort of a momentary coldness on her father's part. The point is worth

---

[29] Jonathan Edwards, *Charity and Its Fruits* (Edinburgh: The Banner of Truth Trust, 1969), p. 188.

generalizing, because some of the resistance to the suggestion that anger essentially involves the desire for hurt comes from not reckoning with the full range of what counts as hurting. Anger *may* include a desire for damnation, deep humiliation, full exclusion, permanent physical injury, or death; but the hurt desired may also be something relatively inconsequential, such as mild irritation, a twinge of guilt, or a slight inconvenience.

Someone might admit that the desire for hurt is very characteristic of anger, and yet still resist my point, by saying that what the angry person wants, ultimately, is the correction of the offense, and it just happens, in human life, that offenses are often corrigible by hurts. So the desire for hurt is only instrumental, and the angry person will be just as happy to correct the offense in some other way – for example, by giving the offender a reward for future good behavior. In view of the fact that nonhurtful ways of correcting offenders are often at least as effective as hurtful ones, we might expect to find the more rational people doing good to their offenders out of anger. Rational people do sometimes undertake nonhurtful ways of correcting the people they are angry at; but it seems to me that they are moved to this not *by their anger,* but by other considerations that require a self-critical control of their anger. This point, too, has more general force: The impression that anger does not always involve ill will may be abetted by the fact that mature people more or less automatically monitor their anger and deny it most of its most hurtful expressions.

How can anger always have nasty dimensions, if it is sometimes morally right to be angry? The answer will have to be that the nasty dimensions are sometimes morally called for, and that they can be morally rightly formed. My analysis says that the angry person sees the offender as bad in some respect and as deserving some degree of hurt. Anger is, no doubt, often an inappropriate and false perception and often leads to injustice. But most moral outlooks allow that people *are* sometimes bad in some respect and deserving of some degree of hurt, in which case anger may be a right perception and lead to justice. No doubt anger is very prone to get out of hand. That is why morally mature persons have the virtues of practical wisdom and self-control, by which they monitor their perceptions and impulses and selectively correct and check them. But anger's proneness to distortion is no argument that it is never right.

Since I have admitted the slippage in our vocabulary about anger – that we sometimes call what isn't anger "anger," and sometimes use other terms for what is really anger – the issue between my resisters and me might seem to be merely about the use of the word "anger." They want a broader, and I want a narrower, scope for the word. But my interest is really not in insisting on a particular usage of a word, but in pointing out the existence, transculturally, of an emotion with a very particular package of logical features, a package that is expressed in the defining proposition that occurs at the end of Section 3.3a.

3.4. FAULT

a. Remorse

In feeling remorse a person construes some particular action or omission of her own as a violation of standards that she regards as right and is concerned to honor. She construes the action or omission as not only her doing, but as something she did intentionally or negligently, and thus blameworthily. She need not believe that it was her fault, but she must so construe it. A child's sled slides onto the icy street and a woman drives over the child, killing him. She was driving attentively and at a speed appropriate to the icy conditions and is in no way at fault. Her family and friends have rehearsed these facts endlessly, and she believes she was not at fault, but she *feels* remorse. Her remorse is irrational; she should be feeling intense regret instead. Perhaps she says to herself such things as "If only I had waited another five minutes to go out for milk," and so by a self-flagellating sophistry she makes it appear to herself that she is to blame. That she feels remorse, rather than regret, is determined by the terms in which she sees herself and the situation: in terms of her blameworthy fault. Remorse's consequent concern (wish or desire) is to make reparation for the offense, to make it right. If some more or less literal reparation is impossible, the remorseful person may find satisfaction in suffering for her offense, or seeking and receiving forgiveness from persons she may have wronged. Remorse, like many emotions, comes in widely ranging degrees of intensity, all the way from a fleeting faint fret involving only a pithless momentary urge to atone, to an enduring burning pain that can reorient an entire life. Remorse's defining proposition is, accordingly, something like this: *It is very important not to do wrong (omit right) in matters like X/Y, and I have blameworthily done X (omitted Y); let me atone for doing X (omitting Y).*

b. Guilt

David Copperfield has come into the dour clutches of Mr. Murdstone, his mother's new husband, and Murdstone's sister Jane, who have taken over David's instruction. These two so intimidate him that, though he knows his lessons, he cannot recite them, and on one occasion Murdstone undertakes to beat the delinquent scholar. The hand by which the man holds him in place for beating comes near David's mouth and he bites it ferociously to the bone.

He beat me then, as if he would have beaten me to death.... How well I remember, when my smart and passion began to cool, how wicked I began to feel! I sat listening for a long while, but there was not a sound. I crawled up from the floor, and saw my face in the glass, so swollen, red, and ugly that it almost frightened me. My stripes were sore and stiff, and made me cry afresh, when I moved; but they were nothing to the guilt I felt. It lay heavier on my breast than if I had been a most atrocious criminal, I dare say (Charles Dickens, *David Copperfield*, Chapter 4).

It is not uncommon for people to speak of feeling guilty when they are feeling remorse, and of remorse when it would be more apt to speak of guilt. Still, when we speak carefully or look for differences, we see that the concepts are distinct. Guilt (not as a moral status but as an emotion denoted by the phrase "feel guilty") differs from remorse in focusing less or not at all on a particular offense and more on the offender's status of being guilty.[30] For David, the most salient thing is his wickedness. Whereas remorse requires reference to some particular act or omission, one can feel guilt in a more generalized, diffuse way; indeed, one can feel guilty without there being any particular offense or set of offenses that one feels guilty about. And even when guilt does focus on a particular offense, it generalizes to an overall or fundamental status of the offender. As Taylor says, guilt is an emotion of self-assessment, not just of act assessment (p. 97). We saw (Section 3.1a) that anger does not separate the sinner from the sin, but smears the offender with badness; the same is true of guilt and remorse, but in remorse one construes oneself as *having committed an offense*; in guilt, as one who is *morally spoiled*.

Obviously the two emotions are closely related: Remorse turns easily into guilt as the subject generalizes from his being an offender in some particular to his being morally spoiled; and guilt often makes reference to some particular purported wrong, such as David's biting of Mr. Murdstone. And it is not strictly right to deny that remorse is an emotion of self-assessment (after all, its defining proposition makes evaluative reference to what "I" have done; its consequent concern is not just that a wrong be righted, but that "I" atone for the wrong); rather, one should say only that it is not an emotion of *general* self-assessment. The difference between remorse and guilt will be, in this respect, one of degree and of focus – of degree, inasmuch as guilt involves a more profound and general impression of the badness of the self; and of focus, inasmuch as in guilt the focus is typically on the self, while in remorse the focus is more typically on the deed and its repair. The word "typical" is considered, because in the kaleidoscopic shiftings of emotional focus, guilt will sometimes focus on the deed, and remorse on the self. But when guilt focuses on the deed, the deed is seen as imparting a general badness to the self, and when remorse focuses on the self, the self is seen as the author of a particular blameworthy deed.

We are not told that David felt remorse for biting Murdstone; in fact we can imagine he was glad to have done it and would do it again if he could

---

[30] Thus Gabriele Taylor errs when she says, "... feelings of guilt are localized in a way in which feelings of shame are not localized; they concern themselves with the wrong done, not with the kind of person one thinks one is" (*Pride, Shame, and Guilt*, p. 89).

avoid the consequent fury. But still, he felt guilty. Why? We get the impression that his sense of being "wicked" is as much due to the violent authoritative punishment he receives, with the rejection and alienation it signifies, as it is due to the "wrong" he has done. Punishments are often physically painful or embarrassing or inconvenient; but for sensitive individuals, their moral meaning can be their most burdensome dimension, for they say "You deserve this treatment because you are bad." Even one who firmly believes that he has not done wrong and is not wicked may be prey to the picture of himself that is conveyed in his punishment. The power of angry judgment and punishment and rejection to induce guilt feelings explains why people who are innocent of any wrongdoing and know themselves to be so will sometimes feel guilty under questioning and accusation, and why people who have committed wrongs and know it may start feeling guilty only after accusations or questions suggesting accusations are put. Cases like this show the advantage of a construal account of emotions over any that require beliefs or judgments of the emotion's propositional content.

One can feel guilt about things other than actions – about wishes (Princess Maria Bolkonsky feels guilty about wishing her father, the old Prince Nikolai, dead[31]), about privilege (being well provided for and at ease when others are starving or suffering in war) – and about actions that one did not perform oneself (e.g., a man born in 1950 feels guilty about the bombing of Hiroshima, another about the sins of his father[32]); but it seems less appropriate to talk about remorse in these kinds of case – presumably because remorse, unlike guilt, does ascribe to oneself personal responsibility for wrongful action. I do not say that guilt in all such cases is (or even can be) rational, but there is a rationale for it – a sense of being blameworthy and morally sullied by the wish, the unjust privilege, or the actions of one's family or nation. As moral rationalists we may feel uncomfortable allowing the sense of blameworthiness to be detached from an ascription of responsibility; but this does seem to be allowed within the concept of guilt as an emotion.

Guilt is a "negative" or unpleasant emotion. People who have no aversion to being morally spoiled will not, in construing themselves as morally spoiled, experience the emotion of guilt, just as people who have no aversion to being the author of moral wrongs will not experience remorse. Thus both guilt and remorse presuppose moral concerns that the subject is likely, upon

[31] Leo Tolstoy, *War and Peace*, Book Three, Part Two, Chapter 8.
[32] Søren Kierkegaard's aesthete writes, "In her childlike piety, the Greek Antigone participates in her father's guilt, and so also does the modern Antigone.... She loves her father with all her soul, and this love draws her out of herself into her father's guilt. As the fruit of such a love, she feels alien to humankind. She feels her guilt the more she loves her father; only with him can she find rest; as equally guilty, they would sorrow with each other" [*Either/Or*, translated by Howard and Edna Hong (Princeton, New Jersey: Princeton University Press, 1987), Volume I, pp. 160–161]. Taylor denies this possibility. See *op. cit.*, p. 91, where she follows Joel Feinberg, *Doing and Deserving* (Oxford: Oxford University Press, 1970), p. 231.

reflection, to think good, and thus both emotions suggest something good in the character of the subject.[33] Because, in guilt, what one is averse to is oneself in a moral aspect, one might think that guilt necessarily involves self-dissociation, a sense that the morally tainted self is not the real self and that the real self identifies with the aversion to moral evil and not with the motive of the guilty action (if there is such an action).[34] On the other hand, it is clear that the pain of guilt depends on seeing the morally sullied self as not alien, as being one's real self. No doubt people sometimes have a sense of their good self when they are feeling guilty, and this sense may both cause them to construe the sullied self as alien and enhance the impression of sully. Also, self-dissociation is no doubt one way to "deal with" guilt – say, as it were, "My guilty self is not the real me." But I don't think it is an essential characteristic of the emotion. The reason is that the self that is represented by the aversion to evil is not necessarily a part of the situational object of the emotion of guilt. The aversion must be operating for the emotion to occur, but the self that this aversion is characteristic of need not be in the picture. The proposal that self-dissociation is essential to guilt seems to confuse the orientation of the concern basic to the emotion with the sense of self essential to the emotion.

Guilt's consequent concern is to be free from the blameworthiness, the moral disfigurement. If the guilt involves reference to an action or omission that grounds the blameworthiness, then the consequent desire may be, as in the case of remorse, to atone for the action or omission. This may take the form of reparation, or of suffering that seems to the subject to "make up" for the misdeed. But if the sense of blameworthiness derives chiefly from the accusatory anger of others, the subject may desire reconciliation to (e.g., forgiveness by) the accuser. If the sense of being morally sullied does not derive from an action or omission, or if the blameworthiness seems irreparable by atonement, then the subject may desire to be free of the sense of blameworthiness by *any* means – by rationalization, drugs, sleep, oblivion, suicide, or psychotherapy.

The defining proposition for guilt will, then, be something like this: *It is very important not to be a bad person and I am a bad person in being blameworthy; let me be free from this stain of blameworthiness.*

c. Contrition

Contrition is an emotion central to the Jewish and Christian traditions of spirituality. It is typically occasioned by the awareness of some particular

---

[33] I say "likely" because of cases like the conscience of Huckleberry Finn, who upon reflection might not think that the concern on which his feelings of guilt or remorse about protecting Jim from capture was good. See Mark Twain, *The Adventures of Huckleberry Finn*, Chapter 16.

[34] Taylor seems to suggest that it is a necessary characteristic of guilt that the subject construes his morally sullied self as alien. See *op. cit.*, pp. 94–97.

wrongdoing or wrong attitude, for which the subject construes himself to
be responsible and blameworthy, and so contrition bears some resemblance
to remorse. It is also like guilt in being an emotion of general self-assessment:
the contrite person generalizes over his entire self, construing himself as a
sinner. Psalm 51 in the Hebrew Bible is a classic expression of contrition
and contains all the propositional content characteristic of this emotion:

> Have mercy on me, O God,
>   according to thy steadfast love;
>   according to thy abundant mercy
>   blot out my transgressions.
> Wash me thoroughly from my iniquity,
>   and cleanse me from my sin!
> For I know my transgressions,
>   and my sin is ever before me.
> Against thee, thee only, have I sinned
>   and done what is evil in thy sight,
> so that thou art justified in thy sentence
>   and blameless in thy judgment.
> Behold, I was brought forth in iniquity,
>   and in sin did my mother conceive me.
> Behold, thou desirest truth in the inward being;
>   therefore teach me wisdom in my secret heart.
> Purge me with hyssop, and I shall be clean;
>   wash me, and I shall be whiter than snow.
> Fill me with joy and gladness;
>   let the bones which thou hast broken rejoice . . .
> Create in me a clean heart, O God,
>   and put a new and right spirit within me.
> Cast me not away from thy presence,
>   and take not thy holy Spirit from me . . .[35]

The first thing we notice is that the psalmist construes himself as standing
in a personal relationship to God – of being an object of God's attitudes.
Properly, Hebrew contrition is never just a construal of oneself as having
violated some social expectation or moral standard; God is the primary
offended party ("against thee, thee only, have I sinned"). Thus the concern
on which contrition is based is not just a general concern to be morally
upright, but is in particular a concern to be righteous in God's sight, to
be in a positive or approved relationship with God. The transgression is
not merely behavioral, but attitudinal ("thou desirest truth in the inward
being," "create in me a clean heart"). This God is alienated, sitting in angry
judgment ("cast me not away from thy presence"), but more dispositionally
he is a God of steadfast love and abundant mercy, who welcomes and restores

---

[35] Verses 1–11, in the Revised Standard Version.

repentant sinners. Though the psalmist construes himself as sullied by his sin ("wash me") and sick (God has broken his bones), he is able rather boldly to plead for mercy because of God's character. Thus true contrition is not a purely negative emotion, but contains positive elements and (as contrasted with extreme remorse and guilt) is never "desperate": It sees the way out of blame, degradation, and alienation in God's basically positive regard; it sees its way to a better self than the spoiled one.[36] One can well imagine someone committing suicide out of remorse or guilt, but not out of contrition. Contrition's consequent concern is for restoration to God's full favor by amendment of one's life. The defining proposition is thus: *It is very important to be righteous in Your sight, O God, and I have blameworthily spoiled myself in Your sight; but You are merciful and will forgive (have forgiven) me; I must amend my life, with Your help.*

3.5. DEFECT

a. Shame

Shame is based on a concern to be "respectable," where this word encompasses both intrinsic personal worthiness of one sort or another (say, in physical appearance, social graces, athletic skill, intellectual aptitude, artistic sensitivity, moral rectitude) and the social appearance of such worthiness. The concern is deep, touching one's sense of value as a person. Shame is a construal of oneself as failing dramatically in such respectability or worthiness. Individuals differ from one another, as do cultures, in what kind of respectability is of concern and how such respectability is measured, and thus in what kind of perceived deficits shame one. But what is common to the cases, and defining for shame, is that the subject perceives himself as falling steeply short in worthiness or respectability of some important kind. The depth of the concern and the angle of the shortfall are nicely suggested in the word "disgrace."

Like guilt, shame is a global negative self-construal, and also like guilt it can be occasioned by faults in other people: A person may be ashamed of his father or his children, and not just of himself. To be ashamed of others is to see them as casting disgrace on oneself, but "oneself" need not be interpreted in a strongly individualistic way. Scottie Pippen might feel ashamed of the Portland Trail Blazers' performance on a given occasion, not because of the disgrace reflected on him as an individual but because of the disgrace reflected on the Trail Blazers as a team. This is still a self-construal, since the Trail Blazers is Scottie's team; but the self is less an "I" self than a "we" self.

[36] See my article, "The Logic and Lyric of Contrition," *Theology Today* 50 (1993): 193–207.

Shame differs from guilt in not necessarily construing the defect as blame-worthy. One can feel guilty for one's father's misdeeds or bad attitudes (say, his racism); but one cannot feel guilty for his shortness of stature – though one can feel ashamed of it.[37] The very same misdeeds of one's father might be the occasion for either guilt or shame: To feel guilty for one's father's racism is to construe oneself (in association with one's father) as *blameworthy* for it, while to feel ashamed of one's father's racism is to construe oneself (in association with one's father) as *demeaned* by it. One might, of course, construe oneself as both blameworthy for and demeaned by one's father's racism, in which case one would feel both guilty and ashamed at the same time.

For most people, perhaps, the social *appearance* of worthiness is a more vital concern than intrinsic worthiness, and so it is typical, though not universal, that shame is triggered by the impression of oneself as perceived *by others* to be disgraced. Thus perceiving ourselves to be the object of other people's contempt or disgust is often the occasion for feeling ashamed of ourselves. Shame that is before others is typically before a limited class of others, rather than all others. The child who is ashamed of her mother's Dutch accent is probably ashamed only among nonimmigrants and feels perfectly comfortable with her mother's accent among the immigrant children whose mothers speak as hers does. Even people who are deeply concerned for intrinsic respectability – say, very serious craftsmen or intellectuals – may sometimes require a public revelation of their unrespectability to catalyze the self-construal that is active shame. But I think it is wrong to make the sense of being perceived by others a necessary feature of shame. The craftsman who compromises his worthiness by cutting corners may feel ashamed of himself even if he is confident that his own name will never be associated in anyone else's mind with the sloppy work.[38] It is true that despite not

---

[37] Crazy exceptions are possible here. A person might construe his father as blameworthy for his father's shortness of stature and, by association with his father, construe himself as sharing the blameworthiness. Such exceptions would just reinforce the point that I am pressing throughout this chapter, that emotion types are defined not by the types of actual situation to which they are responses, but by the kind of terms in which the subject construes them. The proposed view implies no logical limits (and hardly any psychological ones) to what situations can evoke any given type of emotion.

[38] Descartes says that shame (*la honte*) is "the evil . . . that is or has been in us that is referred to the opinion others may have of it" (*The Passions of the Soul*, Article 66, p. 55). Spinoza says that "shame (*pudor*) is pain accompanied by the idea of some action of our own which we imagine others to blame" [*Ethics*, translated by Andrew Boyle (New York: Everyman's Library, 1959), Part III, Definitions of Emotions XXXI, p. 135]. Gabriele Taylor, by contrast, says "it is . . . not necessary for feeling shame that the agent believe or imagine there to be some observer who views him under some description" (*op. cit.*, pp. 65–66, and see p. 58; but see also pp. 57 and 67). Arnold Isenberg, similarly, says "we must allow for the existence of an autonomous conscience, for the fact that a man may feel himself disgraced by something that is unworthy in his own eyes and apart from any judgment but his own" ("Natural Pride and Natural Shame," in *Explaining Emotions*, p. 366).

believing that the work will ever be attributed to him he might construe (imagine) the work as being attributed to him by others. This, too, often produces shame. But I do not think that even the construal of oneself as unworthy in the eyes of others is necessary to shame. Intrinsic shame is possible even if it is rare.

Shame's consequent concern is to restore one's respectability or reduce one's disgrace. Thus people often respond to shaming situations with efforts at self-justification, rationalization, or efforts to avoid similar situations in the future. If others' perception of oneself is prominent in the experience, the desire to reduce disgrace may take the form of an urge to hide from view whatever one is ashamed of, or to hide oneself. The craftsman who is ashamed of cutting corners will want to behave more like a self-respecting craftsman in the future,[39] while the student who is ashamed of his "D" may want to explain it away as a result of inadequate sleep, and the child who is ashamed of her mother's Dutch accent will want to avoid being seen with her mother.

This consequent concern can be manifested in paradoxical complications that look like counterexamples. A couple of Dostoevsky's characters present cases of this. Marmeladov's speech in *Crime and Punishment*, Part I, Chapter 2, suggests a man intensely concerned with his dignity, whose drinking has been the occasion for repeated shameful actions and their shameful consequences. His drinking has cost his family dearly. It has dragged his wife from a respectable social position to poverty, degradation, incessant labor, and mortal disease; it has forced his daughter into prostitution. The speech expresses Marmeladov's sense of shame, and yet most of it is not directly an effort to hide, explain away, or justify his actions (though some of it is); he parades his disgrace in lurid self-flagellating detail before people who very well may abuse him and treat him with contempt. He invites Raskolnikov to judge him a swine and a brute, fit to be crucified rather than pitied. He returns, with Raskolnikov, to his flat, where his wife abuses him verbally and drags him into the room by his hair while neighbors laugh at him:

Marmeladov himself helped her efforts by crawling meekly after her on his knees. "This too is a pleasure for me! It's a plea-ea-sure, my de-ar s-sir," he cried out as he was shaken by the hair, and once he even banged his forehead on the floor.[40]

Several plausible interpretive strategies bring this kind of case under the general claim I have made about shame's consequent concern.

First, Marmeladov may construe his audience in such a way as to lessen his vulnerability to shame. He treats the bystanders in the bar as people whose

---

[39] Like fear, shame can also paralyze. But one might argue that this is really two emotions: shame plus despair.

[40] Translation by Michael Scammell (New York: Washington Square Press, 1963), p. 28.

opinion does not matter, and Raskolnikov may look disreputable enough to be someone who will sympathize with his position. But second, even if he expects the others to condemn him, some of his self-recrimination is so virulent as to suggest that he has abandoned the pursuit of dignity. By giving up the concern for dignity, Marmeladov hides himself, so to speak, and defends himself against the contempt of his sanctioners. Only those who claim dignity can be shamed by disgrace. We might call this the strategy of putting oneself below disgrace. (Admittedly, the concern for respectability is hard to kill; but it may be stifled for a moment, especially if one is drunk.) A third strategy is value dissociation. In displaying himself to abuse and describing himself in highly condemnatory terms, Marmeladov may be taking the evaluative high ground against himself – saying, as it were, "The better part of me thinks just as ill of my behavior as you do." Thus, in a sense he justifies himself, showing himself to himself and others as having a respectable side, with which he identifies. Fourth, Marmeladov's words and behavior have a strong theme of atonement. He says (not very believably) that he drinks to intensify his sufferings, and when he rejoices in his wife's abuse, it is as though the pain and humiliation, and his acceptance of these, make up for the destruction he has wrought in his family. This strategy has the potential to improve his self-respect because his shame is a guilty one; atonement does not apply to all shame.[41] Another common defense against shame, especially when it is grounded in guilt, is anger at those before whom one is ashamed; it is a way of claiming the moral high ground and shifting blame.[42]

So I think that, despite the complicated cases, we might express shame's defining proposition thus: *I am or appear unrespectable (unworthy, disgraced) in some way that it is very important to be or appear respectable (worthy); may I be or appear more respectable.*

b. Embarrassment

Embarrassment might be described as a shallow variant of shame. It is shallower in the following respects: First, embarrassment, being always a sense of one's "audience," lacks the potential autonomy characteristic of the deeper forms of shame. Second, if shame is based on a concern to be respectable or worthy, embarrassment is based on a concern not to be seen in an uncomplimentary or very revealing light; thus third, the consequent concern of embarrassment is not to improve oneself but to get out of certain kinds

---

[41] The other Dostoevskian character I have in mind is Fyodor Karamazov, father of the three brothers. The scene is the visit to the elder Zossima in the monastery (*The Brothers Karamazov*, Part One, Chapter 2). After much buffoonery on the part of the old Karamazov, embarrassing to Alyosha and the other visitors, Zossima comments that Karamazov's demeaning self-display all stems from shame.

[42] See Dostoevsky's *Notes from the Underground*, Part II, Chapter 9 and Section 3.3a.

of light. And finally, while embarrassment is reflexive like shame, it does not seem to go to the core of the self in the way shame does. Disgrace touches dignity, but mere uncomplimentary light does not. Consider some contexts.

Many people are embarrassed to be seen without their clothes. These individuals are not all ashamed to be seen unclothed because they do not construe themselves as demeaned insofar as they are seen naked (almost nobody construes himself as demeaned by being naked, provided that he is not seen), but they are embarrassed, and this for various possible reasons: Some wish to keep their bodies from public view because they take their bodies to be uncomplimentary to them; others, who regard their bodies as beautiful and attractive, may still be embarrassed to display them publicly in all their glory, simply because, when so seen, they construe themselves as strange and vulnerable (they are modest); yet others, who perhaps don't mind being seen and lusted after, may still find it distasteful to be seen as persons who don't mind being seen and lusted after, and so they keep their clothes on even if they would kind of like to take them off. The first and third groups keep their clothes on to avoid being seen in an uncomplimentary light; the second group keep their clothes on to avoid being seen in too revealing a light.

So embarrassment is not always a self-construal as being seen in an uncomplimentary light. One vulnerability to embarrassment is the disposition we call "modesty." This is the concern for privacy, or for not being on display, with respect to some range of things: One can be modest about one's body, one's accomplishments, one's religious practices, one's diseases, and so on, where one does not construe the public display of these as uncomplimentary. You are modest about your accomplishments, and you find yourself being extravagantly complimented in a public setting, thus made the center of intense admiring attention. You are embarrassed and wish you could disappear. (You would need a strange mind to be ashamed in this situation.)

Being embarrassed to be naked differs from being ashamed of one's body. Let us say my body is ugly, and I regard physical ugliness as very degrading. So when I construe myself as being seen in my bodily ugliness I feel shame. If, by contrast, I am only embarrassed about my ugliness, it will be because I have less of my self invested in bodily beauty, and consequently do not feel degraded, but only disapproved by my body's being seen in its ugliness.

We can see how embarrassment is shallower than shame by applying our observations to moral examples. If a person is ashamed of having lied, he construes his having lied as essentially demeaning to him (making him unworthy) as a person; if he is only embarrassed about it, then the issue is not his meanness but his unagreeableness or objectionableness; and it is not his lie as such that embarrasses him, but the fact that others are aware of it. If he feels guilty about having lied, he construes his having lied as causal or symbolic of his blameworthy moral degradation. Or consider a devout monk in conversation with some worldly young blades. The latters' talk turns to their sexual exploits and one of them asks the monk about his. He replies, with a certain emotional uneasiness, that he is a virgin. If his emotion is shame, then his virginity appears to him at this moment, via the consciousness of the others, to make him less than a man (as usual, he need not believe this about himself to feel shame). If, by contrast, his emotion is merely embarrassment, then his personal dignity is not in question, but he does construe himself, uncomfortably, as being seen in an uncomplimentary or too revealing light.

Embarrassment, like shame, can be by association: That is, the uncomplimentary light in which one construes oneself as appearing can be reflected from another. Also, embarrassment can be empathic or a response to a fiction, and the "self" that one wishes to be seen in a complimentary or not too revealing light can be a social or "we" self. An example of Gabriele Taylor's can illustrate these points:

> Some people are gathered together for a light-hearted social evening. Suddenly one of them begins to pray; the other guests are embarrassed (p. 70).[43]

Consider the perspective of Burt, one of the guests. Burt's embarrassment over the prayer could be a case of his construing himself as an individual seen in an uncomplimentary light, if he construes the other guests as associating him with the praying person ("they all think he came with me"). Another possibility is that Burt's embarrassment is empathic, that he feels embarrassed *for* the man who is making himself appear ridiculous by praying. In this case Burt imagines being the other person in this situation and feels accordingly. Burt's imagining, in this case, makes crucial assumptions about the praying person's character because only certain characters, in that situation, would feel embarrassed[44]; and the assumption may be false, in case the praying person, fully aware of the situation, is not such as to feel embarrassed. Still another possibility is that Burt responds to the man's action by imagining *himself* to be praying in this situation, and thus feels a kind of fictional embarrassment (see Section 2.4g).

Another possibility is that Burt is embarrassed not so much *for* the person who is praying as *by* him, yet without construing himself as construed by the others as especially associated with the praying individual. In this case, he sees this person as casting an uncomplimentary light on *us all*. His embarrassment consists in his sense that we look ridiculous because of this person's behavior. The case is not neatly symmetrical with individual embarrassment

---

[43] *Ibid.* My use of the case differs from Taylor's.

[44] I am indebted to Peter Goldie for noticing that such assumptions are crucial to empathic feeling. See his *The Emotions: A Philosophical Exploration* (Oxford: Clarendon Press, 2000), pp. 198–201.

because the eyes in whose view we see ourselves as appearing in an un-complimentary light are none other than those of the people at the party; that is, they are not quite the eyes of "others," but our eyes. Still, they *are* the eyes of others, insofar as, for each individual who feels this communal embarrassment, the eyes are at least partly other than his own.

The defining proposition for embarrassment is thus something like this: *Being concerned to be approved by others or not too apparent to them, I am appearing to others in an uncomplimentary or too revealing light; let me cease to do so.*

c. Humiliation

With the word "humiliation" we designate a special version of shame. Humiliation is a construal of oneself as having been *shown to be* or having been *made to appear* to be unrespectable (unworthy) by some action or event that puts one's real or apparent unworthiness on display for others. It involves, thus, reference to a dramatic transition to disgrace that shame may lack. Revelations of their sordid pasts to their small towns of Middlemarch and Casterbridge occasion not just shame but humiliation for Mr. Bulstrode (George Eliot's *Middlemarch*) and Michael Henchard (Thomas Hardy's *The Mayor of Casterbridge*). In Somerset Maugham's *Of Human Bondage*, Philip Carey is humiliated when some older boys forcibly and closely examine his club foot while commenting on it in such words as "beastly," "rum," "ugh," and "is it hard?" (Chapter XI). Gabriele Taylor writes:

> A person feeling shame will exercise her capacity for self-awareness, and she will do so *dramatically*: from being just an actor absorbed in what she is doing she will *suddenly* become self-aware and self-critical. It is plainly a state of self-consciousness which centrally relies on the concept of another.... The element of drama in the shifting viewpoints and the sudden realization of one's changed position is quite missing in the case of pride (p. 67, italics added).

On my analysis, the properties of dramatic shift and reliance on the concept of an observing other belong not to shame as such, but to the special kind of shame that we call humiliation. Taylor thinks that humiliation differs from shame in that the distinctive mark of humiliation is the judgment *I am regarded as presumptuous* (p. 68).

Humiliation is indeed enhanced by the judgment or construal that not only has my unworthiness been displayed before others by some action or event, but that those others regard me as having presumptuously asserted a worthiness that is roundly disconfirmed by the event. But this is not necessary for humiliation. It is plausible in the cases of Bulstrode and Henchard mentioned above, but to ascribe such a construal to Philip Carey and other similarly humiliated persons, who have shown no presumption and have no reason to suppose it attributed to them, would be gratuitous. The defining proposition for humiliation, then, is *X (some event or action) has shown*

me to be or made me appear to be disgraceful in some way that it is very important to
show myself to be or appear respectable; may I be or appear more respectable.

3.6. LOSS

a. Sadness

I was sad when they said Grandma would never be able to come home again.
Suzy got sad if she thought about the friends she'd left behind in Memphis.
With sadness I saw the bulldozers raze the house we'd lived in for so many
years. We were all sad about Joe and Mary's divorce. Richard is sad when he
thinks about his son's dissolution and addictions. It makes me sad to contemplate the devastation of the rain forests. Daddy is sad, because he lost his job.

Examples like these suggest that sadness is a construal of some event,
or some state of affairs, as a loss of something to which one is "attached":
Grandma being at home, with all that entails for visits and for Grandma's
happiness; the friends in Memphis; the old residence; the marriage of Joe
and Mary; the prospects for Richard's son. Indeed, sadness upon the loss of
something is one of the chief indices of attachment; if you lose something
and feel no sadness about it, chances are good you didn't care much for it.

On the basis of what I have said so far, we might proffer this defining
proposition for sadness: *X, whose continued existence or presence or availability is*
important, is no longer existent, present, or available.

But other usages of "sad" suggest that sadness should be treated as a
generic "downness" of emotions, not necessarily associated with loss. We may
be especially inclined to this view when we consider the range of emotion
terms for which "sad" can stand in as a generic substitute. "Sad" can be used
in contexts of disappointment (we were sad that Auntie was not home when
we visited), regret (Mel is sad that he did not take the opportunity to invest
in Apple), grief (many people were deeply saddened by President Kennedy's
death), despair (having been in the life boat on the open sea for three days,
and seeing no hope of being rescued, we all became very sad), remorse (Sam
was sad when he thought about how he had treated his first wife), homesickness (during the first three weeks of school, Abel became sad whenever
he thought of his family and friends back in Toccoa Falls). These considerations may tempt us to think that sadness is just the generic uncomfortable
element common to the negative emotion types; perhaps we'd better not
try writing a defining proposition for it – it having so little "definition."

But it would be wrong to think of sadness as the generic negative element
in negative emotions because a person is not sad when he is afraid, annoyed,
angry, embarrassed, or contemptuous. Why does "sad" substitute often for
disappointment, regret, grief, despair, and homesickness, but not for terror,
indignation, hatred, horror, disgust and frustration? The loss hypothesis
does seem to throw light on the matter: Loss does not seem to be definitive

for any of the emotions in the last group. We might try to see losses in the other cases: the loss of an opportunity to visit Auntie or to invest in Apple, the loss of hope of being rescued, the loss of contact with the folks in Toccoa Falls.

But the loss needs to be construed as pretty permanent for "sad" to be the right word. Think of cases of only temporary loss – a ball team that has fallen behind, but not yet irrevocably; a businessman who has lost some money, but hopes to gain it back on the next deal. As long as the prospects of reversing the loss seem pretty good, the fan and the businessman will speak of anxiety, annoyance, regret – even of being sorry they made the moves they made – but they won't talk about sadness until the game is over or the money seems unrecoverable. Thus I think we can allow the defining proposition written above to stand. For the phrase, *"no longer existent, present, or available"* is naturally read as suggesting a certain permanence of loss.

Our first reason for denying that sadness is generic negative emotional tone is that sadness is not involved in such negative emotions as fear, annoyance, and contempt, negative though they are. A second reason is that it is not clear that there *is* any emotion that is the general form of negative emotional tone. Among the emotions for which "sad" can stand in place of the more precise term, the negative construal differs significantly; because emotions are construals, it is not possible to hive off the other aspects and be left with a single type of negativity that can be designated as "sadness." The notion of a concern-based construal is that of a perception, the reasons for which are not just exogenously causal of it (see Section 2.6a) but are analytic of it. So it is erroneous to suppose that all of these emotions contain a common mental element named sadness, which in the different cases is caused by different kinds of causes; it is better to say that these emotions are different kinds of sadness – or better yet, "sad" is used rather loosely in this range of cases.

b. Grief

Augustine of Hippo describes the grief he felt on the death of a friend:

My heart was utterly darkened by this sorrow and everywhere I looked I saw death. My native place was a torture room to me and my father's house a strange unhappiness. And all the things I had done with him – now that he was gone – became a frightful torment. My eyes sought him everywhere, but they did not see him; and I hated all places because he was not in them, because they could not say to me, "Look, he is coming," as they did when he was alive and absent. I became a hard riddle to myself. . . . Nothing but tears were sweet to me and they took my friend's place in my heart's desire.[45]

---

45 *Confessions*, translated by Albert C. Outler (Philadelphia: Westminster Press, no date), Book Four, Chapter IV, p. 81.

In a central usage, "grief" is a sense of having suffered an irrevocable loss of a nonfungible object of very great significance to the griever – paradigmatically of a person and by death. The object will be one to which the subject was (is) strongly *attached*, and this term is particularly apt here, inasmuch as the loss seems to disorient the subject – that is, call into question his personal identity or cause him to lose his bearings in evaluative space.[46] By Augustine's attachment to him, his friend afforded a pervasive meaning to the things and activities in Augustine's life, so that to lose him meant the evacuation of vitality from all else. The loss of the sense of value in the ordinary things with which the friend was associated causes Augustine to become "a hard riddle to himself." This is perhaps why we also speak of "grieving" or "mourning" as a *process* that one goes through, at the end of which one has accommodated to the loss, having come to some adjusted sense of oneself.

Augustine, in effect, contrasts his grief with the emotion we call "missing." To miss someone is also to construe oneself and one's surroundings as characterized by the absence of that object of attachment, and to do so with a certain discomfort. But missing, when it differs from grief, does not construe that object as irrevocably lost. So it makes sense to try to reestablish communication with him or her, and that, indeed, is the consequent concern of missing: One wants to "see" the friend, the beloved, and this desire often motivates action. The defining proposition for missing is something like this: *X, to whom (which) I am strongly attached, is absent from my present situation; may X be present to me again.* By contrast, grief is paralyzing or essentially frustrating in that it has a *wish* that *would* be its consequent concern were it not that the subject sees no sense in trying to satisfy it and no prospect that any fortune can satisfy it. So it is as though it had no consequent concern. We might write the defining proposition for grief as follows: *X, to whom (which) I was (am) deeply attached and who (which) is irreplaceable, has been irrevocably taken from me; would that X could be restored to me!*

This account invites three objections. One may doubt whether the object of grief must be of *great significance* to the subject, and whether it must be construed as *nonfungible* and as *irreparably lost*. The most interesting of these objections is the third, but let us begin with the first and second. The first two objections may ignore that emotions are construals. True, people sometimes grieve (or at any rate "grieve" – see Chapter 4) over things that many would regard as unworthy to be grieved over and/or things that most of us would regard as replaceable. People may grieve for their dead pets, their wrecked cars, and their ruined gardens. But as I have argued *ad nauseam*, the propositional content of an emotion does not need to be

---

[46] I borrow this term from Charles Taylor. See his *Sources of the Self: The Making of the Modern Identity* (Cambridge, Masachusetts: Harvard University Press, 1989), Chapter 2.

true – or even believed – to be the content of the emotion. If my remarks about grief are right, the subject need only construe his pet or his wrecked car as being deeply important and irreplaceable. Also, as I have noted before, people use emotion vocabulary loosely. Furthermore, someone may say that he is grieving over his wrecked car, to slightly comic or melodramatic effect.

The third objection is more substantial because we have cases in which grief seems to motivate action intended to restore the lost object. Mr. Peggoty (in Dickens's *David Copperfield*) wanders the world over in search of his lost niece Emily, who has run off with the unscrupulous but galvanizing James Steerforth. Mr. Peggotty meets David in London and tells him about his experiences. He tells about the kindnesses he has received from people along the way and recalls,

They would often put their children – partic'lar their little girls . . . upon my knee; and many a time you might have seen me sitting at their doors, when night was coming in, a'most as if they'd been my Darling's children. Oh, my Darling!

Overpowered by sudden grief, he sobbed aloud (Chapter 40). On the account of emotion offered here, the imagined scene triggers a vivid impression of his loss of Emily, and this impression is his grief. But can the impression be one of irrevocable loss, when his ongoing mission is to find Emily and bring her home? Dickens juxtaposes Mr Peggotty's grief with that of Ham, who had been her fiancé. Ham's grief conforms more straightforwardly to the notion of grief as a perception of irrevocable loss:

"He ain't no care, Mas'r Davy," said Mr Peggotty in a solemn whisper – "keinder no care no-how for his life. When a man's wanted for rough service in rough weather, he's theer. When there's hard duty to be done with danger in it, he steps for'ard afore all his mates. And yet he's as gentle as any child. There ain't a child in Yarmouth that doen't know him" *(ibid.)*.

Ham still acts, but he does nothing to satisfy the wish implied in his grief – the wish to have Emily back. Ham's grief, like Augustine's, takes the point out of everything, and it does so because it is a sense of loss without hope.

I propose that Ham's grief and Mr. Peggotty's differ because of their different relationships to Emily, but not in the attribution of irrevocability to the loss. They differ in what they are grieving *about*: Mr. Peggotty grieves for the innocent Emily that was, and now is gone forever – the Emily that might have married Ham and had children like the ones that the mothers have put on his knee. But as the uncle he can still hope to find the present Emily, the worse for wear, and salvage her life. For Ham the fiancé, by contrast, the only salvaging that would console him would be the Emily he could take to wife, and she is irretrievable.

Specifying more particularly what is construed as lost can help us with other kinds of cases, as well. When spiritually developed Christians grieve dead loved ones, they do not do so without hope. The hope, in effect, limits the *scope* of the irrevocable loss. Christians genuinely grieve, inasmuch as they construe the loved one as irrevocably lost *for this life* and *in the form* in which the person was known and loved. And since for Christians the relationships of this life can be very important, such grief can be extremely painful. And yet, like Mr. Peggotty's grief for Emily, and unlike Ham's, the Christian's grief is not desperate, for she can construe the loved one as retained for another life and in another form. And in virtue of this hope the Christian can even act in the interest of restoration, inasmuch as she can pray for the dead.

The cases of Mr. Peggotty and the spiritual Christian suggest, too, a way of understanding Ilongot grief, which Michelle Rosaldo contrasts with "Western" grief, saying that "mourning, for Ilongots, points not to passivity and calm but to wild violence"[47]—in particular, the violence of headhunting. We have seen (Section 2.9c) that the consequent concern of an emotion type is understandable in terms of the emotion's defining proposition, and that the consequent concern of an instance of emotion is understandable in terms of the emotion's material proposition. If it is true that grief's defining proposition contains the clause *"my loss is irrevocable,"* it is understandable how grief's consequent concern is essentially frustrated or damped out, and the emotion "points . . . to passivity and calm" if not qualified by something like the Christian hope or Mr. Peggotty's hope.

How can the desire to kill be consequent to grief? If it can be understood rationally (and I am supposing throughout that emotions are basically rational states of mind), we will expect the loss to be somehow construed as corrigible or compensated for by killing. The answer seems to lie in the meaning of headhunting for the Ilongots. For them it expresses vitality and thus is a device of renewal:

Ilongots agree that headhunting has a good deal less to do with enemies and victims than with the desire of young men to emulate their "fathers" . . . men recognize that headhunting is an aspect of the process by which children realize in their turn the life and energy once achieved by elders, renewing, through their show of "passion," the experience and vitality of adults.[48]

Rosaldo does not show precisely how killing can "satisfy" grief, but she seems to provide the elements of an explanation. Grief is a perception of loss of some individual or individuals by death. This loss may be of a person to whom one is particularly attached – a brother, a father, a husband or wife – or it may be of more distant kin. The "closer" the lost individual is to the subject of grief, the more will the grief be like the emotion I have been

---

[47] Rosaldo, *op. cit.*, p. 222. "Even extreme grief may ultimately vent itself in violence – but more generally takes the form of apathy. . . ." See Joseph Conrad, *Heart of Darkness*, in *Heart of Darkness & The Secret Sharer* (New York: New American Library, 1960), p. 102.

[48] *Ibid.*, p. 139. See pp. 33–34.

describing in recent paragraphs. But the Ilongots think of this same loss as a loss of a general vitality (*liget*) to the whole community. Even if one construes the lost individual life as irreplaceable and irrevocably lost and as having momentous importance in itself, nevertheless the lost individual life is associated with another momentous loss that is not irrevocable and is of something that is not irreplaceable. Killing cannot restore lost individuals, but because it expresses and produces *liget* and *liget* is vitality, killing can restore vitality to the community that has lost it through the death of individuals. Thus headhunting prevents grief from being an entirely hopeless or necessarily passive emotion. Just as Christian grief and Mr. Peggotty's grief differ from Ham's grief in virtue of their association with hopes, so Ilongot grief is distinctive in virtue of its association with the process of restoring *liget* through headhunting.[49] Here, too, the scope of the irrevocable is circumscribed by a kind of hope. The hope is not quite merely another emotion added to grief – certainly not merely alternating with grief – but actually affects the character of the grief by affecting the reading of the irrevocable.

Because grief is painful, it can also motivate people to escape from it. We see a suggestion of this in Dickens's description of Ham as volunteering for the most dangerous tasks at sea. He is not quite suicidal, but he would not mind escaping from life; and he does finally escape in this way. Other people escape the discomfort by various strategies of denial – for example, by removing from the house all reminders of the beloved. Others may go to a therapist who will help them "work through" their grief. The more blatant and conscious cases seem to be ones in which the subject dissociates from his grief, treating it more or less as an nonrational pain and not as an expression of his deepest self. If getting over deep grief is, as I suggested earlier, a matter of shifting one's psychological identity, the person who seeks therapy for his grief is in effect treating his identity – as constituted by his attachments – as inessential and thus manipulable for the purpose of comfort and "getting on with his life." In any case, the desire to escape from the pain of grief, while it is common enough, is not the consequent concern arising out of the internal logic of this emotion, any more than the desire to escape anger or anxiety by just any available means (drugs, oblivion, therapy) is the consequent concern essential to these emotions. I have argued that the consequent concern of grief is the wish for the restoration of the object of loss, a wish that is rationally frustrated by the construal of the loss as irrevocable. This explains why grief is essentially paralyzing, motivationally,

49 The headhunting approach to grief involves finding something revocable that is analogous to or associated with what one has irrevocably lost. This "strategy" is seen when a mother who has lost her child to a certain disease devotes her time to raising funds for medical research into the disease, or a man who has lost his daughter to a drunk driver campaigns for stricter laws.

and why the actions to which it does give rise are motivated auxiliarily by various forms of associated hope.

c. Regret

In regret, some action, event, or state of affairs in the past, present, or future is construed as contrary to some good and as contrasted with some more propitious alternative (action, omission, occurrence, nonoccurrence, state of affairs); that is, something unfortunate is construed in terms of what might have been. (If what is regretted is taken to be in the future, it nevertheless presents itself as a *fait accompli.*) I might, for example, regret having yelled angrily at my child; or regret that my friends were on the mountain when the storm hit; or regret that I shall die before my grandchildren are old enough to remember me; or regret that the United States is so racist. In each case the object of regret is displayed, as it were, against a background thought: I might have kept my cool; my friends might have been safe in the lodge when the storm hit, or the storm might have hit later; I might have lived to be 90; the United States might have been racially just.

One can see, from the breadth of possibilities here, that regret is a relatively indeterminate, all-purpose emotion type. One might think of sadness, sorrow, and grief, as well as remorse, guilt, and contrition, as variants of regret: In sadness and grief, one regrets a loss; in remorse and guilt, one regrets a misdeed or character defect. Losses, misdeeds, and character defects are all contrary to some good and alternative to it. This is something philosophers, focusing on the formal requirements for regret, might say; but if my friends die in the winter storm, I do not say "I regret that my friends died," and the person feeling deep remorse may feel some impropriety in saying "I regret that I insulted you." "Regret" by itself seems to undersuggest the gravity or pathos appropriate to the situation or felt by the subject. "Deep regret" may do the job, but even this might not quite substitute for "grief," "sorrow," or "contrition."

Also, regret differs from these more particular emotions in accommodating a broader range of basic concerns. Remorse is based on a concern to do what is morally right; guilt on a concern to be morally right; embarrassment on a concern not to be seen in an uncomplimentary light; sadness and grief on attachments to things, places, persons. Regret is less discriminate: It seems that it can be based on any concern whatsoever that can be contravened.

Regret's consideration of what might have been also differentiates it from some of these other emotions: I might feel embarrassed about being seen naked, and yet not regret it, in case I don't construe the mishap in terms of an alternative scenario in which it did not occur. Sadness and grief might occur without regret for the same reason; remorse, guilt, and contrition seem less likely to do so. Of course it sounds odd to say, "I was embarrassed about being seen naked, but didn't regret that I was seen naked," because the expression "... didn't regret X" is conventionally used to mean "... wasn't averse to X." Denying that I regret X might also allude to some good that overrode the embarrassment: I was embarrassed to be photographed in the nude, but didn't regret it because of the big fee I was paid. Waxing analytic, I might go on to say, "Well yes, I do regret that I had to be photographed *naked* to earn the money; but given the fee, I don't regret having done it."

Regret's defining proposition, then, seems to be this: *X (occurrence, nonoccurrence, action, omission, state of affairs), which is contrary to my concern(s), might have been otherwise.*

d. Disappointment

How does Clement's being disappointed in Don's performance at the University differ from his regretting Don's performance? If Clement is disappointed, he says something like "It was important to me for Don to do well, and I expected he would, but he didn't. If he regrets Don's performance, he says instead, "It was important to me for Don to do well, as he might have done, but he didn't." Clement will regret Don's performance if he is disappointed in it because his expecting it to be good implies his thinking it may be good. But Clement will regret Don's performance without being disappointed in it in case he did not expect Don to do well, but nevertheless construes Don's performance in terms of the possibility of his having done well. Disappointment's defining proposition would seem to be: *X (occurrence, nonoccurrence, action, omission, state of affairs), which I wanted and expected, did not occur (fail to occur) or was not done (omitted) or did not obtain.*

e. Depression

If "depression" names an emotion, rather than a mere mood, the emotion so named takes an "object": I am depressed about the state of the economy, about the new president, about my grades, the job market, my lack of philosophical talent. Depression differs from sadness and grief in its not necessarily involving any reference to loss. Instead, it seems to be a view of one's situation in terms of *poor prospects*: My grades, the character of the new president, the job market – all seem to offer reasons for thinking that things will not be going well for me or for people and things I care about. True, a loss may also offer such a reason. If upon losing my job I get depressed, my emotion is depression rather than grief insofar as I construe the loss of job less as a loss of something I am attached to than as boding my future ill. Differently, depression about bad prospects may be *precipitated* by a loss – grief may *cause* one to see only poor prospects and, thus, to be depressed about things one wouldn't otherwise be depressed about. Here the transition from the emotion of grief to the emotion of depression seems to be made by way of a *mood* that we might call depression – a generalized downness in one's view of things that then attaches itself, more or less non-rationally, to "objects" like the new president and my deficit of talent (see Section 2.5d).

If depression as an emotion is future-oriented, we might wonder what its relation is to some of the emotions in the fear family, especially anxiety and dread. Clinically, depression is in fact strongly associated with anxiety; but since anxiety is more likely than depression to motivate avoidant action, we would probably do better to compare it with dread, which, as you will remember, construes an aversive future eventuality as unavoidable (see Section 3.2c). In dread a more or less definite future eventuality is construed as a positive threat, while in depression there may be no definite future eventuality in view, but the depressing event is construed as *depriving* the future of meaning, purpose, and sense. Discouragement seems to me indistinguishable from depression the emotion. The proposition that defines depression as an emotion is, accordingly, *X (an event or state of affairs) implies that for me or persons or things I care about the future is low in prospects for vitality and meaning.*

f. Despair

Despair is a stronger version of depression as an emotion. If depression "says" that future prospects in some important connection of life are dim, despair "says" they are nil. Depression focuses on some event or state of affairs that is construed as dramatically dampening future prospects. Despair is less focused on its "reasons": We speak about being depressed *about X*, where *X* is the reason in terms of which the future looks dim; but when we speak of despairing over or of something, the future prospects themselves are what is primarily in view. Thus I might despair of ever getting an academic job or despair over my prospects of becoming morally mature. Despair is more than just seeing certain future prospects as nil; those prospects must be currently of momentous importance to the subject. Thus despair is like frustration (see Section 3.3d), only absolute and with less focus on the obstacles. Let us say then that the defining proposition for despair is, *X (an eventuality), which is of momentous importance to me, cannot be realized.*

g. Resignation

Resignation is also a way of taking one's situation as not good, but in a less painful way than the depression, despair, regret, or disappointment to which the act or process of resignation is applied. Pain is mitigated because, as we say, one has "reconciled oneself" to the situation's being as it is. What does this mean? To be reconciled to bad prospects is to see them as not so bad after all, which could come from seeing a silver lining in the cloud – say, seeing one's joblessness as a kind of freedom, one's bad grades as a sign of being too creative to be appreciated by the teacher. But *such* a way of seeing bad prospects as not so bad after all is not resignation. In resignation, circumstances that would be depressing or desperate or disappointing or regretful have become less so through a lowering of whatever concern is basic to the emotion. The resigned person says, as it were, "My prospects are not good, but what does it matter?" If one came to care nothing at all for one's prospects, resignation would dispel the emotion altogether. But I think that in most cases, when a person speaks of being resigned, he expresses not no emotion at all, but a milder form of the emotion from which he started, or which he would have without the resignation. So some frustrated concern for what would otherwise be depressing prospects or disappointing results or regrettable circumstances, and so on, continues. If someone says, "I am disappointed to lose the election, but am resigned to it," or "I regret having missed that golden opportunity, but feel resigned to it now," or "it is depressing to have lost my job, but I am resigned," he means to say that the emotion he feels, while it is a version of disappointment, regret, depression, and so on, is mitigated. It may be mild even to the point of not being felt, of having retracted into a more or less purely dispositional form.

Resignation seems to imply that we sometimes have some voluntary control over what we care about. If I am sorely disappointed to have lost an election, I may be able to dim my concern for it by turning my attention to other things, or by placing the objective in a wider context, or by telling myself that it makes no sense to keep caring about what is now impossible. As my reference to regret, disappointment, depression, and despair suggests, resignation is not a separate emotion, but a form of mitigation of these and other negative emotions. Accordingly, it will not have a defining proposition of its own.

h. Romantic Melancholy

Romantic melancholy is a form of sadness or depression in which the negative emotion is an occasion for self-exaltation. The subject looks at himself in his loss or deprivation and in the sufferings that this causes his sensitive soul, and he sees himself as ennobled, as beautiful, as extraordinary. This state is thus an emotion about an emotion, a pride or self-admiration in sadness. The experience partakes of both emotions, so that the suffering is real enough even if the sadness be not quite authentic (see Chapter 4), and the pleasure of self-admiration is likewise real. Thomas Gray's "Elegy Written in a Country Churchyard" is a classic expression. After extolling the unknown peasants who lie buried beneath the lawn, he imagines an old peasant remembering Gray's own last visits here:

> "There at the foot of yonder nodding beech
>   That wreathes its old fantastic roots so high,
> His listless length at noontide would he stretch,
>   And pore upon the brook that babbles by.

> "Hard by yon wood, now smiling as in scorn,
>   Muttering his wayward fancies he would rove;
> Now drooping, woeful-wan, like one forlorn,
>   Or crazed with care, or crossed in hopeless love.

> "One morn I missed him on the customed hill,
>   Along the heath, and near his favorite tree;
> Another came; nor yet beside the rill,
>   Nor up the lawn, nor at the wood was he;

> "The next, with dirges due, in sad array,
>   Slow through the church-way path we saw him borne.
> Approach and read (for thou canst read) the lay,
>   Graved on the stone beneath yon aged thorn."

The loss depicted in the last two quoted stanzas is highlighted by the presentation of the poet's pleasures, vitality and struggles, and the beauty of the setting. The poet is at the center of the stage, the sad hero as it were, and the beauty of the language and imagery frame him and his loss in such a way that he appears to himself noble and great. If we think of the poet as not merely the producer and object of the poem, but also its foremost audience, then the emotion is a sadness about the (anticipated) loss of precious experiences of nature and of human life, but a sadness that is perceived with pride or esthetic/spiritual self-admiration. Thus the defining proposition for romantic melancholy will be something like this: *In my sadness I am noble, beautiful, interesting, and wonderful.*

In my discussions of Ifaluk fear and anger (Sections 3.2b and 3.3b) I noted that the Ifaluk approve these emotions more and differently than North Americans do, and yet I resisted Catherine Lutz's implied inference that this kind of difference is enough to make Ifaluk fear a different emotion from North American fear. I quoted her report about Gatachimang, an Ifaluk man who seemed to be proud of his fear. This would be structurally parallel to the experience of romantic melancholy. Yet here I allow romantic melancholy to be a distinct type of emotion. Am I inconsistent? Should I say that we just have *two* emotions here, namely, sadness and a pride that is directed at it? That does not seem quite right, since the two emotions are locked together in the romantic tradition, and the experience of sadness is quite different when it is part of romantic melancholy than when it is by itself, with no pride being taken in it. Or should I give up my resistance to the idea that an emotion can be determined as to type by a distinct cultural evaluation of it?

Emotions get crossed in lots of ways: people feeling guilty about their pride and proud of their guilt, embarrassed about their anger or their joy, amused by their bewilderment or their anxiety. These crossings may have cultural warrant, or be more idiosyncratic. The more idiosyncratic and less stereotypical ones do not induce us to multiply emotion types, even though it is pretty obvious that the object emotion (the one that the other emotion is about) is experienced differently when the subject emotion is directed at it. If an odd American were frequently proud of his fear, we would not be inclined to think he was having a special and different emotion – even though, let us say, he was having a special and different emotional experience. So one thing that seems to be needed for an emotion crossing to gain the status of a distinct type of emotion is that it have cultural warrant. Both romantic melancholy and Ifaluk *metagu* meet this condition. But romantic melancholy is by definition a crossed emotion, while Ifaluk *metagu* is not. The expressions "romantic melancholy" and "Ifaluk *metagu*" have different scopes. Romantic melancholy does not include just any melancholy experienced by a romantic, but Ifaluk *metagu* does include just any *metagu* experienced by an Ifaluk. Some sadness that is experienced by a romantic will be plain, uncrossed sadness, sadness not exulted in, even though romantic culture warrants such exultation. We distinguish such sadness from romantic melancholy by reserving the epithet for the latter. While the Ifaluk, because of the cultural evaluation of *metagu*, will sometimes take pride in their *metagu*, they do not always do so, and so *metagu* is not, by definition, a crossed emotion. When Lutz says that *metagu* is approved by the Ifaluk, she is not saying that the Ifaluk always have positive emotions about their *metagu*, but at most that they feel good about their *metagu* more often than we feel good about our fear. And certainly we do approve of some instances of our fear and feel good about some instances of it.

i. Acedia

Acedia was identified in ancient Christianity as disruptive of the attitudes and activities of monks. The earliest writers (Evagrius of Pontus, d. 399; John Cassian, c. 420) do not regard acedia as a form of sadness, but it comes to be so regarded with Gregory the Great (d. 604), and this characterization becomes entrenched with Thomas Aquinas's endorsement of it. For this reason I discuss it here, though the classification seems deeply problematic, as will become evident.

"Ἀκηδία" is cognate with "κῆδος" (care, concern) and "κήδομαι" (I heed), and means something like "apathy" or "indifference." In the monastic culture to which our concept belongs, acedia is not, however, a general indifference, but an indifference about – or worse and more characteristically, a repugnance for – the things and activities characteristic of the monk's calling. Cassian tells us that it comes over the monk especially about noon, when the day is hot and the monk is hungry and has been praying and reading alone in his cell for several hours.

And when this [acedia] has taken possession of some unhappy soul, it produces horror of the place, disgust with the cell, and disdain and contempt of the brethren who dwell with him or at a distance, as if they were careless or unspiritual. It also makes the man lazy and sluggish about all manner of work which has to be done within the enclosure of his dormitory. It does not suffer him to stay in his cell, or to take any pains about reading, and he often groans because he can do no good while he stays there, and complains and sighs because he can bear no spiritual fruit as long as he is joined to that society; and he complains that he is cut off from spiritual gain, and is of no use in the place....[50]

As described by Cassian, who is the chief ancient authority, acedia would seem to be not an emotion, but a syndrome of emotions that arise in response, partly irrational, to the sufferings of the monk. Cassian mentions *horror* of the place, *disgust* with the cell, and *disdain* and *contempt* of the brethren. At least some of these emotions differ by type: Horror differs markedly from contempt. But even if we overlook these varieties of construal that seem to go into acedia and reduce them to something generic like repugnance for spiritual things, the two chief suggestions of the tradition – that acedia is indifference and that acedia is a form of sadness – seem misconceived. None of the four emotions that Cassian mentions is indifference; they are all painful construals of their objects. They resemble indifference only in undermining motivation to pray, read spiritually, and persevere in the monastic life.

The other chief suggestion of the tradition is found throughout the discussion of acedia in *Summa Theologiae* 2a2ae, Question 35, where Thomas Aquinas construes acedia as a kind of *tristitia* – sadness or sorrow. He says, for example, "acedia as we are using it here denotes sorrow over spiritual things" (2a2ae, 35,1, reply) and refers to it as the state of being "sorrowful about the Divine good, which charity rejoices in" (2a2ae, 35,2, reply).[51] But Thomas uses "*tristitia*" in an abstract philosophical sense, in which it means, quite generally, "emotional pain" (this is perhaps justified by the fact that *tristis* can mean *harsh* or *bitter*). He speaks of "sorrow, which is the opposite of the joy that is in the soul" (*ibid.*) (as contrasted with physical pain, which is the opposite of the pleasure that is in the body). And he says that "contrition is sorrow about something past, anxiety is sorrow about something future" (1a2ae, 35,2). If Thomas had in mind genuine sorrow over something rightly construed as good, he would not say, "Since, then, a spiritual

[50] *The Institutes of the Coenobia*, translated by Edgar Gibson, in *The Writings of the Nicene and Post-Nicene Fathers of the Christian Church* (Grand Rapids, Michigan: Wm. B. Eerdmans Publishing Company, 1955), Book X, Chapter II, translation slightly altered.
[51] The translation is by Thomas R. Heath, O.P., in *Summa Theologiae* (London: Blackfriars, 1972), Volume 35.

good is a real good, the sorrowing over it is bad in itself" (35,1, reply). The monk in the state of acedia does not literally sorrow over spiritual things; instead he finds them repugnant in one or more of the several ways that we have mentioned.

I conclude that acedia is neither a species of indifference nor of sadness. Indeed, it does not seem to be an emotion, but rather a syndrome of emotions in the repugnance family, directed at spiritual goods and indisposing the subject to pursue them.

3.7. THE WEIGHT OF TIME

The student is bored by the philosophy lecture he doesn't understand, the philosopher by the vacuous and desultory discourse of the society gentleman. "Interesting means not boring; the boring is the not interesting," comments Patricia Meyer Spacks.[52] Boredom is accordingly a construal of one's present situation or activity as dull, unstimulating, unfascinating, unengaging. Sometimes it may seem to be based on a general lassitude of concern or disinterest in everything whatsoever; but taken literally this cannot be a right analysis. It is true that people whose interests are few or narrow will, other things being equal, be prone to boredom in more situations than people with more catholic concerns. But someone who was interested in nothing at all – not even in being interested – would not suffer the kind of emotional discomfort that boredom is. So this construal is based on a concern to have one's attention engaged, to be stimulated, entertained, interested, gripped with fascination.

Boredom is remarkable, among emotion types, for two properties of its basic concern: its reflexivity and its diffuseness. Whereas emotions like shame and embarrassment are reflexive in being based on a concern for oneself as an object, so to speak—to be respectable and to be seen in a good light – boredom is based on a concern to be in a certain state of mind. But the state of mind in question is very diffuse, being not further defined than as *engaged*. So boredom's consequent concern is simply to escape boredom. This emotion comes as close as any to motivating in the way Patricia Greenspan describes: to act as a way of escaping from the discomfort of the emotion (see Section 2.9d).

It is instructive to compare boredom with its relative, impatience. Both emotions motivate their subject to depart from the present situation. Both may be marked by "fidgety" behavior. In both the burden of time is a term of the construal. Boredom often begets impatience, and impatience sometimes begets boredom. But the two emotions are distinct: A person can be bored without being impatient and impatient without being bored.

---

[52] *Boredom: The Literary History of a State of Mind* (Chicago: University of Chicago Press, 1995), p. 116.

The consequent concern of impatience, though it is not defined by the *concept* of impatience (as for example a concern that the offender be punished is defined by the concept of anger), is not diffuse, but something particular, something focused: One is impatient *to do X or that X should happen.* (By contrast, no "X" occurs in the defining proposition for boredom.) Thus the consequent concern of impatience is not, like that of boredom, to be in a certain state of mind. The behaviors that are characteristic of boredom are aimless, or better, have no other aim than to stave off boredom: thumb-twiddling, doodling, sleeping when no more sleep is needed, pacing, eating though not hungry, reading material that would not interest one otherwise. Distinctively impatient behavior, by contrast, is actions designed to hasten the looked-for event. The pregnant woman who, at the beginning of the ninth month, is eager to have her baby and fidgets in painful consciousness of the dragging time is impatient but, being preoccupied with preparations and dreams of her baby and on the *qui vive* for signs of contraction, she is far from bored. Soldiers who are encamped week after week expecting a battle without its coming may be either impatient or bored. If they are primarily concerned to do battle, they are impatient; but if they are just looking for something, little matter what, to divert them, and want the battle for this reason, they are bored. I said that in both emotions the burden of time is a term of the construal. But time weighs differently in the two cases. In impatience, time is construed as the frustrator, the barrier to the wanted event or action; while in boredom, time appears as merely slow and heavy, as a corollary, so to speak, of everything seeming dull. Impatience is born of expectation, but the bored person may lack all expectation.

I mentioned that boredom and impatience can cause one another. Boredom begets impatience when, out of boredom, one fixes on some expedient for relieving it and then becomes impatient that the expedient should be realized or exploited. The bored student in the philosophy lecture may be impatient for the clock to show the end of the hour, but her interest in the hour's ending is only that the burden of the uninteresting should end. Impatience begets boredom, typically, when the impatient subject loses interest in other available objects and activities than the object of impatience and so becomes bored with her surroundings. For example, the pregnant woman may, in her impatience, be so singularly focused on the coming baby that she loses interest in other things that would normally occupy her – people, work, books, and so on – and thus finds them boring.

Let us say that the defining proposition for boredom is, *It is very important for me to be interested, absorbed, to have my attention engaged, but everything I currently behold, and everything I currently might do, is uninteresting; may I soon be free from this state of mind.* And the defining proposition for impatience is this: *It is very important that I do X (or that X should happen), and I am going to do X (or X is going to happen), but circumstances continue to prevent my doing X (or X continues not to happen); may this time of delay pass.*

Spacks points out that the words "bore" and "boring" first appear, with reference to emotion, in the 18th century and that "boredom" appears only in the 19th. She proposes that we try to understand the emotion itself as a newcomer and as a social construction, and identifies many ways in which the understanding of boredom has varied in the last 250 years. Of Samuel Johnson and some of his contemporaries she notes that while they are well-acquainted with the experience of boredom and preoccupied with its problems, they do not (or very seldom) use the words in question. It seems to me likely that the emotion of boredom has occurred throughout history and across cultures, inasmuch as the concern to be interested in one's surroundings and activities seems generically human, and it seems likely that people in all sorts of periods and cultures sometimes find themselves in circumstances and/or states of mind that frustrate this concern. Spacks gives an example of what appears to be boredom from an uncertified century, but tries to dismiss it as not meeting the requirements for genuine boredom:

Hyppolyta, in *A Midsummer Night's Dream*, complains of the actor playing Moonshine, "I am aweary of this moon. Would he would change" (5.1.256). The performance has gone on too long; she's tired of it. To impose the category of boredom on Hyppolyta's reaction would transform it into a weightier judgment, of herself and of the actor, registering her inability to take interest, his incapacity to interest her. Boredom, unlike weariness, carries intimations of despair (p. 11).

But if my analysis is correct, boredom's defining proposition contains no requirement that the subject construe her condition as irremediable or the boring circumstance as inevitably dull. Spacks herself gives many examples of people who fight their boredom, and so presumably do not construe it as irresistible. This indeed is one of the many variables to which boredom is historically subject, according to Spacks.

Spacks documents many different ways boredom has been interpreted since the time of its naming. It has been thought to be a complaint of the working class or of the leisured class; to be a women's complaint or a men's problem. It has been blamed on the self or blamed on the environment. The bored are sometimes condemned as reprehensible, sometimes pitied as victims. Some have been proud of their boredom, others just burdened by it or even ashamed of it. It has been regarded as avoidable and curable or as inevitable and incurable. Sometimes people have not reflected about it much at all, so as to evaluate it. *What* is regarded as boring also differs: Novels that were all the rage in one generation are declared "boring" by the next. Different cures for it have been proposed.

Many, if not all, of these cultural and historical variables affect the way boredom is experienced and when variously combined constitute a dizzying

array of subtlely or not so subtlely diverse possibilities of emotional experience. But none of these attributions is present in the defining proposition
for boredom as I have analyzed it, and none conflicts with that proposition.
Furthermore, even a cultural constructionist like Spacks who stresses the
diversity of experience seems to have a guiding sense of a distinct emotion
type that is *subject* to all these experiential variations, an emotion type that is,
for example, distinct from so close a cousin as *ennui*. I have tried to give some
analytical precision to my account of this essence by comparing boredom
with impatience and formulating its defining proposition. These more reflective stances *about* the emotion, mentioned in the preceding paragraph,
and the experiences that depend on them, require that it be named and
thematized, in a way that the emotion itself does not. Thus Hyppolyta can
experience boredom without having a name for it (though she is able to
talk about it by adapting "weary" to present purposes), but she cannot experience it as *that besetting incurable emotion of our age* or *boredom the moral problem
that we are obliged to struggle against*. For that she needs an established term
such as the one that was coined in the 18th and 19th centuries.

One way boredom seems clearly to be different in the period about which
Spacks writes is quantitative. There seems to be a lot more of it now than
there was 500 years ago. Spacks attributes this, in part, to the modern preoccupation with experience. If boredom is based on a concern to have intense,
engaging, vivid, gripping experience, it stands to reason that a culturally encouraged demand for experience of this sort will increase the incidence of
the corresponding sort of frustration.

3.8. OPPOSITION

a. Hatred

My Grandmother Roberts hated flies. To her they appeared as little black
buzzing emblems of unrelieved evil. I remember the pursed lips and wrin-
kled nose and the fire in her eyes as she went for her weapon; and then
the fervid but controlled swing, bent on total annihilation. I remember the
satisfaction, mixed with repugnance, with which she peered at the little tangle of legs and wings all askew in a blob of gray goo, and wiped them up
with a Kleenex or washed them down the drain. Hatred, like anger, paints
the offender as bad; and the behavior characteristic of hatred – destructive,
harmful, pain-inflicting – is very similar to that which marks anger.

And yet Grandmother could feel hatred for a fly without being angry at
it. I don't deny that people get angry at flies; I have allowed that they get
angry even at motorcycles (Section 2.3b). But unlike anger, hatred does
not necessarily construe its object in terms of a culpable offense. The only
"reason" for the evil look of the hated object may be that it is the object that
it is. To be angry, Grandmother did not have to construe the fly as doing

anything, other than being a fly and being in the house. We do sometimes give reasons for our hatreds, but insofar as they are our real reasons and our emotion is really hatred rather than anger, they will make reference, finally, not to things done, but to states of being. The abused wife may give a long list of reasons for hating her husband, but they come to trait ascriptions: He is a nasty, inconsiderate, selfish *person*. And so may the Palestinian, or the Nazi, for hating the Jew; the offenses, if they were there at all, have by now been compiled into a trait: being a Jew. Thus repeated episodes of anger, in which badness is ascribed to the object on account of culpable misdeeds, may lead to hatred by a kind of accumulation and abstraction: The badness of the object gets distilled from his offenses and acquires the independence and perduration of a personal essence. But hatreds based in prejudice and tradition may be less the effects of a history of anger than its cause.[53]

Hatred is not always itself an emotion. Sometimes it is a concern on which emotions of a number of different types may be based, and which is thus expressed in these other emotions: the joy a person feels in seeing his enemy humiliated or harmed, the hope he feels at such a prospect, the regret at missed opportunities of hurt, the envy of rival malefactors who got there first. But Grandmother's construals of flies are cases of hatred as a distinct emotion. The reason is that they are the direct construal of the hated object as evil and as worthy of suffering and destruction. Let us say, then, that the defining proposition for hatred is this: *X is evil and worthy of damage, suffering, and destruction; may X be damaged, hurt, or destroyed.*

This analysis raises a question about the fit of the paradigm of emotion offered in this book to cases of hatred as an emotion. The paradigm is that emotions are concern-based construals, which is to say that they are construals of objects or situations, one of the terms of which is a concern or the terms of which impinge on a (distinct) concern. But I have been suggesting that hatred lacks the structure of reasons that is found in anger and most other emotion types. You might say that hatred *is* a reason, *is* a concern; and yet in Grandmother's case it is also an emotion. To identify the object as a fly is sufficient "reason" for hating it, because its essence contains its execrableness. Thus paradigm cases of hatred as an emotion seem not to be concern-*based* construals; they seem to be instances of construals that *are*, as such, concerns. It is not a case of "I hate this fly because it polluted my soup (about which I care)," but "I hate this fly because it is a fly, to which species I have an aversion." This must be admitted as one of the kinds of case that do not perfectly fit my proposed paradigm. We will meet parallel cases in Sections 3.15b and 3.15c. But the paradigm is still enlightening and

---

[53] For several illustrations of the reason-independence of hatred, see the opening pages of Jean-Paul Sartre's *Anti-Semite and Jew*, translated by George J. Becker (New York: Schocken Books, 1948). Malice, says David Hume, "gives us a joy in the sufferings and miseries of others, without any offense or injury on their part" (*A Treatise of Human Nature*), p. 372.

pretty close to analyzing hatred. If the object is not seen as evil, then clearly it is not hated. But hatred is not just seeing the object, in a disinterested way, under the "category," so to speak, of evil; the perception of evil must take the form of a concern.

Hume says that the sensation of love is always "agreeable," and that of hatred is always "uneasy."[54] If hatred is taken as a concern, then it is clear that the emotion based on it need not be unpleasant: I have mentioned joy and hope as constructible on the basis of hatred. Is hatred, regarded as an emotion, necessarily "uneasy"? Given our analysis, the question comes to this: To construe something or someone as evil and worthy of suffering or destruction and do so in a concerned way, is it necessary to experience the construal with discomfort? I think the answer is No, but that will depend on what we count as "hatred, regarded as an emotion." When Grandmother was hunting flies in the house, it was not with displeasure, but rather with a grim but pleasant excitement, that she would behold one of the nasty little intruders. At that moment she certainly viewed it as evil and worthy of destruction and did so in a concerned way, but we might be inclined to say that it was not hatred she felt at that moment, but the joy or hope of the hunt. Now it seems clear to me that she was experiencing the joy of the hunt, but not so clear that she wasn't experiencing hatred. She certainly saw the fly as evil and worthy of destruction. Accordingly, I resist Hume's suggestion that hatred, as an emotion, is always unpleasant.

b. Disgust, Repugnance

Hume sometimes lumps together what should be distinguished when discussing the passions; for example, he confuses humility and shame. When he says that hatred is always uneasy, perhaps he has disgust or repugnance in mind. We may be able to assimilate hatred and repugnance as two species of aversion, but feeling repugnance for someone – say, a severely disfigured person – is not at all the same as hating her. The inclination to hurt or destroy is not an aspect of repugnance, as it is of hatred. One might even feel repugnance for a person while wishing her well and trying hard to help her out – though because the consequent concern of repugnance is to avoid the object, one will probably try to overcome one's repugnance in such a case, as it tends to impede the helping. Also, as I just noted, the emotion of hatred may sometimes involve an attraction to and pleasure in the hated object, but it is characteristic of disgust to be repelled and made uneasy by its object. As Noël Carroll observes:

We do not . . . attempt to add some pleasure to a boring afternoon by opening the lid of a steamy trash can in order to savor its unwholesome stew of broken bits of

54 *Ibid.*, p. 331.

meat, moldering fruits and vegetables, and noxious, unrecognizable clumps, riven thoroughly by all manner of crawling things.[55]

If some people do this, a couple of possible explanations are available: They may, for some reason, not be disgusted by deep breathing over hot, ripe garbage. (Perhaps they are like some sewage specialists I have known who are inured by long experience and the need to get on with the work; we can imagine such a worker, five years into retirement, unscrewing the clean-out on her sewer and breathing deeply for nostalgia's sake.) Or they may be disgusted and take a masochistic pleasure in disgusting themselves. Pleasure without disgust provides no counterexample to my proposal that disgust is intrinsically unpleasant; and when one takes masochistic pleasure in an emotional state, the emotion is a crossed or layered one that presupposes the unpleasantness of the emotion it is about. (Though if the disgust is not too intense, the overall experience may be pretty pleasant. See the discussion of romantic melancholy.) In explaining the "paradox" that people *enjoy* horror fiction in which slimy and hideous monstrosities figure as central attractions, Carroll theorizes that our pleasure is not in the disgusting objects as such, but chiefly in the disclosures and discoveries of the narrative in which our piqued curiosity is satisfied.[56] So we might say that the defining proposition for disgust is this: *X is repulsive and worthy to be shunned; may it depart from me.*

Like most human emotions, repugnance usually has a background of thought and belief, which provides "terms" for this construal and reasons for feeling repugnance. For example, someone who is repelled by the worship of idols will typically think that such practice is an offense to the true God; one who is repulsed by English spoken with a rural Kentucky accent will typically have beliefs about what constitutes cultured speech; if you are disgusted by a hair in your soup, you may explain that hair is filthy. The particular object of some episode of repugnance may, then, fall under a more general concern (the importance of worshiping the true God, of cultured speech, of clean food) and be construed in a way that impinges on that concern. In such ways the object of disgust may be apprehended in a concern-based construal, so that the emotion fits the model proposed in this book.

But for some instances of disgust, this analysis is artificially intellectualist. Let us return to Carroll's garbage can, and suppose that someone who has no opinions about germs and corruption is brought to look it full in the mouth from close up while breathing deeply in. If she has normal visual and olfactory equipment, she will probably be disgusted. What are the terms of her construal? What is the concern on which it is based? We look in vain, I think, for something in the background, *in terms of which* she views

---

[55] *The Philosophy of Horror*, p. 158.
[56] See *ibid.*, pp. 178–195. Our interest in the narrative an our curiosity about what is going to happen are intensified by the horror and revoltingness of the monsters.

the garbage – either more general concepts like cleanliness/filth, or the concerns that complement them. She does view the garbage in a certain way, a way determined, it seems, by the native structure of her body (crows and vultures seem not to share this structure, whatever it is, with human beings). The disgust is not a construal in terms of concepts on the basis of a more fundamental or general concern; instead, it seems to be itself a primitive reaction.[57] It is nevertheless a reaction in which we can see both "seeing" and concern. And it is one whose form is well-characterized by the proposition: *X is repulsive and worthy to be shunned.* But we should not suppose either that these words occur to someone experiencing the emotion in this primitive form or that the emotion is formed by a conceptual background made up in crucial part of concepts like *repulsive* and *shun* (see Section 2.5c).

Another way this primitive disgust is unlike many of the paradigm human emotions is indicated by the difficulty of articulating the form of the construal in genuinely analytical (non redundant) terms. Compare disgust with anger. According to our analysis in Section 3.3a, the angry person construes the situational object of his anger in such terms as *offense, bad person, culpable, in a moral position to judge,* and so on. None of these terms is just another way of saying "anger-provoking." But when we turn to analyze disgust, we find ourselves inarticulate in the sense that the terms we come up with for characterizing the object of disgust all tend to reiterate the concept of disgust. The crucial term in my proposed defining proposition for disgust is "repulsive." I might have used "repugnant," except that I felt silly defining repugnance (the emotion) as a matter of construing an object as repugnant. Other possible choices, such as "revolting," "repellent," "fulsome," and "vile," do not seem to advance the project of analysis any better, though they might give that appearance through diversification of vocabulary.

Let us return to the cases of disgust in which we may articulate our reasons for feeling as we do. Here the explanations are (potentially) genuinely analytical (see Section 2.6a). After all, to say that rural Kentucky speech violates standards of high linguistic culture is not just another way of saying that it disgusts (*that* term of construal might enter into annoyance, or contempt, or shame). I say "potentially," because in many cases the explanation of disgust is less a genuine analysis than a rationalization. Someone's explanation of disgust for homosexual practice in terms of its unnaturalness may reverse the order of priority. The disgust may explain the belief rather than the belief the disgust. I do not mean to generalize. Beliefs, especially as they

---

[57] This kind of case reminds us of Hume's comment that " 'Tis altogather impossible to give any definition of the passions of *love* and *hatred*; and that because they produce merely a simple impression, without any mixture or composition" (*Treatise*, p. 329). If Hume's remark were true of emotions in general, the central project of this chapter – to analyze and thus "define" a representative sampling of the variety of emotion types – would be hopeless.

characterize communal life, shape disgusts just as surely as disgusts shape beliefs. Even rather primitive kinds of disgust are subject to beliefs. John Hare mentions that he was disgusted by other people's babies' diapers, but not by those of his own children.

But even when disgust is well-explained by reference to views and concerns distinct from disgust, it seems that the terms referred to are not definitive for disgust in the way that the terms referred to in the defining proposition for anger are definitive for that emotion. None of the ones we have mentioned – *natural/unnatural, loyalty/betrayal, cultured/crude, clean/filthy* – is definitive of disgust in the way that *offense, culpable, bad, action/omission, being in a moral position to judge,* and so on, when combined syntactically in the right way, are definitive for anger. So disgust remains somehow primitive and inarticulate, even in its more sophisticated, propositional instances. One way to express this point would be to say that while instances of disgust may be articulable in a material proposition, they do not have a proper, or analytically informative, defining proposition.

c. Contempt

If the foregoing is correct, then by the standards of the account of emotion I am offering in this book, hatred and repugnance are not quite paradigmatic human emotions. Insofar as they are emotions (we have noted that hatred may instead be a dispositional concern), they are construals characterized by concern; but they are not in all cases concern-*based* construals.

Contempt, by contrast, fits the paradigm. The terms of contempt are excellence/worth/status, lack of these, and claim to these. Consider Buonissimo, who feels contempt for Bosco. Buonissimo is a dean, nearing retirement, who is widely respected in the college but a little self-important. He has, for example, a strong sense of his own piety and wisdom, which he much cherishes and gladly shares. Bosco is twenty-five years his junior and cracks some of Buonissimo's favorite icons. Bosco is pretty self-assertive and vocal in meetings but has not achieved the tokens of honor and publicly recognizable excellence that a few, at his age, have achieved. When Buonissimo thinks about Bosco he tends to construe him as markedly inferior in piety and wisdom, and yet, by his activity and assertiveness, as implying a claim to have these qualities. He has an urge to put Bosco in his proper place, so as to look down on him as precipitously as Bosco's inferiority requires and to induce others to take this same perspective.

Contempt can be felt for things as well as persons. Some people who prize excellent music contemn rock and roll. Perhaps they regard it as lacking refinement, rhythmic subtlety, harmonic and melodic complexity, interest, and development. If they did not construe it as making some claim to be music (and in the mouths and ears of these people, "music" is a term of honor), they might still be annoyed by it and angry at people who subject the public to such a nuisance, but they would not feel contempt for it. True, neither the person nor the thing that is contemned need actually make any claim to equality or excellence, nor does the subject of contempt need to believe that such a claim has been made. It is enough, as in the present case, that a single word – "music" – be used to designate the excellent. The bare fact of Bosco's being on the faculty might be enough, in Buonissimo's eyes, to seem like a claim to equality. Let us say, then, that contempt has the form of the proposition: *S is markedly inferior and unworthy in X important way, yet he (it) obtrudes, pretending to equal status and worth; may he (it) be put in his (its) place.*

Feeling contempt for Bosco differs from what we may call "holding him in contempt," which is not an emotion at all. Buonissimo may hold Bosco in contempt without being much aware of Bosco's existence. He may notice, and assess, him just enough to ascertain that he is of no importance, that it does not matter what he pretends to. Bosco is not even worthy of Buonissimo's attention. But for Buonissimo to *feel* contempt for Bosco, Buonissimo's attention must be fairly strongly fixed on Bosco, who must in fact have a kind of importance for Buonissimo: the importance of an impertinent and inferior pretender to a status that is important to Buonissimo.[58] Thus we can see that at least two concerns are basic to contempt: the concern for the value that the subject construes the object as being deficient in, and his concern about the object's pretending to equality in this respect. If Buonissimo *either* did not care about piety and wisdom, *or* did not care that Bosco was pretending to it, he would not feel contempt for Bosco. Holding in contempt (in the present sense) is not to be confused with unconscious contempt (as an emotion). The difference would show up (if it showed up) in the behavior: The person experiencing unconscious contempt might behave in a way calculated to put the uppity one in his or her place, whereas one who merely holds another in contempt will simply ignore him or her.

3.9. RIVALRY[59]

The jealousy and envy on which I will focus, though they are different emotions, have in common that they involve construing some other person or quasi-person as a rival for some thing, person, advantage, or quality that

---

[58] This formulation may make it sound as though contempt is competitive. This is not true. Envy of the pretender or anxiety for one's own comparative status may enhance irrational contempt, but no element of competition is necessary to contempt.

[59] This section has profited from discussions with Daniel Farrell, Justin D' Arms, and John Hare.

one wants for oneself. "Jealous" often refers to *bona fide* envy, but "envy" is not used for cases of *bona fide* jealousy. Thus we say, "Pam was bad-talking Gretschen's new job, but really she was just jealous"; but nobody would say, "Steve's been seen out dancing with his secretary a lot lately, and his wife is beside herself with envy." Still, it is just possible that Steve's wife is not jealous of the secretary, but envies her. If so, she has an unconventional attitude toward her husband. She sees herself as, in principle, having no more claim on Steve's attentions than the secretary and, I shall argue, wants those attentions primarily for the *personal worth* they imply. Envy has a quite different structure from jealousy. They diverge from each other in the kind of concerns on which they are based and in the particular terms in which the situational object of each emotion is construed.

a. Jealousy

Jealousy belongs in what Daniel Farrell calls a "three-party context."[60] The three main characters in the drama are the "lover" (the jealous person), the "beloved," and the rival. The lover construes the beloved as in process of being lost to the rival, or as already so lost, or as about to be lost; the lover construes the rival as taking, having taken, or about to take the beloved away, so as to have the beloved for him- or herself; the lover construes himself as losing, having lost, or about to lose the beloved to the rival. Any of these characters can be the focus of the construal, and in each case the one focused on is construed in terms of the other two. "Lover" and "beloved" are to be understood with a particular breadth of sense. Erotic attachments and rivalries are paradigmatic for jealousy, but other kinds of attachments may provide the basic concern. For example, a mother is jealous of her daughter's boyfriend (seeing the boyfriend as her rival for the daughter's affection); a friend is jealous of his friend's other friend; a teacher is jealous of his student's other teacher. In each case, the jealous party construes the "beloved" as rightfully in some sense his own, and as being alienated from him by the rival.

We commonly associate jealousy with the lover's being betrayed by the beloved, and so we might think it essential to jealousy that the lover construe the beloved as in process of betraying him, or as having betrayed him, or as in prospect of betraying him. While the ascription of betrayal is perhaps present in the central cases of jealousy, it is not essential to the emotion. A person can be jealous of someone he construes as not committed to him in any way, and thus not in a position to betray him. A lad has his eye on a certain

---

[60] "Jealousy," *The Philosophical Review* **89** (1980): 527–559, and "Of Jealousy and Envy," in Christina Sommers and Fred Sommers (eds.), *Vice and Virtue in Everyday Life*, third edition (New York: Harcourt Brace College Publishers, 1993), pp. 393–417. The latter paper appeared originally in *The Philosophical Review* **100** (1991).

girl and then later sees her on the arm of another. He has a fleeting episode of jealousy: He construes the man as his rival and the girl as rightly his (irrationally, no doubt). But he does not need to construe her as committed to him and thus as having betrayed him. Such fleeting episodes of jealousy are also counterexamples to a claim that is often made about jealousy:

> What sets jealousy apart from other possible responses to a real or imagined infidelity – such as rage or grief – is its quality of obsession.... Jealousy ... is a state of virtual paralysis in which the will races around a single point.[61]

Such dramatic cases are among the most consequential, and thus interesting and salient for us, but if we keep our eyes open we see plenty of nonobsessive jealousy.

Other writers read jealousy as a kind of fear – that is, as essentially a construal of oneself as *threatened* with the loss of the beloved.[62] Jealousy is often like fear in this respect, but not always. A woman who has definitively lost her boyfriend to a rival may continue to feel jealousy just as intensely as when she only saw this loss looming on the horizon. She construes herself no longer as threatened with the loss, but now as having suffered it. Jealousy of this sort is more like grief than fear. But jealousy is no more just a kind of grief than it is of fear. It comes in both forms, as well as intermediate ones.

A jealous person may construe either the rival or the beloved or both as having culpably offended him or her and as deserving punishment. That is, he may be angry at the rival or the beloved for the loss or threatened loss of affection; and such punitive behaviors as murder, mayhem, harsh words, material deprivation, and obstruction of the beloved's access to the children indicate the anger. But imagine that your little daughter seems to prefer a rock star to you. She puts your picture in the drawer and sets his up on her dresser; he has recorded some children's stories and she prefers these tapes to sitting in your lap for stories in the evening. Being only four, she is not old enough to be accountable for her attitude, and the rock star isn't even aware of her devotion. You feel jealous of the rock star, who is receiving your daughter's affection instead of you. You might be angry at either of the parties, but that would be irrational, and being a rational person, you

---

[61] Leslie Farber, *Lying, Despair, Jealousy, Envy, Sex, Suicide, Drugs, and the Good Life* (New York: Harper and Row, 1976), p. 186. Amélie Rorty acknowledges the light cases of jealousy, but says that "if a person is *disposed* to passing light jealousy, when the occasions seem to present no threat, it is because the conditions for dark and heavy jealousy obtain in the background" [*Mind in Action: Essays in the Philosophy of Mind* (Boston: Beacon Press, 1988)], p. 361. It seems to me that virtually everybody is disposed to "dark and heavy" jealousy if we mean by "disposed" that some possible circumstances would evoke it. But a person need not be unusually prone to heavy jealousy to experience some episodes of light jealousy.

[62] See Jerome Neu, "Jealous Thoughts," in Amélie O. Rorty (ed.), *Explaining Emotions* (Berkeley: University of California Press, 1980), pp. 425–463, especially p. 433; and Amélie Rorty, *Mind in Action*, pp. 135–154.

are not angry. You do not blame them or want retribution, but you are jealous.

This last case raises a question about the concern on which jealousy is based. If we focus on the erotic examples, we may suppose that this concern is for the *exclusive* affection of the beloved. But this is not a requirement for jealousy. You would likely be jealous if your wife cared as much about the rock star as she cares about you, and you are jealous of the rock star if he alienates your daughter's affection from you. But as a psychologically normal and rational father, you will not be jealous of your wife if your daughter loves her as much as she loves you: The concern on which your jealousy is based is not a desire for exclusive or unequaled affection from your daughter.

We have seen that neither grief, fear, nor anger is necessary to jealousy. To test and refine our conception, let's now ask, Can one grieve over the loss of the beloved to a rival without being jealous? Can one fear the loss of the beloved to a rival and yet not be jealous? Can one be angry at the beloved or the rival for the loss of the beloved to the rival and yet not be jealous?

One is not jealous when one's beloved is taken away by death because death does not alienate her affections, but simply destroys them. It is essential to jealousy that the loss of the beloved's affection be construed as occurring *by transfer to the rival*. But might a person grieve the loss of his beloved *to a rival* without feeling jealous? This is possible but only on condition that the lover construe the rival in a way that derivalizes him or the beloved in a way that deprives her of agency with respect to directing her affections. If, for example, the lover construes the beloved as under a spell (or a drug, or an abnormally altered state of the brain) that accounts for the diversion of affection, then he might grieve the loss of her affection, without being jealous, even though he sees her affection as being transferred to a rival. Or the rival might seem to the lover so implausible, *as* rival, that he does not see him as a rival in the required sense. He sees him as the object of his lover's affection and the cause of her alienation from himself, but the rival seems to him so stupid, or ugly, or bumbling that he can't take him seriously as a rival. He sees himself, thus, not as suffering loss at the hands of a real competitor but rather (so to speak) as the victim of an inscrutable natural disaster.[63] So he grieves but is not jealous. This thought experiment suggests that in jealousy the beloved is construed as having some real personal agency in conferring or possibly conferring her affection and that the rival is construed as being a viable competitor – not just a successful one.

Can one fear the alienation of one's beloved's affection by a rival, without being jealous? Yes. One hears that a very charming rival, who is likely to succeed if anyone can, has designs on her. So far, however, one's beloved has never seen the fellow and so doesn't give a flip for him. Missing is the

---

[63] Another possibility is that he suffers from wounded vanity: "If she can fall in love with this creep, what does that make *me*?" Wounded vanity, like envy, is sometimes called "jealousy."

actual affective engagement of the beloved in the pictured scene: as actually
charmed, either wholeheartedly or partheartedly or by way of temptation.
(One *might*, of course, be proleptically jealous by anticipating her reaction
to the charmer.) I think, too, that one can fear the loss of the beloved to a
rival without being jealous, if one lacks the vulnerability that is characteristic
of jealousy: I could very much want not to lose the beloved, and construe
myself as in jeopardy of losing her to a rival, and yet not feel jealous, if I didn't
construe this potential loss as threatening my self in the way characteristic
of jealousy. Maybe I like being adored by her and would miss it enough to
fear its loss; but my personal attachment is really all to philosophy, so that
to lose her affection would not require any more revision of my self-concept
than would the loss of any other source of amusement that I like a lot.

Jealousy is based on a special kind of concern that I have called attachment, to some particular individual of some kind of being (paradigmatically
a person) that is capable of reciprocating the concern. Attachments are especially relevant to one's self-concept. If I am attached to my antique Porsche,
then my self-concept is significantly tied to that particular Porsche-token.
A loss of *it* would require some adjustment in my self- concept. People often have such attachment to their pets. Another cocker spaniel to replace
Taffy does not assuage the sense of loss. Dogs are quasi-persons because
they can reciprocate attachment, unlike antique Porsches. So I may be jealous of Taffy if somebody alienates his affections, but it is hard to imagine
being jealous of my Porsche (in the strict sense of jealous) if somebody
makes me an offer for it that I cannot refuse. I can envy the new owner his
Porsche; I can covet it. But to be jealous of it would require a very original turn of mind. The contrasts of this paragraph and the preceding one
highlight two features of jealousy: that it construes the beloved (at least in
imagination) *as actually affectionally alienated* in some degree, and not merely
potentially so; and that the concern it is based on is an attachment to a person or quasi-person that therefore touches one's sense of self in a special
personal way.

So one can one fear the alienation of one's beloved's affection by a rival,
without being jealous. Something similar can be said about anger. If I am
angry at my rival or my beloved for the alienation of my beloved from me
by the rival, and yet not jealous, it may be because the concern on which
the anger is based is not that special kind of attachment to the beloved that
constitutes part of my sense of self. She is my beloved in a different sense, and
he is my rival in a different sense than these terms bear if they express the
propositional content distinctive of jealousy. Take the example of the above
paragraph. I like Elizabeth's attention in much the way I like driving around
in my antique Porsche: It's exciting and pleasant and elicits lots of respect
and attention from my fellow blades. And now Elizabeth takes it from me
and gives it to Frank – with, I might add, Frank's active encouragement. I
am enraged at both of them, and because of the context of this rage many

will take it for jealousy. But it may be only anger. Whether it is only anger or jealous anger will depend on the nature of my attachment to Elizabeth, and thus the nature of my sense of loss. Am I chiefly embarrassed because I've come down in the world in the eyes of the blades? Am I frustrated because I don't get my wonted kicks? Or am I touched in my sense of self by the loss of a special regard and affection by which Elizabeth satisfied my need *for Elizabeth?*

Let us say, then, that the defining proposition for jealousy is: *It is very important that B have a special personal attachment to me, but R is taking (has taken, may take) B's special attachment away from me with B's responsible collusion or consent, with a result of R's having B's special attachment for himself.* In this formulation we have not expressed a consequent concern. Jealousy does motivate actions of various kinds. When it is like fear, the subject is concerned to protect the relationship against the rival. Where it generates anger, the concern will be to punish the beloved, the rival, or both. Where jealousy is more like grief, it may have no other consequent concern than the empty wish to have the beloved back. But none of these concerns is to be written into the defining proposition for jealousy because none of them is definitive of this emotion.

b. Envy

The word "envy" is used for at least three different emotions, one of which I shall especially address here – the kind of envy that might be designated "invidious envy." Sally, who has crooked teeth, envies Marge for her lovely straight ones. Sally feels bad when she sees or thinks about Marge's picture-perfect smile, and she enjoys fantasizing that Marge, who has started taking figure skating lessons, may fall on the ice and disfigure her mouth. Another kind of envy, also rivalrous, is "friendly envy":

"Pell," he used to say to me many a time, "how the blazes you can stand the head-work you do, is a mystery to me." – "Well," I used to answer, " *I* hardly know how I do it, upon my life." – "Pell," he'd add, sighing, and looking at me with a little envy – friendly envy, you know, gentlemen, merely friendly envy; I never minded it – "Pell, you're a wonder; a wonder." Ah! you'd have liked him very much if you had known him, gentlemen (Charles Dickens, *The Pickwick Papers*, Chapter 55).

The Lord Chancellor (whom Pell here casts in the role of envier) sees himself in a somewhat painful light because of his inferiority (so he sighs), but he bears Pell no malice and really enjoys contemplating Pell's excellence. This emotion is a rivalry that overlaps significantly with one kind of admiration. Its defining proposition is something like: *It would be nice to have advantage X in a degree equal or superior to that in which R has X, and I don't; but it's OK for R to have X.* At other times, "envy" is a synonym for "covet." To covet is to wish to have exactly what is somebody else's (not just another exemplar of the same type). "Covet" implies an awareness of the ownership of the thing coveted but does not imply competitiveness or rivalry[64]; the focus may be overwhelmingly on the thing desired. That is why it is not a very good substitute for "envy."

Basic to invidious envy is the concern to establish one's own personal worth through equaling or besting a competitor in some competition, and it is a construal of oneself as losing in that competition or of the rival as winning out over oneself. Thus if Gerald depreciates his brother Samuel's academic accomplishments, and Philip explains the depreciation by remarking that Gerald is envious, Philip is saying that Gerald construes Samuel's accomplishments as detracting from Gerald's personal worth and so wishes to make Samuel's accomplishments appear inconsequential.[65] No beloved figures in envy but only the issues of superiority/inferiority/equality to some other person or persons in the context of some competition for personal worth.

Consider again our young man who fleetingly feels jealous when he sees, on the arm of another, a lass he has been admiring. If he feels envy instead of jealousy, he construes the other as having bested him by getting the girl. The basic issue for him is not that he has lost the girl, but that he has been demeaned, made less important, by the other's good fortune or felicitous action. And the young woman figures not as the beloved but as a status symbol. The rival threatens one's sense of self in both envy and jealousy but in different ways: In jealousy, one's self as constituted by the bond with the beloved is threatened; while in envy, what is threatened is one's worth as established by "doing well" in competition with another.

Envious behavior often has the appearance of punishment, and envy can shade into anger. But anger's consequent concern is to punish the offender, whereas envy's is that the rival be put down, either by his superiority actually decreasing (e.g., by Marge's falling on her face) or by his superiority appearing to be less (e.g., by Gerald's depreciating Samuel's academic accomplishments before some important audience).

The defining proposition for envy, then, would appear to be something like this: *It is important for me to have the personal worth that would be established by my being or appearing to be equal or superior to R in respect X; however, I am or appear to be inferior to R in respect X; may R be or appear to be degraded in respect X.*

---

[64] It is the attitudinal counterpart of stealing: knowing whom the object belongs to (at least that it belongs to someone else) but leaving this out of consideration for purposes of appropriation. The thief does not, simply as thief, regard the owner of the object as a competitor or rival.

[65] The present example, which is typical, gives the worth in question a decidedly public character: Gerald wishes to make Samuel's accomplishment appear inconsequential *to others*. But I do not intend "worth" to be necessarily public. It is often in the privacy of our thoughts that we measure our worth by others' excellences, find ourselves painfully wanting, and take secret joy in glimmers of their faults.

Let me end this discussion by returning briefly to jealousy, so as to defend against a counterexample to my analysis. The analysis of jealousy in terms of lover, beloved, and rival may seem too narrow. For example, a case of "professional jealousy" is offered by Farrell: An old tennis pro gets a lot of gratification from being admired as one of the best players on the pro circuit. But then a younger player emerges, who seems to be attracting to himself much of the admiration formerly enjoyed by the old pro. Farrell imagines him as

jealous because of the attention [the] younger pro is starting to receive. He talks about the latter's bad days a little too much, let us suppose, and about his own good days a little too often.[66]

The terms "lover" and "beloved," while they fit parent–child and friend–friend relationships with a little stretch, do not fit at all the usual relationships between tennis pros and their admirers. Admiration and the enjoyment thereof do not constitute the attachment and its reciprocation that are the basis and the issue, respectively, of jealousy. Instead, they seem to be about what envy is about: what I have called "personal worth." Furthermore, talking about the rival's bad days and one's own good days seems to go with a concern to lower the relative status of the rival and raise one's own. Farrell acknowledges that envy can occur in three-party contexts, so why does he think the old pro's emotion is jealousy rather than envy?

One possible reason is that we do not normally speak of a person as "envious" who currently enjoys or has recently enjoyed high status and who construes his status as threatened or in decline. We describe him, instead, as suffering from threatened or wounded vanity, but if we are speaking loosely we may say that he is jealous of the person who displaces him. So "jealous" serves as a broad term, encompassing even more than envy and jealousy, to denote what one feels when losing out to a rival. But the terms of wounded vanity are very similar to those of envy and quite different from those of strict jealousy as I have analyzed it: The concern basic to wounded vanity is for personal worth rather than for reciprocation of an attachment. It is true that the old pro might be suffering jealousy, rather than envy or wounded vanity: It is remotely possible that he thinks of his admirers as friends or lovers whose affection has been alienated by the young pro. But more likely, his concern about their admiration is a concern for personal worth.

However, Farrell's stated reason for interpreting the old pro's emotion as jealousy rather than envy is its *focus*. He says that in cases where envy occurs in a three-party context, it is envy rather than jealousy because the subject focuses not on the fact that the rival is *receiving* the desideratum (in the old pro case, the admiration of the groupies) *from the third party*, but simply on the fact that the rival *has* the desideratum and the subject lacks it

---

[66] *Vice and Virtue in Everyday Life*, third edition, p. 395.

(see p. 398). Thus Farrell seems to allow that an episode of jealousy might have exactly the same terms as an episode of envy, the only difference being the focus of the construal (Farrell does not speak of construal).

But even if the old pro focuses on the players' transfer of their favor from him to the young pro, the old pro's emotion may still be envy and not jealousy. If what concerns the old pro is professional status – shown here by the allegiance of the players – then the fact that he sees the players' allegiance as alienated by the young pro is not enough to make the old pro's emotion jealousy as contrasted with envy. On the other hand, if the old pro is personally attached to particular players – with something like friendship or love – and sees the due reciprocation of *this* as being transferred from himself to the young pro, then in my analysis he is suffering from jealousy proper. In general, emotions' focus may differ considerably within a type; envy differs from jealousy in the strict sense not in focus, but in the terms of the construal and the character of the concern on which it is based. (On focus and terms, see Section 2.3c.)

3.10. EXCELLENCE

a. Admiration

To admire a colleague for her scholarly work is to construe her as excellent in some way (e.g., skilled, industrious, intelligent, high-minded, wise) as evidenced by her work. So far, the description is compatible with envy, because to envy a colleague may also involve seeing her as excellent as evidenced by her work. The difference is that envy would be a reluctant or distressing perception of another's excellence, while admiration is pleasant. We have seen that the discomfort in envy comes from the subject's sense of being demeaned by the excellence or good fortune of the other: He sees himself as losing in a competition for personal worth. Thus to see the other as winning the competition is to be frustrated in one's concern for personal worth. In admiration, by contrast, the excellence of the other either does not raise the issue of one's own worth at all (the emotion is self-ignoring) or, if one's worth is one of the terms of the construal, the perception of oneself as less excellent than the admired one is not painful; one is not reluctant to perceive the other as superior because one is comfortable with being inferior in some respect (perhaps resigned to this, or confident or hopeful of self-improvement). Søren Kierkegaard may have this self-comparing admiration in mind when he says that "admiration is happy self-surrender; envy is unhappy self-assertion."[67] The perception is not painful because it does not frustrate, but indeed satisfies, the concerns on which it is based – the

---

[67] *The Sickness Unto Death*, edited and translated by Edna and Howard Hong (Princeton, New Jersey: Princeton University Press, 1980), p. 86.

love of excellence of some kind, and well-wishing toward the person who exhibits it. So the kind of concern basic to cases of admiration differs from the kind basic to invidious envy.[68] Self-ignoring admiration is built on a straightforward concern for one or another kind of excellence, and without any concern for relative worth, while self- comparing admiration is based on some concern for personal worth, but without the ideology that the other's comparative excellence spells one's own diminution (in this sense it involves "self-surrender").

Admiration differs from envy in two other ways. First, envy is always directed at persons, or anyway at beings construed as enough like persons to be rivals; but nonpersons can be perfectly well-admired. I might admire my colleague's work but not the colleague. Indeed, one can admire an excellent rose or sunset. To do so is to perceive it as excellent and to take pleasure in it for this reason. Second, admiration seems to require attribution of excellence, but envy does not. I might envy my neighbor his lottery win, but I would not admire him for it, unless I could find some way to construe it as evidencing his excellence (maybe I think of it as exhibiting his persevering optimism in buying tickets week after week over the years, or maybe my metaphysics entails that luckiness is a form of personal excellence).

We have identified three kinds of admiration. Whether we regard these as distinct but related emotion types or as variants of one emotion type depends on our categorial interests. It might be worthwhile, in moral psychology, to distinguish admiration of nonpersons (simple admiration) from admiration of persons, as well as to distinguish self-ignoring admiration of persons from self-comparing. Thus the defining proposition for simple admiration would be roughly: *Excellence of X kind is important, and Z has excellence of X kind, as evidenced in quality Y.* For self-ignoring admiration of persons, by contrast, the proposition would be: *Excellence of X kind is important, and it is important for S in particular to be excellent; S has excellence of X kind, as evidenced in Y; so it is fine for S to have excellence X.* And for self-comparing admiration of persons, the proposition would be, *Excellence of X kind is important, and it is important for S in particular to be excellent; S has excellence of X kind, as evidenced in Y, which I would like to have too but fall short in; but it is fine for S to have excellence X, even if I don't.*

b. Respect

Respect is another emotion in which we construe things and persons in terms of their excellences, but the kinds of excellence appropriate to respect form a narrower range than those of admiration. If I am articulate about the deep respect I feel for the University of Chicago, I will feel this for

---

[68] Self-comparing admiration is very similar to what I called friendly envy in Section 3.9b.

such things as its achievements in the sciences and arts. I may also admire it for these achievements. I will be much less likely to respect it for its excellent shrubbery and lawns, though I may very naturally admire it for these reasons. Similarly, while you may be pleased by my declarations that I admire both your integrity and your curly hair, and that I respect your integrity, you will be puzzled if I tell you that I respect your curls. These contrasts suggest that the kind of excellence posited by respect is broadly "moral." I say "broadly" because the connection to morality can be made in a variety of ways. The scientific achievements of a great university are broadly moral in that they are advances in truth and/or they result from deep commitment and arduous work. Thus if someone did see the University's shrubbery as an analogous achievement, it might just make sense to feel respect for it. But the connection to morality need not be made via achievement. We also speak of respecting unborn human life, and here the word "dignity" suggests itself. Unborn human beings have dignity not because of their achievements but because of their potential – again, for living a life of "reason," of "love," of social responsibility, and so on. And I think that when people insist that we should respect nonhuman animals, and even plant life, they see some analogue of such dignity there – or they see these beings as created by some divine principle that invests the creatures with such dignity. Let us use the word "worthy" to capture this notion of a broadly moral excellence and say that the defining proposition for ordinary respect is: *X is worthy in Y important way and deserves benign attention and good treatment on account of Y; may he (it) be so treated.*

Respect is not always an emotion. We may say that someone respects the rules when we mean only that he intentionally avoids violating them, for whatever reason. And similarly a child can be said to treat his elders "with respect" when there is no question of his attitude, but only of his behavior, toward them. This, too, will sometimes explain the insistence on respecting nonpersonal life.

Respect differs from admiration in requiring less articulateness. One might respect the University of Chicago while having only a vague idea what makes the University worthy of respect. People can feel respect for dignitaries whose roles and titles to respect they do not understand, their reason for respecting them being simply that these people are *presented* as worthy of special regard, as persons who are respected by others. By contrast, if we lack knowledge of what makes the University or these dignitaries worthy of admiration, it is not good English to say we *admire* them.

Respect also differs from admiration in not necessarily distinguishing persons who do, from persons who do not, warrant the response. We do, of course, accord differential respect to persons, marking moral differences between them. If we are rational, we feel greater respect for persons of integrity and high moral achievement than for moral slackers and the vicious. But the moral life, in some traditions, requires a respect for persons that is blind to such differences (while still being an attribution of a broadly moral property). We are trading on one or another concept of universal respect when we say "Bigots are people who are short on respect for people of other races" or "The Vanderbilts treat their servants with respect." (Contrast, "The Vanderbilts respect their chief butler for his assiduity and precision.")

Immanuel Kant articulates a concept of universal respect (*Achtung, reverentia*) that is central to his moral philosophy. In Kant's version, moral respect is a construal of a person as a being that can legislate his or her own actions in universal (and thus purely rational) terms – that is, not as being passively subject to causal laws (predictive laws of nature), but as actively giving *itself* laws of obligation and thus determining its *own* behavior. This rational power of will, or freedom, is what makes a being a person, in Kant's view, which is to say, a being with *dignity*.[69] All persons have dignity in this sense and are thus worthy of respect, however unadmirable they may be. Not just anyone who has Kant's concept of dignity, and thus the ability to construe persons as having dignity, will be disposed to feel *Achtung*. If the account of emotions offered in this book is correct, only people who care about dignity will, in construing individuals as having dignity, feel Kantian respect for them. This concern, then, is basic to the emotion.

Does Kantian respect also have a consequent concern? To see persons as beings with Kantian dignity is to set a certain limit to one's behavior toward them; in particular, respect generates an aversion to treating people merely as means to one's own ends. If the Vanderbilts have Kantian moral respect for their servants, they will be interested in doing what is in the interest of the servants themselves and will not take those interests into account merely as factors needing to be addressed in the pursuit of the Vanderbilts' interests. The defining proposition for Kantian moral respect will be something like this: *The dignity of each person, as a rational moral chooser and thus as the subject of possible rational interests, is of surpassing importance; S has such dignity; may S's own interests therefore be taken as strict limits in dealing with him.*

Kantian respect is just one among several possible kinds of universal respect that have in common that they fix on some universal broadly moral feature of human persons, independent of their particular achievements or qualities, as making them worthy and setting limits, in some way, to our behavior toward them. Descartes says that the *généreux*, who esteem themselves for their ability to determine freely their volitions and for their firm resolution to use this power well, easily persuade themselves that other people have the same grounds for esteeming themselves; thus the *généreux* do not

---

[69] See *Grounding for the Metaphysics of Morals*, translated by James W. Elllington, in *Ethical Philosophy* (Indianapolis: Hackett, 1983), p. 43f (Akademie, pp. 439–440). I am not suggesting that Kant would agree to my account of emotions as concern-based construals, but showing how my view would assimilate his account of moral respect.

scorn anyone.[70] Existentialist moral respect construes persons in terms of their self-determining powers but without any suggestion of universal *legislation*. Buddhist moral respect construes persons in terms of their ability to be selfless in some peculiar Buddhist sense of "selfless." I am less confident to speak of such emotions than I am to speak of Christian universal respect, in which persons are construed as made in the image of God, the defining proposition of which would be something like this: *The dignity of each person, as a creature made in the image of God, is of surpassing importance; S has such dignity; may S's own interests therefore be taken seriously in dealing with him.*

Other cultures or life views (such as the Aristotelian or Nietzschean ethics) that find nothing morally worthy in human persons independent of their distinguishing accomplishments, abilities, and traits lack an emotion of universal respect, though they have emotions of admiration and respect, one of the reasons for which would be virtues such as generosity, justice, and truthfulness.

c. Reverence

An acknowledging subjective response to something excellent in a personal (moral or spiritual) way, but qualitatively above oneself, is reverence. Thus it is not adequate to say that the well-formed orthodox Jew respects the Torah, much less that he admires it, because these words do not suggest the sense of qualitative elevation above himself of the excellence that he acknowledges in God's word. (Imagine such a Jew praying, "Lord God, King of the universe, creator of heaven and earth, I admire and respect you.") Some people feel reverence for kings and prophets; Plato may have felt it for Socrates. "Reverence" seems to fit better Kant's moral emotion when he thinks of it as directed to the moral law as such than when he thinks of it as directed toward human agents, because in the former case it seems to have a halo somewhat like the Torah's, including a slightly suggested personal reference to God as its source. If we sense in Tolstoy or Brahms something deeper, even, than great artistry, we may revere them. Some people seem to feel reverence for Elvis Presley. But on the whole, reverence falls on hard times in highly egalitarian and secularized settings. The consequent concern of reverence is to express acknowledgment of the qualitative exaltation of its object – thus to praise, worship, and bow down before it. Let us say that the defining proposition for reverence is: *Moral or spiritual excellence is of great importance and X possesses such excellence in a degree and quality far beyond any attributable to beings like me; let X be praised and honored.*

[70] See *The Passions of the Soul*, Articles 153–154. The reference to the firm resolution to use their free will properly seems to attribute a rather irrationally generous inference to the *généreux*; but it is clear that Descartes is looking for an emotion analogous to Kantian respect for persons.

3.11. THE BEYOND

a. Awe

When we feel awe, we perceive something's greatness in any one of a variety of ways of being great: vast (the Grand Canyon, the Milky Way), intricate (the biochemistry of cell reproduction), beautiful (sunrise in the Lake District), violent (a volcano, a storm at sea), or in the way of some great human achievement (Bach's B Minor Mass, Hegel's *Phenomenology of Spirit*, Michael Jordan's hang time). The perception of greatness seems to require some standard of comparison. Hegel's *Phenomenology* inspires awe because it is so far beyond anything that most philosophers produce; the Grand Canyon is awesome by comparison with the ditches we are used to seeing.

"Great" is neutral with respect to morality and spirituality. This is how awe differs from reverence. Awe is a fitting response to the destructive power of the hydrogen bomb, but reverence is not. You can properly be in awe before God, but if you are *only* in awe, you are missing something important about God as he is understood in the Hebrew–Christian tradition. You could be struck with awe at the intricately balanced interactions of organisms in a niche, and yet be equally impressed with the moral indifference of the whole system, fraught as it appears to you to be with suffering, death, and waste. It might even seem to you, despite your awe, that it is not better, on balance, that there be this great thing than that it not be; yet you are struck by its greatness.

Is awe based on a concern? It sounds a little peculiar to speak of a concern for greatness or caring about greatness. It certainly sounds odd to say, "I am concerned that galaxies and volcanoes be great," perhaps because it sounds as though we might be able to do something about this. We are more comfortable speaking of a sensitivity to greatness. This will differentiate people who look at the Winchester Cathedral and say, "So what? Another big building. Let's get lunch," from people who gape at it in awe of the human achievement it represents. But what is this sensitivity? In part, it is a matter of having available a fairly detailed standard of comparison, of knowing how it usually goes with buildings and how it goes with this one. But we can imagine a person who can reliably pick out great buildings, and in that sense has a sensitivity to greatness, yet does not feel awe when contemplating ones that are well beyond the others in greatness. If awe is a special way of perceiving greatness, in which the greatness as a value of the great thing strikes the person with a perceptionlike immediacy, then the added dimension of this sensitivity must be a readiness to perceive the value of greatness. And this added dimension is in the family of what I have been calling concerns. The emotion of awe will be possible only in persons for whom greatness matters.

The person struck with awe sometimes construes himself as lacking personal adequacy to "deal with" the object of awe – to understand or otherwise get control of it; awe will then involve a construal of oneself as passive, helpless, small, inadequate, incapable of fathoming or appreciating what one contemplates (this term of the construal often forms a retiring background to the thing that obtrudes as surpassingly great), and so on. Thus, when experiencing awe before something, people may speak of being overwhelmed. To the extent that one construes oneself as overwhelmed by the object, the emotion is based not only on a concern for what is great, but also on a concern to be in control. But I do not think that, in general, awe is a reflexive emotion. The perceived greatness seems to need a comparison, in the background, but the comparison need not involve the subject's self. We could, I suppose, think of awe that is reflexive in the way I have just described as a special kind, since it will have a different defining proposition than the awe I have mostly been discussing. However, the defining proposition for the awe I have mainly discussed will be something like this: *Greatness of kind Y is important and X exhibits a surpassing greatness of kind Y.*

b. The Feeling of Absolute Dependence

Friedrich Schleiermacher is well known for constructing a systematic theology around an emotion type. He describes this emotion in terms of a formal dialectic between self, other, and their interaction. The human self stands in two relations to "the other": on the one hand we are acted on by it and thus *depend* on it for changes in ourselves. For example, one kind of other is the peanut butter sandwich, and I depend on it or something similar to it for periodic changes in my self without which I could not go on breathing, philosophizing, dancing, and reglazing old window sashes. People are another kind of other on which I depend in various ways. On the other hand, the other also depends on me for changes in it. The peanut butter sandwich needs cutting and spreading; and people need my advice, my helping hand, my company, and so on. My relation to the other that depends on me Schleiermacher calls *freedom*. We might call it, more naturally, *effective agency*.

Associated with these relations to the other are the *feelings* of dependence and freedom. Our feeling of freedom is never absolute, in the sense that it is unmixed with any feeling of dependence, for such freedom would mean that the other had no "influence . . . upon our receptivity."[71] And the very idea of something's being an object for us requires that it have such an influence. Nor have we ever, toward things *within* the world, a feeling of pure dependence unmixed with freedom because we always have a possibility of influencing them, in some small way at least: "For upon such an object there

[71] H. R. Macintosh and J. S. Stewart (eds.). *The Christian Faith* (New York: Harper and Row, 1963), proposition 4.3.

would always be a counter-influence, and even a voluntary renunciation of this would always involve a feeling of freedom" (*ibid.*). So we always feel, in relation to things within the world, a reciprocity between our dependence and our freedom – that is, only a relative dependence and a relative freedom. However, if we think in these terms yet think not of the interrelation of *parts* of the world but now construe the *whole* world as one of the terms in the relation, then we are construing the world (ourselves included) as "absolutely dependent"; and the relation of the other to the world as "absolutely free." Thus the construal of oneself as part of the world conceived as a whole is the feeling of absolute dependence (see proposition 46).

Since the issue in the dialectic governing the feeling of absolute dependence is that of agency and passivity, perhaps we are warranted in supposing that a concern about these is basic to this emotion. If an agent is concerned to have some agency in all the connections of his life, then the construal of himself as absolutely "dependent" will be an uncomfortable emotion. On the other hand, if he welcomes being completely without agency in this connection, the feeling will be positive. Perhaps human beings are by nature ambivalent on this issue, having some concern in both directions; in that case, the feeling of absolute dependence might be pleasant and uncomfortable by turns, or even a simultaneous mixture of pleasure and discomfort. The following formulation of the defining proposition for the emotion should be read as leaving the above question undecided: *Agency is important, and in relation to the Other beyond all existence, I am utterly without power of influence.*

Schleiermacher's account of this religious emotion cries out for critical comment. He vacillates between the highly "cognitive" interpretation of the feeling that I have just expounded and a concertedly non-"cognitive" one (see proposition 3.2). Furthermore, the emotion does not seem to be really a feeling of absolute *dependence*. Dependency is quite different from an inability to influence, and the feeling is a construal of the world and oneself as utterly incapable of influencing the "other"; on Schleiermacher's description of the emotion, it would be better called the feeling of absolute impotence. And since the "Other" posited by this emotion is not a being, not anything that exists, but simply the Beyond of everything that does exist – the Void on the other side of existence – it seems unfit to serve the theological agenda to which Schleiermacher assigns it. It seems to be meant to supply an interpretation of such traditional religious emotions as gratitude to God for his gifts, awe of God, reverence and love of God as expressed in praiseful worship, and so on. But the "Other" of the feeling of absolute dependence is not construed as having any of the properties – existence, providential agency, good will – which must be attributed for such emotions to occur.[72]

---

[72] For a development of some of these criticisms, see my paper "The Feeling of Absolute Dependence," *The Journal of Religion* **57** (1977): 252–266. The paper contains some errors,

c. Other Emotions of Radical Transcendence

The feeling of absolute dependence is just one of a class of emotions that we might designate "emotions of radical transcendence." Ludwig Wittgenstein describes an emotion of radical awe:

> I believe the best way of describing [this experience] is to say that when I have it *I wonder at the existence of the world.* And I am then inclined to use such phrases as "how extraordinary that anything should exist" or "how extraordinary that the world should exist."[73]

It is not the extraordinariness of anything *within* the world that impresses one (e.g., a magnificent mountain or the number of the galaxies), but that there is a world at all:

> It is not *how* things are in the world that is mystical, but *that* it exists. . . . To view the world sub specie aeterni is to view it as a whole – a limited whole. Feeling the world as a limited whole – it is this that is mystical.[74]

I remarked that standard awe involves some comparison, thus some standard of the normal by reference to which the awesome thing is extraordinarily great. In the feeling that Wittgenstein reports, it is as though the subject takes a standpoint outside the world and contemplates it and thinks to herself, How extraordinary that it's there! It is as though she takes there being nothing as what one would expect, in the normal run of things – and from the vantage of this norm the fact that there is a world impresses her as amazing. The emotion is clearly a construal; and the unusual, transcendent sense of the normal, which we might describe, stretching language, as a sense of "what one would expect," functions analogously to a concern. A little later (Section 3.16) we will examine some nontranscendent emotions – surprise, puzzlement, amazement, and amusement – that are based on expectations or something in that neighborhood, rather than on concerns proper. Martin Heidegger voices a similar "unworldly" or "mystical" wonderment:

> "Why are there beings, why is there anything at all, rather than nothing?". . . Many . . . never encounter this question, if by encounter we mean not merely to hear and read about it [but] to feel its inevitability. And yet each of us is grazed at least once . . . by the hidden power of this question, even if he is not aware of what is happening to him.[75]

---

by the standard of the present book, but I have adapted some material from it for this and the following subsection.

[73] "A Lecture on Ethics," *The Philosophical Review* **74** (1965): 3–12; 8; italics in the original.

[74] *Tractatus Logico-Philosophicus*, translated by D. F. Pears and B. F. McGuinness (New York: Humanities Press, 1961), 6.44, 6.45; italics in the original.

[75] *An Introduction to Metaphysics*, translated by Ralph Mannheim (Garden City, New York: Anchor Boooks, 1961), p. 1.

When Heidegger expresses the emotion in this question – a question taken very seriously in the larger context of his thought – he suggests a somewhat different emotion from Wittgenstein's. The question suggests that this emotion is based on a real concern, namely an interest in explanation, or at least in understanding. Heidegger's radical wonderer is more an inquirer than Wittgenstein's. If Wittgenstein's emotion is a transcendent amazement, Heidegger's is a transcendent puzzlement (for a comparison of amazement and puzzlement, see Section 3.16a). The defining proposition for transcendent amazement might be written as follows: *It is not to be expected that there should be a world, but there it is!* For transcendent puzzlement the proposition would be this: *It is important for me to understand why there is a world, but I do not understand it; may I understand.*

Heidegger speaks also of a transcendent form of anxiety, an anxiety that is not about any particular threat, but about "Being-in-the-world as such"[76] :

That in the face of which one is anxious is completely indefinite. Not only does this indefiniteness leave factically undecided which entity within-the-world is threatening us, but it also tells us that entities within-the-world are not "relevant" at all (p. 231).

One who is anxious in this special way construes himself as detached from and beyond the world, as "uncanny" [*unheimlich*: not-at-home (p. 233)]. In his anxiety he thus finds *himself* insofar as he is a being not to be identified within the ordinary order of things, a being of a completely different kind from what is merely and determinately factual. He is himself what transcends the world. He, unlike all of the items that populate his world, is indeterminate in his being, and this "openness" or freedom is what vaguely threatens him (see Section 3.2c). Again, the determinateness of the things within-the-world creates a backdrop of normalcy against which the individual's own indeterminacy has a striking salience. Transcendent anxiety of a Heideggerian type will be based on a concern for the comfort and "safety" of the determinate, the reliable, the predictable, the established, and so on. Its defining proposition will accordingly be this: *It is important that my world be determinate, reliable, and predictable; but I, unlike things within-my-world, may do or be virtually anything; let me therefore escape from myself.*

Immediately following the passage in which Wittgenstein speaks of the feeling of radical amazement, he speaks of another emotion:

I will mention another experience straight away which I also know and which others of you might be acquainted with: it is, what one might call, the experience of feeling absolutely safe. I mean the state of mind in which one is inclined to say "I am safe, nothing can injure me whatever happens."

---

[76] *Being and Time*, translated by John Macquarrie and Edward Robinson (New York: Harper & Row, 1962), p. 230. "Being-in-the-world" is one of Heidegger's favorite expressions for being human; thus the anxiety under discussion is a construal of oneself as the source of threat—in particular, one's freedom, the fact that life is not preset for one, but needs to be chosen.

A feeling of safety is, in an obvious way, the opposite of anxiety. The person experiencing this emotion has in view not the threat of his own freedom, but the threat of what Heidegger would call "things within-the-world" – ordinary threats like mad dogs, cancer, and plane crashes. But since the subject is viewing the world *sub specie aeterni* – as a whole of which he, the subject, is *not* a part – such "threats" cannot touch him. The onrushing foaming Doberman looks like a character in a distant world from which the subject is thoroughly dissociated. Accordingly, the defining proposition for the feeling of transcendent safety would be something like the following: *It is important that I be safe from the aversive eventualities of this life; from my vantage beyond the world, no such eventuality can touch me.* Both the radical anxiety that Heidegger describes and the sense of radical safety that Wittgenstein describes are based on a concern to be safe. The safety in the first case is that of an established and predictable order of things; in the second it is a safety from the ordinary dangers of life.

3.12. ENHANCEMENT OF SELF

Pride, when an emotion rather than a trait, is a construal of oneself as enhanced or confirmed in one's worth, or a construal of some accomplishment or attribute or possession associated with oneself as enhancing or confirming one's worth. Based as it is on a concern for worth, it is a form of emotional satisfaction or pleasure. Let me now elaborate this account by addressing some questions: How shall we interpret "oneself" – is pride necessarily egoistic, or can the "self" in question be communal? How shall we interpret "worth" – in particular, is the worth that pride is concerned for always comparative or competitive? How shall we interpret "associated with" – what is the essence or range of associations pertinent to pride? I shall end with some comments about the role of beliefs in pride, and Hume's distinction between pride's "object" and "cause."

Hume is right to say, "When self enters not into the consideration, there is no room . . . for pride . . . ."[77] But he errs a few pages later when he elaborates that claim:

. . . 'tis absolutely impossible, from the primary constitution of the mind, that [pride] shou'd ever look beyond self, or that individual person, of whose actions and sentiments each of us is intimately conscious (p. 286).

In being proud of the bicycle paths, the well-dredged canals, and the beautiful parks of the Netherlands, a Dutch person need not construe them as a credit to herself as an *individual*. She construes them, instead, as a credit to "us" Dutch. One might think that to take such emotional pleasure she must perform a second mental act, in which she construes the worth of the Dutch as confirming her own individual worth. This claim strikes me as a

[77] *A Treatise of Human Nature*, p. 277.

speculative posit of *a priori* egoist psychology rather than observation. However, I admit that in much pride the self that is construed as enhanced is the individual.

In much pride, too, a person sees the enhancement or confirmation of his worth as following from the *superiority* of his accomplishment, abilities, and so on, to that of some specifiable others. Such pride is thus a construal in terms of ranking, of oneself as successful in a competition against rivals. Is what one is proud of always that one is superior to others? Does taking this kind of pleasure in one's accomplishments require the thought that others have accomplished less? Some have thought so,[78] but this seems to me too strong a requirement on pride. The thought essential to pride is that the accomplishment, attribute, or whatever, is good, not that it is superior. We are led to think that pride is always competitive because academic, athletic, musical, and many other kinds of excellence become manifest among us only through comparisons. But the fact that we can know I am a first-rate guitarist only by knowing that I'm quite a bit better than quite a lot of other guitarists does not imply that when I feel proud of my guitar playing, I am construing it as quite a bit better than quite a few other people's playing. Thus I think we must distinguish two kinds of pride: invidious or comparative pride and plain pride.

Hume says that "every cause of pride, by its peculiar qualities, produces a separate pleasure . . ." (p. 285). He means that one cannot be proud of something unless one takes pleasure in that thing, independently of its power to confer value on oneself. Thus I can be proud of my beautiful house only if it is something I would take pleasure in, whether or not it was mine. This seems incorrect. I might be proud of having read Shakespeare's *King Lear* or attended Alban Berg's *Wozzeck*, yet without enjoying them. Donald Davidson revises Hume's claim to be not that the proud person must take a separate pleasure in what he is proud of, but that it must be something that he more generally approves of.[79] This seems correct. Thus if I feel proud about attending Wozzeck, though I don't like it and don't value *it* in any way, I have to be disposed to construe people who attend *Wozzeck* as sophisticated, or gritty, or cool, or some such thing; and this will count as approving of attending *Wozzeck*.

The proud person perceives whatever he is proud of as associated with himself in some way – as an attribute of himself (he is a homeowner) as something he did (he finished his dissertation), as something that belongs to him (his house) or is a part of him (his handsome face), as some attribute of, or something done or possessed by, someone related to him or associated with him (his son is a homeowner, his daughter finished her dissertation, his

---

[78] See R. S. Lazarus, *Emotion and Adaption*, p. 273.
[79] *Essays on Actions and Events*, p. 280f. Gabriel Taylor proposes a similar revision. See *Pride, Shame, and Guilt*, p. 25.

navy possesses powerful submarines), and so on. We are tempted to try to reduce this attributed relationship to some essence. Gabriele Taylor claims that *belonging* is the essence of the relationship. But this move requires her to stretch the meaning of "belonging" pretty far. For example, in the case of a person who is proud of owning a house (as distinguished from being proud of his house) " 'owning a house' is now what he sees as . . . 'belonging' to him." Similarly, "his handsome face or his sense of humour, may be said to be belongings of his" (p. 32). The various kinds of relationship to himself in terms of which the proud person may construe whatever he is proud of may not be captured in any single current concept. Perhaps we can do no better than to enumerate the kinds of relationship in terms of which people can feel pride; the essential point is that, whatever these are, they are such that the subject sees whatever he is proud of as reflecting well on his own worth.

A person can acknowledge that he stands in one of these relationships to something that he takes to be worthy of approval, and yet not feel pride in it. I may, for example, acknowledge that I have just won a footrace and approve of this, yet not be proud of it. Taylor, trading on her general view that emotions are formations of "identificatory" and "explanatory" beliefs, explains this by the principle that "What a person is proud of is to him an achievement in that it goes beyond his norm of expectations" (p. 38). But this seems incorrect. Let us say that I fully expect to win the race, and to win it gloriously. Will my expectation prevent me from feeling proud of winning, when I do? I need not be surprised in any way by the value of what I am proud of, but I do need to be *impressed* by it. Thus Hume is on the right track in his general theory that emotions are a kind of impression (p. 275), as contrasted with interpreters like Taylor and Davidson, who attempt to translate his insights into claims about beliefs. Taylor says that "at the time of [the emotion's] occurrence the person feeling pride believes that in a certain respect her own worth is confirmed or enhanced" (p. 24). Not necessarily so. I have just bought a car; but I fight against feelings of pride in owning this car, precisely because I disbelieve that such a thing enhances my worth. My *impression* is of enhanced self-worth, but I don't believe it.

Hume distinguishes pride's "object" from its "cause" (p. 277). Its object is always the self, while its cause is whatever consideration causes the person to take a high view of himself. Thus one who is proud of his beautiful house makes himself the *object* of his attention, but appreciates himself (this pleasure being the pride itself) *because* this house is beautiful and belongs to him. On the view that I am advancing what Hume calls the emotion's object is called its focus. The notion of a construal is that of a unitary organization of an array of aspects, some of which could be called objects. Thus I do not so much speak of the object of an emotion, as of its *situational* object – the entire array that is taken in and organized in a way formally characteristic of an emotion type. Within the array, the focus may shift rather fluidly. For example, in anger the focus may be oneself as injured, or the injury as directed to oneself, or the offender as doer of the injury, or even the culpability of the offender. The emotion is anger not in virtue of some particular focus (Humean "object"), but because *whatever* of the various elements of anger is the focus is construed in terms of this particular configuration of considerations. In pride the self is sometimes the focus, but not always. The subject may attend to his own person as enhanced or confirmed in its status by what he is proud of, but just as likely the object of his attention will be whatever he is proud of – an accomplishment, a possession, an attribute – with the consideration that it is his, and thus prospers his worth, somewhat in the background. That is, he may construe the accomplishment as enhancing or confirming his person, and not necessarily construe his person in terms of its enhancing accomplishment. If asked why he is so pleased with himself, the proud person may answer by referring to his accomplishment; this is the paradigm case on Hume's accounting of object and cause. But equally, if asked why he is so pleased with his accomplishment, the proud person may answer by pointing to its relation to himself or what it has done for his worth. In this last case the accomplishment is the Humean "object" of pride, and the relation to the self, or the self itself, is (part of) its "cause."

I propose, then, the following formula for the defining proposition of pride: *It is important for me to have high worth; and X (attribute, possession, accomplishment, associate), by its goodness and its association with me, confers, enhances, or confirms such worth.*

3.13. GOODNESS

A number of expressions in current English can be used to denote an emotion, or slight variants of an emotion, that we may generically term "joy." Thus I am pleased that my son was admitted to a good college, or happy about it or glad of it, or delighted with it, or perhaps even elated or ecstatic or exultant. The various expressions seem to designate, not different emotions, but different intensities of the same emotion. If I rejoice about my son's admission, my emotion is on the upper end of the intensity scale, but less dramatically I may be pleased or take a quiet joy in this turn of events. I experience a different but related emotion if I am contented with his admission, and yet another if I am relieved about it or by it. An even more different emotion is nostalgia about it. Let's begin with joy, distinguishing it from a couple of other kinds of pleasure or "enjoyment," and then comment about the differences between joy and some of the related emotions.

a. Joy

Some physical sensations are naturally pleasant – the smell of lilacs, the taste of honey, sensations produced by a back massage or sexual intercourse. Other physical pleasures depend more on the correction of a prior state of deprivation or discomfort: warming one's hands by the fire when they are chilled, drinking a glass of water when thirsty, resting one's muscles after intense exertion. Both kinds of sensory pleasure differ markedly from gladness or emotional delight. The pleasant sensation is localized in one's nose, mouth, back, genitals, hands, but joy does not occur at any location in the body, nor is the pleasure of it a bodily pleasure. The sensation is caused by the application of some stimulus to the relevant organ – honey to the tongue, pressure on the back, friction of the sex organ, water on the gullet – but the emotion is caused by whatever it takes to come to "see" a situation in a certain light, finding satisfaction of a concern in that "seeing." The sensation in the deprived gullet is normally *of* the water flowing over it, and the sensation in the sex organ is normally *of* the partner's organ, but taken just as a sensation it is not necessary to the sensation or its pleasantness that the stimulus be identified in one way or another. By contrast, it is essential to joy that what it is about be identified by the subject in the particular way that satisfies the prior concern and distinguishes this joy from other joys. The pleasantness of my gladness that my son was accepted by a good college depends on my construing, and in this sense identifying, the situation as I do, and not on my body's being impinged upon by any stimulus.

However, though it is not essential to sensory pleasure that the stimulus be identified in any particular way, or even identified at all, I do think that most human pleasures of sensation have an emotional dimension, since the construal of the stimulus is so important to the pleasure. The pleasure of eating a perfectly broiled salmon steak is not, in adult human beings, a purely sensory pleasure, as is shown by the fact that it can be spoiled by the information that the steak was fished out of Lake Michigan near the paper mills. Nor is the pleasure of sexual intercourse purely sensory, as is shown by the importance, to that pleasure (for many people, at any rate), of the partner's identity and attitude. The difference between the pleasures of sensation and emotional pleasure is that emotional pleasure lacks pleasure of sensation; it is not that the pleasures of sensation lack a dimension of construal.

Another phenomenon related to joy that is not an emotion proper, or at any rate does not fit my paradigm, is that of taking pleasure in an activity. The difference between the phenomena is brought out by cases in which joy about an activity is independent of, or opposed to, enjoyment of the same activity. For example, I may be glad that I am helping my child with her homework, without enjoying the activity. Again, without being glad that I am playing bridge (I may think that bridge right now is a waste of my time, and thus regret having gotten myself into the game), I may take pleasure in playing bridge.[80] Aristotle makes a great deal of activity pleasure

[80] See Elizabeth Anscombe, "On the Grammar of 'Enjoy'" *Journal of Philosophy* **64** (1967): 607–614, especially 609. Gilbert Ryle makes a threefold distinction similar to mine between pleasant sensations, pleasure in activity, and being emotionally pleased, in "Pleasure" *Collected Papers 2: Collected Essays 1929–1968* (London: Hutchinson: 1971), pp. 326–335.

in his account of the virtues and moral education. But what is this family of emotions that I am calling joy?

I am surrounded by my children, who are playing happily, conversing brightly, joking, running vigorously, looking out kindly for one another – in short, showing signs of flourishing, of growing well in body, mind, and spirit. As I contemplate this goodly scene, I am filled with joy. On my analysis of emotion, my joy amounts to a concern-based construal of my children: I "see" them in terms of their well-being, and this term impinges satisfyingly on my concern for their well-being. If I do not see them in terms of this or some similar aspect of the scene (let us say I merely perceive the noise and motion as an impediment to my reading), then I will not feel joy; or if I perceive them in terms of their flourishing but without this perception's impinging on my concern (I am assessing them clinically, with perfect detachment, and give them a high grade), then likewise I do not feel joy. Let us say, then, that joy is a construal of something in terms that satisfy one or more of one's concerns. What kind of joy one exemplifies – whether one is pleased, happy, glad, delighted, elated, ecstatic, or exultant – will be determined by the intensity of the emotion, that is, by the strength of the concern, the vivacity of the construal, and the rate of impingement of the terms on the concern (see Section 2.10). The defining proposition for joy, then, is something like this: *It is important that X be in condition Y; and X is in condition Y.*

Clearly, this definition does not distinguish joy from any number of other positive emotions – hope, gratitude, pride, relief, nostalgia, even romantic melancholy. They are all, in one way or another, construals that impinge satisfyingly on one or another concern of the subject. Thus we might say that joy is the general form of the positive emotions; it is emotional satisfaction. I hasten to add that this is not to say anything very profound, and indeed is in a sense to detract from joy – to attribute it to somebody is to give less information about that person's state of mind than would be given by ascribing hope, gratitude, or pride to her. Let me now give a brief account of three emotions that are similar to joy, and yet are not merely joy in one of its degrees of intensity.

b. Relief

If I am relieved that my children are flourishing, then I am perceiving them in some terms that impinge satisfyingly on my concern for them, but I am also construing them as having been not flourishing, or under some threat of not flourishing. Thus it is to construe my children's present, gratifying condition, or the security of it or my knowledge of it, as a notable change from earlier. Relief's defining proposition is this: *It is important that X be in condition Y; and X is in condition Y, though X was not, or might not have been, or was not known to me to be, in condition Y.*

c. Contentment

To feel contented with my children's flourishing is to say to myself, as it were, "It is good enough." The concept *enough* is not essential to plain joy, but here a measure of good in terms of which a perception of enough can supervene is required. What one is contented with is perceived in terms of how its goodness might have been exceeded, yet in such a way that not its falling short, but its attainment of this goodness, is salient. This analysis perhaps explains why contentment is a moderate form of joy; the contented person does not rejoice or exult; he is not ecstatic, yet he perceives whatever he is contented with as gratifying. Contentment's defining proposition, then, is this: *It is important that X be in condition Y; and X is in condition Y; and I ask no more.* We sometimes ascribe contentment to people to whom the question of enough has not occurred: for example, the contented inhabitants of a primitive culture, whom *we* see as not missing fast food, laptops, and cellular phones. To ascribe contentment to such people is to ascribe the absence of the emotions of discontent: frustration, longing, and disappointment; it is not to ascribe to them the emotion of contentment.

d. Nostalgia

Often when we smell flowers in springtime – gardenias, lilacs – we not only have a pleasant olfactory sensation, but experience a rush of nostalgia as well. On the present account of emotions, we would say that we smell the flower in terms of pleasant scenes from our past. If able to articulate our olfactory nostalgia, we might say, "That fragrance carries me back to happy springtimes of my youth in grandmother's garden," but often the terms of the construal are vague. *Some* pleasant memory is mingling with the present lovely smells, but one can't pin it down.

I treat nostalgia here in connection with joy, because it is a pleasant experience; people often seek out settings and stimuli that will bring on nostalgia; they take "nostalgia trips." Nostalgia can be self-enhancing: The earlier pleasure is exaggerated or gilded; in memory, it becomes fantastic. But often the pleasure of the pleasant memory is tinged with pain that the experienced good is past and gone, never to be retrieved or fully duplicated. The pain may be very slight; sometimes, however, "nostalgia" is used as a synonym for "regret," as in T. S. Eliot's reference to "Dante's . . . nostalgia, his bitter regrets for past happiness." In this case, too, something present is construed in terms of a sweet memory, but now that memory occasions a disadvantageous comparison that embitters the present. It is not precisely *regret* – not a pain at what might have been but was not; rather, it is a pain at what is *lost*. Hence Eliot would have written more precisely of Dante's bitter grief for past happiness. If we treat such painful nostalgia as a form of grief, perhaps we can reserve for nostalgia proper a place among the joys.

What are the defining propositions of nostalgia? Plain nostalgia: *X reminds me of Y (pleasant memory)*. Nostalgia with pain: *X reminds me of Y (pleasant memory), and would (per impossibile) that lost Y might be again!* Nostalgia with pain shades into nostalgic grief when the last clause intensely dominates the construal.

3.14. PROSPECTS

a. Hope

Hope can be regarded as the positive mirror image of fear (Section 3.2). If to fear some eventuality is to construe it as presenting a bad possibility possessing a significant degree of probability, to have hope for some eventuality is to construe it as presenting a good possibility possessing a significant degree of probability. Thus if I feel hopeful about my child's prospects of being admitted to Yale, I construe that eventuality as both good and fairly likely to occur. Just as what is feared can be something construed as bad in itself (disease, dysfunction, pain) or something construed as making such an eventuality more probable (unavailability of needed medicine), so what one hopes for can be some eventuality construed as good in itself (admission to Yale) or something construed as making such an eventuality more probable (high SAT scores). Just as we distinguish what is feared (a fall on the ice) from the grounds of fear (the fact that one's shoes have bad traction on ice), saying "I fear X because of Y," so we distinguish what is hoped for (admission to Yale) from the grounds of the hope (high SAT scores). In some but not all cases, we can speak of either the thing hoped for or the grounds of hope as hoped for. We hope for high SAT scores as well as admission to Yale; but if my hope of recovery rests on the skill of the doctor, I may hope for recovery but not hope for the doctor's skill, which I may construe not at all in terms of probability: His skill may appear to me as fully established. An analogous point is true about the grounds of fear: I fear falling on ice because of my shoes' bad traction, without fearing my shoes' bad traction.

I have been presenting hope as a positive emotion counterpart of fear. But in modern English, "hope" may mean little more than "wish." "I'm pretty sure it won't happen, but I hope it will" is not an expression of hope as an emotion, but rather of the continued wish that this prospect, almost relinquished, will occur. If it assesses the probability positively,[81] it is only in the faintest way. Still, it is a *little* more than a wish; if the prospect were completely resigned, the use of "hope" here would be bad English; the right expression would be "wish" with some contrary-to-fact expression such as "I wish it would," or "if only it had been possible." The positive emotion of

[81] "Positive" assessment of probability does not mean "above .5." Depending on prior expectations a probability of .1 could be a term in a hopeful construal of a situation.

hope is expressed less ambiguously by some locution involving "hopeful" or "hope" as a noun: Thus it seems contradictory to say "I'm pretty sure it won't happen, but I am hopeful [or: I have hope] that it will." So the defining proposition for hope will be something like this: *X presents an attractive possibility possessing a significant degree of probability; may X or its attractive consequences be accomplished.*

"Faith," says the book of Hebrews, "is the assurance (ὑπόστασις) of things hoped for, the conviction (ἔλεγχος) of things not seen" (11.1). In the terms of our analysis so far, the suggestion would seem to be that proper faith in God makes the probability construal of future good as good as 1.0. Most of what is called hope in modern English is less confident than this. If we think our investment is completely invulnerable, we are not likely to speak of hoping for a good outcome or being hopeful, but, instead, we speak of expecting. This is due in part to our usage of "hope," which we do not readily apply to cases of certainty of outcome, but it is also due in part to our grounding our construals of future good on conditions to which it makes sense to ascribe degrees of probability – for example, the likelihood of a solid stock market for the next ten years. But the ground of Christian hope is not such a set of conditions, but instead the character of God and the character of faith in him, which is not a calculation but a venture of one's life. Thus it seems that Christian hope does not have quite the same defining proposition as the hope that I have described. The prospect in view is a kingdom of justice and love in which God is honored as God and human relations are peaceful and mutually benevolent. But this attractive possibility is not construed, in fully Christian hope, as merely having an excellent chance of occurring; it is construed as a completely assured prospect. Calculation of probabilities is not in order here. Such assurance might seem to rule against the propriety of calling this state of mind hope. But the analog of the nonassurance that characterizes ordinary hope is the "invisibility" of what is hoped for. We may take this invisibility to be more than ordinary nonpresence (the person who calculates the probability, and thus his hopes, of recovery also hopes for what is "not seen") because of the striking discontinuity of the happy prospect with the way things go in this present visible world. The defining proposition for Christian hope would be something like this: *The kingdom of justice and love presents an enormously attractive possibility that our God is sure to actualize, contrary to present appearances; may it come.*

I noted in Section 3.1b that similarities and differences among emotion types come in a variety of kinds. Fear is not the only "opposite" of hope; in a different way, despair is an opposite as well. I said in Section 3.6e that despair is like frustration (Section 3.3d): The subject is deeply concerned for some good (say, a life project, the well-being of a loved one) that he or she construes as impossible. Hope is the opposite of despair in being a construal of such a good as possible and even significantly probable. Thus hope and despair are both based on a concern for some good, but are on opposite ends of the probability/improbability continuum. The comparison with fear highlights hope's expectation of *good*; the comparison with despair highlights hope's posit of a *significant probability* of good. Again, in Christian hope, "significant probability" is not the right word for this element of the construal.

b. Expectation

When we expect something we are ready for it to occur or appear. She's expecting a baby in two months; guests are expected for dinner. Wow, I didn't expect to see that tree gone. When we speak of something "unexpected" happening, we are usually saying not just that we were not ready for it, but that we *were* ready for some rather strongly contrasting eventuality or merely the ordinary expected flow of things; that is, we are usually expressing something like surprise or bewilderment at its occurring. (One is not surprised by what does not contravene positive expectations. Thus very small children are unresponsive to magic shows.)

We have lots of robust expectations that we are not currently aware of. I expect my students to be sitting around the seminar table when I arrive for class and would be surprised to find them standing on their heads or huddling under the table; but my expectation does not consist in mentally anticipating their sitting posture. I am simply ready for them to be sitting. (But if *asked* what posture I expect them to be in when I arrive, I can easily say.)

Unlike contravened expectations, which result in surprise, most fulfilled expectations are not emotions. I walk by the tree that I have come to expect to see on that corner; it is indeed there, and I feel nothing about it. By contrast, the moment at which one comes to know of the fulfillment of a fairly strong desire is typically a moment of joy; and the moment at which one comes to know that a fairly strong desire has been contravened is typically a moment of disappointment or frustration (provided that the desired thing was somewhat expected). As a readiness to be surprised or unsurprised, expectation is less like an emotion than like the concern that is a disposition to a range of emotions. And we've seen that expectation is in a way an aspect of emotions like fear, dread, and hope.

An expectation is a kind of construal, whose defining proposition is the very formal *X will occur* (or *be so*). But it is neither a concern nor a concern-based construal. Expectations are not concerns, though one can be concerned (pro or con) for what one expects. When we claim that somebody expects a certain tree to be standing on the familiar corner, we do not suggest that she cares one way or the other whether the tree is there. But the readiness is *analogous* to a concern: It prepares us to respond to the event as either a satisfaction or a contravention of our expectation. Given this understanding of expectation, it does not seem to me very natural to call expectation an emotion.

3.15. THE BELOVED

a. Introduction

The manyness of love's splendors may be traced, in part, to its many varieties. Parents love their children; teenagers fall in love for an afternoon; spouses sometimes love one another more after forty years than they did on their wedding day; friends love one another; some people love chocolate and others love waterskiing; Christians and Jews love God; patriots love the fatherland; a mother loves her newborn immediately, but the father's love may come on more gradually; some non-Italians love Italy; after many years it dawns on a man that he loves the family farm that earlier he only wanted to depart from; benevolence for humanity is sometimes called love; Mother Teresa showed love for the dying outcasts of Calcutta. These different "loves" entail widely different behaviors, have different biological backgrounds, are explained by reference to different kinds of reasons, and are or involve very different ways of construing what is loved.

It is barely possible that all loves are emotions, and it is not very likely that nothing we call love is an emotion. So to answer "Is love an emotion?" with a simple Yes or No is probably out of the question. Our answer will turn on analysis and distinctions; I will try to indicate the kinds of love that are emotions and the kinds that are not and I will attempt give reasons for the specifications. Themes and family resemblances pervade the variety of examples in the above paragraph. A number of the loves can be regarded as forms of attachment (to children, to spouse, to friends, to the fatherland, etc.), and I want to start with a couple of examples of this kind. Family resemblances make for a natural transition to erotic or romantic love; then, with insights thus garnered, I will turn to the love that Christians call agape. Finally, I shall comment briefly about a number of concepts that border on or belong to the category of forms of love, such as gratitude, compassion, sympathy, benevolence, mercy, and fondness.

The proposal that emotions are concern-based construals is that we address situations, or supposed situations, from the standpoint of some desire, interest, preference, or attachment, and we "see" the situation in some way that impinges on that desire, preference, or attachment (generically, concern). This view is an informative heuristic paradigm that fits and illuminates a vast number of cases and illuminates even the cases that it does not fit, such as the musical emotions (see Sections 2.5g–2.5j); it is not a universal theory of emotion. Our thesis is the Wittgensteinian one that while the concept of emotion is coherent, no informative set of properties runs through every instance of the class.

A potential weakness in the paradigm, already discussed in Section 2.7d, is that the distinction between concerns and emotions cannot be made clear enough – that concerns are themselves construals, and that some of what we call emotions are not concern-based construals, but are just concerns. The difficulty arises in a special way in connection with love, inasmuch as "love" seems to denote, in some of its uses anyway, what I have called a concern, while love is also widely thought to be an emotion. I shall now look at some of the main things that we call love, asking how they relate to emotions conceived as concern-based construals.

b. Attachment

By definition, an object of attachment is *special to the subject.* One is not attached to just anything, but only to certain things. The psychological determination of their specialness seems to be that they are then "seen" in a certain way. They have a "meaning" for the subject that constitutes the attachment. Thus an old cup that I have drunk coffee from for years is special to me. It is unique: Losing *it* (rather than just "a cup") is an occasion for mild distress, and finding it after a period of loss is a mild relief and joy. If I am very attached to this cup, then were I convinced that someone had switched my cup for a different one of the very same design, and with identically configured chips and stains, I might not feel the same about the new cup (I might find myself pretending that this is my cup). But I want to focus on attachments to persons because these are of much greater significance to most people.

In terms of purely sensory qualities, my daughter Maria is not very different from thousands of other seventeen-year-old girls. Of course she has sensory properties *somewhat* different from all those others, in virtue of which I can pick her out, infallibly, from among others who resemble her. Most of these distinguishing properties are ones I cannot specify, and the ones I can specify I can describe only in rather general terms; but despite my inarticulateness, I can "see" the difference. Among the qualities that constitute Maria's "meaning" to me (what I "see" in her), some are sensory and some are not. She is beautiful to look at, and that visual impression feeds into my attachment, just as my attachment colors my impression of her beauty. However, the meaning she has for me is not just that of a beautiful young woman but is constituted of properties that are not sensory at all and that are "seen" by me only because of the history that I have lived through with her.

The qualities in terms of which I am attached to Maria can be summarized in the predicate *is Maria,* where "Maria" functions as a uniquely referring term. Thus if asked in virtue of what qualities of Maria I care about her, I have to answer, "in virtue of her *being Maria.*" What makes this girl the one and only Maria (*my* Maria)? It is she whose diapers I changed, who used to crawl up on my lap for stories, whom I have nurtured in countless ways these past seventeen years, and who calls me "Dad." These things are not seen with the eyes, but they feed into and determine my experience of Maria whenever I see her or talk to her or think about her. In short, she is identified in terms of this history, which involves me. The elements of our common narrative need not be in the foreground of my consciousness or rehearsed in any explicit way to determine my "perception" of her.

For an attachment to form, it is not enough to have a long history of *association* with another person; one might have such a history and hate the other. To found attachment, the history has to be one that promotes an impression of the goodness of the object of attachment. This impression can be achieved in a variety of ways. Mothers seems to have a biological mechanism by which they normally see their baby as a momentous good. This impression is furthered by the mother's "investment" in the child, in nurturing it (we might say that the child *has* to have positive value because of what it has cost the mother). And in the normal case this is followed by the child's positive valuation of the mother and the gratifying responses (smiles, caresses, cute behavior, etc.) of the child. To be attached to someone involves experiencing him or her in terms of that self-involving, good-showing history. Something analogous can no doubt be detailed for the history that eventuates in attachment to nonpersonal objects like cups, houses, animals, and fatherlands.

So far I have not spoken of any emotion, though the attachment I have described is closely connected with emotions. A significant part of the evidence that a person has an attachment to someone is the emotions that he or she experiences in response to the vicissitudes of the attachment's object. I take joy in Maria's successes, her happiness, her virtues, and in other evidences and instances of her flourishing, because of what she means to me; but similarly I will be angry if someone treats her maliciously, anxious if she is endangered, grateful if someone helps her in some striking way, and grief-stricken if I lose her – and all because I am attached to her. I will not experience these emotions, or anyway experience them with the same intensity or regularity, in connection with people I am not attached to. The variety of the emotions that give evidence of an attachment and the mutual contrariety among some of them suggest that attachment is not an emotion. Instead, the attachment seems to be a basis for many possible emotions. If this is right, then it seems that an attachment as such does not have any particular emotional feel (it is not positive or negative).

And yet we do speak of a parent's *feeling* love, *feeling* affection, for his or her child. Is "love" in this claim just a stand-in for the range of emotions in which the attachment is actualized and evidenced? In other words, when a person speaks of feeling love for his child, is he simply saying that, in matters touching the child's weal and woe, he sometimes feels joy, sometimes anger, sometimes disappointment, sometimes anxiety, and so forth? This is, I think, sometimes the force of speaking of feeling love or feeling attachment; but in cases of some particular emotion episodes that arise out of an attachment, we would resist saying that we are feeling love. When, upon losing our beloved, we are sad, we do not usually call the sadness a feeling of love, though we might say, "I didn't realize until I felt that sadness how much I loved her." Similarly, if I am disappointed at Maria's missing a golden opportunity, or anxious about her well-being, I am not likely to say that what I am feeling is love or attachment. In an episode of anger at someone who spreads malicious rumors about Maria, it is not natural to say, "I am feeling love for Maria." The reason is perhaps that the more salient objects of the emotion are the *offense* against Maria and the *offender*. Maria does figure in the situational object of the emotion, but she is not at the center of the stage. When someone says, "I'm angry!" the natural question is, "Whom at?" or "What about?" and in answer I indicate the offender and the offense, not the one I am attached to, except as an auxiliary in the characterization of the whom or the what. Maria is not the "object" of my anger, though she figures in its situational object.

In other cases of the particular emotions arising out of an attachment, we speak much more comfortably about feeling love. When Maria was little I would take intense pleasure in seeing her sleep peacefully, or play vigorously, or display intelligence in her remarks about things. I think we are more comfortable saying that in such episodes of emotion I was feeling love for her, even if this is just one of many emotions that arise out of my attachment to her. Three explanations of this difference come to mind. First, attachment (love) is fundamentally a pro-attitude or good-seeing disposition, and so is the joy in contemplating Maria's beauty, health, or intelligence. So the basic attachment attitude is more similar to the perception constituting joy and some of its emotional cousins than it is to anger, disappointment, and grief. Second, the attachment will not get formed in the first place without some (indeed, plenty of) good-seeing in its history. As Søren Kierkegaard comments, "Even if love can give birth to pain, it is not brought forth in pain."[82] Unless a mother takes delight in her infant, we may well suppose, she will never become attached to it; unless people take pleasure in one another and in their presence, they will never become friends; had a lover never delighted in the aspect of her beloved, she had never fallen in love with him. So the emotions that see the attachment object in terms of loss, deficiency, or damage are secondary and derivative from the ones that see her in terms of flourishing and beauty. Third, unlike the anger and disappointment discussed above, Maria is center-stage in the situational object of this joy, making the expression "feels love for Maria" more fitting. Both positive emotions and negative ones that we are not much inclined to call feelings of love arise out of an attachment. For example, when Maria performs her Chopin Waltz smashingly and I am very happy about her accomplishment, I am more inclined to say that I rejoice with her, or am proud of her, or am delighted that she played so well but not so inclined to say, "At that moment

---

[82] *Three Discourses on Imagined Occasions*, translated by Howard and Edna Hong (Princeton, New Jersey: Princeton, University Press, 1993), p. 47.

I felt so much love for her." And the reason, perhaps, is that here the focus of the emotion is not Maria herself, but her accomplishment, or even her accomplishment's enhancement of me as her father.

So far, I have suggested that love, in the dispositional sense of attachment, is not an emotion but a disposition to a range of emotions, and, that some of the emotions in this range – in particular the positive ones that take the attachment object as a central focus of the emotion's situational object – are naturally identified as love for the object of attachment. But these are not, I think, the only kinds of experience that deserve the name "love as an emotion." Perhaps they are not even the most deserving. I have said that what distinguishes attachment as a construal from the emotions as construals is that whereas emotions are *situational* construals of the object of concern, attachment is a construal that *identifies* the object of concern.

For the most part, the identifying construal of Maria as good and as mine is dispositional: It is part of my character, actualized in various emotion episodes (situational construals) and actions. But this identifying construal or some part of it also has *episodes*. I think of Maria and experience an excited pleasure. Or I look at her and listen to her voice and take intense pleasure in her excellence, her goodness, her beauty, and so on. Such experiences are emotions, yet they do not quite fit the paradigm that I have been proposing in this book; they are not best analyzed as concern-based construals. Here the construal is not laid over – does not impinge on – some concern; it *is* the concern. And it is not a construal of the object of the concern as in some particular circumstance but is just a perception of the object of concern in what we might call its "identity." The object of the emotion is not Maria-in-a-circumstance or a circumstance as it impinges on Maria but just *Maria*. This sort of emotion is analogous to the ecstasy or appreciation that one sometimes experiences in the presence of natural phenomena – a sunset, a mountain lake, a tree or flower. One might call this an "experience of attachment," but I think it is natural also to reserve "attachment" for the disposition and to call this experience an emotion of love. The defining proposition for attachment love as an emotion would be something like this: *My special S is essentially wonderful.*

Let me summarize my analysis of attachment love. Like an emotion, an attachment is a construal because it is a way of "seeing" the object of the attachment. This seeing is usually a historical accretion that includes a preponderance of positive experiences with the object of attachment. But an attachment, as a construal, differs in two ways from an emotion: An attachment is dispositional, and so not strictly a perception; and it is a seeing, not in terms of the more or less local and episodic *circumstances* of the object of attachment, as is typical of emotions, but instead in terms of enduring predicates of the object *herself*. Furthermore, this seeing is constitutive of the value of the object for the subject of the attachment; it is not a construal that *impinges* on a concern, as in the case of most emotions, but a construal that *constitutes* a concern. The construal constitutes the object as good (special) to the subject. Being dispositional, an attachment is not felt, except as one feels the episodes of particular emotions to which the attachment gives rise. Of the emotions to which the attachment gives rise we can distinguish three kinds: (1) emotions that we are not inclined to call feelings of love because they are negative and/or the object of attachment is not the focus of the construal that is based on the attachment; (2) emotions that we are inclined to call feelings of love but are nevertheless circumstantial construals of the object of attachment; and (3) noncircumstantial or "identifying" construals of the object of attachment. Emotions of this last type deviate from the paradigm for emotions that is offered in this book; they are not concern-based construals.

c. Erotic Love

Let us turn to the case of romantic or erotic love. By "erotic love" we do not mean sexual intercourse, nor mere sexual attraction and desire, nor even erotic fascination with an individual; we are speaking, instead, of the phenomenon of being "in love."

In a scene of Leo Tolstoy's *War and Peace*,[83] Pierre Bezuhov falls in love (though not wholeheartedly) with Hélène Kuragin. Pierre is an awkward, goodhearted, intelligent, naive young man whose recent inheritance of a fortune and a title have opened up possibilities of matrimony unavailable to the fortuneless illegitimate son of a count that he formerly was. With Pierre's enormous new fortune, Hélène's father wishes him to marry his beautiful daughter, and he and others in their circle, including Hélène, plant suggestions in Pierre's mind that such a thing is possible. In a situation engineered to fix an attachment to Hélène, he finds himself perceiving her from up close:

She was...wearing a gown cut in the fashion of the day, very low back and front. Her bosom, which always reminded Pierre of marble, was so close to him that his short-sighted eyes could not but perceive the living charm of her neck and shoulders, so near to his lips that he need only stoop a little to have touched them....He saw not her marble beauty forming a single whole with her gown, but all the fascination of her body, which was only veiled by her clothes. And once having seen this, his eye refused to see her in any other way, just as we cannot reinstate an illusion that has been explained.

She looked up, straight at him, her dark eyes sparkling, and smiled. "So you have never noticed before how beautiful I am," Hélène seemed to say. "You had not noticed that I am a woman? Yes, I am a woman, who might belong to anyone – might even belong to you," said her eyes. And at that moment Pierre was conscious that Hélène not only could but must become his wife....

[83] Translated by Rosemary Edmonds (London: Penguin Books, 1957).

Pierre dropped his eyes, then lifted them, and tried to see her again as a distant beauty removed from him, the way he had seen her every day until then, but found it no longer possible. He could not do it any more than a man who has been staring through the mist at a tuft of steppe grass and taking it for a tree can see it as a tree once he has recognized it for a tuft of grass. . . .

Back at home Pierre could not get to sleep for a long while for thinking of what had happened. What had happened? Nothing. He had merely discovered that a woman he had known as a child, a woman of whom he had been able to say indifferently, "Yes, she's nice-looking" when anyone told him that Hélène was a beauty, might be his.

"But she's brainless, I have always said so," he thought. "No, this isn't love. On the contrary, there's something nasty, something not right in the feeling she excites in me. Didn't I hear that her own brother Anatole was in love with her and she with him, that there was a regular scandal and that was the reason he was sent away? . . ." he reflected, but while he was thus musing . . . he caught himself smiling and was conscious that another line of thought had sprung up and while meditating on her worthlessness he was also dreaming of how she would be his wife, how she would love him, how she might become quite different, and how all he had heard and thought about her might be untrue. And he again saw her not as Prince Vasili's daughter but visualized her whole body only veiled by her grey gown. "But no, why did this idea never enter my mind before?" and again he told himself that it was impossible, that there would be something nasty and unnatural in this marriage, something which seemed dishonourable. . . . But at the very time he was expressing this conviction to himself, in another part of his mind her image rose in all its womanly beauty (Book One, Part 3, Chapter 1).

This is not a case of full-fledged erotic love, but it contains what is distinctive in that state and exhibits the features that most incline us to suppose that such love is an emotion. Pierre's love for Hélène is a quite definite experience, a concern-based way of seeing her that is all the more striking for being completely new to Pierre; and this way of seeing is, from his wonted perspective, circumstantial or situational in the way that I take to be paradigmatic for emotions. The emotion is the one expressed in Pierre's smile at the thought of Hélène's being his wife and loving him. Erotic love, in this emotional sense, is an interest in an individual construed in terms of such thoughts as *she is (or can be) mine* and *she is very good* and *I am (or ought to be) the unique object of her love.* Such thoughts define a situation vis-à-vis Pierre's sexual interest that is analogous to the situation defined by *my life is endangered by cancer* vis-à-vis my interest in surviving or *he has insulted my dignity* vis-à-vis my interest in being treated with respect. In addition to Pierre's sexual interest, his experience of erotic love is based on the interest in having a partner and being a special (unique) object of that person's love. Pierre's response to Hélène, insofar as it is the *emotion* of erotic love, is a form of joy or hope, a *satisfaction* of his erotic interests.

I say Pierre's case is not full-fledged because he is ambivalent; one moment he sees Hélène in this "loving" light, and the next he sees her in a quite contrary light, and even as he yields more and more to the idea of marrying her, his yielding is fatalistic, not wholehearted as out-and-out erotic love is. In particular, he is not fully confident about the proposition *she is very good*; and later in the novel, when he finally decides he does not love her and in fact was never really in love with her, his reason is that he was deceiving himself about the fact that she was a "depraved woman" (Book Two, Part One, Chapter 6).

What is full-fledged erotic love, and how does it stand vis-à-vis emotions? For one thing it is more settled and stable than Pierre's construal of Hélène. It ceases to be merely an emotion and becomes a trait of the lovers, a part of their identity: Who is she? Mine. Who am I? Hers. This construal is not just *based on* the sexual interest and the interest in having a partner, as Pierre's construal of Hélène is; we should say rather that the sexual interest and the interest in having a partner *are* the attachment to this other person. The attachment is the form those interests take. In one sense the attachment is a construal, for the partner is certainly "seen" in a very particular way, determined by the history of their relationship. But the "as" in "see as" seems inappropriate here as it is not in Pierre's case (see Section 2.3b, especially C12). In full-fledged romantic love, my experience is not of seeing my beloved *as* mine; that she is mine is rather the basic form of my attachment (concern). It is not a situational aspect of my life; it is a central aspect of my identity, that which situations of my life are situations *of*. Pierre's ambivalence about Hélène means that the attributes attributed to her and himself in his emotion do not form for him parts of his and her identities.

However, let us suppose that his ambivalence subsides and he falls in full-fledged love with her. He continues to experience her, from time to time, with the joy that marked the dawning of his love, but this joy is not the whole of his love, nor is it, in the vicissitudes of their life and relationship, the only emotional indicator of his love for her. Often, when engaged in conversation with her, he feels no emotion at all respecting *her* (if he feels emotion, it is about whatever they are discussing), yet he is as much in love with her as ever. Sometimes, when he contemplates her in a certain way, she strikes him with that former joy that partially duplicates the circumstantial construal that people tend to identify as romantic love, but his love is now marked as well by his anxiety for her health and hope for her recovery when she is ill, disappointment at her failures, and exultation in her triumphs. In other words, Pierre's erotic love for Hélène has become an attachment. The construal of Hélène as "mine" and "beautiful" and "good" and "loves me" is still there, and it is still connected with his sexual interest, but these predicates have ceased, for the most part, to be *circumstantial* of Hélène or of Pierre's sexual interest and have become *identificatory* of Hélène herself as an object of Pierre's concern (attachment). Though the terms of the two construals are much the same, the one construal constitutes an emotion, the other an attachment. The defining proposition for romantic love as an emotion is: *S is mine and I am hers (his); she (he) is uniquely wonderful and sexually attractive; we belong together forever.*

d. Agape

The love that Christians call "agape" is directed at both God and one's fellow humans, in a way that connects the two objects. The background of agape is the story of God's demonstrated goodness to us in Jesus Christ, in rescuing us from sin and death, reconciling us to himself and making us members of his people. Thus in agape God is "seen" with the eyes of the heart (Ephesians 1.18) through the determinants of this narrative. When agape is directed at fellow human beings, it has this same story and construal of God as background. That is, fellow human beings are seen as ones with whom Christ identified in his incarnation and for whom he died and was raised, as ones who on this account are being welcomed by God to membership in his people.

Mother Teresa of Calcutta composed the following prayer for daily use in her Children's Home:

Dearest Lord, may I see you today and every day in the person of your sick, and, whilst nursing them, minister unto you.

Though you hide yourself behind the unattractive disguise of the irritable, the exacting, the unreasonable, may I still recognize you, and say:

"Jesus, my patient, how sweet it is to serve you."

Lord, give me this seeing faith, then my work will never be monotonous. I will ever find joy in humouring the fancies and gratifying the wishes of all poor sufferers.

O beloved sick, how doubly dear you are to me, when you personify Christ; and what a privilege is mine to be allowed to tend you. Sweetest Lord, make me appreciative of the dignity of my high vocation, and its many responsibilities. Never permit me to disgrace it by giving way to coldness, unkindness, or impatience.

And O God, while you are Jesus, my patient, deign also to be to me a patient Jesus, bearing with my faults, looking only to my intention, which is to love and serve you in the person of each of your sick. Lord, increase my faith, bless my efforts and work, now and for evermore. Amen.

Mother Teresa's love for God consists in a construal of God as good, glorious, kind, wonderful, beneficent Father. It has, as I said, the background of the narratives of God's kindness to his people, especially the narrative of God's grace in Jesus Christ. The goodness of these acts of God appears to a believer against a background of caring about what they represent: the hungering and thirsting for righteousness that Jesus speaks of (Matthew 5.6). Without the caring, the construal of God in evangelical terms is not the love of God. This hungering and thirsting is not definable apart from the concept of the very God in question, because the righteousness in question is righteousness *before this God*. The hungering and thirsting is not the same as the joy of its fulfilment because one can also *suffer* emotionally (frustration, guilt, disappointment) on the basis of this hungering and thirsting.[84] But in such suffering the focus of the construal is not God in his goodness, glory, and so on, but typically it is oneself as a moral–spiritual failure. God is in the picture, as it were, but now a bit farther in the background, as the one who defines the sought-for righteousness and as the one the sought-for righteousness honors and in the relationship to whom it would consist.

We are disinclined to say that the emotions of guilt, frustration, or disappointment are feelings of love, though these emotions are symptoms or indications of one's love for God. This is partly because love, if it is an emotion, seems to need to be a happy one; and partly because the focus of any emotion that counts as love is the beloved, and the focus of these emotions is the (failed) lover (viz., the believer). The love in question in cases like this is the *concern* (to be in a good relationship with God) on which the guilt, and so on, are *based*. In another kind of case, God is actually construed, not in his aspect of goodness, graciousness, and so on, but as one who at the moment is being unhelpful [see some of the Psalms (13, 22, 42) in which the Psalmist expresses anger or disappointment at God]. This kind of case, though it is based on the love of God in the sense of a concern to be in a happy relationship with him, is even farther from being an emotion of love than the guilt and frustration just mentioned. Being a form of anger or disappointment, it construes God in some aspect of evil such as negligent, absent, or uncaring. God as good is still in the background, however. In all three of the Psalms I mentioned, the psalmist's complaint against God is followed by some form of praise or expression of confidence in God's goodness.

Much of the love of God, then, parallel to the attachment love and the erotic love that we have examined, is not an emotion but a concern on which a range of emotions are based, which in this way "express" the subject's love for God. Some of these emotions are better candidates than others for the expression "feeling of love for God." But as in the other cases, instances of one emotion type most deserve the expression "feeling love for God," namely the emotion in which a subject is simply "impressed" with the goodness, glory, or beauty of God. This emotion is sometimes called adoration. In the context of orthodox Christianity or Judaism, these ascriptions always have their background in the salvation narratives. But that background can yield a foreground in which these predicates are hardly at all circumstantial and are almost purely identificatory of God. When the subject feels this emotion, it is as though the concern on which the range of emotions "expressive" of love is based has itself become episodic and felt in the form of an emotion.

---

[84] See Søren Kierkegaard, *Concluding Unscientific Postscript*, translated by H. Hong and E. Hong (Princeton, New Jersey: Princeton University Press, 1992), pp. 431–525. For a version of this suffering from which a sense of guilt seems to be absent, see Romans 7.21–7.24.

This emotion deviates from the paradigm of emotion offered in this book in a way that parallels its counterpart in attachment love and erotic love.

What shall we say of the agape for human persons that Mother Teresa expresses in the prayer I quoted? In agape for the persons to whom she ministered, Mother Teresa saw them in an aspect of goodness: It is a "privilege" to attend them; she finds "joy" in doing so; they are "dear" to her; they are very much *worth* helping. Their "beauty" comes in large part from her construing them as personifying Christ: They belong to Him; they are ones whom he loves and for whom he died, ones with whom he identified in his incarnation and death. She would not have been able to love these sufferers as she did if she had not seen Christ in them. The story of Christ's ministry and death provides the distinctive character of Christian love for human persons. But the persons to whom Mother Teresa speaks of ministering do have a beauty, a goodness, in themselves: They are "doubly" dear. This goodness may be invisible without the construal in terms of Christ, but once it is seen it has a certain independence. Their humanity is itself beautiful and good. Much of her agape for them, we may surmise, consists in emotions expressive of her concern for them: compassion for them in their sickness, hope for their recovery, fear of their taking a turn for the worse, gladness when they recover. Yet these sufferers, and in general one's enemies and neighbors (paradigm objects of agape in Christian tradition), take on a stable identity, in the mind of the mature Christian, as good and beautiful. The neighbor's status as belonging to Christ is not merely circumstantial, but identificatory, and so an emotion of love in the strictest sense is possible (see the discussions of attachment love and erotic love). The defining proposition for agape as an emotion is this: *S is wonderful because S personifies Jesus Christ and is loved by him; may S's true interests be promoted.*

e. Gratitude, Compassion, Sympathy, Benevolence, Mercy, Fondness

Gratitude, as a pro-attitude toward a benefactor and a disposition to do kind and helpful things for the benefactor (to return favors, to say thank-you or otherwise express one's gladness to be benefited by the benefactor), is a kind of love. It is, however, clearly a circumstantial construal, inasmuch as the grateful one construes the benefactor as benefactor on the basis of some particular benefice or set of benefices. Gratitude's defining proposition is something like this: *S has fittingly, benevolently and freely conferred X (some benefit) on me, so I am attached to S by a sort of debt; let me express my indebtedness and attachment in some token return benefit to S.* To say that S has conferred X benevolently is to say that she did it out of good will to me – for my good. To say she did it freely is to say that she did it not under compulsion – not even under the "compulsion" of duty. To say that S has *fittingly* benefited me expresses that I care to be benefited in this way *by S*. When people we dislike or do not want to be attached to confer benefits on us, we are either ungrateful for the benefit (though we may be glad to have it) or we soften in our dislike and resistance to attachment. This openness to be benefited by S can be regarded as a sort of concern, or at least the absence of a negative concern, a repugnance to being helped by S. Other things being equal, we are gladder to receive benefits from those to whom we are attached by bonds of affection than from strangers or, *a fortiori*, enemies; thus we are more prone to be grateful to those to whom we are attached. But the gratitude may also be not so much a consequence of an already formed attachment as a precipitating condition of its formation. For a case of this sort, see the progress of Esther Summerson's attachment to John Jarndyce in Dickens's *Bleak House*, or of Smike to Nicholas in *Nicholas Nickleby*. Even when gratitude is dispositional, it is still circumstantial because the beneficent act or acts need to be mentioned to indicate the construal.[85] But in cases where the benefice is very generalized, it can become something like an essential predicate of the benefactor.

When compassion is an emotion rather than a character trait, it is a construal of some person or other sentient being as in distress or some significant deficiency. Being based on a concern for the sufferer's well-being, the construal is distressful to the subject and begets a consequent concern to alleviate the suffering or make up the deficiency, or at least to see it alleviated or made up. Thus the defining proposition for compassion is something like *It is important for S to be flourishing, but S is in distress or deficient in X way; may S's distress be relieved or S's deficiency made up.* Because of the concern on which it is based and the behavior that characteristically issues from it, the emotion of compassion counts as a form of love. Such compassion is thus a circumstantial construal – a construal of the object in terms of an "accidental" characteristic, namely its suffering or deficiency. In ordinary contemporary English, "sympathy" is a near synonym for "compassion" in the sense of an emotion. We speak of feeling sympathy for those who are grieving or suffering other adversities. Compassion as a trait is a disposition to feel compassion as an emotion and to act on it. The disposition is a concern that we might call benevolence.

Benevolence is a concern for the well-being of people and other sentient creatures, for their sake (not, say, as a means to something independent of their interests). It is consequently a disposition to take emotional pleasure in their well-being for their sake and to experience emotional distress about their suffering or deficiency for their sake. It is also, via these positive and negative emotions, a disposition to promote the well-being of such

---

[85] Such dispositional gratitude to *someone* differs from the virtue of gratitude, which is a high proneness to experience the emotion in a range of cases and toward a range of possible benefactors. For further discussion of gratitude as an emotion and as a virtue, see my paper "The Blessings of Gratitude: A Conceptual Analysis," in Robert Emmons and Michael McCullough (eds.), *The Psychology of Gratitude* (New York: Oxford University Press, 2002).

creatures. As such, benevolence is not itself an emotion, but is a readiness for a range of both positive and negative emotions. One can feel benevolent, but this is not an emotion based in benevolent concern, as are joy in the news of a healthy baby's birth or distress at bad news about a birth. Instead, this is a feeling of construed condition (see Section 2.2), usually with a note of self-congratulation. Benevolence is broader than attachment; one is usually benevolent toward persons to whom one is attached; but one may be benevolent also to one's "neighbor," toward all comers. The benevolent person acts benevolently toward particular persons rather than humanity in general, but it need not be in virtue of their particular attributes (*is mine, is beautiful, is Maria*) that particular persons become objects of benevolence; it may be in virtue of generic attributes such as *is human, is sentient*. If we want to say that benevolence is a construal or a disposition to construe, then such generic attributes are the terms of construal, and benevolence is not, like emotions, a construal that is *based on* a concern, but rather the construal is the *form of* the concern itself; the terms of the construal – *person, fellow creature, sentient* – are the terms in which this kind of being is of concern to the subject. Compassion in the trait sense is just a part of benevolence; it is benevolence insofar as it is directed at beings who are suffering or deficient. It is possible that some people's benevolence is actually partial in this sense, that they are moved more by human and animal distress than by human and animal flourishing. We might say that benevolence comes in various traditional versions, of which Christian agape is one.

"Mercy" is sometimes a synonym of "compassion," as when an order of nuns is named Sisters of Mercy, or one speaks of mercy killing. But another, perhaps more usual sense of the word denotes the state of affairs of an offender's receiving a less severe punishment than he or she deserves. The motive of such action may be strategic or "political" or self-serving in some way; to that extent we will deny that the act was motivated by mercy, however merciful the result of the action may be. What, then, is the motive characteristic of acts of mercy, and is it an emotion? It seems to me that the motive of such actions is compassion. It is an aversion, for the offender's sake, either to what he or she has already suffered, or to the punishment that would fulfill strict justice, or to the accumulation of both. In that case, while legal mercy is not an emotion, acts of legal mercy, insofar as they are true acts *of mercy*, are characteristically motivated by compassion.

A person can be fond of fondue, of waterskiing, of Karl Richter's interpretation of the Brandenburg Concerti, of a certain special uncle, and so on. To be fond of something is to prefer it, to be disposed to enjoy it, but in a sort of "esthetic" way. "Fond," like "prefer," suggests little pretension to the objective importance of the object and no very deep personal attachment. Of the kinds of attachment that I discussed in Sections 3.15b and 3.15c, it would be understatement with a comic tinge to speak of fondness: My fondness for Maria, Pierre's fondness for Hélène. "Passionately fond" sounds like a joke. In my quasi-technical sense of "concern," a fondness is a concern. That is, it can be the basis for emotions: I am delighted to hear that the menu includes fondue, or angry because my boss gave me a schedule that prevents my waterskiing, or disappointed to hear that the recording of the Brandenburg Concerti that we'll be using is not Richter's. Thus fondness is not an emotion. If, when we speak of *feeling* fond of that special uncle, we have any particular emotion in mind, my guess is that it is the enjoyment of being in his company or the excitement of anticipating his arrival rather than the disappointment or anger that are equally grounded in our fondness (preference). "I'm feeling so fond of Uncle Teddy," if it is ever said at all, is not a good substitute for saying, "I'm mad" or "I'm disappointed," even when the anger or disappointment is based on a fondness for Uncle Teddy.

3.16. DISORIENTATION

a. Surprise and Puzzlement

Some surprises are pleasant, others painful; still others are just surprises. Ralph Nickleby comments about Madeline Bray's response to an unwonted display of fatherly affection: "I saw a tear of surprise in her eye. There'll be a few more tears of surprise there before long, though of a different kind" (Charles Dickens, *Nicholas Nickleby*, Chapter 47, last paragraph). The phrase "tear of surprise" is surprising and puzzling, but the context resolves the puzzle: Madeline was not *just* surprised, but touched by her father's solicitude and affection. And the tears of surprise that are expected presently are tears of dismay and horror at being given in marriage to the hideous and evil old Mr. Arthur Gride.

Surprise is the mental state we are in when we are struck by a deviation from what we expected (on expectation, see Section 3.14b). Madeline is surprised by her father's concern that she is overtaxing herself because such solicitude is contrary to what she has come to expect of him. Madeline's surprise reflects a moral perception-readiness about her father. Such a readiness can also be toward oneself. Thus,

The most appalling feature of the morning after I nearly committed adultery was my lack of surprise. I was scared out of my wits, racked by regret and almost prostrated by shame, but a virtuous amazement was notably absent. For some time my life had resembled a ball of wool kidnapped by a kitten, and now, after the preliminary unravelling, I was apparently experiencing the start of the inevitable tangled mess (Susan Howatch, *Ultimate Prizes*, the opening paragraph).

Neville Aysgarth has several virtuous emotions with regard to his near act, but thinks a better person would also have been surprised that he could come so close to committing adultery: A good person would expect better of himself. He explains that he already had indications his life was getting out of control. His lack of surprise is testimony to the advanced progress of his weakness and moral disorientation.

As these examples indicate, surprise can be mingled with other emotions. Perhaps all the morally interesting cases are like this. But surprise by itself is not evaluative, as fear, hope, anger, and envy are. Its lack of hedonic tone goes with the lack of the usual kind of basis; surprise is a construal, but not of the situation as satisfying or contravening any concern. It is a construal of the situation as contravening expectations. I look out, and to my surprise, the squirrel sitting on the limb outside my window is white as snow. I have no *stake* in squirrels' being gray or red, but I strongly expect them to be; thus my surprise. If I *wanted* to see a white squirrel, I would perhaps be delighted to see this one. If I thought white squirrels a bad omen, and thus wanted *not* to see one, I might experience anxiety. Delight and anxiety can take the form of happy and unhappy surprises. But no such concern is required for surprise at the white squirrel; it is enough that I expect squirrels to be red or gray.

Because surprise is not based on a concern, it also has no consequent concern; it does not motivate actions [though it does sometimes precipitate behavior – e.g., the characteristic facial expression, the double take (on the distinction between action and behavior, see Section 2.9b)]. It may seem to motivate investigative actions, but this appearance is dispelled if we distinguish surprise from puzzlement, which it sometimes arouses. Surprised that the squirrel is white, I start being puzzled when I get the urge to explain this fact or explain it away. I may then undertake to verify that it is really a squirrel, or read up on albinism. Puzzlement is based on a concern to understand, and is thus a discomfort with paradoxes or unexplained facts. So it fits better than surprise does the model of an emotion as a concern-based construal. But surprising things do not always puzzle us. Sometimes the explanation is as patent as the fact (I can be surprised at the white squirrel in my tree while fully informed about albino squirrels); sometimes explanation is not in the least called for.

Astonishment seems to be intense or dramatic surprise. One can be surprised by relatively insignificant contraventions of expectations (or contraventions of rather insignificant expectations); one can also be mildly surprised. But one cannot be astonished at insignificant contraventions of expectations (or contraventions of rather insignificant expectations); and to be mildly astonished is to be pretty intensely surprised. Some surprise is astonishment, and all astonishment is surprise. The issue of the intensity of surprise calls for a refinement of my denial that surprise is a concern-based construal. While expectations are not themselves concerns, some expectations are more significant than others to the subject of surprise, and this significance is both a factor in the intensity of the surprise and something like a concern.

The reader will remember that I analyzed the strength of emotions (Section 2.10b) as "determined by the strength of the underlying concern, the vivacity of the construal, and the rate of impingement of the other terms of the construal on the concern." Similarly, we might analyze the strength of surprise as determined by the strength of the expectation (the probability estimate, so to speak), the vivacity of the construal of the situation as contravening the expectation, and the rate of impingement of the construal on the expectation. But what is the rate of impingement in this case? I think we have to see that while surprise is not *based* on concerns, but rather on expectations, the strength of something like what I have been calling a concern is a factor determining the intensity of this emotion. While I need not care what color a squirrel is, to be surprised when I encounter a white one, squirrel color does need to be the sort of thing that *interests* me. And in general I will be more surprised by contraventions of expectations about things that interest me more than by contraventions that interest me less. Consider a surprise party. You are visiting a friend, expecting a quiet evening of conversation *à deux*, when the doorbell rings and a group of your friend's friends pile into the house laden with refreshments to celebrate the acceptance of your friend's manuscript by a major university press. Both of you are surprised (you had equally firm expectations for the evening; and you see equally clearly what is happening), but it is reasonable to suppose that your surprise will be less intense than that of your friend, who is more "interested" in the case.[86] One might think that what seems to be the greater intensity of your friend's surprise in this case is just the presence or greater intensity of other emotions such as joy, gratitude, irritation, embarrassment, and the like; she is not feeling any more *surprise* than you. No doubt it is difficult to separate the intensity of the surprise from the other emotions; but I think it is plausible that the surprise itself is more intense because of the friend's greater "interest" in the case.

We might distinguish bipolar from unipolar concerns. The concerns on which the vast majority of standard human emotions are based are bipolar. If I am attached to somebody, I am concerned *for* certain states of affairs with respect to him and so *against* others. If I desire that *p*, then I am averse to not-*p*. Interests, by contrast, are unipolar. I can be interested in a baseball game without caring who wins; the interest keeps my attention on the game, even if I have no desires with respect to its outcome. As long as the game keeps "moving," my interest is satisfied. In this case I can be surprised by its outcome (in case it is not what I expected), but without any of the paradigm case emotions. I can be interested in the color of the squirrel without caring which color it is. An interest, in this special sense, is satisfied not by one state or another of the object, but by the object; I am satisfied by being involved with it perceptually and perhaps otherwise. Interests and bipolar concerns are connected in at least the following ways: We become interested

---

[86] I owe the example to Maria Roberts.

in *kinds* of objects, the particular instances of which we care about. Interests are involved not only in surprise, but in such other mental responses as amazement and amusement, as we will see.

We are sometimes surprised by things we are not very concerned about, but we must be interested enough in them to pay attention to them or at least to have our attention aroused by anomalies in them. Things we do not notice will not surprise us. I may not care whether the tree whose absence on my walk surprises me is there or not. But expectation itself seems to imply some interest. And most of what surprises us does so because it concerns us. Still, surprise differs from the paradigm case emotions in that what the construal impinges on is not some concern, but some expectation. Let us say, then, that the defining proposition for surprise is X *deviates strikingly from my prior expectation.* The defining proposition for puzzlement is X *is paradoxical (or in need of explanation); may I have an explanation of X.*

"Amazement" and "surprise" are sometimes used interchangeably, but careful modern English distinguishes two emotion types here. Most notably, amazement does not involve a straightforward contravention of expectations. "I never cease to be amazed" at the beauty and depth and inventiveness of Bach's music; but having listened to it now for almost sixty years I am hardly surprised by these qualities. We might say that amazement is subjunctive surprise: The beauty, depth, and inventiveness are not the sort of thing one *would* expect. And when I experience amazement, again and again, despite my confident expectation of hearing something great, that extraordinariness of Bach's music strikes me again with the force of perception. Amazement, when it is not surprise, is pretty much the same as awe (see Section 3.11a for a defining proposition). One can be amazed at great evil as well as at great good: "I never cease to be amazed at the cruelty of which humans are capable." In this sense, amazement is not evaluative of its object. And yet, one must care about greatness (whether good *or* bad) to be awed or amazed; and this unipolar concern corresponds to the interest that is involved in surprise. A difference between amazement and awe seems to be that, in general, awe construes its object as of greater extraordinariness than amazement does.

b. Amusement[87]

I shall now discuss amusement as a response to comical presentations – jokes as well as incidents of real life and of more extended fictional narratives that we regard as funny. Like surprise, amusement in this sense of the word sometimes has marks analogous to some of the paradigm case emotions: a typical

---

[87] Some of the material in this subsection is borrowed from my papers "Is Amusement An Emotion?" *American Philosophical Quarterly* **25** (1988): 269–274 and "Humor and the Virtues" *Inquiry* **31** (1988): 127–149.

facial expression, convulsion of the chest, and the vocalizations of laughter. (In milder forms it may provoke only a smile or no behavior at all.) But even when it lacks those marks, it is a construal: Someone for whom the comical situation does not come into focus *as* comical will not have the characteristic experience. Thus jokes are more than "stimuli," and it takes more than knowing what the point of a joke is to find it funny. Unlike surprise and like some of the paradigm case emotions, amusement is intrinsically pleasant. But the pleasure of it seems quite different from that of the paradigm pleasant emotions, which lend themselves to analysis as satisfactions of concerns. Like surprise, amusement is not based on any bipolar concern about its object; instead, it is based on a sense of the normal – a readiness analogous to (but not the same as) an expectation. Anger, jealousy, and fear, being based on concerns, move their subjects to particular kinds of intentional actions; but amusement, like surprise, seems to have only behavioral marks.

Amusement is an emotionlike pleasure taken in the perception of a certain range of incongruities as such. I say "as such" to distinguish amusement from pleasure taken in paradoxes as puzzles to be resolved.[88] Thus when Harry Frankfurt publishes an article entitled "On Bullshit"[89] and, using the methods of analytic philosophy, carefully distinguishes bullshitting from lying, bluffing, and humbug as to the exact character of their respective "misrepresentational intent," and undertakes to answer the question, Why is there so much bullshit?, the impression is amusing because of the incongruity between the academic style and setting of the paper and the word's normal associations. And it seems that we delight in such incongruities, not because of anything they produce or anything we can do with them; we just delight in *them*.

However, incongruity is amusing only if not too painful. To continue the barnyard theme: My mother was not amused, despite the incongruity, when she spied my father lying atop the manure pile with one arm plunged in to the elbow, for she thought he might be dead or injured. Tragedy takes all the fun out of incongruity. When it was discovered that he lay there quite happily with a copy of *Prevention* magazine open before him trying to relieve his arthritis in the heat of the wild bacterial action below, the story was good for some family amusement because of the incongruousness of this medical expedient. Some humor goes too far in the tragic or dark direction and thus is not amusing to those for whom this painful aspect of the communication stands out. For some people, jokes involving teenage suicide or

---

[88] John Morreall distinguishes these in "Funny Ha-Ha, Funny Strange, and Other Reactions to Incongruity," in John Morreall (ed.), *The Philosophy of Laughter and Humor* (Albany: State University of New York Press, 1987).

[89] *The Importance of What We Care About: Philosophical Essays* (Cambridge: Cambridge University Press, 1988), pp. 117–133.

parents beating their children with coat hangers are not amusing, no matter how well crafted they are to bring out situational incongruities. We might speculate that people who are amused by such incongruous presentations are insensitive to the tragedy they represent. Other kinds of negativity that, if too powerfully salient to the subject, can prevent an incongruity from amusing are the disgusting and the immoral. There may be others.

Roger Scruton has argued that the enjoyment of incongruities as such is not even a necessary condition for being amused by humor.

> The caricature amuses, not because it does not fit Mrs. Thatcher, but because it does fit her, all too well . . . satire at least possesses, when successful, the quality of accuracy, and satire has its equivalent in everyday life, when a character acts true to himself. What amuses us, it could be said, is the total congruence between the idea of the man and his action.[90]

Scruton has not looked hard enough for the perceptions of incongruity in the kinds of amusement he mentions. It is true that a caricature is not good unless it looks like its subject, but perfect congruence in itself is never amusing. A perfect-likeness photograph of Ronald Reagan in one of his most normal poses will not be amusing unless something is added to it by a humorist – a comment, a subtitle – that renders visible an incongruity in the pose, or in something with which the pose can be associated (say, the incongruity of having a grade-B movie actor for president, or a president who understands only the most simplistic memos on international affairs). However accurate a caricature may be, it must also highlight some feature that, when highlighted, looks incongruous. Looking at Mrs. Thatcher through the caricature, one sees her swooped-up hairdo as an incongruity. When Garrison Keillor gently satirizes the small-town Minnesotans, his characterization is funny, it is true, only because we respond with something like "Yes, that's how they are." But how they are is just what, with the help of the comic characterization, looks incongruous to us sophisticates who have escaped all that.

Another limit on the incongruity, and one that Scruton's comment highlights, is that the incongruity cannot be too extreme. Just as the perfect-likeness photograph cannot, without help, be humorously perceived, neither can the incongruity be so great that the ensemble completely lacks verisimilitude. If Reagan has a dainty nose but a caricaturist gives him a very large one, the incongruity is even greater than if she had exaggerated some feature already prominent; but the effect is very likely not comical, because the incongruity has overshot the bounds. It is partly because, as Frankfurt's clever article makes clear, the concept of bullshit does have enough depth and complication to make an adroit philosophical

[90] "Laughter," *Proceedings of the Aristotelian Society,* Supplement Volume **56** (1982): 197–212; 202; reprinted in *ibid.,* p. 161.

analysis of it possible, that the article is so amusing. We might say that the incongruity becomes "invisible" if it is too extreme: It can still be conceptualized and thus understood as an incongruity, but to be amusing it needs to strike the subject with the immediacy of perception.

But even if we limit the objects of amusement to pleasant incongruities that are neither tragic nor extreme to the point of lacking verisimilitude, we do not have a sufficient condition for objects of amusement. Not all enjoyment of middle-range nontragic incongruities as such is amusement. Mike Martin has pointed out that we enjoy the incongruities in some of Picasso's paintings, or the dramatic ironies in *Oedipus Rex*, and enjoy them as such, yet without finding them funny.[91] Can we specify more closely what kind of incongruities are the object of amusement? Clyde Lee Miller, examining ironic incidents such as shouting at one's children to make them quiet, or the wealthiest woman in the country club winning the state lottery, speaks rightly of their "appropriate impropriety." But when he tries to specify the required appropriateness, he narrows it artificially:

> What eventuates may counter conventional or normal expectations, but it also functions as the "just deserts," whether good or bad, of those attempting, awaiting or just hoping for and believing in the opposite. Normal outcomes have been thwarted, only to have "poetic justice" (which may prosaically reward as well as punish) done.[92]

A kind of justice is indeed wrought in one of Miller's examples:

> Most blind dates she had were real "dogs" so she did not want another one. She got her roommate to go instead and he was this beautiful guy.

One could say that in ironically missing the beautiful guy she got what she deserved because she gave up too soon on blind dates, or was too cautious, or was unjustly trying to foist a bad situation on her roommate. But it is hard to see the justice in a rich lady winning the lottery or a man yelling at his children to quiet them. In the case of the yelling father the congruousness of the incongruity, and part of what makes it amusing, is that this behavior is so typical of parents. Similarly, being rich and winning the lottery are the same kind of thing. It would not be ironic for the richest lady also to outlive all her contemporaries, because longevity is not connected directly enough with being rich.

Why are the blind date story and Frankfurt's article funny, but Picasso's incongruous (yet clearly recognizable and nontragic) paintings are not? I am sorry to say that at present I do not know how to specify adequately the form of the construal that is amusement. So I am even less ready to hazard a defining proposition for amusement than I have been for the majority of

---

[91] "Humor and the Aesthetic Enjoyment of Incongruities," *British Journal of Aesthetics* **23** (1983): 74–85; reprinted in *ibid.*

[92] "Ironic or Not?" *American Philosophical Quarterly* **13** (1976): 309–313; 310.

the emotion types. The best I can do at present is to say that to be amused is to construe a situation pleasantly as having an appropriate impropriety or limited incongruity that is not tragic or anyway not very tragic.

It is clear, however, that amusement is a kind of construal. A deft analysis of the concept of bullshit would not be amusing in the way Frankfurt's is if the word did not constantly induce us to hear the discussion in terms of something normally foreign to the academic essay. The image of my father lying on the manure pile amuses, in part, because I grasp it in terms of the background of canons of human propriety that exclude manure piles as reclining places for persons of dignity. The image of my father's hand plunged twenty inches deep in hot dung takes on a further amusing quality when I construe it as a medical procedure, with medicine's associations with white linen, sterile instruments, and high costs. So amusement is a kind of construal. But I have suggested that it is a bit like surprise in not being a concern-based construal. Let us explore this aspect further.

John Morreall tells us that emotions all involve a pro or con attitude to the object of the emotion, whereas amusement does not require a pro or con attitude to what is amusing.[93] To feel proud of my pet chimpanzee I have to have a pro attitude toward her (construe her as excellent in some way that I care about, and as conferring some positive status on me), but to be amused at some chimpanzees in a cage I need not love them or care about something on which they may impinge. But do we really take *no* pro attitude toward chimpanzees when we are amused by their antics? They waddle, swing from branches by their long arms, irritate one another, hug and play with one another, and make "faces." Put together, these things compose an amusing scene to many of the somewhat brighter primates outside the cage, because we see them as incongruous humans. Their bodies and movements resemble our own enough to incline us to see them in human terms; but as humans they are bizarre, and yet in an untragic way. Is there no pro attitude here?

Our amusement at chimpanzees is not based on any care we may have regarding them (wishing them well, wishing them ill), or concern about something they might do to us (bite us) or for us (make us money). In this sense, amusement at chimpanzees, unlike compassion for a suffering one or fear of an attacking one, is "disinterested." But in another way it is quite literally "interested," and this makes for a certain similarity between amusement and the paradigm case emotions.

Just as we cannot have emotions if we do not care (pro or con) about anything on which the terms of the construal impinge, so an incongruity does not come into comic focus for us if the matter containing the incongruity in no way interests us. Part of the reason chimpanzees amuse us is that

---

[93] John Morreall, "Humor and Emotion" *American Philosophical Quarterly* **20** (1983): 297–304; reprinted in *The Philosophy of Laughter and Humor*, pp. 214ff.

our attention is naturally attracted to things that resemble us. Furthermore, just as the intensity of our concern with something predicts (other things being equal) the intensity of whatever emotion is based on it, the intensity of interest in something predicts (all else being equal) the intensity of our amusement at it. In general, members of my own family find the story of Dad on the manure pile more amusing than would nonmembers, and friends find it more amusing than would strangers, and strangers with fathers find it more amusing than would fatherless strangers, and human beings find it more amusing than would, say, Martians who can understand our language (and thus grasp the incongruity) but somehow function without fathers or manure piles. This decrease, from group to group, of amusability is a function of decreasing interest in the subject matter of the story and consequent decreasing impact of the incongruity. We meet daily with incongruous juxtapositions of things that do not in the least amuse us; and one ground of their failure to do so is that we take no interest in them, or no interest in that aspect of them in whose terms we perceive them as incongruous. Morreall goes too far when he says that "amusement... involves a non-practical attitude toward some present or non-present... situation, that need have no relation at all to us."[94] He is right that the kind of interest that is basic to amusement is not practical in the sense of motivating action (that is what I have called a bipolar concern). But amusement does depend on our attention's being engaged; and this in turn requires a kind of interest that we might call esthetic or curious (a unipolar concern).

Interest, in this sense, and concern are not just analogous; they are psychologically connected. Usually our disposition to pay attention to something is grounded in our concern with it or with something on which it impinges. Someone is interested in the quality of education in her school district because she cares about her children's education, and she is concerned about that because she loves her children. It is plausible that we are interested in chimpanzees because we care about human beings (at least ourselves). We do not much notice things unconnected with what we care about.

Morreall comments that "Babies enjoy peekaboo only with familiar faces of people they feel *attached to*."[95] Mere familiarity does not seem to be enough. Michael Clark says, "Why are we amused by the behavior of our children and not by the same behavior in other people's children? Presumably because our own children are more endearing to us. Many jokes are effective because of their topicality and are completely unfunny when their references cease to be topical."[96] Bullshit is a funnier topic than many because it borders on the embarrassing. Damasio's "Elliot" seems to confirm my general claim about the difference between amusement and the paradigm

[94] *The Philosophy of Laughter and Humor*, p. 217.
[95] *Ibid.*, p. 135; my italics.
[96] "Humor and Incongruity," in *ibid.*, p. 141.

case emotions, while calling for a qualification of the speculation of the present paragraph. Elliot, who because of his brain damage was generally flat of affect, was nevertheless "quietly humorous."[97] I argued in Section 2.7e that Elliot's frontal lobe damage deprived him of the capacity for longer-term concerns. This explains, on my account of the paradigm case emotions, why Elliot does not have them. The fact that he retains the capacity for amusement suggests that amusement does not depend on *such* concerns. Elliot was still intelligent, and thus could appreciate incongruities, and he had enough capacity to be interested in things to "interrupt the activity he had engaged, to turn to something he found more captivating. . . ."[98] Perhaps we should say that while in neurologically normal people interests are held in place, in large part, by bipolar concerns, people like "Elliot" show that the capacity for interest is not wholly dependent on the capacity for concerns.

The difference between an interest and a concern implies another difference between amusement and the standard emotions, with respect to the roles that pro and con attitudes play in them. The concern basic to an emotion is typically connected logically to its consequent desire if it has one (see Section 2.9c). Furthermore, the affective tone (pleasure or discomfort) of the emotion is transparently connected with the care on which the emotion is based, given the construal. But the interest that is instrumental in cases of amusement does not generate, by the logic of the construal, any desire; nor is the connection between the interest and the pleasure of the amusement transparent. Compare the motivating anxiety my mother felt upon seeing Dad lying on the manure pile with the amusement we experienced in this connection, and the pleasure of her joy at noting the open copy of *Prevention* magazine. Indeed, it might be better not to say that amusement is *based on* the interest; instead, it is based on a sense of the normal (just as surprise is based on an expectation and amazement is based on a would-be expectation), and the interest is a fixation of attention on the incongruity.

A final difference between amusement and the paradigm cases of emotions is their relation to beliefs. Throughout this study I have argued against theories that claim that emotions either are, or necessarily involve, judgments. But in the central cases of rational anger, fear, hope, compassion, and many other emotions, the propositions in terms of which the various foci of the emotion are construed are taken by the subject to be true. Encountering a person who does not believe some of the propositions in terms of which he hopes or fears or is angry, we are usually inclined to think him irrational. But someone who does not believe the propositions of a joke he heartily enjoys, or a person who laughs at the antics of chimpanzees without thinking that they really are human beings, is under no suspicion of irrationality on that account. Indeed, the concept of irrational amusement

[97] *Descartes' Error*, p. 44.
[98] *Ibid.*, p. 36.

seems to lack application (though the concept of perverse amusement has it).

Philosophers have sometimes made it a condition of amusement that the comic element in the representation be *unexpected* by the subject. Thus René Descartes says, "when it springs up unexpectedly (*inopinément*), the surprise of Wonder (*la surprise de l'admiration*) causes us to break into laughter."[99] Immanuel Kant says that "In the exhibition involved in jest, the understanding, failing to find what it expected (*das Erwartete*), suddenly (*plötzlich*) relaxes, so that we feel the effect of this slackening in the body by the vibration of our organs...."[100] Arthur Schopenhauer says, "In every case, laughter results from nothing but the suddenly (*plötzlich*) perceived incongruity between a concept and the real objects that had been thought through it in some relation.... All laughter is therefore occasioned by a paradoxical, and hence unexpected (*unerwarteten*), subsumption...."[101] But the fact that we are amused and laugh at our own jokes and the "old" jokes of others, and that we find familiar incongruities funny, suggests that we need not be surprised by the comical aspect to experience amusement. And it is not plausible to suppose that we continue to find a familiar joke amusing only if, each time we laugh, we discover in it some new dimension of incongruity.[102]

I think that in speaking about surprise, these authors are trying to get at a feature of amusement that I call freshness. It might also be called punch, or vividness, or even vision. For when we are amused by an incongruity, it "lives" for us in an especially fresh or vivid way. It is this that a joke loses for us when it gets "old." We do not necessarily cease to know, believe, or judge that an incongruity is being presented to us. We may even be able to give an accurate account of it to someone who wants to know what others are laughing at, but for us it has become stale.

The jokester's art is to find ways to make incongruities vivid for us, and she has a number of them: facial expression, bodily attitude, vocal inflection, stress, choice of vocabulary, and so on. One important expedient is "setup": The jokester has to prepare her hearer for the punch line, to give him a context in which the punch line punches him. One important strategy of setup is to minimize the hearer's "expectation" of the punch line. I put "expectation" in scare quotes because it is not literally expectation that is minimized here; if the hearer has heard the joke before, he may expect exactly the punch line, and yet the setup remains an important condition for

---

[99] *Passions of the Soul*, translated by Stephen H. Voss (Indianapolis: Hackett, 1989), article 178; see also article 181.

[100] *Critique of Judgment*, translated by Werner S. Pluhar (Indianapolis: Hackett, 1987), Section 54.

[101] *The World as Will and Representation*, translated by E. F. J. Payne (New York: Dover, 1969), Section 13; see also John Morreall, *Taking Laughter Seriously* (Albany: State University of New York Press, 1983), Chapter 5.

[102] See Morreal, *ibid.*, p. 50.

his appreciating the joke. I suggest that it is the importance of setup for the effectiveness of many jokes, and the similarity between what is accomplished here and setting somebody up for a surprise, that has led people to think surprise essential to amusement. What *is* essential, however, is what setup is intended to effect, and which in the case of much amusement is fostered by genuine surprise, namely the freshness or liveliness of the perception of incongruity.[103]

We have seen both similarities and differences between amusement and the paradigm types of emotion. Fear and amusement are both construals, typically (but not necessarily) involving involuntary or half-voluntary bodily changes and characterized by "affect" (positive in amusement, negative in fear). The interest on which amusement depends is analogous to and connected with, but different from, the concerns on which emotions are typically based; the terms of the amused construal do not impinge on the interest in the way the terms of a standard emotional construal impinge on the underlying concern. Lacking a basic bipolar concern, amusement has no consequent concern either, and thus it does not motivate actions in the way many of the paradigm emotions do. Nor is the affect in amusement connected logically to the interest via the terms of the construal. The rational person is not at all presumed to believe whatever propositions may supply the terms of his amusement. This mix of similarities and differences explains, I think, our ambivalence about classing amusement as an emotion. If we wish to write a defining proposition for amusement, it would seem to be something like this: *X, which is at most minimally tragic, disgusting, immoral, or otherwise painful, appears in a delightfully incongruous aspect.* This defining proposition is inadequate in at least two ways. Crucially, it does not distinguish delightfully incongruous representations that are amusing from ones like the Picasso paintings that are not. Also, it employs "delightfully," which itself seems to be an emotion word. "Delightfully" needs to be included here, but not in the defining proposition of positive standard emotions, because in the latter, but not in amusement, the positive character of the mental state is a function of the satisfaction of the basic concern(s), and that satisfaction is indicated in other parts of the defining proposition.

c. Startle

I have entitled Section 3.16 "Disorientation" because in the case of each emotion type treated here some "orientation" – an expectation, a would-be expectation, a sense of the normal, a sense of what makes sense, an accustomed level of sensory stimulus – is contravened, and a mental state ensues that is marked by a departure from the presupposed orientation. Insofar as

---

[103] For further discussion of freshness, see Karl Pfeifer, "Laughter, Freshness, and Titillation," *Inquiry* **40** (1998): 307–322.

the state has a situational object, this object is construed as departing from the presupposed orientation. I say "insofar as it has a situational object" in introducing the startle response because, though it has the character of a departure from an orientation, the startle response lacks a situational object. Carney Landis and William Hunt stress the difference between the startle stimulus and the object of a fear response, as perceived by the subject:

When we speak of the startle pattern as a general flexion response it should not be considered a directional response involving movement *away from* the stimulus. The response is quite independent of the sound source, and the flexion is in no way changed by the direction from which the stimulus comes.[104]

In being thus "unperceptual," startle is more like a bodily reflex than like the paradigm emotions to which this book gives chief attention. And yet, like some of the emotions and unlike the knee-jerk reflex, it is conditionable (pp. 52–59) and can vary with expectation.

Startle is an involuntary bodily reaction to the sudden onset of a strong sensory stimulus such as a gunshot or a dash of ice water on one's back. Landis and Hunt used high-speed cinematography to demonstrate that the startle response in human beings is a complex stereotyped pattern of bodily movements. A complete startle response

includes blinking of the eyes, head movement forward, a characteristic facial expression, raising and drawing forward of the shoulders, abduction of the upper arms, bending of the elbows, pronation of the lower arms, flexion of the fingers, forward movement of the trunk, contraction of the abdomen, and bending of the knees (p. 21).

This is a list of elements comprising what Landis and Hunt call "a complete startle response." Not every element is present in every case of startle, but the eyeblink is virtually invariable and the head movement and facial expression are very common. Compared to most emotions, the reaction has very short duration, lasting less than a half second in most cases (p. 27).

Landis and Hunt found that habituating their subjects to the gunshots reduced the extent of the startle reaction in some subjects, but did not obliterate it in any (p. 32f). Their photography showed that even expert marksmen of many years' experience pulling their own triggers startled very briefly at the sound of their guns, all of them exhibiting the eyeblink with every shot and most of them the head movement as well. They were surprised, upon viewing the films, to see that they "made faces" when they shot. Expectation of the stimulus reduced the extent of the startle response in some subjects (though not all), but the case of the marksmen shows that unexpectedness is not a necessary condition of the response, as it is of surprise.

---

[104] *The Startle Pattern* (New York: Farrar and Rinehart, 1939; reprint New York: Johnson Reprint, 1968), p. 31, italics in the original.

Not having a situational object, startle is not a construal, not even to the extent that highly stereotyped animal fear responses to predators are construals (see Section 2.5e) because even in cases in which the fear response is a function of the less discriminating "older" part of the brain, the animal is discriminating to some extent – distinguishing predator-potential situations from safe ones. By comparison the startle-stimulus is situationally blank, like a tap on the knee. The only dimensions of articulation that it possesses are suddenness (rise time) and intensity. Startle, like other bodily reflexes, does not have a defining proposition. Nor is startle concern-based, any more than the knee jerk. Having no basic concern, the startle response also does not motivate any kind of action; it is purely behavioral.

Surprise and amusement, though they are not concern-based and deviate in related ways from the paradigm case emotions, belong among the emotions that are of interest to the moral psychologist. They are capable of great sophistication and vary with the moral character of their subject. None of this is true of the startle response.

Is startle an emotion type? It fits poorly the analysis I have been promoting of most of the main human emotion types. But whether it belongs among the emotions is largely a question of our interests and the groupings of things that go with those interests (see Sections 1.3, 1.5a–e, and 3.1c). For someone who stresses the behavioral and neurological concomitants of emotions, the features of the startle response may make it an important emotion. It has even been proposed as providing the central paradigm of emotion.[105] But for the explorer of emotions in their relevance to the moral psychology of the virtues and vices, startle is far indeed from the central paradigm cases. The disposition to startle does not seem to be any more interesting for the moral psychologist than the disposition to shiver.

3.17. TRAITS AND EMOTIONS

As I noted in Sections 2.1 and 3.1a, trait terms such as "vanity," "avarice," "indolence," and "ambition" sometimes appear in lists of emotion types. Gilbert Ryle, trying to show that emotions do not require feelings of emotions, comments about the supposed emotion of vanity:

> To put it quite dogmatically, the vain man never feels vain. Certainly, when thwarted, he feels acute dudgeon and when unexpectedly successful, he feels buoyant. There is no special thrill or pang which we call a 'feeling of vanity'. Indeed, if there were such a recognisable specific feeling, and the vain man was constantly experiencing it, he would be the first instead of the last person to recognise how vain he was.[106]

---

[105] See Jenefer Robinson, "Startle," *Journal of Philosophy* **92** (1995): 53–74.
[106] *The Concept of Mind*, p. 87.

Ryle admits that some felt emotions are *symptomatic* of vanity, without stop-
ping to consider that vanity itself is better thought of not as an emotion, but
as a trait that has emotional indicators. Vanity is what in this book is called
a concern (in particular, it is an excessive concern to be well-regarded by
other people, for the social importance their regard confers on oneself),
and as such it can be expected to issue in a variety of positive and negative
emotions, depending on how the vain person construes himself and his situations in the vicissitudes of his life. Anthony Kenny comments on Ryle's
comment:

> This argument appears to rest on a confusion between feeling vain and having vain
> feelings. To feel vain is to feel that one is vain. It is possible, therefore, to have a
> vain feeling without feeling vain, in a way in which it is not possible to have a hungry
> feeling without feeling hungry. A woman, surveying her face in the mirror, may bask
> cosily in the thought 'how beautiful I am!' . . . But it is not necessary that she should
> recognise this feeling as a vain feeling; and only if she does will she, then or later,
> feel vain.[107]

Kenny is giving the name "vain feelings" to vanity's emotional indicators,
which, as he correctly notes, do not themselves identify the subject of the
emotions as vain in the sense that the material propositions of the vain
emotions include a description of the subject as vain. But a person who
understands, even if only intuitively, that emotions indicate traits may very
well recognize himself as vain *by* his feeling, say, of acute dudgeon at being
thwarted in his excessive efforts to be well-regarded by others for the sake
of the social importance their recognition confers on him. Then he will
perhaps have *another* emotion that we might call, with Kenny, "feeling vain,"
and this emotion's material proposition will include a clause to the effect
that the subject is vain.

But it will probably not do to suppose that this feeing vain is a distinct
emotion type, for it is very likely to be a case of disappointment (in case one
has been trying to overcome one's vanity and now sees that the efforts have
been less successful than one hoped) or shame (in case one sets considerable store with being unvain and considers vanity a disgrace) or pride (in
the unlikely case that one regards vanity as a feather in one's cap) or another
emotion of some rather standard type. Which of the reflexive emotions one
feels about being vain will depend on one's concerns with respect to being
vain, and how one construes one's vanity. But neither of these ways that
vanity can be involved with the emotions justifies supposing that vanity *is* a
type of emotion.

In Section 2.2 I identified a class of feelings that I called "feelings of
construed condition" or "feelings of self-estimate." The emotions about
one's vanity, as occasioned by emotions indicative of one's vanity, would

---

[107] *Action, Emotion, and Will*, p. 15.

all be feelings of self-estimate (provided the subject was conscious of them). In that earlier discussion, however, I entertained the possibility that there might be types of feeling of self-estimate that did not coincide with any of the named emotion categories. With respect to vocabulary, these emotions would be more like beliefs and desires, which we identify by specifying what is believed or desired (see Section 3.1a) – thus feeling triumphant, feeling awkward, and so on. Might there be an analogous feeling of vanity – that is, one that did not get subsumed under another category such as shame or pride? I suppose this is possible. If so, the existence of this category as a separate emotion type would seem to depend on its not being assimilable to such standard case emotions as shame and pride, but also on the social and psychological importance and salience, to some community, of vanity as a personal attribute.

These comments about vanity can be transferred to any number of other traits. On the same basis we might identify special emotion types of feeling avaricious, feeling righteous, feeling ambitious, feeling indolent, feeling patriotic, and so on. These will have the best claim to separate type status if they have instances that are not subsumable under other, more standard emotion categories and if the communities in which they are identified are particularly concerned about the attributed trait. However, it is clear that the emotions so identified are not the same as the traits that the subjects of these emotions construe themselves as possessing.

3.18. CONCLUSION

In the present chapter I have surveyed a representative sample of the kinds of states of persons that have been called emotions. One purpose has been to test my proposal that we think of emotions as concern-based construals and to test it against a broad enough range of examples to avoid the selectivity that makes so many "theories" of emotion initially plausible but finally unsustainable. Treated as such a test, this analytic survey has shown that a number of items that have been called emotions deviate, in one way or another, from the proposed paradigm. The startle response is not a construal; it is more like a bodily reflex. Surprise, amusement, and some related states of mind are construals but not concern-based. Love, in one sense of the word, is a concerned construal, but the construal does not seem to be *based on* any concern; it seems instead to *be* the concern. Vanity and other traits have been called emotions, for reasons that become clear on reflection.

I have tried to be very liberal and nonstipulative in my use of "emotion" here, but I must admit sympathy of intuition with some theorists who want to deny that the startle reflex and perhaps even amusement at jokes, are emotions. They do not seem to be at the center of most people's concept of emotion, even if people can sometimes be caught calling them emotions. So I do not claim that all emotions are concern-based construals, and thus the paradigm is just that: not a theory, but a suggestive paradigm. It does, however, lend itself beautifully to a rich analysis and understanding of the vast majority of those adult human mental states that are indisputably emotions, and it throws light, by comparison and contrast, on the items that deviate from the paradigm. It is also a subtle tool for the work of moral psychology.

A second purpose of the chapter has been to provide a fairly detailed account of the structure of many emotion types. The analyses bring out the rich variety of human emotions and begin to show the many parallels and interconnections among them. I have thought this intrinsically interesting and interesting for moral psychology.

Third, although I myself have offered a particular organization of the discussion of the emotion types, as reflected in the section headings of this chapter, I have hoped to bring out the variety of possible ways of dividing up the human emotional territory, as a way of establishing the interest relativity of any scheme of "basic emotions." Yet, in the case of some emotion types, such as anger and fear, I have also tried to show that some anthropologists' efforts to show that emotion types vary culturally are overblown. Emotions do vary in many ways from society to society, but if we take my proposal that emotion *type* is best construed as given in the emotion's defining proposition, then it seems that the anthropological studies that I have sampled do not refute the claim that such emotions as anger and fear are cross-culturally universal. Another value of the paradigm offered in this book is the framework it provides for a more fine-grained analysis than anthropologists have so far offered of cross-cultural emotional similarities and differences (see Section 3.3c for a summary).

The remaining chapter of this volume begins to broach the moral psychology of the emotions proper by exploring the relationships between emotions and feelings of emotions, especially as these bear on selfhood and self-knowledge.

4

The Play of Emotional Feelings

4.1. EMOTIONAL ERROR

In Section 2.2 I noted that when philosophers distinguish emotions from feelings, the feelings they usually have in mind are the sensations of body states that typically accompany some strong emotions: muscular tightness in face and neck and arms, goose pimples, abdominal perturbations, and so on. I agreed that *such* feelings are not emotions, and was led into the exposition of my basic account of emotions by identifying a kind of feeling that is very far from being a bodily sensation, namely feelings of triumph, of awkwardness, of having been ripped off, and so on. These feelings of states or qualities of the self I called feelings of construed condition. This observation gave us the concept of a kind of feeling that is, for ordinary purposes, indistinguishable from emotion. It is this concept of a feeling of *an emotion* – and not that of a sensation that may or may not *accompany* an emotion – that justifies the interchangeability in many ordinary language contexts of "emotion" and "feeling."

Robert Kraut once tried out the thesis that emotions are feelings in a certain kind of context: "Just as a piece of wood, when caught up in the appropriate conventions, qualifies as a pawn, a certain feeling, when occupying a specifiable position relative to the causal order and the order of social practices and communal norms, qualifies as an emotion."[1] In the context of his proposal, Kraut seems to assume that feelings are something like bare sensations which thus need a "context" if they are to be identified as, for example, feelings of fear or indignation. But in the end he admits that the proposal will not work: "Feelings, insofar as they are individuated [by reference to the social contexts in which they are felt], appear to have richer content than we were led to believe by those obsessed with tickles and itches; indeed, the content of feeling is sufficiently rich to ground the

---

[1] "Feelings in Context," *Journal of Philosophy* **83** (1986): 645.

emotional distinctions in question. Annoyance does not feel like indignation, after all" (p. 651). And he ends by saying what to my mind is exactly right: "We shouldn't have tried to put feelings in context; the context is already in the feelings" (p. 652). Paradigmatically, for adult human beings to be angry is to feel angry and to feel angry in just the way one *is* angry; and to feel angry is to be angry, in just the degree and toward just those objects and for just those reasons that one *feels* angry.

But the paradigm cases are not the only ones; nor are they, surely, the majority of the cases. One can be episodically anxious without feeling anxious, angry without feeling angry, envious without feeling envious, embarrassed without feeling embarrassed. I can be talking about what makes me anxious or angry (thus concentrating on the "object" of the emotion), and even exhibiting some bodily or behavioral symptoms of it, and yet not feel it. Feeling the sensations associated with anger, or becoming aware of, say, scowling and speaking in a loud voice, does not guarantee that one feels angry, but noticing such symptoms may be the first step in a dawning awareness that I am anxious or angry. Whether this pattern is possible with all emotion types is debatable, though I am inclined to think it is. If we think a person cannot be joyful without feeling joy, it is because we are concentrating on a narrow set of examples. Malicious joy is more likely to be unfelt than a joy there is no reason to have qualms about. Similarly, one may be having the emotion of gratitude without feeling it, if what one is grateful for, or the person one is grateful to, is a cause for embarrassment.

It is also possible to feel anxious when one is not. Perhaps stomach flu is just coming on, but hasn't yet declared itself. Zack has a test coming up, so his "anxiety" has the propositional content: *This test is vaguely a threat to my standing as a bright student.* Then with the progress of the disease he realizes what is causing the uneasiness in his abdomen, whereupon the feeling of anxiety disappears and that of being sick settles on him. The evidence that he is not anxious, despite feeling so, might be such things as: He has not recently experienced anxiety about tests like this; he is not currently displaying any behavior characteristic of anxiety about this test; when he becomes convinced he has stomach flu, he ceases feeling anxious. This is a case of feeling an emotion of a given type without being in that *type* of emotional state. In other cases the feeling is mistaken, not about the type of emotion one is in, but about what the emotion is of or about. Thus classic cases in psychoanalysis: You feel angry at your wife, but you're really angry at your mother. You feel in love with your therapist, but you are "transferring" onto her emotions that are properly about your mother. Here you are not wrong about feeling angry or in love, but about whom you are angry at or what you are angry about. But if we grant that an episode of emotion is identified by what it is of, about, to, for, and so on, then the formula, "feeling an emotion without having it," still applies.

So Descartes errs when he says that the passions

are so close and internal to our soul that it is impossible it should feel them without their truly being as it feels them. ... even though we be asleep and dreaming, we cannot feel sad, or moved by any other passion, unless it be quite true that the soul has that passion within itself.[2]

Like Descartes, Peter Kivy seems to identify feeling and emotion when he says,

Is my imaginary fear, as opposed to my real fear, intelligible? While I am imagining I am fearful, am I not *fearful*, with all that implies? ... and I suggest, further, that "He has an imaginary emotion" is, *prima facie*, more like "He has an imaginary pain" than "He has an imaginary illness." It must mean something like "He has an emotion caused by his imaginings".... But the emotion is real: real fear, real anger, real anguish.[3]

Just as the idea of a felt pain that is not really there as pain or does not have the quality or quantity that it is felt as having seems to be an incoherent idea, so the idea of a feeling of fear that does not correspond to one's real fear is incoherent, thinks Kivy.

We can sympathize with these philosophers. Someone who feels fear or sadness has an experience of these emotions. And perhaps in the moment of the feeling he cannot be wrong about the felt quality of the experience. But this incorrigibility may be like the incorrigibility of the visual experience of the stick in water: The stick has, incorrigibly, a bent *look*, but the experience is certainly corrigible in another sense. We correct it by judging the contrary. A still closer analogy is that of someone who walks into a room and sees his friend with what appears to be an angry look on his face.[4] The facial expression makes the friend look angry, but conversation reveals that he is only puzzling over a difficult logic problem; the look is really one of hard concentration. With fuller information about the friend's mind, the facial expression, unlike the stick, may, without changing physically, take on a different look: He may cease to look angry and start looking like a man who is concentrating hard. My point is that in this case, unlike that of the stick in the bucket, the perceptual experience – and not just one's believing – is corrigible through the influence of information or

---

[2] *The Passions of the Soul*, Article 26, translation slightly altered. Annette Baier points out that Descartes's own descriptions of our emotions carry us well beyond what is available to the unreflective in the immediacy of his emotional feelings. For example, the passion of abhorrence, even if it is only experienced at the touch of a worm, "represents to the soul a sudden and unexpected death" (Article 89). See Baier, "Getting in Touch with Our Own Feelings" *Topoi* 6 (1987): 89–97.

[3] *Sound Sentiment: An Essay on the Musical Emotions* (Philadelphia: Temple University Press, 1989), p. 252.

[4] I owe the example to Bill Tolhurst. See his "Seemings," *American Philosophical Quarterly* 35 (1998): 293–302.

other interpretation. Similarly, in psychotherapy, coming to have a different view of our emotions may alter the way we feel them.

So feelings of emotions can be true or false representations of the emotions they are of. The whole drift of the account of emotions that I am advocating in this book is that they too can be true or false. As a concern-based construal the emotion makes two kinds of claims, first about what we might call the *structure* of the situation that the emotion is about, and second about its *importance* or *bearing*. The idea that both emotions and feelings are representations analogous to sense perceptions, which can thus be correct or incorrect (or partially correct) as representations, suggests the following typology of affective error:

1. **Object Misrepresentation** (error in emotion).
   A. *Situation-Misrepresentation.* Al is afraid that the salmon he ate will give him cancer, but his reason for fearing this (that the salmon is poisoned with dioxin) is a false proposition. (He sees his situation as threatening, but it isn't.)
   B. *Importance-Misrepresentation.* Al is angry at Bud for putting a finger print on the hood of his 1924 Rolls Royce. The intensity of his anger is incommensurate with the importance of the offense. (He sees the offense as more important than it is.)
2. **Misrepresentation of the Emotion** (error in feeling).
   A. *Type-Misrepresentation.* Al feels anxious, but is not; it is the stomach flu coming on. Al is embarrassed, but feels "excited" instead. Al feels compassion for Sue, but what he is feeling is really anxiety about himself.
   B. *Object-Misrepresentation.* Al feels angry at his therapist, but is really angry at his father. This feeling is a misrepresentation of his anger, because the anger he feels (at the therapist) differs from his actual anger (at his father).

This typology represents possibilities in respect of truth and error, not in respect of justification or the lack thereof. Thus a person might correctly fear that the salmon will give him cancer because it is laden with dioxin (it is in fact so laden), but base his belief on very unreliable information or faulty reasoning. Thus in seeing it as a threat to his health he sees it as it is, but is not justified in so seeing it. Similarly, I suppose, a person might feel anxious when he is, but be brought to perceive himself in this way by a false cue – say, the onset of the flu. Thus again his feeling is veridical yet unjustified. The reverse of this kind of case would be ones in which the perception is false but justified. Thus Al wrongly sees the salmon as a mortal threat, but arrives at this perception by an epistemically virtuous process – for example, he has no way of knowing he is being lied to by an expert on lake pollution. Or he feels angry at his therapist while really angry at his father, but this self-misperception comes about as a result of a developmental process that does not involve culpable epistemic misbehavior. In this chapter I am interested chiefly in veridical and false feelings of emotion, and not particularly in the issue of justification, though the truth criteria for feelings that I expound in Section 4.5 are relevant to that issue.

The concept of a feeling of an emotion, in human life, is intimately connected with the possibility of error. Emotions of subhuman animals resemble human emotions in being susceptible to 1.A., situation-misrepresentation: Dogs can be "afraid" of a gun that is not loaded, "angry" at someone who is not in fact an intruder, "hopeful" of catching a prey that in fact there is no chance of catching, and so on. It is less clear what to say about 1.B., importance-misrepresentation. But it seems clear that dogs do not feel emotions they don't have, either according to type or according to object. They are not capable of perceiving their own emotional states rightly or wrongly. Thus they do not *feel* their emotions in this distinctively human sense.

4.2. EMOTIONS AND FEELINGS

Sam feels compassion is ambiguous analogously to *Sam sees water in the road.* In one sense the latter sentence implies that water is in the road and that it stands in a certain causal relation to Sam's visual apparatus; here we may undertake checks to determine whether water is in the road (and, in some unusual cases, whether that water was causing Sam to seem to see water). Such checks may undermine the claim that Sam sees water in the road without calling into question the quality of his experience. In the other sense, *Sam sees water in the road* implies only that Sam is in a conscious state in which he seems to himself to be seeing water in the road. Analogously, *Sam feels compassion for Susan* may be true only if Sam *has* compassion for Susan, and there will be in principle nonphenomenological tests of the claim. Does Sam have a history of genuine compassion? Does Sam go to some trouble to help Susan? Do Sam's vocal and facial expressions express compassion? Are the conditions ripe for Sam's deceiving himself about the extent or character of his compassion; for example, does he have a desperate desire to think of himself as compassionate? And so on. Trading on this sense, if Sam claims to feel compassion for Susan we may, on investigation, controvert him and say that whatever he feels, it isn't compassion for Susan. In the other sense, Sam can be said to feel compassion for Susan without his having any real compassion for Susan – if only he experiences himself, in a certain immediate and quasi-perceptual way, as having compassion for Susan. In the latter, but not in the former sense of "feel," Descartes and Kivy are right that emotional feelings are incorrigible.

This immediate and quasi-perceptual grasp of oneself as in a certain emotional state is paradigmatic for emotions. But what is it like? It is the experience one has of oneself when one is conscious of being, for example, angry, gripped by compassion, fearful, struck with hopefulness, envious, and so on. We notice the feeling of emotion, as distinct from the emotion, especially in cases where the feeling comes after the emotion. For example, I see the snake in my boat and react with the characteristic actions and behavior (this suggests that I see the *snake* in the way characteristic of fear), but only seconds or minutes later do I begin to feel the fear (on the proposed view, I am now aware of *myself* as in a state of fear). Or you may realize, at some point in a conversation in which someone has been subtly insulting you, that you are behaving hostilely toward your insulter, and noticing this triggers an awareness of the state you are in, and you begin to *feel* angry. Or in some intense athletic game you notice at a certain point that for the last few minutes you have become hopeful of winning, and now you begin to *feel* hopeful.

Let us contrast the feeling of an emotion both with the feeling of a sensation that is associated with the emotion and with mere knowledge that one is in a certain emotional state. You can feel a tightening in your shoulders or burning sensation in your abdomen (or something pretty similar to these) that are concomitants of an episode of anxiety, yet without feeling the anxiety. Your therapist may have to teach you that these are symptoms of anxiety. But concluding "I am anxious" from these symptoms (plus circumstantial clues) is not the same as feeling anxious. By contrast with this inferential knowledge, feeling anxious is an immediate awareness of being anxious. Merely knowing that one is anxious is to feeling anxious, as the knowledge that it is snowing outdoors, inferred from a weather report plus a knowledge of one's geographical location, is to seeing the falling snow with one's own eyes and feeling it against one's cheeks.

How do my present claims about feelings fit with the basic suggestion of this book that emotions are concern-based construals? To say that Bud's anger at his wife for cleaning up the workshop (thereby making it hard for him to find his tools) is a concern-based construal is to say that he sees her in terms of a set of propositions, among which will certainly be *She has made it hard for me to find my tools; it is quite important for me to be able to find my tools easily; she is culpable and worthy of punishment for this misdeed.* To say that he perceives her in terms of this proposition is not to say he is conscious of doing so. Especially if he has some strong motive for disallowing himself awareness of his anger, he may show punitive behavior toward her traceable to his perceiving her in these terms without being aware, at the time of the behavior, of so perceiving her. But if he also feels his anger, he perceives himself in terms of another proposition, namely, *I am angry.* This construal is, as it were, about the other propositions as operative in his grasp of the situation: It identifies them as the terms in which he is seeing his situation. It is a richly constructive perception of himself.

Emotions and feelings, then, are both construals. A paradigmatically self-conscious emotion (one that is felt as the emotion that in fact it is) will have the following structure: It will be a concern-based construal that its subject consciously construes himself as currently performing/undergoing. We cannot straightforwardly use the language of construal to characterize what the subject construes himself to be doing in having an emotion, because the construal account of emotion has features not current in an everyday understanding of emotion. But the adult feeler of the emotion will identify it by its grammatical features, that is, by the types of its propositional content, including the actions, if any, that he is inclined to perform in consequence of seeing the situation as he does.

Let us use subscripts to distinguish the two construals, a subscript 1 for the emotion and a subscript 2 for the feeling, and place brackets around the word "construal" to indicate that the ordinary subject does not experience his emotion in terms of the concept of a construal. Thus, to feel angry at Sally is to $construe_2$ oneself as [$construing_1$] Sally as having culpably offended in some matter that one strongly cares about. To feel proud of Nathan is to $construe_2$ myself as [$construing_1$] myself as increased in status because of Nathan's attributes. To feel contrite is to $construe_2$ myself as [$construing_1$] myself as being or having done something contrary to some moral or quasi-moral standard that I am strongly concerned to meet.

$Construing_2$ will always be conscious, and indeed consciousness of self, but $construing_1$, in the absence of $construing_2$, will not be consciousness of being in a state of emotion, and it may not even be consciousness of the true object of the emotion. (I may not only be not perceiving my anger as I confront someone I concernfully perceive as offending me; the person I am aware of as offending me may not be the real object of my anger.) Consciousness of the object in the way characteristic of the emotion does not necessitate consciousness of the emotion, but because emotions are self-involving in being based on some concern of the subject, consciousness of the object of the emotion powerfully *predisposes* the subject to be conscious of himself as in the emotional state. In the case of such emotions as pride, shame, and guilt, a salient object of the $construal_1$ will be oneself; but even where this construal is conscious, it is not consciousness of oneself as in that state of emotion. That is, in the case of essentially reflexive emotions it is one thing to be conscious of oneself in the terms characteristic of the emotion and another to feel the emotion.

Like sense perceptions of things, feelings of emotions come in degrees of awareness and degrees of accuracy. As in the phenomenon of "blind sight" produced by a certain kind of brain damage the subject may visually respond to things without any conscious visual impression of them, genuinely unconscious emotions operate without any awareness of them at all. But in many cases the feeling of an emotion may be analogous to what is sometimes called "subception," a state of mind in which one is aware of something without noticing being aware of it – so that when one's attention is called to it, one remembers a kind of peripheral awareness of it. "Yes, I was in fact feeling envious of his new position, though I didn't notice it until you remarked about how Bridget had reacted to the news." Such subception of emotion admits of degrees of awareness, and on the other end of the spectrum are emotions that are felt with "full" consciousness. As to accuracy, we noted in Section 4.1 that emotions may be felt rightly or wrongly with regard to type and with regard to what they are about. We might regard a feeling that identifies an emotion rightly with regard to what it is about as more accurate than one that merely identifies the emotion rightly with regard to its type. There will also be degrees of accuracy of feelings with respect to what the emotion is about. Thus a man may rightly feel angry at his father, yet not be aware of his reasons for being angry at his father.

My account suggests that nothing strictly feels *emotions* unless it has an emotion vocabulary, a categorial scheme in terms of which it recognizes emotional states in itself. This is not to deny that infants and animals feel *something* when in emotional states but only to deny that they feel these states as emotions of particular types – types that for human beings have various kinds of social significance, implications about relationships with others and with the world, and implications about one's own character as a person. This significance is itself often an emotional significance. One might be ashamed of envy or fear, or feel guilty about a certain joy, or be glad to feel guilt about something. I see no reason why a dog should not have sensations of its heightened heartbeat, or of baring teeth, or of running away from a fearsome object; if a dog is conscious, it will be conscious of the object of the emotion under some aspect (e.g., threatening or offensive – or rather, the aspect under which the dog sees it is something like what we call threat or offense). But it seems clear that dogs are not capable of feeling their emotions in the sense that enables human beings to be mistaken about their own emotions. A dog does not perceive itself as anxious when it's not because it has no concept of anxiety, nor does it feel angry at one thing while really angry at another because it does not *feel angry* in the appropriate sense at all. A dog sees elm trees all right but because of a category deficit sees nothing *as* an elm tree; it is thus without access to a certain recognitional experience. In a similar way it never feels anger or fear, though it may be in states analogous to human anger and fear, being conscious of their objects and feeling concomitant physical changes and behavioral consequences.

It may be objected that the feeling of emotions cannot be as dependent on emotion vocabularies as my account suggests they are because we sometimes develop new vocabularies to talk about what we are already feeling. I do not suggest that we cannot feel an emotion (in my sense of "feel") unless we have a *name* for the emotion. The important thing is that we have ways of conceptualizing ourselves, and I should think it obvious that we have a lot more concepts than we have concept words. Because of the concept words we do have, we can invent new concepts for various purposes, one of which may be the identification of experiences of ourselves. I can imagine that people in a culture without a specific term for feeling triumphant might feel triumphant. But this would be because they have some concepts of self-reference, among them emotion concepts, and they have a concept of triumph – whether or not they have a vocabulary item that corresponds exactly to our "triumph." My view is this: The feeling of whatever emotion a person feels in feeling triumphant can be felt in the absence of that emotion only by a person who has a concept of that emotion.

Some have felt that my account of emotional feelings attributes too much reflectiveness to people. Surely, the critics say, we can feel our emotions without construing ourselves as in one or another state of emotion. That presupposes that we have a concept of self, and a concept of the emotion we construe ourselves to be in. And besides, it is psychologically implausible to claim that whenever we are conscious of being in some emotional state we perform a mental act in addition to whatever occurs in having the emotion, this act of construing ourselves to be having the emotion.

My account does presuppose a certain reflectiveness on the part of people who feel their emotions, but not more than can plausibly be attributed to them. When I say feelings of emotion are perceptions determined by an emotion vocabulary, I am not saying that to feel an emotion one must rehearse some sentence or other in which this vocabulary occurs. No one who holds that visual perceptions are influenced by concepts would impose such a requirement. With our native languages we learn a system of concepts for attributing emotion states, as part of a larger system of concepts of attributes that together constitute a concept of the self. At an early stage of development we have conceptual wherewithal for construing ourselves to be in some state of emotion. Without this repertoire we could have *some* awareness of our emotional state. I granted earlier that the dog may notice (if that is not too strong a word) the pounding in its chest when frightened. But the awareness of such items is not what the six-year-old child reports when she says she feels afraid. She is reporting an experience that is culturally shaped, by a concept that brings together the various aspects of fear into a unitary experience that cannot be had by a being that does not have the concept of fear. To feel emotions whole in such a way as to be able to be correct or in error about one's emotional states requires a minimal understanding of the language of emotion.

The second part of the objection attributes to me the view that whenever we are conscious of being in some emotional state we perform a mental act in addition to whatever occurs in having the emotion. I'm not sure what to say about this because I don't know how to individuate mental events. I am not committed to any story about temporal priority. I would think that in the normal case my emotion and my construal of myself as in that emotional state would be simultaneous; indeed, despite the fact that one can feel an emotion one doesn't have and have an emotion one doesn't feel, I'm inclined to say that when one *does* feel an emotion, the feeling and the emotion are two aspects of one mental state, rather than two separate ones.

4.3. FEELINGS AS AWARENESS OF SELF

In somewhat diagnostic contexts we speak of feeling anger, embarrassment, fear, and so forth. This kind of expression, which substantivizes the emotion, seems to support the view I am promoting – that feelings of emotions are conscious intentional states taking emotions as their objects. But it is more usual to speak of feeling angry, embarrassed, or afraid, thus making the self the object of the feeling and the emotion a qualifying condition of that self.[5] This suggests that what we are aware of in feeling an emotion is our self. Putting these two data together, I suggest that emotions are states of the self, and that to feel an emotion is to perceive oneself in such a state. Feelings of emotion belong to a class that William P. Alston has called "adjectival feelings," which include feeling generous, adventurous, sleepy, energetic, and cheerful, as well as feeling in such various states of emotion as embarrassed, elated, and depressed.[6] My point is that the adjective always qualifies the self of the one having the feeling. In this the emotion differs from the feeling: Whereas the feeling is always of the self-as-in-a-given-state, the emotion is often or typically directed "outward," toward things other than the self.

One possible reason for confusing sensation concomitants of an emotion with the feeling of the emotion is a certain analogy between them that follows the analogy between the human body and the self. The body is a natural representation and representative of the self, yet without being identical with the self. The sensations that are concomitant to emotions are bodily sensations, in the sense that they are (phenomenologically) *of* one's body, rather than of something "external." For example, physically speaking, perspiration is felt in part due to air currents passing over one's skin; and in many situations in which we perspire, our focus of attention might be those air currents. In such situations, if asked, "What do you feel?" you might respond, "A breeze." But if asked what you feel when you feel embarrassment accompanied by perspiring, you might say, "I feel sweaty." Thus you talk about your body, rather than something external to it. Analogously, the feeling of embarrassment or anger is an awareness of a state of oneself, rather than of something external – even though what one is embarrassed or angry about may be in large part something external to oneself.

Awareness of states and attributes of the self is analogous to (and possibly inclusive of) awareness of attributes of the body, but not identical with awareness of these. The self (the person, the individual) has bodily states, but not all states of the self are bodily states. For example, Tom's having just insulted his boss is a state of Tom's self (a fact about Tom), but not a state of

---

[5] For some emotions the first kind of locution is more natural: We speak of feeling compassion rather than feeling compassionate, of feeling contempt rather than feeling contemptuous.

[6] See "Feelings" *The Philosophical Review* **76** (1969): 3–34.

his body. Being the father of Nathan Roberts is a state of my self, but not of my body. Being a person who played the guitar badly for Andrés Segovia in 1963 is a state of my self, but not of my body. Being still embarrassed about having played badly for Segovia is a state of my self, but not of my body.

Because states of the body are states of the self, feelings of itches and throbs are also self-perceptions: An itch on my left elbow is after all a state that *I* am in. But emotions are states of the self in a more significant and personal sense. Being concern-based construals, a person's anger, hope, gratitude, or embarrassment gather together, focus, and actualize some concerns (which may be central to the personality) in terms of some concepts and models for viewing the world (which are often of ethical relevance). The subject's emotions embody her projects, attachments, and commitments, even ones she is not clear about herself, and her ways of understanding herself and her life. In a person's emotions (admittedly in some more than others) we have indicators of her character that are as potent as her actions. Indeed, her actions would not have the identity they have, as actions, were they not tied to the personality in the way they are via the emotions. So if we ask, Of *what* are emotional states states? the most plausible answer is not, Of the body, nor even Of the mind (taking mind to be something less than the entire personality). The most plausible answer is, Of the self (the person). What is the self, that it may be perceived in feelings of emotion?

A self is a construct of agential powers, mental and physical dispositions and attributes, relationships (personal and nonpersonal), and past actions and relevant events. A self is centered in a particular body and particular mind, but because it also has relational and narrative properties, it is not strictly identical with its body and mind. As such a complex construct, it is never more than partially known by itself or anybody else, but still it is the sort of thing that gets characterized in biographies and less formally in answers to the request, Tell me about yourself. Who are you? What are you like? You answer this question by citing significant events and accomplishments in your personal history, by situating yourself in a geographical and cultural context, telling about (illustrating) your traits, your potentials and abilities, your relationships with significant others; you tell about your hopes and fears, what angers you and what gives you joy, what you admire and what you deplore – that is, the patterns of your emotions and motivations.

Some facts about a person can simply be noted: when and where he was born, where he grew up, who his family are, his bodily characteristics, and so on. But these rather external facts of his life must be connected in various ways with his psychological attributes (concerns, abilities, outlook) if they are to reveal much of interest about his self. A good biography is a narrative selection of episodes that reveal his dispositions to emotion and action and their development from one period of his life to another. The self as a whole is like a wheel with a hub and spokes fanning out to a periphery.

At the hub, where most of the (e)motion is transmitted to the periphery, is a set of organizing cares – attachments to persons, interests in projects, the concern to survive, the concern to be well thought of, the concern for power, the concern for moral rectitude. I am not saying that all people have all these types of concerns but am pointing to the kinds of concerns that are typically at the center of a person's selfhood and which are typically the ones that explain many of a person's actions and are the basis for many of his or her emotions.

If emotions are states of the self and indeed states quite directly related to the self's core, and the feeling of an emotion is a conscious, quasi-perceptual awareness of being in such a state, it would seem that emotional feelings are a very special and important form of self-knowledge. To the extent that we are "out of touch with our feelings" (for "feelings" read "emotions"; for "be in touch with" read "feel") – to the extent that we do not feel the resentment, envy, anxiety, and fear that characterize us or do feel a compassion, joy, and gratitude that do not characterize us; to the extent that the objects of the emotions we feel are not quite the objects of our real emotions – to that extent we are blind to ourselves. True, there is a kind of self-knowledge that falls short of conscious quasi-perceptual awareness. It is the theoretical *mere* knowledge I referred to earlier, in which one knows by inference, by trusting in a theory or an authority, about the distortions of self-view created by one's feelings or lack thereof.

Let me illustrate. Emma feels intense grief for her dead dog, thus representing herself to herself as deeply attached to that dog. But her grief is largely histrionics; she is grieving, but not so intensely as she feels. By presenting her grief to her as more intense than it is, her feeling misrepresents the degree of the importance of the dog to her, the intensity of her concern for the dog, and thus misrepresents her self. We may suspect that this is the point of the distortion in perception: Emma has some need to think of herself as deeply attached to the dog. But histrionics is a way of life for Emma, and so this false self-perception is deep and tenacious. She is suffering terribly and makes an appointment with a counselor. Making and keeping (and paying for!) the appointments is no doubt part of the histrionics, but I want to emphasize that Emma really is suffering from her sham grief. The therapist has seen Emma before, and his strategy is to lead her, in the safety of his empathy, to a different understanding of her grief, and thereby to a more accurate feeling of it. He explains, in terms of her childhood experiences, her need to think of herself as very attached to the dog and gently suggests that the Emma she is presenting to herself in her feeling of grief is less the real Emma than a worked-up persona. He gives her some behavior exercises involving abstinence from dramatizing her dog's death and telling herself exaggerated stories about what the loss means to her. Emma may accept the therapist's account without immediately getting over her feeling for the dog. If we assume that the therapist is right in identifying

the real Emma and that her confidence in him justifies her believing his
account, we can say that Emma knows herself in this respect. But she does
not yet have a just *perception* of herself with respect to her grief, so she still
has some way to go in self-knowledge.

Note that in Emma's case (and I take this to be typical for feelings) the
feeling has a significance in Emma's self-understanding that Emma does not
perceive – or even understand. Thus while feelings are necessarily conscious
states, they are surrounded by unconscious or only semiconscious meaning.
The difference between false feelings and veridical ones is not that the veridical ones lack this unconscious meaning, but that the unconscious meaning
is not such as to distort the feeling. Consider Emma after successful therapy.
After a period of ceasing to dramatize daily her dog's death and exaggerate
its impact on her life, she gradually calms down. She still misses the dog,
but her feeling now matches better the way she actually views the dog, herself, and her loss. Her self-perception in the feeling is thus more accurate, a
better representation of her actual mind. But the feeling, which is a state of
consciousness, still has a dimension of unconscious meaning. There is still
the question, which *might* be explored in therapy, of what it means for her
to feel the loss of her dog in just the way she does. But now the exploration
is somewhat less complex, being a matter of how her present grief connects
with forgotten or unforgotten losses, other loves, past and present, and so
on – not a question of why she is distorting her present perception of her
mental state.

If emotional feelings are liable to error, it would seem that whether feeling
one's emotions is a more *reliable* way of knowing about them than inference
will depend on factors that differ from person to person. Just as people's
sense-perceptual experiences – say, when examining microscope slides or
looking for defects in a job of dry-wall – differ in their reliability depending
on training and on such intellectual virtues as honesty, tenacity, and objectivity, so the reliability of emotional feelings will depend on whose feelings
they are. So I have not made the superiority of self-knowledge based in feelings to turn on their greater reliability than inference. How then might we
characterize their superiority?

First, perception is first-hand. For years I could not see the young woman
in the old lady/young woman gestalt figure (see Section 2.3b). I knew it was
there, because reliable people told me it was. Now I can see it for myself, and
it seems obvious to me that I am now in an improved epistemic condition.
Other things being equal, experience is an enrichment of knowledge. If
emotions are as central to selfhood as I claim, then anybody who thinks self-
knowledge a good thing ought for this reason to be dissatisfied with merely
knowing what his emotions are. He should want to feel them, as well.

In addition to the sheer value of experience, another kind of advantage
of perceptual knowledge is an availability of detail that is often lacking in
nonperceptual knowledge. To take our figure again, one who sees for herself

the young woman in the figure is able to say other things about the figure than that there is a young woman to be seen there. She can point out which part of the figure is her ear, which her headdress, which her neck, can say fairly precisely at just which angle she is looking away from the viewer, and so on. This is not an absolute superiority of perceptual knowledge, because it is possible that somebody knows all these things by inference, but is blind to the young lady. But such a knower would be the exception; in cases like this, perceivers are generally better able to "go on." Is someone who feels her emotions for herself analogously better able to go on? I suspect she is. Given equal linguistic ability and IQ, one who is affectively in touch with herself will write a richer and more interesting autobiography than people who rely heavily for their knowledge of their emotions on their therapist or on psychological theories plus relevant information about their own behavior and psychological condition.

I have been arguing that emotional feelings are putative perceptions of emotional states, and that they are sometimes veridical and sometimes not. When they are veridical, I have said, they are correct perceptions of *oneself.* The following case seems to be a counterexample of my view. I hear that a colleague, who is also a good friend, of about my age and achievements, has been offered a job at a prestigious university. A feeling of dark envy engulfs me, but as soon as I feel it I dissociate from it as something unworthy and uncharacteristic of me. Let us say that this act of dissociation does not dispel the feeling: I continue to feel envious but judge, with some dismay, that this is not the true me. Now if the feeling is veridical, it is a perception of something about my character: I see my friend as a competitor, am a deficient friend to her, and so on. It is because I recoil from this self-perception that I dissociate myself from the emotion. But if I recoil, it is because I take the feeling to be veridical: I am really perceiving *my* emotion. Yet if I dissociate from it I am saying, as it were, that it is not *mine*, not a predicate of my *self*. Thus we seem to have a case of a veridical feeling of an emotion that is, nevertheless, not a veridical self-perception.[7]

To answer this objection we must distinguish our true self from our actual self. Typically, mature people have some real dispositions that they own as belonging to themselves in a normative sense of "self" and other dispositions that, while belonging to their actual selves, are such that they wish to dissociate themselves from them. A vivid illustration is found in the seventh chapter of St. Paul's letter to the Romans where he says of some of his actions:

I do not do what I want, but I do the very thing I hate. Now if I do what I do not want, I agree that the law is good. So then it is no longer I that do it, but sin that dwells within me (vv.15b-17).

---

[7] I owe this objection to William R. Schroeder.

Paul is not simply denying that he performed these actions that are uncharacteristic of the new self that he has in Christ; but he is saying that it is not the *real* Paul who performed them. They were performed by a remnant of Paul's old sinful self. Since emotions are as much indicators of selfhood as actions, the same sort of ambiguity and a similar disambiguation are possible in their case. Thus the invidious self from which I dissociate is both me (in the sense of actual self) and not me (in the sense of true self). In condemning this emotion in myself, I do not deny that it is a real emotion, nor that it belongs to my actual self; and feeling this envy is one of the ways that I get in touch with that actual self that is nevertheless not the real me.

4.4. HOW FALSE FEELINGS COME ABOUT

We somehow know pretheoretically that in feeling grief over a loss, indignation about some moral evil, or envy of a colleague's success, we are seeing ourselves. Often we don't like what we see through our feelings; and sometimes we have a positive stake in seeing ourselves in some particular way. We are under social pressure to have emotions that show us to be a good wife or parent or friend or patriot. These self-image considerations are not the only motives for false feelings: Grief or compassion may be so painful in itself, apart from what it says about us (which may be complimentary), that we opt to feel something else. So false feelings are often, in part, a motivated product of self-deception. But our motivation to misfeel our emotions is only part of the story of how they come about. We are sometimes more or less passive victims of this deception, and sometimes false feelings are not even deceptive: We may see through them, while still feeling them.

In the previous sections of this chapter I have hinted at parts of an account of how false feelings are generated, and now I want to make this account more explicit. In general, I suggest that they are generated by acts or events (overt *and* mental) of self-presentation under an aspect or set of aspects. Consider this passage from Gilbert Ryle:

And there is a special reason for not paying much heed to the feelings had by a person whose motives are under investigation, namely that we know that lively and frequent feelings are felt by sentimentalists whose positive actions show quite clearly that their patriotism, e.g. is a self-indulgent make-believe. Their hearts duly sink when they hear that their country's plight is desperate, but their appetites are unaffected and the routines of their lives are unmodified. Their bosoms swell at a march-past, but they avoid marching themselves. They are rather like theatregoers and novel readers, who also feel genuine pangs, glows, flutters and twinges of despair, indignation, exhilaration and disgust, with the difference that the theatregoers and novel readers realize that they are making-believe.[8]

8 *The Concept of Mind*, pp. 89–90.

We can begin by noting that the sentimentalist does not just "feel genuine pangs, glows, flutters and twinges," but that these are twinges, and so on, "of indignation, exhilaration and disgust" (presumably emotions). As far as I know, Ryle has no explanation of what makes a given pang a pang *of* some given emotion, especially if the emotion does not go on and issue in actions of indignation or disgust, as those of his sentimentalist do not.

According to the account of feelings I have just sketched, and assuming that a twinge is a bodily sensation, we will not say that the twinge itself is the feeling of indignation. But the twinge is a sensation that typically accompanies (and this is the sense of "of") strong indignation. The feeling of indignation, by contrast, is a conscious perception of oneself as indignant. According to Section 3.3d, indignation is the construal$_1$ of a person or group of persons as having shockingly offended in some important particular, of the agent(s) as bad and deserving punishment, and of oneself as in a strong position to judge. The feeling of indignation is, accordingly, the construal$_2$ of oneself as [construing$_1$] someone as having shockingly offended, and so on. The twinge, as an item of consciousness typically associated with indignation, will often trigger the feeling of indignation (the true or false perception of indignation in oneself), and becomes an ingredient in the feeling, in the sense that the feeling of indignation is, among other things, the construal *of such twinges* as features of indignation. How does this analysis help explain the occurrence of false feelings?

Let us say the indignation is about how one's country is regarded by the Nazis. Thus the twinge appears as a symptom of patriotism (a virtue, a possible constituent of one's self, a kind of character-constitutive caring). We are clued in to the shamness of the feeling, Ryle suggests, by the fact that the feeler of it never takes appropriate action. The twinge in question is (let us say) a conjunction of a momentary sensation of slight constriction in the area of the speech apparatus, with a mildly unpleasant glow in the abdomen. How does this twinge become a twinge of (sham) indignation? The indignation in question would be a construal$_1$ of one's country as insulted by Nazi behavior, or alternatively a construal$_1$ of Nazi behavior as insulting to one's country, based on a strong concern for the dignity of one's country. Let us say it is an empirical fact that construals$_1$ of things held dear as insulted, or of actions as insulting things held dear, tend to cause such twinges. Findings of neuroscientists that particular emotion types have particular neurologies with their special implications for behavior and Paul Ekman's finding that some emotion types have specific facial expressions would account for such associations (see Sections 1.3c, 1.3e, and 4.5). If so, then if the *circumstances* are such as to lend themselves to construal$_1$ of some behavior as insulting-to-things-held-dear, then given a *wish* to [construe$_2$] oneself as patriotic, the occurrence of such a *twinge*, because of its association with such construals$_1$, may be enough to bring about a construal$_2$ of oneself as indignant. It is a feature of construals that they are constructions of data that by themselves underdetermine the construal (see Section 2.3).

So the twinge can *seem* to the subject to be a twinge of indignation, without being such, if the subject construes$_2$ himself, in consequence of the twinge, as concernfully [construing$_1$] some behavior as an outrage-against-things-held-dear, when in fact the subject is not construing$_1$ some behavior as an outrage-against-things-held-dear. Thus we have a sham feeling of indignation. But how can this be? How can a person perceive himself to be [construing$_1$] his situation in one way, when in fact he is construing it in another? One part of the answer is that emotions (construals$_1$) are not necessarily conscious states; so it is not a foregone conclusion that one will always perceive which one of them one is in, and not perceive oneself as in one while being in another (or none). Another part of the answer is that there will nearly always be some ground, in the person's actual state, for the misperception. In the present example, this is the function of the twinge and the circumstances: It is a twinge very much like twinges characteristic of indignation, and it occurs in a situation to which indignation is appropriate and perhaps one's companions are expressing indignation. If in addition to feeling the twinge I respond to this situation by behaving in ways characteristic of indignation, then I am adding still further encouragement for perceiving myself as indignant. Thus I may say something like "blasted Nazis," gesture indignantly, turn red in the face, and so forth.

But, someone may be thinking, if I recognize the situation as calling for indignation – I see these Nazis as insulting my country, I see my country as victimized by them, and let us say I even evaluate this situation as a bad thing – then, if in addition I'm saying "blasted pig Nazis" and feeling twinges characteristic of indignation, surely my feeling of indignation is veridical and not sham. But I think Ryle's reason for suspicion is excellent: In the larger context of my life, I systematically lack the actions characteristic of one who has the care/concern that is basic to indignation about insults to my country. On this book's account of emotion a construal is not an emotion unless it is based on an appropriate concern, and that is the same concern that, in the case of such motivational emotions as indignation, gets transfigured, via the construal, into a motive for action (see Section 2.9c). Thus lack of proper motivation is, for these emotions, a strong indicator that the emotion itself is absent. If the individual feels it nevertheless, the feeling is sham.[9] In a

9 Ronald de Sousa [*The Rationality of Emotion* (Cambridge, Massachusetts: MIT Press, 1987)] discusses what may happen when a person feigns emotional expression and thus induces in himself what I am calling a false feeling. He rightly notes that such cases are "not merely a matter of acquiring false beliefs about one's own emotions" (p. 242). But because he does not distinguish emotions from feelings of them, and thus does not distinguish the two main kinds of emotional error (see Section 4.1), he goes on to say, "Rather, [the feigning of expression] *induces* an emotion, which is itself erroneous in its ascription of a characteristic property to

related way, diagnostic suspicion of my feeling may turn on doubts about whether I adequately understand the situation – whether I have sufficient mastery of the concepts required for indignation, whether I am capable of appreciating the import of what the Nazis are doing or threatening to do to my country. Thus we may suspect that the feelings of indignation felt by children in the presence of their indignant elders are typically false.

It is possible that the construal of myself as indignant causes me actually to *become* indignant. This will depend on my character: on whether I have in me the resources for concernfully construing certain acts as outrages against my country. These resources will be things like a mastery of such concepts as dignity and moral outrageousness, an understanding of the present situation, and above all a concern for my country (which I may not realize I have, until such time as I begin to feel indignant and go on to show, by my subsequent life, the truth of that feeling). The Ryle quotation suggests that the construals of the world that the sentimentalist perceives in himself are somehow not authentic, not *his* (he is like a theatregoer or a novel reader, as compared with someone who is experiencing his *own* life). They do not arise out of his heart, but are closer to being construals that he "entertains" (though he, unlike the theatregoers, is not clear that he is only entertaining them). On this book's account of emotion, a major form of the gap between the "emotion" and the self is the construal's failure to *impinge* on the self – which is to say, its failure to impinge on some sufficiently strong concern of the individual.

Ryle's comparison of sham feelings with the emotions of a theatergoer is reminiscent of Kendall Walton's theory of emotional responses to fiction that I discussed in Section 2.4g. Walton says that emotional responses to fiction are only "quasi"-emotions because he thinks that the subject of a real emotion believes its propositional content. I argued to the contrary that emotional responses to fiction can be as real as any other emotions because belief in their propositional content is not a necessary condition of emotions. So if Ryle were to hold (as he does not, to my knowledge) that emotional feelings in response to fiction are all sham, I would disagree with him as well. Some feelings in response to literature are false, and in the following section I shall exploit the distinction between real and false feelings in response to literature to explain how literature may have a morally educative function.

Ryle compares the person deluded by his emotional feelings to a theatregoer. But it is more apt to compare him with an actor. The actor who raises his voice to an angry pitch, scowls, gesticulates angrily, and causes himself to turn red in the face generates in himself sensations characteristic

an object" (p. 242f, de Sousa's italics). But error in the feeling is compatible with truth in the (supposed) emotion. In my example, the error is not in what the (supposed) emotion ascribes to its object (the property of moral outrageousness to Nazi behavior), but in what the feeling ascribes to its subject (real indignation).

of anger, and he construes himself and the actor he is "angry" at in terms of the history and present situation of the characters as given or suggested in the play. Into this construal of self and other in terms of the play enter the sensations of the actor's physical movements and state; the result can be an extraordinarily lifelike subjective simulation of anger as *his*. We know the emotion that he feels is not his – and that his feeling of it is thus not a proper self-perception – because it belongs properly not to him, but to the character. Further evidence is that the actor can step out of character, and thus out of his emotional feelings, more or less instantaneously, and this is not typical of genuine emotion. But Ryle's analogy of the theatregoer is appropriate after all; for in this case the actor is also the audience: The point of this kind of acting, as far as sham feelings go, is to bring about a false self-perception.

When we experience false feelings we, like the actor who feels an anger that is not his own, do so by presenting ourselves to ourselves (or just being presented to ourselves) in systematically misleading ways. The deception is not merely propositional (*telling* ourselves lies – though this is certainly *one* mode of false self-presentation); it is a holistic coming to *look* to ourselves emotionally otherwise than we are. False feelings come in varying depths of deceptiveness and varying degrees of deliberateness as well: An insane actor may confuse himself with his role, but most actors know, while in role, that their feelings are stage feelings. Analogously, false moral feelings range from ones that are practically nondeceptive, to ones that are self-deceptive, to ones that are so deeply deceptive that the deceived does little or nothing intentionally (not even subconsciously) to bring about the deception.

4.5. TRUTH CRITERIA FOR FEELINGS

I now propose some criteria for sorting out veridical from nonveridical feelings. Discussing these should also deepen our understanding of the relationships between emotions and the feelings of them. I shall end the section by considering the role of theoretical frameworks in formulating criteria of veridicality of feelings and query the theoretical commitments of the present proposal. The criteria I propose are expression, action, character, situational fit, lack of motivation, causal normality, and survival of reflection. No one of these criteria's being met guarantees the veridicality of an emotional feeling. On the other hand, a feeling may be veridical without meeting all the criteria. But if a feeling can meet any of the criteria without being veridical and can violate any of the criteria while being veridical, how are the criteria to be applied? I can only say, "judiciously." But I can say with some confidence that if a feeling violates all or most of the criteria, it is certainly false; and if a feeling meets all or most of the criteria it is surely veridical. The discussion that follows should help to clarify what "judiciously" amounts to in this connection.

NATURAL EXPRESSION. Many who write about emotions, Darwin being the best known, point out that emotions have natural behavioral expressions – facial, vocal, postural, and so on. They usually emphasize that such expressions signal to others the emotional state one is in, and thus the further behavior that others may expect from one. It is less often remarked that they also may signal one's emotional state to oneself. Thus if someone feels at peace but notices that his knuckles are white with gripping the arms of his chair, he has reason to doubt that he is in touch with his real emotions. Those who can see his face may also be able to read anxiety in it. If a young existentialist is feeling despair about the universe, the lilt in his step and the enthusiasm in his voice as he expounds the gloomy doctrine may suggest to his mother that the self he presents to himself is not quite the real one. Emotions are hard to fake behaviorally, and that is the power in this criterion, but most false feelings are not *just* faked in any straightforward sense, and that is its limitation. One of the sources of the feeling of peace experienced by the anxious person in the above example may be the calm and assured tone in which he speaks. If he were *just* faking, his thespian powers might well be too meager to sustain the illusion; but the voice is part of a larger complex mask, by which he himself is largely taken in. Most of us are far better actors of the various parts we assign ourselves or find ourselves assigned to than we are when we try out for a play or try outright to deceive someone.

APPROPRIATE ACTION. I noted in Section 2.9 that some emotions, such as anger and gratitude, involve motivation to characteristic actions. The absence of such motivation indicates a lack or weakness of the concern on which the emotion is based, or a failure to see the situation in the terms characteristic of the emotion. Consequently, actions of a certain type – for example, punitive or corrective actions for anger, danger-avoidant actions for fear, favor-returning or favor-acknowledging actions for gratitude – can serve as loose criteria of the reality of these emotions. The reality of the emotion of a person who feels indignant about Nazi behavior toward the fatherland can be indicated by whether he takes some kind of corrective or punitive action, somewhere along the way, toward the Nazis. The application of the criterion is not very straightforward because opportunities for action may be rare or not noticed, and a truly indignant person might pass up some opportunities for reasons that do not undermine the ascription of indignation. Furthermore, action may require courage, and it is just possible that if someone is paralyzed enough by fear he may be really indignant without taking any such actions, though under such conditions indignation will tend to become resentment (see Section 3.3d). If a person is indignant, and yet does not act on clear opportunities, then we will expect another emotion – guilt – to corroborate the seriousness on which the reality of his indignation depends. Despite these qualifications and others that might be thought of, the absence of appropriate action is often an indicator, as Ryle suggests, that one's emotions are not as one's feelings depict them.

CHARACTER. A person's feelings may be corroborated or called into question by reference to his larger established dispositions of emotion, action, and thought. Luke is highly competitive but also rather insecure, as evidenced by the low view he tends to take of himself when he loses in competitions. Losing depresses him, but often he does not recognize his depression, which comes out in irritability and blaming others and his situation for defects in his life. Recently he has felt strong contempt for the person and work of his colleague Arthur, who was promoted to a position just above Luke, from a position just below him. Luke's friends do not question the sincerity of his avowals of contempt, but knowing Luke, they think that if he were clearer about himself he would be feeling not contempt but envy and wounded pride.

SITUATIONAL FIT. Luke's friends would be more cautious in their judgment, were it not that Arthur is not in the least contemptible. He is competent, in fact somewhat more competent than Luke, and besides this a gracious and likable person. Luke's *apparent* (to him) construal of Arthur as incompetent and sleazy seems to be a construction by Luke (largely unconscious, no doubt) in the service of Luke's concern to deny that he has lost in his competition with Arthur, rather than a response to the obvious features of the situation. I say obvious, not because I believe in something that could be called the intrinsically obvious features of any situation, but because some features of *this* situation – notably Arthur's ascendancy in the business and his greater competence and likability – are obvious to Luke's colleagues and are also in some sense salient to Luke as the content of the envy to which his colleagues attribute his feelings of contempt.[10]

The appropriateness of the emotion to the situation it is apparently about is a major criterion used by Freud to distinguish real emotions from transference emotions.

... the patient has transferred on to the doctor intense feelings of affection which are justified neither by the doctor's behaviour nor by the situation that has developed during the treatment. ... [These feelings develop] under the most unfavourable conditions and where there are positively grotesque incongruities, even in elderly women and in relation to grey-bearded men, even where, in our judgment, there is nothing of any kind to entice. ... We can be in no doubt that the hostile feelings towards the doctor deserve to be called a "transference", since the situation in the treatment certainly offers no adequate grounds for their origin. ...[11]

The relation between transference emotions and what is really going on in the analysand's mind according to Freud's theory is not the same as the relation between Luke's purported feeling of contempt and his real

---

[10] Note that Luke's sham feeling of contempt would undoubtedly satisfy, as veridical, the criteria of natural expression and appropriate action.

[11] James Strachey (ed.), *The Standard Edition of the Complete Psychological Works of Sigmund Freud*, Volume 16 (London: The Hogarth Press, 1963), pp. 440f, 442, 443.

emotion of envy. In the latter case, as I have described it, Luke's purported construal of Arthur is a defense against his real construal of him, and there is no question about whom the emotion is directed toward. It is Arthur. Furthermore, the terms of the purported construal differ significantly from those of the real one, a difference that changes the type of emotion from envy to contempt.[12] By contrast, transferred emotions are of the same type as their originals – love of analyst corresponding to love of parent, anger at analyst to anger at parent – and the transferred emotion is not typically a defense against the original, but a confused "memory." My main point here is just that an emotional feeling's being wildly inappropriate to what it is about is a strong indication that the felt emotion is not the real one. It is not a guarantee. Wild misconstruals of the situation can be genuine emotions, and accurate ones can be false feelings.

LACK OF MOTIVATION. As concern-based construals, emotions *contain* something like a motivation, what I have called the basic concern; and some *produce* a motivation, what I have called the consequent concern. But emotions or their simulacra may also be motivated; that is, they can be a kind of performance or action that is itself effected for a reason. And I wish now to suggest that when an emotion is deployed for a reason, the chances are good that it is fake. Nico Frijda neatly summarizes some of the possible motives for having emotions:

Emotions produce gains that differ from one emotion to another. Anger intimidates and instills docility. Fear saves the efforts of trying to overcome risks. Guilt feelings for misdeeds done confer high moral standing. Grief provides excuses, confers the right to be treated with consideration, and gives off calls for help. Often, when crying in distress or anger, one casts half an eye for signs of sympathy or mollification. Anticipation of such consequences, it can be argued, belongs to the factors that generate one particular situational meaning structure rather than another, and thus brings one particular emotion rather than another into existence. The mechanism involved is transparent. One focuses, for instance, on the idea that another is to blame *in order to permit emergence of* an anger that makes the other refrain from what he or she is doing.[13]

When people's motivation for an emotion is very obvious, we sometimes call their bluff and say, "You're not really mad, you're just trying to intimidate me," or "You're not really afraid, you just don't want to take the risk," or "She's not really grieving that much, she just likes the attention." Our challenge may be chastened somewhat if we are convinced they are not *simply* faking, but have worked themselves into a real feeling of anger, grief, or whatever. But even so, knowledge of such an etiology strongly reduces our inclination to take the emotion seriously; we feel that it is superficial.

---

[12] For an account of these differences, see Sections 3.9b and 3.8d.
[13] "The Laws of Emotion" *The American Psychologist* **43** (1988): 356 (italics added).

In an effort to make emotions out to be "rational," Robert Solomon focuses on such cases, pointing out that an emotion is rational insofar as it is used strategically.[14] His central case, which we have visited before in another connection (Section 1.4a), is a husband who flies into a rage about his wife's failure to pick up his shirts at the laundry, even though he has plenty of shirts and the ones that have been left at the laundry don't differ much from those hanging in his closet. To understand this seemingly irrational anger, says Solomon, is to see the *purpose* it serves. The husband is using his anger to distract his wife from her effort to get him to go to a party with her. One might think the strategy would as well be served by feigning anger as by actually working up the feeling. Solomon does not deny this possibility, but points out how natural it is to slide from feigning into actually being (I should say feeling) angry. Someone might actually make himself angry through such acting. But in the described case the husband's anger at the wife does not arise naturally out of the impingement of his perception of an offense on some concern of his about his rights, and so on. Instead, it arises eccentrically out of a desire not to go to a party, so that the supposed concern-impinging perception of offense has to be got up artificially. That it is being used as an instrument to accomplish a purpose suggests a certain dissociation – perhaps conscious, perhaps not – of the man from the emotion. And this dissociation remains, no matter how intensely the emotion is felt in the moment.

NORMALITY OF CAUSATION. In a famous experiment Stanley Schachter and Jerome Singer[15] attempted to show that emotions are states of roughly generic physiological arousal that the subject "labels" in terms of his or her "immediate situation as interpreted by past experience." Thus if someone has sensations of arousal in a situation that he recognizes, from past experience, as threatening, he will label his bodily state as fear; if he has the same sensations in a situation of erotic encounter, he will label them love, and so on. Thus Schachter's and Singer's theory of *emotion* resembles, at some distance, my account of emotional *feelings*.

They injected subjects with epinephrine (adrenaline), which fairly closely mimics the autonomic arousal associated with some strong emotions (increased pulse rate, trembling of hands, flushing of face, etc.). All subjects were told the injection was vitamins, but some were correctly informed what effects to expect, others were misinformed (told, for example, that their feet would get numb), and others were told the shot would have no side effects (these were called ignorant). Another set of subjects received a saline

[14] "Emotions and Choice," *Review of Metaphysics* 27 (1973): 20–41. I agree that a person who uses an emotion for some purpose may be rational in a minimal instrumental sense. But most emotions that are rational in this way are *ipso facto* irrational in the way of situational fit; and the feelings of such emotions are also often irrational in being false self-perceptions.
[15] "Cognitive, Social, and Physiological Determinants of Emotional State," *Psychological Review* 69 (1962): 379–399.

solution placebo. The subjects were divided into an anger group and a euphoria group. Within a minute or so of being injected with the "vitamins," each subject was left alone in a room with a stooge who purported to be another participant in the vitamin experiment. Subjects in the anger group had to fill out a questionnaire that included a lot of privacy-invading questions, and they were put with an "angry" stooge who complained volubly about the questionnaire and ended by ripping it angrily to shreds and stomping out of the room. Subjects in the euphoria group got a "silly" stooge who in his gaiety made an outrageous mess of the room by shooting baskets with crumpled paper, making paper airplanes, shooting down a tower of file folders with a slingshot and paper ammunition, and hula-hooping around the room. Thus the one group were encouraged to interpret their bodily arousal in terms of the offensiveness of the questionnaire, and thus to become angry, and the other to interpret theirs in terms of the gaiety of the situation.

Schachter and Singer found that by measures of self-report and behavioral observation through a one-way mirror the subjects who had received epinephrine and did not know the true explanation of their arousal – subjects in the ignorant and misinformed categories – felt far more anger or euphoria than ones who had a proper explanation of their arousal; and they had somewhat more anger or euphoria than those who had received a placebo. Schachter and Singer concluded that emotions require both an arousal state (because the subjects who were less aroused experienced less emotion) and a situational interpretation of that state because both anger and euphoria were produced with the same kind of artificial arousal and were thus differentiated only by the interpretation and because, when the purely chemical interpretation of their arousal was dominant for them, they tended to feel no emotion.

Equipped with the distinction between real emotions and emotions that are merely felt, we may read this experiment as suggesting a criterion of reality for emotions. For the fact that the knowledge that one's arousal state is due to an injection greatly reduces one's tendency to feel the arousal state as an emotion suggests that the arousal state's being due to an injection is a reason for calling into question the veridicality of feelings of emotions so produced. Toward the end of their paper, Schachter and Singer report that in interviews taken after the experiment was over some of the subjects who had received epinephrine but had been left in the dark about the effects to be expected had, on their own, become suspicious that their palpitations and tremor had been caused by the injection. This group was just as low on the scales of emotional feeling and behavior as the officially informed. I can well imagine somebody in this group starting to feel angry or euphoric and then smelling a rat in the psychology lab and settling into a better view of himself. It seems to me it would be quite natural for him to say, at that moment of turning, that the anger or euphoria he had just felt was fake, because of the artificiality of the setup that had brought it on. Similarly, someone who had developed an intense feeling of anger, along with angry behavior, during the experiment, and had only later learned of the chemical manipulation, might justifiably look back on that episode of "emotion" as illusory, as not really belonging to him, to his own character and life history in the same way as natural episodes of anger.

On the other hand, the mere fact of chemical manipulation does not guarantee the shamness of the generated feelings. Imagine someone like our suspecter mentioned above. She has been aroused, without her knowledge, by the injection, but begins to suspect that the injection is causing it. Then the larger scenario begins to emerge in vague outline, and suspicion becomes conviction: This experiment is not what it was advertised to be. I've been lied to and am being manipulated by underhanded scientists. Now she is angry as a matter of conviction. She realizes that her anger is intensified by the drug, but she is not out of control and decides to "go with it." Here, despite the nonstandard causation of her emotion, the emotion is real and is hers; the feeling is veridical.

A different way that nonstandard causation undermines the reality of a felt emotion is illustrated in an article in which Paul Ekman, Robert Levenson, and Wallace Friesen[16] attempt to refute Schachter's and Singer's supposition that types of emotions may not be differentiated at the physiological level. Professional actors and scientists who study the face were attached to autonomic monitoring devices. Then, in accordance with knowledge of which muscles are contracted to form the facial expressions of anger, fear, sadness, happiness, surprise, and disgust, the subjects were directed to tighten their facial muscles in various configurations. Names of emotions were not used in the directions; for example, the instructions testing for autonomic activity in fear went as follows: "(A) 'raise your brows and pull them together,' (B) 'now raise your upper eyelids,' (C) 'now also stretch your lips horizontally, back toward your ears.'" The muscle configurations were held for ten seconds, and autonomic activity was monitored. The investigators found that heart rate increased significantly more in conjunction with facial expressions characteristic of anger, fear, and sadness than in those of happiness, surprise, and disgust; and that finger temperatures increased significantly more in anger than in any of the other emotions. As ordinary experience might have predicted, fear and disgust actually decreased finger temperature somewhat.

Studies showed that such manipulation of the facial muscles resulted not only in the autonomic activity characteristic of the corresponding emotion types, but also in the subjective experience of the emotion.[17] Ekman

---

[16] "Autonomic Nervous System Activity Distinguishes Among Emotions," *Science* **221** (1983): 1208–1210.

[17] See Ekman's "Facial Expressions of Emotions: New Findings, New Questions" *Psychological Science* **3** (1992): 34–38.

summarizes: "[In] a number of studies . . . we have found that deliberately performing the entire muscular configuration for an emotion [type] generates the physiology and often the subjective experience of [that] emotion [type]."[18] That is, when a person succeeds in disposing his facial muscles in just the pattern characteristic of disgust or fear, he feels something like disgust or fear, or feels somewhat as he would feel were he in a state of disgust or fear. On my proposed view of emotional feelings, this is a self-construal (perception) in terms of disgust or fear, to which, we may suppose, the individual is strongly disposed by his or her facial kinesthetic sensations. The feeling of emotion is not just an experience of these sensations, any more than seeing the duck-rabbit as a rabbit is just a visual impression of the lines of the duck-rabbit. Instead, just as the rabbit-reminiscent shape of the duck-rabbit establishes a channel for the experience of the figure as a rabbit, so this facial set establishes a channel for the experience of oneself as in a state of disgust or fear. Just as some familiarity with rabbits is presupposed by the experience of the duck-rabbit as a rabbit, so, I argued in Section 4.2, no one will experience certain kinesthetic sensations as a state of disgust or fear unless he has a set of emotion concepts. If Ekman and company are right that such facial muscle configurations are also accompanied by differentiated patterns of autonomic activity, these would further set the channel for such self-construals.

Such a self-construal, if generated as in the directed facial action task, is not a feeling of an emotion in the sense in which it may seem to the subject to be such. A person who is really fearful fears *something*, even if this something is somewhat ill-defined; a person who is really disgusted is disgusted by or about *something*. Furthermore, by identifying what the person fears or is disgusted about, and his reasons for fear or disgust, we can discern the concern that lies behind these emotions in the personality and the person's characteristic ways of conceptualizing his or her situation. But none of this is possible in the case of a feeling of fear or disgust generated by just manipulating the facial muscles. Such a feeling is a self-perception, all right, but it has no depth; it is more like the self-perception involved in feeling an itch. The difference, however, is that this feeling is phenomenologically not just a sensation or set of sensations indicating a state of the body, but a self-construal in emotion terms; that is, it is an impression of being in an

---

[18] Paul Ekman, "Facial Expression and Emotion" *American Psychologist* **48** (1993): 384–392; 390. Ekman thinks that these phenomena do not result from sensory feedback from the face, but instead from "direct connections among different brain areas" (p. 391). I fail to see why the two hypotheses could not both be true. In general, adult human emotional phenomena are causally a tangled mixture of the automatic-unconscious-physiological and the more or less deliberate-conscious-cultural. My account, being a moral psychology of the emotions, stresses the latter without denying the former. For evidence supporting the feedback hypothesis, see Stuart Valins, "Cognitive Effects of False Heart-Rate Feedback" *Journal of Personality and Social Psychology* **4** (1966): 400–408.

emotional state. Because the scenario is set up in such a way that the subject may very well not be in the emotional state that he appears to himself to be in, such feelings are very likely to be false.

Contrast the feelings generated by Ekman's other method. In the relived emotion task the subject imagines himself into a past situation of natural fear or disgust. Here the emotion may very well be real; after all, the emotion that is being relived in all likelihood occurred in a real situation, construed in terms natural to the subject, on the basis of a real self-manifesting concern of the subject. It is true that the self revealed in the emotion may be not the current self of the subject, but perhaps an infantile self or other past self that the subject no longer, or only partially, identifies with. In that case we might say that what is currently felt is a past, though real, emotion. If it is felt *as* past, it seems to me it would count as a genuine feeling of emotion, but with the oddity that what one currently feels is not one's current emotion.

SURVIVAL OF REFLECTION. Reflective people are often unsure what emotion they are feeling. In such situations you may be very clear that you are feeling *some* emotion (you are feeling vaguely elated, or upset), yet you are puzzled as to which more particular emotion it is. (It is part of self-knowledge and articulateness about oneself to have a subtle repertoire of emotion categories in terms of which to feel, and to be more or less insistent on getting one's feelings right.) Or circumstances and behavior may lead you first to feel frustrated and then on reflection you realize you are really angry (and you start feeling so), or first to feel a vague excitement and then to realize that you are hopeful of what will transpire in the meeting with the boss later this morning. Such cases are sometimes hard to distinguish from ones in which reflection brings about a change in the emotion, but I am suggesting that in many cases the emotion remains the same and the change is in the feeling of it. Amélie Rorty is on the right track when she says, "Although it is often difficult to distinguish regretful feelings from closely allied emotion with similar painful feeling tones – shame, guilt, remorse, self-recrimination – they are distinguished by their related characteristic thoughts."[19] In Chapter 3 I went to some lengths to illustrate my thesis that types of emotion are distinguished by the kinds of terms in which what they are directed toward is construed. When I wonder what emotion I am feeling, a proper question to ask is, "In what kind of terms am I seeing my situation?" This kind of reflection is a test of our feelings: If I feel regretful, and upon careful reflection determine that I am indeed seeing the situation in terms characteristic of regret, I have confirmed my feeling. This criterion, like others, is fallible. I may lack resolve, or honesty, or skill, or opportunity, or conceptual resources, to carry it through. And even if it turns out that I am,

---

[19] "Agent Regret" in *Explaining Emotions*, p. 498.

as best I can determine, construing the situation in the terms characteristic of regret, the emotion may still not be mine if I lack the concern on which it would be based.

How does one go about thinking one's feeling through? In the simpler cases one may be able to query one's "thoughts" directly: What have I been thinking about and in what terms have I been thinking of it? What have I been saying to myself? What kind of imagery has been going through my head? What kind of perceptions have I just now been subjected to? What did I dream last night? What have I been reading lately? Virtually all the other criteria that we have examined in this section may be brought to bear in such reflection. My facial and vocal expressions may be a clue to how I am seeing my situation. The action I am taking or notice myself inclined to take may indicate whether the emotion I am feeling is the one that is operative. I can ask myself, "Is it *like me* to be seeing this kind of situation in just these terms?" or "Is it plausible that in *this situation* I would be thinking in these terms?" or "Do I have any special motivation to be seeing the situation as I seem to be seeing it?" or "Is there anything odd in the causes by which my state of seeming to perceive my situation in this way was brought on?"

Large theories of personality sometimes offer wholesale ways to sort veridical from nonveridical feelings of emotion. Freud held that all adult concerns for other persons – such as are involved in relationships of sympathy and friendship – are rooted in "sexual" desires that now, under the pressures and training of socialization, manifest themselves, as far as conscious self-perception goes, in the disguise of civilized emotions like admiration and respect. Thus such feelings are *never* what they seem phenomenologically to be. Only under the tutelage of an analyst armed with the theory of sexuality will we come to know what our real emotions are; and even then it is not the aim of psychoanalysis to get us "in touch with our feelings" in the sense that we simply feel our "admiration" and "respect" *as libido.* Instead, we learn the theory of what our emotions really are, but continue to feel them more or less as admiration and respect [20] because civilization requires these misperceptions and civilization cannot be forsworn. Nietzsche, in a similar vein, says that what people always really want is their own power and magnificence. So when we feel emotions based on a concern for unfortunates (e.g., pity and compassion, or joy in helping them or seeing them

[20] I say "more or less" because intensive psychoanalysis of a willing and believing patient will certainly have its effect on how the patient construes$_2$ such emotions as admiration and respect. In particular, it will have an ironizing effect on his feelings, especially in his more reflective moments. A moralist may have doubts about the salubriousness of ironizing a person's experience of such morally central emotions as admiration and respect. Freud seems to have intended to debunk the moral emotions, and from the point of view of a number of moral outlooks, this ironizing of feeling is a falsifying and morally lamentable result.

helped), or on a concern for moral rectitude (contrition and shame), the emotions we feel cannot be our real emotions, and the self-perception involved must be distorted. Feelings of Christian love are really misperceptions of envy, resentment, and hatred, born of a failed competition for power and magnificence. By contrast with Freud, Nietzsche does prescribe that (some) people come to have fully veridical feelings of their emotions, especially a self-glorying joy based transparently on the will to power. Similarly, one can imagine a Christian personality theory along Augustinian lines that tells a corrective story about many feelings. The restless heart, anxious about reputation and security in this world or joyful about successes, angry about frustrations, and sad over losses, is in fact longing for a perfect object of praise and gratitude. As in Freud and Nietzsche, so also in this Augustinian psychology, since the concern on which these emotions are based is other than it seems to be, the emotions themselves are other than they are felt to be, and the self they manifest is otherwise than it is construed$_2$ to be. The theory offers the conceptual resources for a corrective construal$_2$ of the emotions, in which what was formerly felt as (for example) sadness and anxiety at the prospect of death comes to be felt as (also) a yearning for fellowship with God.

Such theories, insofar as they offer really wholesale revisionary accounts of our emotional life, are not very plausible unless they include *some* way of acknowledging the reality of many of our apparent emotions. The distinction I mentioned briefly earlier, between a person's actual self and his true self, is one promising device for making such theories more plausible. Thus Freud can admit that there is a reality to the character formation that results from civilization, even though a more fundamental characterization of the person is possible; the Nietzschean psychologist can admit that, say, Saint Francis's actual character is such that it is manifested in the emotions of Christian love, while his deeper or true self is envious, resentful, rancorous, and spiteful. And the Christian psychologist can admit that many people are anxious about their reputation, and so on, while insisting that this is the degenerate or sinful self, not the true one.

The account of emotions I am presenting in this book is not tied to a personality theory that provides wholesale criteria for distinguishing true from false feelings. I have tried, in the present section, to discuss seven criteria that are neutral as between such grand theories, are more finely differentiating, and allow for the reality of emotions belonging to any number of possible world views. The criteria I have presented do not offer much prospect of certainty in the difficult cases, or of widespread agreement about which feelings that an individual might have are veridical and which are not. In addition to the considerations I offered in the opening paragraph of this section, the fact that so many thinking adults are, at least implicitly, partisans of one or another large-scale view of what is basic to human personality contributes significantly to this indeterminacy.

4.6. RESPONSE TO LITERATURE

When we read literature or attend fictional or historical narrative representations on stage or in the movie theater, we feel an ebb and flow of emotion that follows the narrative. Sometimes the emotion is sympathetic: We feel what some character is feeling. Sometimes it is straightforwardly that of spectator: We feel an anxiety or compassion for the heroine that she herself does not feel, or an outrage at injustice or a joy at the spectacle of noble love or a comeuppance, or an admiration for virtue that takes a different perspective from any that the characters could have. Largely we bring our sensibilities, our emotional responsiveness, to the work. It is a soundboard of our character in which the themes of our soul – or at least our apparent soul – become audible to us. But the author, if consequential, may also be an educator, one who can draw us from a state of lesser emotional/moral maturity to a state of greater – where "lesser" and "greater" are measured by the author's moral lights. The author may change our responsiveness by trading on concerns and sensibilities already present in us to draw us into angers and compassions, shocks and amusements, joys and admirations that are actually beyond us.

Because the novelist is a manufacturer of emotion, and herself occupies, often, a general outlook on life differing from the reader's,[21] there is much potential here for discrepancy between what the reader feels in response to the narrative and what the reader is really like as a person. The reader himself, if responsive, may be fictionalized by the work. He may find himself sympathizing with characters he would on principle not sympathize with in life, or brought to tears by goings-on that he hardly regards as worthy of serious sadness. In these cases the reader may decide that the disreputable emotional manifestations show what, contrary to his self-concept, he is really like; or he may judge himself to have been manipulated, or caught in a weak moment, and may regard the feelings as sham. In the other direction, the reader may find himself feeling sympathies and outrages higher than any he thought he had in him, and again he may treat them as self-revelatory or as sham. In identifying these possibilities I am giving thematic definition to experiences that, in all likelihood, are only subceived: The normal reader, absorbed in the novel, will mostly just feel the emotions, without much conscious reflective self-monitoring or hypothesis formation about himself.

Picking up François Mauriac's *Vipers' Tangle*,[22] a reader is alerted to the author's Christian orientation by the epigraph from St. Teresa of Avila and the frontispiece exhortation to have pity on the hateful and avaricious central

---

[21] I shall write as though I am speaking of a novel reader, but I mean the following comments to apply to the consumer of other forms of narrative art as well.

[22] Translation by Warre B. Wells of *Le Nœud de Vipères* (Paris: Éditions Bernard Grasset, 1933; translation Garden City, New York: Doubleday, 1957). In quoted passages I have touched up the translation here and there.

character Louis, since the real object of Louis's yearning is neither revenge
nor money, but some to-be-named and dawning Good. . . . Louis, near death,
begins to write a letter to his wife to make his humanity known to her after
a forty-year marriage of resentment incomunicado. The letter, in which he
depicts her as having created the momentary illusion that he was lovable and
then destroyed this salvation by letting slip that he was just a convenient solution to a bad situation, grows into a novel-length diary in which he reports
on his hatred of her and of their children and grandchildren, on his plans to
avenge himself by cutting them off from an enormous inheritance, and on
the information he garners by eavesdropping on their conversations about
strategies to prevent his cutting them off. Louis's humanity shows not only
in his resentment-filled revelation of his need for Isa's love, but also in his
attachment to his daughter Marie (who dies as a child) and a nephew Luc, as
well as in intimations of a higher order of things which he was loathe to admit
experiencing, as he spent his life resisting Isa's family's Catholicism. That
religion, it becomes evident, is pretty superficial, being a little bit more than
varnish on a life whose master passion, like Louis's, is the love of money.
But as he writes, Louis begins to notice changes that he would not have
predicted – a yearning for reconciliation with Isa and a detachment from
his money begotten of a force that, as he says, is "perhaps love. . . . "

Louis goes to Paris to arrange for giving his fortune to a son Robert he has
never met, whom he fathered in an affair twenty-some years earlier. When he
meets the young man, he is appalled at Robert's stupidity and exasperated
by his and his mother's suspiciousness of an arrangement that is to catapult
them overnight from poverty into fabulous wealth. So suspicious are they
that Robert notifies the family in Bordeaux, thinking it safer to cut a deal
with them. It happens, though, that Louis is drinking a glass of Vichy in
the café where his son Hubert and son-in-law Alfred have arranged to meet
Robert. Louis follows them into the church of St.-Germain-des-Prés and
watches as Hubert intimidates Robert into agreeing to forgo a fortune of
millions in return for an annual income of 12,000 francs. Louis, the infidel,
is particularly irritated that as Hubert left the church he "plunged his hand
into the holy water font, turned towards the high altar, and made a large
sign of the Cross" (p. 141).

While Louis is in Paris, Isa dies of a stroke, and he returns to Bordeaux
where the family is gathered. Prevented by his physical condition from going
with the funeral procession,

I spoke the first words that came into my head.
   "I should have liked so much to accompany her to the end, since I was not here
to say 'Good-bye' to her."
   I repeated, like an actor trying to get the right tone: "Since I was not here to say
'Good-bye' to her"; and these trite words, intended only to save appearances, which
came to me because they were a part of my rôle in the funeral rites, awakened in
me, with sudden power, the emotion of which they were the expression (p. 156).

Louis confronts the family with his knowledge of their plot. He finds satisfaction in catching them in their lies and in making them squirm. This experience of moral triumph, combined with the articulation of his resentments
and his loves that his "diary" represents and the discovery of his capacity to
grieve for Isa, elicit a new self-understanding. It is as though a different self,
which was not quite not there before but was unavailable and undeveloped,
now emerges or begins to emerge. Louis surprises his children with the offer
to divide his property among them – in effect, to impoverish himself for the
sake of these who hate him. He finds an unprecedented peace in giving
up the two things that hitherto had composed the centers of his emotional
life – his property and revenge against his family.

I am especially interested in what he feels – or doesn't feel – toward
this family whom earlier he hated as enemies. As avaricious as ever, their
one object, it seems, is to get their hands on Louis's fortune. Louis invites
Hubert to open the envelop in which the dimensions of the fortune are
detailed.

He went quickly over to the window and slit open the envelope. He read as though he
were eating. Geneviève, unable to restrain herself any longer, got up and stretched
a greedy head over her brother's shoulder.

I looked at that fraternal couple. There was nothing there for me to regard with
horror. A business man threatened with ruin, the father and the mother of a family,
had suddenly rediscovered millions that they had thought lost. No, they did not
strike me as horrible (p. 166f).

Having lost his own avarice, Louis loses his emotional eye for it in his children. What stands out for him is their humanity. They are "the father and
the mother of a family." But Louis is aware that they have not changed.
Geneviève expresses the opinion that 18,000 francs a year is too much for
Robert to have.

Their terror of "losing out" has made them take the comic decision to divide the
complete sets of damask linen and of glassware. They would cut a tapestry in two
rather than let any one of them have the benefit of it. . . .

What do they think about me? That I have been beaten, no doubt, that I have
surrendered. They have "got me." Still, at every visit they show me great respect
and gratitude. All the same, I surprise them. Hubert especially keeps me under
observation; he distrusts me, he is not sure that I am disarmed (p. 170).

But these attitudes in his children no longer elicit from Louis the feelings
of anger and malicious joy they once did. Instead he finds in himself compassion for them, and yearning for a return of love. This seems to come
from a principle of vision by which he sees through the surfaces that people
present, to their humanity.

Robert's stupidity had been what struck me about him, and I had confined myself to
that superficial feature. Never had the appearance of other people presented itself to

me as something that must be broken through, something that must be penetrated, before one could reach them (p. 173f).

This principle of depth-vision of persons comes from a new sense of who he is and what matters.

...I experienced a sense of profound peace. Bereft of everything, isolated, living under a terrible threat of death, I remained calm, interested, active-minded. The thought of my sad life did not overwhelm me. I did not feel the weight of those wasted years. ...
    It was as though I were not an old man and very ill; as though I still had before me a whole lifetime; as though this peace which possessed me were Someone (p. 185).

I have expounded this novel at some length (though not enough to convey its power) so as to discuss possibilities of the reader's response to it. A typical reader (if there is such a creature) finds himself sharing the joy of triumph with Louis as he confronts Robert with his betrayal. There is cruelty in Louis's enjoyment of making Robert squirm. It is not simple cruelty, but one born of a sense of justice: Robert "deserves" to squirm. It is also, to Louis's credit, a playful cruelty that does not keep his interest. He soon feels more disgusted – with Robert and with himself – than triumphant. The typical reader tracks Louis's emotions as he reads: He feels joy at the justice of Louis's triumph, amusement at Louis's playful devices for making Robert squirm, and finally a mixture of disgust, pity, and contempt for Robert and for the whole proceeding.

I have spoken of the typical reader, because there is no guarantee that a reader will respond as I have described. A compassionate reader who is horrified from the beginning with Louis's cat-and-mouse game is also possible. Robert is such a pathetic figure; there is nothing just or amusing here. Louis is simply despicable. He should tell Robert, as gently as possible, that he's been found out, tell him about the income he's providing, and be done with it. Another (we might call her the cruel reader) thoroughly enjoys the cat-and-mouse game, wishes it could have gone on longer, never comes to feel disgusted with it, and feels irritation that Louis ends by giving Robert an income. I think that neither of these readers has responded as Mauriac intended. The narrative artist is a conductor of the free reader's feelings. The narrative is not rigid tracks but a walking path that gently guides the flow of feeling, even if wandering from it is frequent and easy.

It seems to me that, other things being equal, the narratively eccentric feelings of our compassionate and cruel readers are more likely to be veridical – that is, to reveal states of the reader's self – than those of the typical reader. The reason is that the typical reader's feelings are more conditioned by the narrative art, while the others' responses, because they are less subject to the "manipulations" of the novelist, are more likely to be the spontaneous and normal issue of the reader's character. The skillful narrative artist has ways of drawing us into the world of the work of art, and into the heart of the protagonist, that may – if that world and heart are quite alien from our own – undermine the reliability of our feeling responses. Notice that I said "other things being equal," for as we saw in Section 4.5, the reliability of our feelings may be undermined in a variety of ways. On the other hand, our typical reader is a better *reader*. He submits to the narrative art, gets into the narrative, participates imaginatively in the world of the novel and the heart of the protagonist, and so on.

Robert is a small character in the novel. Far more central to Mauriac's purpose are Louis's feelings (and the reader's) toward Louis's legitimate children – in particular, Hubert. We have seen that the novel narrates a Christian conversion, the transformation of a man's emotional responses to his world and himself, in accordance with a quite particular outlook on what the world and human beings are like and what human flourishing consists in. The change in Louis is nowhere more significant and stark than in his feelings toward Hubert. The narrative art guides the reader to duplicate, in his feelings toward Hubert, those of Louis. The transformation becomes most evident in Chapter XVII, when Louis returns to Bordeaux for his wife's funeral and confronts Hubert and the rest of the family with their plot to wrest the inheritance from Robert. It comes naturally to the typical reader to take pleasure, with Louis, in his moral triumph when he reveals to the greedy liars that he knows exactly what they have been up to. It comes less naturally, and thus requires more in the way of artful help from the novelist, for the reader, with Louis, to feel compassion for them and to see through their greed to their humanity. It seems to me to be one of Mauriac's main purposes to bring the reader to this perception.

Vipers' Tangle ends, after Louis's death, with two letters concerning the "diary" that constitutes the main body of the book. In the first, Hubert offers his interpretation of the diary to his sister Geneviève, along with a plea to destroy it after reading it. In the second, Janine (Geneviève's daughter) begs Hubert for permission to read it, and gives some details of the last weeks of Louis's life that the diary did not include. The letter from Hubert is of special interest, because it tests the reader's ability to feel compassion for him. Hubert presents himself as superior to his father in every respect other than financial acuity. It was by his cleverness and strenuous efforts that the family fortune was saved. The diary justifies his judgment that his father was mentally unbalanced, and thus the unsuccessful efforts to have him locked up to insure the fortune. Louis's handing it over was not generosity or detachment, but a cynical and desperate stratagem for saving face when all plans to deprive his children of their due had gone awry. "We have no occasion to put ourselves to the expense of admiration or gratitude" (p. 193).

Is there any trace, I ask myself, of real Christianity in his case? No, a man as informed as I am about such matters knows that, if you give such people an inch, they take a yard. This false mysticism, I am bound to say, provokes in me an insurmountable disgust (p. 195).

Most of us would naturally incline to dismiss Hubert with disgust and contempt. If we do manage to see him, despite his arrogance and stupidity, in that gentler way in which Louis, at the end, had come to see him, it is probably due to Mauriac's art. It will be because we have come to see him through Louis's eyes. I call this letter a test because the narrative that sustains the Christian feeling more directly is now in the past; the reader is on his own against this letter, with only the memory of the narrative to support him. So the letter tends to call for moral growth on the reader's part, a sort of autonomy of proper feeling.

But who is the reader, that Louis's feeling of compassion should characterize her? She might be a Christian in one or another state of spiritual vitality. If she has intimate knowledge of that Someone who is Louis's peace and is, on that basis, in the habit of perceiving the humanity in the most outrageous sinners, then the feeling of compassion for Hubert may be an experience of her actual self. It is perhaps elicited by the narrative, but not created by it. If she is a cultural Christian with no personal knowledge of the peace that Louis found, but is seeking it quite intentionally, we will be less inclined to say that the feeling of compassion elicited by the narrative is of an emotion actually present in her. We might want to say that, through the narrative, she gets an experience of her true self that is not an experience of her actual self. Or perhaps she self-consciously rejects Christianity, but nevertheless, by getting into the narrative, sustains her feeling of compassion for Hubert right through his arrogant letter. In this case she (and we) will judge the feeling to be an artificial construct, an artifact of the work of art in concert with the reader's imagination.

But who are the "we" referred to in the last parentheses? I noted at the end of Section 4.5 that what counts as a feeling of genuine emotion may be relative to a larger account of personality. Clearly, Mauriac is a partisan of the Augustinian psychology that I mentioned. The epigraph of *Vipers' Tangle*, from St. Teresa of Avila, reads,

Lord, consider that we do not understand ourselves and do not know what we want, and that we depart infinitely from what we desire.

On this account, even the self-conscious rejecter of Christianity, like Louis during most of his adult life, really wants more than anything else to be in communion with God and fellow human beings. If "we" are Augustinian, then we will not judge the reader's feeling of compassion for Hubert that is created by the novelist's narrative art to be *merely* an artificial construct. Rather, that feeling will reflect the reader's true self, even though it is sham, or an artificial construct, with regard to her actual personality. It is as though she looks in the mirror of the reading experience and sees herself with a

mask created by the narrative, a mask that misrepresents her actual dispositions, her desires, her outlook on life; and yet unknown to her, the mask is
a true picture of her soul.

If, on the other hand, "we" are partisans of another personality
theory – say, a Freudian or Nietzschean view – our judgments about the
artificiality or otherwise of the feelings created by the narrative art will be
quite different. We will hold that any emotion based on attachment to God
must be accounted for in terms of some process of deception about one's
real concerns; such emotion cannot fully be what it appears in feeling to be.
If Mauriac manages to make a reader feel something like Louis's compassion
for Hubert, then "we" Nietzscheans may admit that that feeling is veridical
with respect to the reader's personality (in case the reader is a Christian),
but if the reader is not a Christian, then the feeling must be *sheer* sham.
And for any reader, regardless of her actual personality, the construction of
feeling created by the novel is a misrepresentation of her deepest self.

In the present section we have seen that narratives may draw us into
emotional ways of feeling that are to one degree or another, and in one way
or another, misrepresentations of ourselves. I have distinguished between
a person's actual self, or personality, and his true self and have suggested
that the representation of one's actual self in feeling may be veridical while
that same feeling may misrepresent one's true self; and similarly that the
representation of one's actual self in feeling created by the narrative may be
false while as a representation of one's true self it is true. I have also suggested
that judgments about true selfhood – and judgments about the veridicality
of feelings that presuppose judgments about what the true self is like –
are the products of contestable personality psychologies. It is not within
the scope of this book to argue for one personality psychology as against
the alternatives, and so my account of veridicality and falsehood of feelings
remains to that extent formal. (I suspect that even after the most rigorous
arguments possible, any personality theory remains contestable.) However,
I do think that the criteria offered in Section 4.5 (which are criteria of
veridicality vis-à-vis the actual self or personality) are relatively independent
of personality theory. One topic remains for this chapter: What is the role
of feelings in emotional education?

4.7. EMOTIONAL EDUCATION

The view of emotions, feelings, and self that I have been presenting is
"realist" in that the emotion is not taken to be just constituted by the feeling
of it, nor is one's self just whatever one perceives oneself to be. But our orientation should not hide from us how the feeling of an emotion contributes
to the emotion and how awareness of self alters the self. A person who is
self-aware differs – as a self – from one who is oblivious to himself. Self-
awareness has large implications, investing us with powers of self-assessment

and self-management, responsibility, potential for change, and courses of action, and these powers are themselves attributes of the selves that possess them. Similarly, the feeling of an emotion feeds back on the emotion and changes it. In feeling an emotion I construe it as belonging with the set of attributes that make up *me*. Thus it gets placed in a particular set of associations, where it is likely to be altered in some ways. At Isa's funeral, Louis utters a formula for grief, tries it again, this time with feeling, and is surprised to find that the emotion is there to be felt. This awareness takes its place in a dawning construct that is a self that truly surprises him, a self he did not know he was. The felt emotion is not an isolated sensation, but an echoing depth, a locus of meaning, a datum glistening with uncountable associations, and so on. Coming to *feel* a variety of emotions – compassion for his children, peace with God, grief for Isa and so on – is crucial not just to something we might call Louis's self-understanding, as though this could be somehow separated from his *being* the self that he is; that these emotions should come to be felt is crucial to the transformation of Louis from the hateful miser that he was, to the gentler, generous spirit that he became.

When Louis comes to feel grief for Isa, he is coming (Mauriac would have us know) to perceive in himself an emotion that was already there. And yet, I have commented, this claim cannot be separated from the fact that Louis changes through this and similar events of self-perception. In any case there is no question here of artifice: Louis does not work himself up, does not create in himself an artificial perception of emotion, a false sense of who he is. But what about artificial feelings? Can feelings that do *not* accurately represent the self have any educational value?

False feelings need not be deceptive, any more than misperceptions must in general deceive. The Nietzschean reader of *Vipers' Tangle* who is induced by the narrative to feel something like Louis's compassion for Hubert need not think this emotion actually characterizes *her*. Nor need feelings, if deceptive, be self-deceptive. The deception may have its ground more in social influences than in the self's own agency. But even if a feeling is deceptive or even self-deceptive, it may be, all things considered, a good thing. False feelings can be indications, and even strategies, of moral aspiration. They may be a stage of moral growth, serving as an important leverage in the development of character. Let us first consider the novel reader and then the typical child.

Let us return to our nominal Christian reader of *Vipers' Tangle* who passes the "test" of Hubert's letter. That is, despite Hubert's self-importance and blind cynicism, she feels compassion for him, inspired by Louis's converted eyes. This is not at all her wonted way of seeing obnoxious people, so we may suppose it to be a false feeling, created for the moment by the novelist's art. Might it have an effect on her character? Might it be a lever by which she is lifted to a more authentic Christian character in which such compassion for difficult people is a natural and spontaneous response? It might, and whether it does is a matter of the use to which it gets put. The feeling is a sort of experimental or hypothetical emotion[23]: This is how I would feel toward Hubert and his ilk were I a somewhat different person than I am. Thus it is an experiential introduction to being a different kind of person. If the reader is well-disposed toward being a Christian, she can take the experience not *just* as an experience, "an interesting possibility," but as an invitation to a way of life. Future courses of action may be affected by this glimpse of another possibility of soul, actions that begin to bring about its actuality. These processes of assessment and undertaking may be more *or less* consciously chosen and conducted. On the other hand, if, like our Nietschean reader, she is not well-disposed to Christianity, the use to which the experience gets put will be different. She may treat it as merely an interesting glimpse into another world, or may even be mildly horrified by it and undertake actions to mitigate its seductive power.

I think that experimenting with emotions, via artificial feelings, is a natural and everyday part of human development. When a child models herself on her parent, she picks up not only behavioral patterns but also attitudes, among which are emotional responses. Her mother's indignation at the exploitation of powerless people becomes a pattern of response in her too, and when she feels it she feels it as an attribute of her self. Because she belongs to a language community in which the vocabulary of emotion is current, she perceives herself as perceiving powerless people in the way her mother does. But at an early stage of growth the child is necessarily missing something here. The emotion is not hers in the way it is her mother's; indeed it is a kind of illusion she creates by her imagination and her power to imitate her mother's gestures and speech. Not that she perceives *nothing* of what her mother, in her indignation, perceives. She can recognize exploited people; she can see that they are suffering; she has some notion of the responsibility of their exploiters. But it is implausible to attribute real indignation to an eight-year-old, because her personality is not yet constructed with the full complement of discriminations, and especially concerns, needed for appreciating proper objects of indignation as such. In the perception that she perceives in herself, she does not grasp the import of the exploitation in the way characteristic of people with real moral indignation.

But this feeling may well be a stage in the development of genuine indignation and of a self that is characterized by such states. It is a subjective qualification for participating in a way of life that, in its mature form, involves those concerns and those moral discriminations that the child is not yet capable of. Through participating, as a quasi-self, in a community of persons with those concerns and those discriminatory powers, the child eventually comes to be subject to genuine indignation.

---

[23] For an argument that hypothetical emotions are not possible, see Ronald de Sousa, *The Rationality of Emotion*, pp. 156–158.

4.8. CONCLUSION

In this chapter I have investigated the relations between emotions and the feelings of them, with special interest in the possibility that one's feelings may not accurately represent one's actual emotional state, the criteria for assessing feelings' truth or falsity, the ways that feelings are generated, and their developmental importance. With these questions we have begun to explore the moral importance of the emotions and their relations to the virtues. In the projected succeeding volume of this work I plan to address the variety of ways that emotions and emotion dispositions interact with and constitute aspects of the moral life. Through the analysis of several kinds of virtues, I will clarify the important relations that emotions bear to moral judgments, actions, personal relationships, and human well-being.

Index

thalamus, 22

therapy, 26, 44, 81, 90–2, 110–11, 113, 117, 164, 219, 225, 239, 315–17, 319, 325–7

Tolstoy, Leo, 4, 224, 268

Tomkins, Sylvan, 152–4, 190

Trollope, Anthony, 1

Twain, Mark, 225

type concepts, 13

unconscious, conscious, 7, 16, 21, 31–5, 43–5, 55, 59, 68–9, 72, 80, 165–6, 178, 319–328

Valins, Stuart, 339

vanity, 259, 310–12

virtues, 2, 3

Walton, Kendall, 95, 331

Williford, James, 90

Wittgensgein, Ludwig, 3, 67, 113, 173, 272–4

Wollheim, Richard, 36

Wood, Jay, 52

Zagzebski, Linda, 146